DATE DUE			
JUN 2 6 '91			

TWENTY LECTURES: SOCIOLOGICAL THEORY
SINCE WORLD WAR II

TWENTY LECTURES
SOCIOLOGICAL THEORY
SINCE WORLD WAR II

—

JEFFREY C. ALEXANDER

COLUMBIA UNIVERSITY PRESS
NEW YORK   1987

Library of Congress Cataloging-in-Publication Data

Alexander, Jeffrey C.
Twenty lectures.

Includes index.
1. Sociology—Methodology. I. Title. II. Title:
Sociological theory since World War II.
HM24.A466 1986   301'.09   86-17106
ISBN 0-231-06210-9

Book design by Laiying Chong.

Columbia University Press
New York
Copyright © 1987 Columbia University Press
All rights reserved

Printed in the United States of America

This book is Smyth-sewn.

To the memory of Felix Bloch

CONTENTS

viii   *Contents*

PREFACE AND ACKNOWLEDGMENTS

In one sense these lectures take off from where my last book, *Theoretical Logic in Sociology*, left off. Whereas in that earlier work the theoretical scheme I developed was applied to theoretical sociology from the classics up through Talcott Parsons, in the present work I use the "logic" to interpret sociological theory right up to the present day.

In another sense, however, these lectures represent new theoretical development. In that earlier work I left the individual approach to order as something of a black box, concentrating mainly on collectivist approaches in their rationalist, normative, and multidimensional form. While investigating the full panoply of assumptions about action, in order words, I limited myself to only one of the two major approaches to the problem of order. Whether that self-imposed limitation was right or not will not be argued here. Suffice it to say that the reasons for that choice were made explicit at the time, and that the length of that earlier work proved unwieldly as it was. In the present work, by contrast, I explore the individualist approach to order at great length. There are minor differences of emphasis in the present work as well. For example, I am here more interested in exploring the social and ideological dimension of theoretical development than I was in *Theoretical Logic*.

Though reworked many times over, this book really did begin as a series of lectures to undergraduates at UCLA. I would like to record my thanks here to those undergraduates for their sharp and stimulating questions, which often pointed me in new directions. I would also like to thank the graduate students who audited the course, especially Geoffrey Gilbert-Hammerling, whose critical and perceptive remarks helped me to get a clearer sense of the project as a whole.

In many ways this book is a product of my eight years in residence at UCLA and of the peculiar, highly stimulating intellectual mix of its sociology department. My colleagues here have forced me to come to terms with microsociology in a way I had never thought necessary before. In this regard I would like to note especially the friendly provocations of Emmanuel Schegloff, Harold Garfinkel, Melvin Pollner, and Jack Katz.

Science, of course, is never a purely local affair, and I have been fortunate in having the assistance of many scholars both here and abroad. Bernard Barber closely read the early chapters of this book and gave me sound advice. Steven Seidman has been an important sounding board and wise critic throughout. Richard Münch read large parts of the manuscript and gave me his thoughtful response. Nicholas Dirks and Ron Eyerman challenged and instructed me about different aspects of contemporary theorizing. Nancy Chodorow and Lewis Coser made some specific and important suggestions. Needless to say, I hold none of these thinkers, nor my colleagues here at UCLA, responsible for the interpretations set forth in what follows.

My wife, Ruth Bloch, provided the final and closest reading of these lectures. Her probing criticism I gratefully accepted.

I have a vivid memory of my first encounter with Raymond Aron's lectures on sociologial theory, translated as *Main Currents in Sociological Thought*. It was the summer of 1971 in Palo Alto, California, and I was reading in the late afternoon sun in the backyard of my wife's parents' home. Aron's ideas were clear and compelling, and it seemed to me that the intimacy of his lectures allowed them to be communicated in a particularly effective way. Imitation is the highest form of flattery. The present lectures are an earnest homage to the memory of that great Frenchman. I would like to dedicate these lectures, however, to the living memory of another great man who died in the same year—to Felix Bloch, in whose house I first read Aron's lectures and from whose association and friendship I gained so much.

Los Angeles

TWENTY LECTURES: SOCIOLOGICAL THEORY
SINCE WORLD WAR II

LECTURE ONE
WHAT IS THEORY?

FOR PEOPLE interested in the real world—and that, I take it, is why most of you are here—a course of lectures on sociological theory might seem a bit off the point. Sociology, of course, is fine. It's about society, and that's why you are here. But "theory"? That sounds too much like philosophy, like ideas for their own sake. Studying theory sounds like it might be dry as dust.

I want to suggest to you, however, that a course about theory is not really as dry and abstract as you might think. True, theories are things that abstract from the particulars of a particular time and place. So we must often talk quite abstractly when we consider them. But there is an important thing that counteracts this abstracting urge. Theories, we must never forget, are written by people. So in studying theories we are looking not at free-floating abstractions but at things people do. To get to know theories, then, we must get to know a bit about the people who wrote them— when they lived, how they lived, where they worked, and, most important of all, how they thought. We have to know these things because we will always be trying to figure out why they said what they said, why they did not say something else, and often why they changed their minds. Most of the time I will try finding answers to these questions inside the theories themselves, but I will try never to forget that behind these theoretical texts are the people and their minds.

Moreover, these lectures are not just about any old sociological theory, but about theory in the present day. One of the attractive things about a course on contemporary theory is, indeed, that we get to talk about our own time. We talk about contemporary life, first of all, because it has had such a great effect on contemporary theory. In the course of my lectures, I will suggest, for example, that the Great Depression of the 1930s and the world war that followed it decisively affected sociological theory in the contemporary period. The utopian hopes for social reconstruction in the postwar world were vital in shaping the nature of the theory which first emerged. As the 1950s turned into the 1960s, these hopes were dashed. The anger and disappointment which followed played a major role in subsequent theoretical work, for it stimulated new theories which challenged those which were dominant in the period of postwar consensus.

I will be talking about contemporary society, however, not just because it has affected the course of contemporary theory but also because it is this contemporary society, after all, that contemporary theory is at least partly about. There is a lot about theory that is timeless, that generalizes from particulars to establish "laws" or "models" which are intended to hold good for all time. But precisely because those who create these theories are affected by their times, their theories can be read as directed toward them in turn. In discussing these theories, I will move continually from theoretical abstractions to the empirically concrete, to the American society you know today, to the conflicts which threaten and inspire us, to the mundane realties of our everyday lives. If my lectures do not get you thinking about empirical things—about everything from the sublime to the ridiculous—in new and intriguing ways, then I have certainly failed.

Before we can get into the "sociological" side of sociological theory, however, we must obviously enter the world of "theory" itself. At least one lecture is going to have to be pretty dry and abstract, and it is only natural that it be the first one. To begin a course you must get first things first. The first thing in a course about theory is, of course, what *is* theory? I will begin with a simple definition. Theory is a generalization separated from particulars, an abstraction separated from a concrete case. Let me give some examples of this process of abstraction. Economic actors are concrete particulars. For example, the president of Chrysler, the automobile company, is a specific person, Lee Iacoca. If we wanted to describe what Lee Iacoca does at Chrysler Corporation, we would not be doing theory. On the other hand, the "presidents of automobile companies" are a *class* of people. Now we are abstracting from a concrete case. If we want to think about what "presidents" of auto companies do, we would have to generalize from particular individuals; we would be making up theories of administrative behavior in automobile companies. If we wanted to study "presidents of American corporations," we would have still another level of abstraction. Let's take another example closer to home. If we look at a child interacting with his or her parents, we would be studying a concrete case. If we wanted to look at many cases of children interacting with many parents, we would be generalizing away from concrete cases and making theories about child/parent interaction. We would be making theories about socialization.

In this course, however, I am interested not just in theory but in general theory. Sociology is replete with special theories, for example theories about stratification, socialization, politics, and administration. You can study these in other, more specialized courses. What *general* theories do is take these special theories and bring them together. General theories are theories about everything, about "societies" as such, about modernity rather than about any particular modern society, about "interaction" rather than about any particular form or genre of interaction. There are special theories about economic classes in society, about the middle class, the working class, and the upper class. But a general class theory, for example Marxian theory, combines all these special theories about classes into a single theory about economic development and class relations as such.

Now that I have defined very provisionally what theory is, let me talk a little about its significance. There is much debate today about the role of theory in science and particularly in social science. The position I take here, which will inform this entire course of lectures, is that theory is crucial, indeed that it is the heart of science. Although theories are always involved with and relate closely to factual "reality," in the practice of social science it is theories themselves that generate the experiments which test facts; it is theories, indeed, which structure the very reality—the "facts"— which scientists study.

Let me give an example. A great deal of social science work today is devoted to finding reasons for Japan's economic success.

In these studies social scientists have often discovered the high value young Japanese students place on achievement, on the "socialization for achievement" which is eventually translated into hard work and discipline in the adult economic world. But how is the "fact" of such socialization actually found? Is it because the reality of this socialization for achievement forces itself upon the social scientific observer? Not really. Studies of socialization have been appearing because many social scientists are imbued before they arrive in Japan with the theoretical notion that childhood socialization is decisive for determining how adults work.

Let's continue with another illustration from the Japanese case. There is a debate raging throughout Europe and the United States about the historical reasons for Japan's rapid economic development. Some scholars argue that it is the protected military position that Japan has enjoyed since World War II which has allowed it to prosper; others, in a similar vein, have cited the protectionist policies of the Japanese government. Still other scholars, however, have argued that these factors are not decisive, that we must look to the cohesiveness of Japanese values and to the solidarity that ties workers and capitalists. These fundamental differences of scientific opinion cannot, I believe, be resolved simply from a closer look at the facts, although look closely we must. These differences are based upon the general theories scientists hold about what motivates people to act and what kinds of forces hold society together. If we believe that people are naturally competitive and invariably selfish, we will look more toward material factors like government and military policy; if we believe, on the other hand, that feelings and morality are vital aspects of the social bond, we are much more likely to be led to such "ideal" factors as values and solidarity.

But the significance of theory can be brought still closer to home. American society has been undergoing the revolution called "Reaganomics." It is a practical program in the most practical of all realms, the marketplace. Yet was this practical policy generated simply as a scientific solution for contemporary economic problems? Not at all. Reaganomics is based on ideas, in the first instance on the ideas of Milton Friedman, but, in a longer time frame, on ideas that go back more than 200 years to the theories of Adam Smith and, before him, to John Locke. It was actually John Maynard Keynes, the great economist opposed to such free market theories, who said that ideas are the most powerful economic force of all.

How are theories generated? Many scientists will admit that theories are more general than facts and are equally important in generating scientific ideas. Yet the most significant question still remains: how are theories produced?

Is theory induced from data, that is, from empirical facts? According to such a notion, we would study a lot of specific cases and gradually make generalizations based on the common qualities between them. The theory which is so generated, a "covering law," would then be acknowledged to play a decisive role in further empirical work. This notion of induction sounds good, but it is simply untrue. Theory cannot be built without facts, but it cannot be built only with them either. Now some philosophers of science acknowledge that theory does precede any attempt at generalization—that we go out into the world of facts armed with theory— yet they maintain, nonetheless, that we use atheoretical facts to verify or falsify our general theoretical concepts. But this position is no more true than the last, especially for the kinds of general theories with which we will be concerned. Such theories cannot finally and conclusively be tested by facts, even though a reference to facts is a vital part of every theoretical test. Facts can challenge some specific propositions in a theory, but a purely factual challenge is limited in two ways. First, the facts which we use to challenge a theory are themselves informed by theories which we are not testing at this time. Second, even if we allow a specific proposition to be falsified, we will rarely give up the general theory of which it is only a small part. Instead, we will launch some revision of the general theory to align its propositions more closely with these new "factual" reports.

How, then, are theories actually generated? I agree, certainly, that the real world puts terribly strict limits on our theorizing. It would be hard, for example, for a social scientist to suggest that American society is undergoing a political revolution, just as "reality" would make it hard to write a theory of Soviet society which said that it was capitalist rather than communist. Yet a few scientists actually have said that American society is undergoing a political revolution, and others have sought to demonstrate that Russia is a capitalist, not a communist country. This shows *in extremis* how theoretical reasoning has relative autonomy vis-à-vis the "real world." Indeed, I have felt compelled to put this last phrase in quotation marks. Because the limits reality places on science are always mediated by prior commitments, it is impossible for us to know, at any particular time, what exactly reality is.

Theories, then, are generated as much by the nonfactual or nonempirical processes that precede scientific contact with the real world as they are by this "real world" structure. By nonfactual processes I mean such things as graduate school dogma, intellectual socialization, and the imaginative speculation of the scientist, which is based as much on his personal fantasy as on external reality itself. In the construction of scientific theories, all these processes are modified by the real world, but they are never eliminated. There is, then, a double-sided relation between theories and facts.

I will call the nonempirical part of science the a priori element. This element is carried not through observations but by traditions. Such a claim might strike you as rather odd. You would normally view science, the prototype of rationality and modernity, as antithetical to tradition. In my view, however, science—even when it is rational—vitally depends on tradition. Sociology is an empirical social science, committed to rigorous testing, to facts, to the discipline of proof and falsification. Yet all these scientific activities, in my view, occur within taken-for-granted traditions which are not subject to strictly empirical evaluation.

What are these scientific traditions? We can agree, no doubt, that they are most likely composed of the basic components of social science. The problem is that people conceptualize these basic components in different ways. It is fair to say, indeed, that these different, often antithetical ways of conceptualizing the basic components of social science are exactly what contemporary theoretical

Diagram 1.1.

The Continuum of Scientific Thought

"Nonfactual" theoretical environment   "Factual" empirical environment

debate is all about. Still, identify the basic components we must, for only in this way will we be able to identify the basic traditions which inform the nonempirical basis of the discipline.

This task is more difficult than it might seem, for in social science a range of nonempirical elements are important. It is not only beliefs about what these elements are, but which among them is more important, that is passed down from one generation of sociologists to the next. I would like to conceive of these elements as forming a continuum of scientific thought (see diagram 1.2).

Different traditions of social theory usually take one level of this continuum as more determinate than others. They often argue, in fact, that this or that level alone is of ultimate importance. It follows, then, that the various theoretical understandings of the component which is taken to be decisive are the basis for the principal sociological traditions.

Many theorists argue, for example, that it is the ideological level that is decisive. The nonempirical element which determines the substance of social scientific findings, they claim, is the political beliefs of the scientists. Sociology is seen as divided between conservative, liberal, and radical traditions. Though this perspective on sociological theory—like the others I will discuss—has been with us for centuries, in the postwar period it reemerged in the social conflicts of the 1960s. Critical sociologists came to view academic sociology as an "establishment" or "priestly" discipline, an ideological theory challenged by the revolutionary or prophetic sociology of the New Left.

Diagram 1.2.

The Scientific Continuum and Its Components

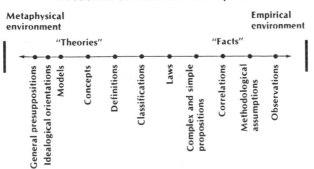

Metaphysical environment

Empirical environment

"Theories"

"Facts"

General presuppositions
Idealogical orientations
Models
Concepts
Definitions
Classifications
Laws
Complex and simple propositions
Correlations
Methodological assumptions
Observations

Other social scientists argue, just as strongly, that it is the model level that determines the fundamental nature of sociological thought. Models are deliberately simplified, highly abstract pictures of the world. There are models, for example, which describe society as a functioning system, like the physiological system of the body or the mechanical system of an internal combustion engine. Other models view society as composed of separate institutions without any integral, systemic relationship to one another. For those who emphasize the model level above all else, it is the decision about functional versus institutional models that is responsible for the complexion of a social theory. Whereas the ideological approach argues that a scientist's political decisions generate models, this second group of theorists argues that it is decisions about functional vs. institutional models that generate ideological commitments. They have frequently argued, for example, that functionalist models lead to conservative ideology. Ideological theorists, by contrast, have often argued in the opposite way, that conservative political beliefs lead to the adoption of functional models.

Another level of the sociological continuum that has often been taken to be decisive is the methodological. It is argued that decisions about whether to pursue quantitative versus qualitative techniques, or comparative analysis in contrast to case studies, are decisive in structuring general sociological theories. At a less technical level, methodological disputes focus on the role of abstract theorizing versus empirical fact gathering. This, of course, is the very dispute I have just engaged in here! Adherents to different sides in these methodological debates often share a belief which I do not: they often believe that it is from these decisions about methodology that commitments to models and ideologies arise. It is not, they believe, the other way around.

Finally, there are a number of social theorists today who argue that a sociologist's decision about whether the world is in equilibrium or in conflict is the most absolute and decisive one he can make. "Conflict theory," for example, insists that if assumptions are made that society is consensual, then models will be chosen that are functional, systemic ideological positions taken that are conservative, and methodologies employed that are empiricist and antitheoretical.

From what I have said, you have probably picked up a note of skepticism. I do not want you to get the idea, however, that I regard these discussions as irrelevant. Each of the nonempirical assumptions they focus on is, in my view, vital for sociological theorizing. I will have occasion throughout these lectures to focus on each of these different levels—model, method, ideology, empirical conflict, or consensus—and to argue for its importance in determining the shape of a particular theoretical position or theoretical change.

At the same time, I would like to argue that each of these strongly held theoretical positions is reductionistic. While each of these levels is significant, no single level actually has the determinate power often attributed to it. Ideology is important, but it is quite wrong to try to reduce theory to the influence of political assumptions. It is not at all unusual, indeed, to find that theorists with very different political ideas produce theories that are similar in significant ways. Just so, it is wrong to think of models as so decisive. Models are important, but they cannot determine the other assumptions that theorists make. Functional models, for example, are promoted today by radical Marxists as well as by conservatives. Some functionalists see system requirements as contradictory and ultimately self-destructive; others see them as complementary and self-maintaining. In the same way, there are functionalists who are empiricists and others who appreciate the independence of the nonempirical side of theory. To consider another typical reduction, it seems awfully wrongheaded to attribute decisive power to methodological commitments. In the history of sociology, the same methodology has substantiated the most radically conflicting positions. There are, for example, both quantitative Marxist theories of class formation and quantitative liberal theories which replace class with status. The methodological commitments are the same, but the theories are very different. Finally, whether or not a theorist takes the world to be in a state of conflict simply cannot, in my view, determine the other characteristics of his theory. Marx saw society as in conflict, but so did Hegel, and few would put their theories into the same camp.

But the problem with these contemporary debates is not simply that they are reductionist, that they conflate what are actually

relatively independent levels. The problem is also that most of
these contemporary debates ignore the most general nonempirical
level of all. I will call this the level of presuppositions. In the
second part of this lecture, I will outline what these presuppositions
are, and I will suggest that they form the dominant traditions in
social thought. In my conclusion, I will finally come back to my
topic of contemporary sociological theory. I will bring this abstract
discussion of traditions down to earth by discussing the intellectual
and social forces which brought the center of theoretical debate
to the United States in the period immediately after World War
II.

By presuppositions, I refer to the most general assumptions that
every sociologist makes—what he "presupposes"—when he encounters reality. It seems obvious, I hope, that the first thing a
student of social life presupposes is the nature of action. When
you are thinking about what action is like, you usually think about
whether it is rational or not. The "problem of action," then, is
whether we assume actors are rational or nonrational. Now I do
not mean to imply here the commonsense equation of rational with
good and smart, and nonrational with bad and stupid. I do not
mean, in other words, that nonrational action is "irrational." In
social theory, rather, this dichotomy refers to whether people are
selfish (rational) or idealistic (nonrational), whether they are normative and moral (nonrational) in their approach to the world or
purely instrumental (rational), whether they act in terms of max-
imizing efficiency (rationally) or whether they are governed by
emotions and unconscious desires (nonrationally). All these dichotomies relate to the vital question of the internal versus external
reference of action. Rationalistic approaches to action portray the
actor as taking his bearings from forces outside of himself, whereas
nonrational approaches imply that action is motivated from within.

By calling this choice presuppositional, I am suggesting that every
social theory and every empirical work takes an a priori position
on this problem of action. Each does not, however, necessarily have
to choose one side to the exclusion of the other. Action may be
portrayed, though it usually is not, as having both rational and
nonrational elements.

Yet to answer the central question about action is not enough.
A second major issue needs to be presupposed. I will call this the

problem of order. Sociologists are sociologists because they believe there are patterns to society, that there are structures separate from the individuals who compose it. Yet while all sociologists believe this, they often disagree sharply about how such an order is actually produced. I will call this an argument between individualistic and collectivist approaches to order.

If thinkers presuppose a collectivist position, they see social patterns as existing prior to any specific individual act, as, in a sense, the product of history. Social order confronts the newborn individual as an established fact that is "outside" of him. Now, if they are writing about adults, collectivists may well acknowledge that social order exists as much inside the individual as without; in fact, this is an important point to which we will return. The issue here, however, is that whether it is conceptualized as inside or outside an actor, social order from the collectivist perspective is not seen as the product of purely this-instant, this-moment considerations. Any individual act, according to collectivist theory, is pushed in the direction of preexisting structure, although this direction remains only a probability for those collectivists who acknowledge that action has an element of freedom. Thus, for collectivist theory, it is the economy that determines the direction of individual economic actors, not entrepreneurs who create the economy; it is the religious system that determines the behavior of an individual believer, rather than the church which springs from faith; it is the party organizations that produce politicians, not politicians who make parties.

Individualistic theorists often acknowledge that there do appear to be such extra-individual structures in society, and they certainly recognize that there are intelligible patterns. But they insist, all the same, that these patterns are the result of individual negotiation, that they are the upshot of individual choice. They believe not simply that structures are "carried" by individuals but that they are actually produced by actors in the concrete, ongoing processes of individual interaction. For them, it is not only that individuals have an element of freedom but that they can alter the fundaments of social order at every successive point in historical time. Individuals, in this view, do not carry order inside of them. Rather, they follow or rebel against social order—even their own values—according to their individual desires.

I do not regard the problems of action and order as "optional." I believe that every theory takes some position on both. But I will go even further than this. I want to argue that the logical permutations among presuppositions form the fundamental traditions of sociology. There have been rational-individualistic theories and rational-collectivist theories. Theories have been normative-individualistic and normative-collectivist. There have also been some attempts in the history of social thought—too few and far between—to transcend these dichotomies in a multidimensional way.

These presuppositional issues are of much more than academic concern. Whatever position theorists take, fundamental values are at stake. The study of society revolves around the questions of freedom and order, and every theory is pulled between these poles. This is, I think, a peculiarly Western dilemma, or better yet, a peculiarly modern one. As modern men and women, we believe that individuals have free will—in religious terms, that every human being has an inviolable soul—and because of this, we believe, each person has the capacity to act in a responsible way. Such cultural beliefs have been, to one degree or another, institutionalized in every Western society. The individual has been set apart as a special unit. There have been elaborate legal efforts to protect him or her from the group, from the state, and from other, culturally "coercive" organs like the church.

Sociological theorists have usually taken these developments quite seriously, and like other citizens of Western society have tried to protect this individual freedom. Indeed, sociology emerged as a discipline from this very differentiation of the individual in society, for it was the independence of the individual, the growth of his powers to think freely about society, which allowed society itself to be conceived of as an independent object of study. It is the independence of the individual that makes "order" problematic, and it is this problematizing of order that makes sociology possible. At the same time, sociologists acknowledge that there are patterns even in this modern order and that the everyday life of individuals has a deeply structured quality. This is just what makes the values of "freedom" and "individuality" so precious. It is this tension between freedom and order that provides the intellectual and moral rationale for sociology: sociology explores the nature of social order in large part because it is concerned about its implications for individual freedom.

Individualistic theories are attractive and powerful because they preserve individual freedom in an overt, explicit, and complete way. Their a priori postulates assume the integrity of the rational or moral individual, taking for granted that the actor is free of his situation defined either as material coercion or moral influence. Yet the freedom of the individualistic position, in my view, is achieved at great theoretical cost. It gives an unrealistic and artificial voluntarism to the actor in society. In this sense individualistic theory does freedom no real service. It ignores the real threats that social structure often poses to freedom and, by the same token, the great sustenance to freedom that social structures can provide. It seems to me that the moral design of individualistic theory encourages the illusion that individuals have no need for others or for society as a whole.

Collectivist theory, on the other hand, acknowledges that social controls exist, and by doing so it can subject these controls to explicit analysis. In this sense collectivist thought represents a great gain over individualistic thought, both morally and theoretically. The question, of course, is whether this gain can be achieved only at an unacceptable price. What does such collectivist theorizing lose? How is the collective force it postulates related to the individual will, to voluntarism, and to self-control? Before we try to answer this decisive question, we must be clear about a vital fact: assumptions about order do not entail any particular assumptions about action. Because of this indeterminacy, there are very different kinds of collectivist theory.

The way I see it, the crucial and decisive question of whether collective theory is worth the cost hinges on whether it presupposes instrumental or moral action. Many collectivist theories assume that actions are motivated by a narrow, merely technically efficient form of rationality. When this happens, collective structures are portrayed as if they were external to individuals in a physical sense. These seemingly external-material structures, like political or economic systems, are said to control actors from without, whether they like it or not. They do so by arranging punitive sanctions and positive rewards for an actor who is reduced to a calculator of pleasure and pain. Because this actor is assumed to respond objectively to outside influences, "motives" are eliminated as a theoretical concern. Subjectivity drops out of collectivist analysis when it takes a rationalist form, for it is then assumed that the actor's response can be predicted from the analysis of his external environment. This environment, not the nature or extent of the actor's personal involvement with it, is considered determinate. I am arguing, then, that rational-collectivist theories explain order only by sacrificing the subject, by eliminating the very notion of the self. In classical sociology, reductionistic forms of Marxist theory presents the most formidable example of this development, but it also pervades the sociology of Weber and Utilitarian theory as well.

If, by contrast, collectivist theory allows that action may be nonrational, it perceives actors as guided by ideals and emotion. Ideals and emotion are located within rather than without. It is true, of course, that this internal realm of subjectivity is initially structured by encounters with "external" objects—with parents, teachers, siblings, and books, with all the varied sorts of cultural carriers and object attachments encountered by young "social initiates." Yet according to nonrational collective theory, in the process of socialization such extra-individual structures become internal to the self. Only if this process of internalization is acknowledged can subjectivity and motivation become fundamental topics for social theory, for if internalization is accepted it is obvious that some vital relationship exists between the "inside" and the "outside" of any act. Individual volition becomes part of social order, and real social life involves negotiation not between the asocial individual and his world but between the social self and the social world. Such thinking leads to what Talcott Parsons called a voluntaristic approach to order, though, I should warn you, this is not voluntarism in an individualistic sense. To the contrary, voluntarism might be said to be exemplified by theories which see individuals as socialized by cultural systems.

The dangers that such theorizing encounters are quite the opposite from those encountered by collectivist theories of a more rationalistic sort. Moralistic and idealist theories often underestimate the ever present tension between individual volition and collective order. There is a strong tendency to assume an innate complementarity between the social self and that self's world—in religious terms, between the individual soul and the will of God, in political terms between individual and collective will.

I hope that this brief discussion of the strengths and the weaknesses of instrumental and moral forms of collectivist theory gives you some idea of how important a synthesis between them might be. While each has its achievements, each by itself tends toward a dangerous one-dimensionality which overlooks vital aspects of the human condition. I would argue on both moral and scientific grounds that theory should interweave the internal and external elements of collective control. I will not even try to tell you at this point what such a multidimensional theory might look like. My goal for these lectures is to outline one. I will do so through a critical reconstruction of sociological theory since World War II.

Presuppositions about action and order are the "tracks" along which sociology runs. Whether theorists or not, sociologists make presuppositional decisions and they must live with the consequences. What these presuppositions are, and what their consequences have been, will be my point of departure throughout this course.

Presuppositional choices determine not only theoretical possibilities in a positive sense but also constraints and vulnerabilities. Every presuppositional position closes off certain avenues even while it opens up others. Theorists often have second thoughts about leaving some possibilities out, and in this sense their presuppositions are straitjackets from which they try to escape. The problem is that if they escape too far they will become different theorists altogether. There are, indeed, often decisive "breaks" in a theorist's work. The early and later thought of Marx is the most famous example, and in the lectures which follow I will talk about similar ruptures in the theories of Garfinkel and Geertz. But theorists rarely want to change their ideas so abruptly. More often, they want to maintain the dominant thrust of their ideas while avoiding some of their consequences. The result is that they introduce revisions only in an ad hoc way. The new concepts become ambiguous, so the "old" theory can still be sustained. I will call these ad hoc concepts residual categories because they are outside the theorist's explicit and systematic line of argument. You might think of residual categories as theoretical afterthoughts: a theorist invents them to respond to nagging worries that he has ignored some crucial point.

In the course of these lectures we will find that even master theorists move uneasily between ambiguous revisions and the reassertion of their original presuppositional position "in the last instance." I will suggest that these options form the poles of a dilemma from which theorists cannot easily escape. Every theoretical position, I believe, produces its own particular dilemma. It is often the followers of master theorists who are particularly sensitive to the dilemmas they faced. They want to defend themselves against criticism, but they also want to be loyal to the orthodox work. As a result, they may seize on a tradition's residual categories and try to work them up in a more systematic way. Still, they have not escaped from the original theoretical dilemma. If they want to remain loyal to the master's tradition, they can rework his residual categories only up to a certain point. In the end, they must be allowed to retain their residual status, for only in this way can the "typical" elements of the original theory be preserved.

Just as I will focus in the following lectures on the presuppositions which determine the tracks along which various theories run, I will also try to show you how every presuppositional position leads to strains which can derail it. I will describe the residual categories which invariably appear and the theoretical dilemmas which are typical of sociological theory in the contemporary period. In this way I should be able to trace not just the basic structures of contemporary theory, but its internal dynamics as well, the strains and conflicts which lead to subtraditions, countertraditions, and to theoretical change.

I will not, however, focus on presuppositions alone. At some point in the course of these lectures every different level of the sociological continuum will emerge as important, sometimes as decisive. It would be foolish to ignore, for example, the vast ramifications of ideology. Sociological theories are not simply attempts to explain the world, but also efforts to evaluate it, to come to terms with broader questions of meaning. Because they are existential statements and not just scientific ones, they invariably have enormous political implications. For this reason, they must always be read against the politics of their day. How a theorist resolves the presuppositional tension between freedom and control is related to —though not determined by—the ideological response he makes to this tension as it appears, for example, in the political conflict between capitalism and socialism.

Nor will I neglect the enormous impact on more general assumptions of changes in the organization of the empirical world itself. If a theory cannot be useful for concrete empirical analysis, it fails. If a theory is perceived as depending upon empirical propositions that are wrong, it is discredited. It is for this reason that the changing empirical environment of sociological theory— the ebb and flow of war and peace, the increasing differentiation and rationalization of politics and economics, the confidence or disillusion in public life—have had an enormous impact on the development of contemporary social theory itself.

So far I have spent a great deal of time on a few extremely abstract theoretical issues. This is the end of the "dry as dust" introduction that is necessary for our discussion to proceed. It is time to come back to earth. The transition is easy to make, because the "logical possibilities" I have described are concretized in the history of social thought by specific intellectual traditions. Each logical position, indeed, was articulated by one of the sociological traditions which defined the "classical" period of sociology between 1850 and 1920. These concrete embodiments of analytical possibilities formed the resources from which sociological theory in the contemporary period has drawn.

Karl Marx assumed that the exploitative economy of capitalist society produced alienated, instrumentally motivated men and women who had no access to nonrational feelings and ideals. Oppressed by the overarching structures of the capitalist economy, these very collective structures would lead them, reward them, and punish them into revolt against capitalism and toward socialist reconstruction. Emile Durkheim theorized in an opposite way. He tended to view society as a cultural and symbolic realm in which the most telling social ties are those of solidarity and affect. In contrast to a world of exploitation, he described a kind of secularized religious world in which socially structured volition was the real stuff of social life. Max Weber sometimes tried to combine these materialist and idealist positions. He believed, for example, that the historical

origins of modern rationality could be traced to nonrational ethical
and religious beliefs. Yet his theory of modern society ended up
developing a political version of rational-collectivist theory. Not
just economics—here he departed empirically from Marx—but the
state, the law, and bureaucracy were viewed as structures that
dominated modern individuals from without.

In my view, these are the main threads, the dominant traditions,
which constitute the inheritance of contemporary sociological theory. Yet there are other classical traditions as well, and we must
be aware of these, too, if we are to understand the full range of
resources with which contemporary theory began. Adam Smith
wrote long before the major formulators of the modern sociological
discipline, yet his "classical economic theory" of market rationality
and cost maximization has continued to form an important reference point for all attempts at social theory which seek an individualistic and rationalistic form. The theories of Simmel, Mead,
and Freud also had individualistic elements, but these were much
more ambiguously formulated than were Adam Smith's. Indeed,
in my view their theories should be seen more in terms of microscopic versus macroscopic empirical foci than in terms of individualistic versus collectivist presuppositions. They studied individuals
and groups—a "micro" emphasis—rather than "macro" things like
institutions or societies as a whole. Yet the traditions they established
did contain individualistic elements, and these provided important
reference points for contemporary efforts to maintain such a presuppositional stance.

Sociological theory, then, exists in time and space and not just
along some abstract scientific continuum. It is carried by traditions
and made up by real human beings. In this last part of my lecture,
I would like to talk a bit about the time and place in which
contemporary sociological theory began.

The classical traditions of sociology were formed more or less
by the end of World War I. This first period of world war, and
the twilight zone which interceded between it and the next, were
decisive in affecting the character of contemporary thought. But
if this establishes the time reference for theory, what about its
"space"? In the beginning, these classical traditions were, with the
exception of Mead and pragmatism, entirely European. In the post-

World War II period, theory underwent a sea change. It moved decisively toward America.

Why did the European traditions of sociological theory not continue in the immediate, post-World War II period? Its originators produced great ideas. Why this temporal hiatus and geographical shift?

European sociology suffered greatly in the period between the two world wars. The story of this interlude has never been told in a satisfactory way, but I think certain basic points are clear. There were, first of all, intellectual and institutional problems. Enormous organizational barriers to sociology existed in European universities, which were old and venerable institutions committed to classical scholarship and humanities. Durkheim, for example, was for a good part of his career unable to acquire a "chair" in sociology, and when he finally did so it was a professorship in sociology and education. Simmel could not find a major position until the end of his career, although this had as much to do with anti-Semitism as institutional opposition. While there were idiosyncratic reasons for Weber's failure to hold an important university position as well, it is not accidental that he was regarded as much as a historical economist as a sociologist for most of his life.

As for the intellectual barriers to European sociology, there existed in Europe few strong traditions of empirical research to legitimate and concretize social theory. In part this was because of the intellectual hegemony of classicism and humanism, but it was also because of the radical cultural and intellectual antagonism among many European intellectuals to contemporary society itself. The European alternative to sociology was Marxism, and though Marxism certainly flourished it often assumed a practical, politicized form that was opposed to the rarified discussions of "high" intellectual life. The most important and sophisticated Marxist intellectuals, moreover, were for political reasons often detached or excluded from sociology as an academic discipline.

There were also social and ideological forces behind the difficulties of European sociology in the interwar period. These can, rather melodramatically, be described as the crisis of European civilization itself. Europe between the years 1914 and 1945 was inhospitable to the continuity of any intellectual traditions. Sociological theories, moreover, were not just any traditions but traditions of a very particular type. Classical sociological theory was inspired by an optimistic faith that reasonable solutions could be found for the problems of secular industrial society. It was premised upon the assumption that, despite social upheaval, important elements of individuality and reason would be preserved. True, some of the classical theorists were more pessimistic about the chances for reform than others: Marx demanded a thorough reconstruction if his faith and hope were to be redeemed. Other classical theorists seemed—from our present perspective—much too optimistic about achieving rationality and freedom in their own time. One thinks here of Mead, and sometimes of Durkheim. But only Weber was a truly pessimistic man. Still, he was liberal, if a liberal in despair. Classical theory was written not simply with the hope but the expectation that people could gain control over their society and maintain freedom as well. These imminent changes—whether reform or revolution—would mix reason with social control.

In Europe between the wars, however, these hopes of the sociological founders were dashed. The leading members of Durkheim's school were killed during World War I. Durkheim and Weber, indeed, both died at relatively early ages from causes related to the war itself. In this period as well, the Enlightenment hopes of Marxism were sharply set back. With the onset of the war European working class movements abandoned internationalism and pacifism for the militant patriotism of their respective national struggles. By the 1930s, European civilization was engulfed by the growing tide of irrationalism and instability. Sometimes European intellectuals did not see the extent of the problem. When they did, they usually felt helpless to prevent it. Many of the leading students of the great sociological founders eventually fled Europe for the United States.

In America the situation was entirely different, and sociology came to have a very different place. Intellectually and institutionally, American sociology was able to avoid the debilitating forces experienced by its European counterpart. Because American universities were relatively new, without sharply differentiated status groups or established institutional cores, the new discipline of sociology was given more of a chance. Often it was received with open arms.

Politically, sociology was associated not with a radical tradition but with a more socially integrative and reformist one. The relatively progressive and liberal character of American society made "antisociological" intellectual movements like Marxism less likely to emerge.

Socially and ideologically, moreover, America remained relatively unaffected by the growing crisis of European civilization. American intellectual life, influenced decisively by pragmatism, remained optimistic and self-confident about reconstructing the Western world. "Chicago sociology," which flourished in the Middle West from the beginning of the century, produced countless empirical studies oriented to the liberal control and reform of social conflict.

Yet American sociology in the interwar period, though more secure than its European counterpart, was not entirely untroubled. American sociology in general and Chicago sociology in particular were, by and large, alarmingly atheoretical and deeply empiricist. They were haunted by theories of instinctualism and vestiges of Social Darwinism, by individualistic forms of pragmatism, and by an enduring anti-philosophical bias that made the creation of systematic sociological theory next to impossible.

By the later 1930s, the situation of sociology might be described as follows. On the one hand, there were theoretical traditions without a nation; on the other, there was a nation without a theory. This paradox set the background for the emergence of Talcott Parsons, the figure who, I will argue, created the framework for contemporary debate.

The theoretical legacy of classical thought and the institutional and cultural situation of the first third of the twentieth century provide the time and space for Parsons' emergence as a major figure. As a theorist, he was bent on the reconstruction of European sociology, providing a synthesis which would eliminate the warring schools which had divided it. As an American, he was confident enough to think that in doing so he could find a path to restore reason to culture and individual control to society. That he was not entirely successful in doing either does not detract from the greatness of his effort, though it certainly explains the success of the "anti-Parsonian" movements which eventually succeeded it.

LECTURE TWO
PARSONS' FIRST SYNTHESIS

I N 1937 an extraordinary book appeared. Little noticed at the
time, it would eventually become the most important and
influential publication of any sociologist since Weber's *Economy
and Society* appeared in the mid-1920s. This book was the *Structure
of Social Action*.[1]

Though Parsons once described himself as an "incurable" theorist, the ideological and social ambition of his first great work must
also be clearly understood. In the early pages of *Structure* Parsons
indicates that he is fully aware that his intellectual effort to develop
a new system of abstract theory must be seen as part of the intense
social crisis of his time. He introduces the work by suggesting a
critical dilemma. Western society places great faith in the integrity
of the individual and in his capacity for rationality, yet both these
objects of traditional faith have been placed in dire jeopardy during
the events of the interwar period. Though Parsons acknowledges
that there are obvious social reasons for this threat to individualism
and rationality, he is writing a theoretical work, and he lays part
of the burden for the contemporary crisis on internal intellectual
developments themselves. It is, at least in part, the simplistic ideology of progress and evolution that has made the cherished ideas
of Western society so vulnerable. This ideology reflects the old-
fashioned nineteenth-century liberalism which, Parsons believes,
remains omnipresent in the English-speaking world. He identifies
this ideology with the theory of laissez-faire capitalism—elsewhere
he calls it the theory of business civilization; he insists that laissez-
faire theory (initiated by Adam Smith) denies any role to the
collective good and denies the possibility for emotional and ethical

[1] Talcott Parsons, *The Structure of Social Action* (New York: Free Press, 1937).

self-expression. It is, in other words, a simplistic theory, not just a simplistic ideology.

Classical liberal theory assumes that if individuals just act naturally they will be rational, and if they just pursue their own selfish interests as individuals then society will "automatically" be stable and every individual want be satisfied. Parsons calls this the postulate of an "automatic self-regulating mechanism." But, he points out, this automatic self-regulation clearly has not occurred. The West in the 1930s was in a state of conflict approaching chaos. The autonomy of the individual was under fire from the political right and left, and the supremacy of reason was subject to increasing attack—"various kinds of individualism have been under increasingly heavy fire [and] the role of reason, and the status of scientific knowledge . . . have been attacked again and again." From the right the threat was Nazism—"we have been overwhelmed by a flood of anti-intellectualist theories"—from the left it was communism—"socialistic, collectivistic, organic theories of all sorts."[2] Parsons suggests that it was against the inadequacies of liberal ideology and theory that these collectivist traditions of left and right had raised their ugly heads. If the integrity of the individual were to be saved, and the capacity of reason sustained, then this liberal theory must be changed. This ambition launched Parsons on his famous book. To revive and reformulate liberal ideology was the great moral injunction under which his new theory was born.

Parsons' enemy is nineteenth-century liberal theory, not just the ideology that corresponded to it. He calls this theoretical system "Utilitarianism." Individualistic and rationalistic theory to its core, Utilitarianism, according to Parsons, is pervasive in Western social thought. There are clear social reasons, I might add, for this omnipresence. In a more or less modern and differentiated society, individuality and rationality correspond to the common sense of everyday life. They also correspond to the self-interest of the rising middle classes and to the ideological hopes of Western men and women more generally. Yet common sense and ideology should not define social theory. Indeed, Parsons believes they must be

[2] *Structure*, p. 5.

sharply separated. To understand what he has in mind, we have to examine in some detail the technical "frame of reference" which he develops to criticize Utilitariansim and upon which he builds his alternative.

At the center of this alternative theory is what Parsons describes as the "unit act." This is a hypothetical actor in a hypothetical situation, a model that consists of effort, ends or goals, conditions, means, and norms. Every person, according to this model, has the capacity for agency: people act, they have purposes, they manifest will. With his notion of agency, or what he calls "effort," Parsons grants that every actor has free will, that free will is an indispensable part of every theory. But he goes on to assert that individuals cannot realize their goals automatically, that is, simply as the manifestation of their effort. Acts occur within "situations," realities which in some sense are outside an actor's control. The situation refers to material elements which constrain agency. Because effort is exerted, some of these constraining situational elements can be pared away and molded to the actor's purpose. These become the "means" of action. But some of these constraints are unalterable: they become the "conditions" of action. There is one more vital element to be explained: norms. To say that action is normative is to say that it involves interpretation, that actors interject their subjective judgment into every action and situation. Interpretation demands standards according to which the situation can be judged and the unfolding action related. These standards are norms. Every pursuit of ends is guided by normative considerations, by ideal standards and expectations which guide interpretation and agency. Effort is always expressed through the normative pursuit of ends.

We can say, then, that there are subjective and objectives components of the unit act. Ends, effort, and norms constitute the subjective parts, while conditions and means refer to the objective elements. All action, Parsons maintains, involves tension between norms and conditions, between subjective and objective components. It is clear that Parsons invented this model to include elements of each of the partial traditions that preceded him. Idealist traditions focus on norms if they are collectivist, effort if they are individualist. Materialist traditions focus on conditions if they are collectivist, means if they are individualist. Parsons' model of the unit is act designed to include each of these emphases without surrendering to any their one-sided concerns.

Each of these partial, one-sided historical traditions defines the abstract elements of the unit act in a specific and concrete way. Utilitarianism, for example, insists that the norms which guide action are always ones that demand absolute rationality and efficiency. Because of this insistence, it is the external conditions of action which become theoretically paramount. One cannot "calculate" one's subjective values to see if they are "efficient"; such commitments must be accepted on nonrational or irrational grounds or not at all. The only elements toward which an actor can actually adopt a purely rational and calculating attitude are normative elements from his material environment of action, or, possibly, elements in which he no longer believes but which are backed by threats of material sanction. By assuming that an actor is guided only by the norm of rational efficiency, therefore, Utilitarianism assumes that actors are oriented only to problems of adaptation vis-à-vis external conditions. If a theorist believes this is true, the subjective aspect of action ceases to be his concern, and the analysis of motive drops out of his theory.

For Parsons, the prototypical example of such Utilitarian thinking is classical economic theory, which portrays the economic actor as motivated only by the lowest price. If a good becomes too expensive, this economizing actor will not buy it. Parsons insists that this is not always the case, that factors other than expense or utility invariably intrude. The Utilitarain approach, he believes, radically simplifies action. But the really negative implications of the Utilitarian approach to action become visible only when it is seen in the light of its approach to order. Parsons believed that the individualism of nineteenth-century liberal theory made it highly unstable. Individualism suggests atomism, and if this atomistic quality is maintained social order becomes random and unpredictable. But what if liberal theory wants to overcome individualism, as it must, for example, if it wishes to explain the breakdown of social order? If the framework of instrumental action is to be maintained, such collectivist theorizing must become antivoluntaristic. Why? The reasons can be found in Parsons' insistence on the objectivist effects of any purely rationalistic approach to action. Because the "rational" actor is conceived as oriented only toward the situation, reference to his subjectivity drops out. Now, what if these actions are aggregated to form collective order? If action is not seen as involving subjective agency and effort, then the only possible source of order is external, conditional structure. Such collective structure can coordinate individual actions only through coercion or reward.

In our economic example, the actions of individual actors are controlled by a market over which no one has control. In Marxist theory, this market is itself conceived as being controlled by the distribution of wealth and property. When a theorist analyzes a market in Utilitarian terms, concepts like intention, effort, and interpretive standards are unnecessary. By looking at the prices of commodities and at collective supply and demand, it is assumed we can predict the response of individuals in a determinate way. The same conceptual narrowing is true for Marxist theory, only here the objective evolution of the mode of production determines class conflict and change. Parsons acknowledges that such an emphasis on material conditions is not the only way that Utilitarianism has sought to escape from the randomizing consequences of individualism. The tradition has also developed a theory of determinate instincts, which holds that individual actions are coordinated not by individual decisions but by genetically coded biological commands.

This elimination of voluntarism by the collective version of utilitarian theory, Parsons believes, creates the "Utilitarian dilemma." If Utilitarianism wishes to maintain subjectivity and freedom, it has to remain individualistic. If it wishes to explain order in a more positive way, it has to eliminate agency and fall back to an emphasis on the unalterable elements of human interaction, to either heredity (biological instincts) or environment (material conditions). The latter are conditions the actor cannot control, things which have nothing to do with his identity or will.

I might add that such a resort to explanations based on heredity and environment is not simply a historical artifact of Utilitarianism; it is still basic to a great deal of social theory today and to much of our commonsense thinking as well. One constantly hears people claim, for example, that political institutions with which we have nothing whatever to do "really" run our societies, or that all powerful economic institutions pull invisible strings that make human puppets of us all. We also find a continuing resort to instinctualist theories, which decry the "population bomb," biological "limits to growth," or the genetic "territorial imperative" which supposedly undergirds private property. The social theory of individualistic liberalism has not, therefore, by any means entirely disappeared, nor has the resort to anti-individualistic theories which cannot dispense with its rationalistic view of human action. This collectivist solution to the Utilitarian dilemma, moreover, continues to be motivated by the destabilizing crises of Western social life, crises that demand extra-individual explanations.

We can see now what Parsons accomplished. He developed a model in purely analytical and theoretical terms, yet with this model he was able to demonstrate the intellectual underpinnings of the ideological challenges to reason and freedom about which he had earlier complained. Thus, the instinct theories which he describes as one unsatisfactory response to the Utilitarian dilemma clearly refer, on the other hand, to the Social Darwinian ideology of competitive capitalism which so destabilized late nineteenth-century and early twentieth-century society and, on the other, to the fascist movements which sought to address this instability in the period between the wars. Similarly, the environmental theories which sought to resolve the "Utilitarian dilemma" by emphasizing external and conditional controls, and which by doing so threatened reason and individuality in a different way, clearly correspond to the Communist regime being developed in Russia, which was a different kind of response to growing "bourgeois" instability. Parsons has succeeded in showing that the social developments which threatened liberalism had theoretical dimensions. The "Utilitarian dilemma" in theory was an existential dilemma as well. Parsons has linked this liberal cirsis to the "theoretical logic" of nineteenth-century liberal theory. What is his theoretical alternative?

To overcome these theoretical challenges to reason and freedom, the roles of human agency, interpretation, and moral standards must be restored. But this cannot be done, Parsons believes, simply by emphasizing the traditional individualism of liberal theory, for it was the latter's naiveté which had promoted the very hyperstructural, rationalistic ideas that must now be overcome. The correct path is to acknowledge social structure in a way that does not threaten subjectivity and freedom. This can be done only if Utilitarian assumptions about action are changed when its position on order is revised. If nonrational action is recognized as significant, then moral and normative elements can themselves be seen as organized structures or "systems." On the one hand, these subjective systems act "over and above" any specific individual, creating supra-individual standards against which reality must be judged. On the other hand, such systems have an intimate relation to agency, interpretation, and subjectivity, for the "structure" they embody can be realized only through effort and the pursuit of individual ends. Remember, according to Parsons' abstract schema, human agency is inseparable from the act of interpretation.

Constructing such a "voluntaristic structuralism" would amount to a theoretical revolution against the dominant strand of nineteenth-century thought. This revolutionary intent is precisely what Parsons attributes to the classical theorists he examines in *The Structure of Social Action*. Weber and Durkheim are foremost among them. These theorists, Parsons demonstrates through detailed exegesis of their work, discovered the significance of normative order and, in the process, established the possibility for a more voluntaristic sociology. Their "voluntaristic theory of action"—the name which Parsons gives this new approach—interrelates norms and values, and therefore human agency and effort, with the unalterable, coercive conditions opposing them. While acknowledging that there must always be a push for efficiency, this new theory insists that this push is always mediated by a variety of norms.

Only such a voluntaristic theory, Parsons believes, can provide the basis for a stable, humanistic, and democratic society. Individual integrity and reason are recognized but not in a naive way, for in contrast to the restricted vision of nineteenth-century liberalism both are themselves treated as part of the process of a broader, social control. If this idea reminds us of the Protestant theory of self-control and congregational as opposed to institutional religious organization, it is hardly an accident. Parsons' family was steeped in Congregationalism and it is certainly from the Puritan milieu of American society that Parsons' theory emerged. The "voluntarist theory of action," then, contains both a moral vision and an analytical structure. The revision of classical liberalism that Parsons carried out in *Structure* contained a theoretical system pregnant with ideological implications. Though the "scientist" in him recognized only the theory, it was to be Parsons' life work to flesh both these implications out.

Analytically and ideologically, Parsons' model has been the initial reference point for every major movement of contemporary sociological theory. Each movement, we will see, has developed its own understanding of what this early model was. I will argue at many points in the pages following that they often "got it wrong," that contemporary theoretical movements have either misunderstood this original theory or strategically misinterpreted its central parts. This said, a vital point must be acknowledged. It is difficult to comprehend Parsons' early work because Parsons himself was not entirely certain of his proposal, nor of his objections to the theories it was designed to replace.

There are three major, fateful ambiguities in this early work. I will consider each of them separately, although we will eventually see that they are interconnected.

The first concerns the status of the Utilitarian solution to order and the meaning of Parsons' alternative, his "voluntaristic theory." Parsons rightly rejects a purely rationalistic alternative to individualism on the grounds that it denies the voluntary element, and he insists on many occasions in *Structure* that he is proposing a multidimensional alternative which combines both voluntarism and constraint. Yet there are also many occasions when Parsons himself slips into an either/or approach to the order problem. When he does so he argues not only that rationalist theory must be replaced by a theory that gives more consideration to subjectivity but, much more one-sidedly, that the rationalistic element of action must completely give way to the nonrational or normative element. For example, in his conclusion to *Structure,* he suggests the following:

> The solution of the power question . . . involves a common reference to the fact of integration of individuals with reference to a common value system, manifested in the legitimacy of institutional norms, in the common ultimate ends of action, in ritual and in various modes of expression. All of these phenomena may be referred back to a single emergent prop-

erty of social action systems which may be called "common value integration."[3]

This statement is troubling in a number of ways. By the "power question," of course, Parsons refers to one kind of determinate "condition" stressed by the rationalistic alternative to Utilitarian individualism, a stress which acknowledges that there must be some supra-individual force in society. But why is a "common" value system referred to as the only solution to the power question rather than simply "value systems" as such? Moreover, can the power problem ever be "solved"? Should it not, instead, be considered as an empirical fact of collective life, a fact that inevitably makes instrumental motives a permanent element in every society? Parsons seems to be proposing here a *purely* voluntaristic theory. It is revealing, in this respect, that he spends much more of his time in *Structure* attacking the Utilitarian approach to collective order than he does criticizing the purely idealist one.

This ambiguity is not something that appears only in the final steps of Parsons' argument. The passage I have just quoted shows that Parsons is trying to *replace* instrumental with normative action rather than to synthesize the two. In Part One of *Structure,* a crucial passage indicates that he is tempted to make the same either/or case for the problem of order as well. "Order," Parsons writes, "means that process takes place in conformity with the cause laid down in the normative system".[4] Instead of treating order as a generic problem referring to collective patterns per se, Parsons here distinguishes normative from factual order and equates a truly collective order with the former alone. There is, in fact, a prominent strand of Parsons' argument in *Structure* which insists that instrumental approaches to order are not really solutions at all, that order can only be achieved through normative control. This strand, of course, contradicts the multidimensional perspective which in other strands of his argument he so forcefully presented.

This tendency toward idealism indicates a fundamental ambiguity on the presuppositional level of Parsons' work. There are also potential problems in terms of his ideological commitments and

---

[3] Parsons, p. 768.
[4] Parsons, p. 92.

his descriptions of more empirical processes. Parsons often conflates order in the sense of collective patterning with order in the sense of social consensus versus social conflict. Notice how in the first passage I have quoted above Parsons talks about "legitimate" norms, a "common" value system, and the need for the "integration" of individuals. Yet one could grant Parsons that normative order is terribly significant, indeed an undeniable factor in the relationship between individuals, without claiming for a moment that all the individuals in any given collectivity or society share the *same* normative commitments or, further, that the norms they do share are politically legitimate ones.

Parsons is wrong here to identify normative agreement with social cohesion and consensus. This is an illegitimate conflation of relatively autonomous theoretical levels. Normative agreement within one group of actors may lead them to promote social conflict and increase social instability. When Parsons denies that material factors represent an acceptable version of collective order, he is practicing theoretical conflation in a similar way: he argues not that material forces are astructural but that the structures they produce are associated with the struggle for existence and even with chaos. He has equated presuppositional argument (the problem of order as pattern) with empirical assertion (that material structures lead to conflict). In regard to the latter, empirical contention, moreover, Parsons seems certainly mistaken. In the history of human civilization coercion has often been very effective in creating orderly social behavior, patterns that often have been far from precarious. But I have said that this conflation also involves ideology. If the presuppositions of Parsons' theory really are linked to social stability rather than to conflict, then they must be judged conservative and anti-egalitarian. To allow for the systematic analysis of change and conflict is not necessarily democratic or liberal, but to deny the very possibility for such analysis does, in fact, imply an antidemocratic stance.

These three central problems—presuppositional, empirical, and ideological—are illuminated by Parsons' problematic definition of the field of sociology. His multidimensional theory would seem to indicate that sociology, and each of the other social science disciplines, must be concerned with the interplay of norms and conditions. How, then, in his conclusion to *Structure,* can Parsons make the following statement? "Sociology may . . . be defined as the 'science which attempts to develop an analytical theory of social action systems insofar as these systems can be understood in terms of the property of common value integration .' "[5] Why should sociology limit itself to the study of common value integration alone? The thrust of Parson's multidimensional model would seem to argue against this restrictive specialization. Once again, we are forced to recognize in Parsons' work a narrow, idealist strand.

Here lies the paradox of Parsons' first great book. On the one hand, he has forcefully gone beyond individualistic theory, producing a brilliant analytical scheme with the potential for integrating different traditions and for ending sectarian intellectual strife. At the same time, however, side by side with this synthetic model one finds a more idealistic and one-sided stance, a model that implies a flight from the real conditions of modern society rather than a serious attempt to confront them.

We shall see that this paradoxical quality created enormous problems in the reception of Parsons' work. Anticipating my discussion of this reception, two other problems in *Structure* should be mentioned, since they, too, became references in the later critical debate. They are not, to my mind, so much mistakes as they are limited emphases which undermine the generality of Parsons' book. The first concerns the status of what Parsons called the concrete, or empirical, individual. One of Parsons' major points, you will recall, was to demonstrate that one could account for collective order without eliminating subjectivity. This subjectivity, which is the source of Parsons' voluntaristic theory, is *not* the same as individuality in a free will, or analytical sense. Voluntarism cannot be based on the theory of free will; social order places great constraints on the exercise of individualism in this radical sense. Individualism in this analytic, or theoretical, sense must be overcome. But empirical individualism, the notion that social structures are based on the actions of real, living, breathing actors, remains. Empirical individuals *do* exercise free will, or agency, though they do so within great social constraints. Parsons never intended to

[5] Parsons, p. 768.

eliminate human agency, or free will, in this more restricted sense. Human agency is what allowed Parsons to differentiate the components of collective life, to develop the contrast between conditions, means, and ends, and to illuminate the manner in which normative interpretation is brought into play. Indeed, it is revealing that in his descriptive justification of the components of the unit act Parsons emphasized temporality, for temporality is, as Parsons clearly realized, the fundamental reference point for the most individualistic, "agentic" philosophy of the twentieth century, Heidegger's existential phenomenology. It is the utterly contingent quality of time that allows Parsons to differentiate subjective from objective elements. "For purposes of definition," he writes, "the act must have an 'end,' a future state of affairs toward which the process of action is oriented."

> It must be initiated in a "situation" of which the trends of development differ in one or more important respects from the state of affairs to which the action is oriented, the end. . . . An act is always a process in time. The time category is basic to the scheme. The concept end always implies a future reference, to a state which is either not yet in existence and which would not come into existence if something were not done about it by the actor, or, if already existent, would not remain unchanged.[6]

To focus on institutions or on systemic patterns does not, therefore, deny free will and contingency. It would be perfectly legitimate for collectivist theory—which denies individualism in an *analytic* sense—to focus on concrete *empirical* individuals and the processes through which they construct their own contingent versions of social order. In principle, Parsons is arguing not against the importance of the empirical individual but against individualism as an analytic position, a position which, he believes, conceives individuals in an asocial way.

Collectivist theory, this reasoning implies, can just as well take a microsociological as macrosociological form. In the former, it can explore the relations of actual individuals, the role of "effort"

[6] Parsons, pp. 44–45.

and "interpretation" in the ongoing construction of a given social pattern. As a macrosociology, by contrast, collectivist theory abstracts from these elements and studies the "noncontingent" (though not unchanging) elements of order in themselves, either as norms or conditions. Parsons makes an *empirical* choice for macrosociology. He studies large-scale systems and not actors. Yet, though his theory does not preclude an empirical focus on individuals, its empirical focus appears, on the surface, to militate against it. This appearance becomes central in the later debates over his work.

The last problem I would like to consider concerns the abstraction of Parsons' theoretical enterprise. Parsons states quite clearly in *Structure* that he wants to develop a theory of analytical elements, that is, a theory which defines elements abstractly rather than in relationship to a historically specific period of time or a specific empirical situation. He will leave such a "concrete specification" to other thinkers and other occasions. In fact, in his later work Parsons himself often carries much of this specification out. But in *Structure* he focuses on presuppositions and general models, not on propositions or even on concepts which are specific enough to have an immediate empirical reference. Neither does Parsons discuss methodology or attempt to explain any particular situation. He leaves open, in other words, the character of the real world in factually detailed terms. This bracketing of the concrete and historically specific also proved to be an enormous frustration for many of the theorists who followed him.

What happened to *The Structure of Social Action?* At first, its author's rather recondite voice was hardly heard, except by the immediate circle of Harvard graduate students (who were terribly impressed!). After World War II, however, the book emerged as a powerful document in creating a new theoretical tradition. As I have already mentioned, the conditions leading up to this war, and the war itself, provoked a massive intellectual migration from Europe to the United States, a migration which helped establish sociology departments in eastern universities like Harvard and Columbia. This institutional factor, along with the other factors I spoke about earlier, undermined the prestige of the empirical, home-grown, "American sociology" of the Chicago school. Harvard and Columbia took Chicago's place. It was Parsons who dominated

Harvard after World War II and his students, like Merton and Barber, who created the theoretical character of Columbia. As American sociology became the center of prestige and power in Western sociology, Parsons and Harvard became the center of American sociology in turn.

The postwar period, which extended through the middle of the 1960s, represented one of the most stable and optimistic periods in Western history. During those postwar years it looked as if the integrity of the individual were finally safe and that reason would eventually prevail. Consensual, stable democracies seemed to be the order of the day, and coercion and conflict within Western countries appeared to be decreasing. These internal developments were reinforced by the climate of foreign affairs. Rather than disrupting domestic stability, the capitalist/communist conflict was now projected outward on the international plane. The hostility generated by the Cold War made Marxism—the major inheritor of collectivist Utilitarianism—a dirty word. It was in this flushed and confident period of Western democratic expansion that Parsons developed his mature sociological theory, which he called "structural-functionalism."

LECTURE THREE
STRUCTURAL-FUNCTIONALISM

PARSONS' FIRST BOOK dealt with extremely general and abstract—presuppositional—questions. His professed intention was to integrate the instrumental and idealist traditions, synthesizing pure voluntarism with pure coercion theory by developing a general schema that would mark the beginning of a new "postclassical" sociological theory. This theory, he hoped, would lay the basis for the restoration of the autonomous individual and would place human reason on firmer ground; in doing so, it would contribute not only to the restoration of Western social theory but to Western society itself. In light of these multiple goals, it should not be suprising that in the years after 1937 Parsons devoted himself to a series of empirical essays directed toward the practical problems of the day, applying his theory to the social crisis of the interwar period and to the Western struggle against fascism. These essays push the general and abstract schema of *Structure* in a much more specific and empirical direction. They developed a "model" of society as a functioning system, and they articulated a number of concepts, definitions, and propositions which greatly clarified the implications of Parsons' general thinking for the practical, "real world."[1] This middle period in Parsons' work culminated with two book-length theoretical statements published in 1951, which sought to combine this new specificity with a return to a high level of abstract generalization. With Edward Shils, Parsons wrote "Values, Motives, and Systems of Action," and he wrote *The Social System*—perhaps his most famous work—him-

[1] In terms of the scientific continuum on P. 0, above, Parsons work now moved "rightward" in this post-1937 period.

self.[2] My discussion today draws on both these works. Only in my next lecture will I examine the empirical essays which actually preceded them. In this way, we will be able to place the empirical essays inside the general theory which emerged from this middle period of Parsons' career.

The first thing that strikes us about the theory of this middle period is that Parsons has encountered Freud. In *The Structure of Social Action*, Parsons argued that Weber and Durkheim had created normative theories which allowed a voluntaristic stance. He uses Freudian theory to add more detailed and convincing evidence about the nature of this voluntaristic order. What he learns from Freud is a new way of theorizing the relation between subject and object, which Freud approached in his theory of the superego. Parsons "goes beyond" Freud by extending this superego theory to the entire range of relationships between an actor and his social objects.

In his theory of superego formation, Freud suggested that "cathexis"—his technical term for affection or love—leads an actor, a subject, to identify with the object of his love; further, he suggested that this identification leads to the introjection, or internalization, of the object by the actor. The young child, Freud believed, focuses his affection on objects who are sources of great pleasure, usually his parents. The child, in other words, cathects his parent. Because of this deep cathexis, the child identifies with his parent, that is, he sees himself as like this parent in crucial ways. This identification causes certain aspects of the cathected person to become introjected into the child's personality. Key parts of the parent's character actually become part of the child's self. These introjected qualities are the origin of the superego, locus of the moral sensibility within children.

What Parsons found extraordinary about this theory of superego development was the way in which it provided new evidence to support his criticisms of nineteenth-century liberal theory. Freud demonstrated that after the earliest stages of personality develop-

[2] Talcott Parsons and Edward A. Shils, "Values, Motives, and Systems of Action," in Parsons and Shils, eds., *Towards a General Theory of Action* (New York: Harper and Row, 1951), pp. 47–275; Talcott Parsons, *The Social System* (New York: Free Press, 1951).

ment external reality ("conditions" in Parsons' vocabulary) is always mediated by moral expectations (Parsons' "norms"). Parsons takes this theory of superego formation, in other words, as the proto-typical explanation for the internalization of norms. In doing so he takes Freud much further than he himself wanted to go, for Parsons claims that infants cathect external objects from the very beginning of their lives. Identification, introjection, and internali-zation ensue almost from birth, ensuring that every element of the self is a social one.

Parsons has taken Freud's brilliant insight into the process of superego formation and generalized it, converting it into one aspect of his overarching theory. According to Freud, once the superego is formed people model every authority they encounter on the internalized authority of their parents. According to Parsons, this internalization does not apply simply to authority: few objects are ever encountered by a person without his having had some previous experience of things "like" them. The existence of external objects is usually guided, therefore, by internalized models about what they should be. Of course, there is always a first time for a new kind of object, yet during this first encounter these objects invariably become the basis for cathexis and internalization. In Parsons' and Shils' words, "objects, by the significance and cathexes attached to them, become organized into the actor's system of orientations."[3] When we see a woman, a man, or a student, or even a chair, a classroom, or a fight, we never really see these objects as external to ourselves—unless, of course, we are encountering such things for the very, very first time in our lives, and even then only small parts of them will be really new. Instead, Parsons suggests, we encounter these objects as in crucial ways already familiar ones, encountering them, as it were, from "within" rather than from "without." This is so because we already have internalized expec-tations (norms) about what such objects or situations will entail. If this were not so, Parsons believes, if we lived with and encountered completely unfamiliar objects, then we would have no intuitive understanding of the world in which we live. Utilitarian theory-would be right: objects would be external to us and we could act toward them only in an impersonal, instrumental, mechanistic way.

---

[3] Parsons and Shils, p. 54.

Parsons' reinterpretation of introjection and internalization suggests that childhood generalization should be seen as critical not
only to the construction of the self but to the formation of society.
These considerations, in turn, point to the relationship between
socialization and cultural values on the one hand, and to the
relationship between socialization and social "objects" on the other.
It was undoubtedly this line of thinking that led Parsons to develop,
during this same period, his crucially important model of the three
different systems of action: personality, society, and culture.

Personality systems, social systems, and cultural systems are analytic distinctions, not concrete ones. They correspond to different
levels or dimensions of all social life, not to distinct physical entities.
Any concrete entity—a person, a social situation, an institution—
can be understood in terms of each of these dimensions; each exists
in all three systems at once. Indeed, Parsons uses the distinction
to argue for the interpenetration of the individual self, his social
objects, and the society's cultural values.

The personality, Parsons reasons, refers to the need dispositions
of the individual person. These need dispositions are a combination
of organic and emotional needs, and they become organized into
an individual "identity" through the process of socialization, through
the individual's evolving experience with society. This personality
level is the source of a distinctive and unique self. Still, it does not
imply an individual self in the atomistic sense of Utilitarianism.
Although the physical separateness of individuals from one another
may contribute to such an impression, Parsons warns us that this
is an illusion. Physiological differentiation does not correspond to
social or cultural differentiation. The personality is a distinct level
of social life, and it does connote the uniqueness of the person.
But this uniqueness is itself the product of an encounter with
society.

The social system level refers to the interaction between different
personalities or, in commonsense terms, to the interdependence of
people. But remember, this is a presuppositional point, not a directly
empirical one. Although the social system is the level of interaction,
this may be interaction of a cooperative or antagonistic sort. Indeed,
interaction means there is more than one person, and whenever
we have two or more people we are faced with the problem of

the distribution of goods. The social system, then, is subject to the pressures of scarcity and organization. It includes a range of institutions and structures whose "function" it is to deal with scarcity and to provide organization, imperatives which in their turn raise the issues of legitimacy and justice.

Finally, there is the cultural system. Culture does not refer to the need dispositions in people, nor to the nature of actual interactions, but rather to broad symbolic patterns of meaning and value. Cultural patterns inform specific interactions and need dispositions but there is always a gap between the generality of a cultural value and the particular way its meaning becomes formulated by a society or a personality.

The differentiation between levels of culture, society, and personality can be illustrated if we consider the symbolic value "liberty." This implies a commitment by the cultural system, let us say, to the ideal that individuals should have freedom. As such, it is an extremely general and diffuse commitment which may be shared by societies and personalities that differ in many ways. In terms of social system organization, the level of specific institutions, we can think of a number of different organizational patterns which attempt to produce economic liberty. Early capitalist society emphasized one kind of liberty, particularly the liberty to buy and sell. Later welfare-state capitalism organized liberty in a different way, emphasizing the freedom of less powerful people to control their own movements and resources. In the earlier phase of capitalism freedom was more accessible to the upper classes, whereas the increased freedom which later capitalism provided for lower income groups comes at the expense of restrictions on owners property. My point is that both kinds of social system organization are consistent with the more general cultural commitment to liberty. If we move down to the even more specific level of the personality, the same relative autonomy of these systems obtains: "liberty" can become a need disposition for the personality in a number of different ways. It could, for example, be articulated by a strongly disciplined personality with strict superego controls. In this case, freedom becomes a matter of self-discipline and purposeful control. Yet a personality could also act "freely" by responding to spontaneous needs for sexual expression. Each of these need dispositions, in turn, could be further specified in different ways, for example, they could be either selfish or altruistic.

The analytic autonomy of these levels should not blind us to the fact that there is almost always some correspondence between them. The organization of scarce resources must be affected by the universe of meanings upon which people draw to understand the world, and the personalities which people develop must be based upon the social and cultural objects which are available for internalization. Symbolic ideals about freedom, then, tend to occur alongside social systems capable of allowing freedom, and both symbols and societies typically interrelate with personality systems capable of acting in a "free" way.

Yet if we look at the history of Western societies, and at developing societies in the process of modernization today, we see that the analytical levels of culture, society, and personality often correspond to uneven levels of empirical development, and that rather than complementary interrelationships there is strain and disequilibrium. In the eighteenth century, for example, significant areas of French intellectual life (part of the cultural system) became influenced by the ideal of freedom. Yet equally significant areas of the social system remained organized in feudal and aristocratic structures which denied political and economic freedom to those very sections of the society most culturally committed to it. This incompatibility might be one way of conceptualizing the origins of the French Revolution. Or to take another historical example, a small religious group, the English Puritans, encouraged the formation of personalities which, in turn, fostered autonomy and disciplined self-control. Yet neither the culture nor the social system of seventeenth-century England was organized in a way that was complementary with this psychological asceticism. How was this empirical incompatibility resolved? The Puritan personality gradually changed the English cultural climate to make it more consistent with cultural asceticism. This cultural change also contributed to fundamental reorganization in the social system.

In many developing societies today, one can see powerful cultural commitments to modernity—sometimes to freedom, sometimes to equality—yet one often finds precious little ability to realize these ideals in social system terms, or, sometimes, on the level of personality. On the other hand, modernizing societies often have the social system resources to realize a given cultural value, for example, they may have established fine centers of higher education. Yet this social system capacity might occur without cultural patterns that are strong enough to make this higher education seem valuable or necessary.

The differentiation between culture, personality, and society, then, allows one to appreciate the interpenetration of individual and society even while it highlights the fact that the links between socialized individuals, psychologically affected societies, and socialized cultures may actually be quite precarious. This notion of precarious interrelation brings us to the issue of Parsons' systemic model of social (as opposed to psychological or cultural) life. This is the heart of his early structural-functional theory. In what remains of today's lecture, I will examine this model in a highly simplified form, as the paradigm of interaction and social roles.

Parsons believes that the social system should not be conceptualized in terms of material structures or institutions but, instead, as a complicated series of social "roles." Roles are impersonal social niches which consist of obligations to perform in specific ways. The material structures, institutions, and organizations of society, he believes, are significant not for themselves but for the kinds of roles which they provide. These abstract yet quite definite role obligations are, of course, themselves the products of different pressures and resources. I will speak about these pressures and resources later. For now, let us simply acknowledge, with Parsons, that roles exist, for example, that "teacher" is a real role in the social system with definite obligations attached to it. Such a role is neither the simple product of personality, nor the automatic emanation of culture. It is a detailed set of obligations for interaction in the real world. It is, in other words, part of the social system.

Now, how can such a role be understood in terms of a voluntaristic theory? How can it be understood in a manner that does not make it seem to be something completely outside of the actors who obey it? According to Parsons' three-system model, personality needs should more or less complement the role requirements of the social system. In the case of our teacher, his or her personality needs should correspond to the demands and obligations established by the teacher role. As Parsons and Shils put it, "there must be a fundamental correspondence between the actor's own self-categorizations or 'self-image' and the place he occupies in the category system of the society of which he is a part."[4]

This correspondence sounds as if it were utterly simple, but it really is not. You and I know many persons whose personality needs do not correspond with the roles they play: teachers who don't want to teach, who feel they are not qualified or have developed different cultural goals. For these teachers, their role commitment is incompatible with their psychological or cultural commitments. Incompatibility between system levels produces strains which all societies strive to resolve. Discontented teachers may quit; they may be "resocialized" by the school; they may be threatened through discipline; they may sometimes be fired. Often, of course, the strain simply continues to exist with continuing disequilibrium the result.

How does Parsons think such disequilibrium can—at least in principle—be avoided? How can role obligations, personalities, and cultural ideals be coordinated by the social system? In the first place, there is usually a subtle correspondence established between the roles that are offered by the social system and the socialization paths that are laid out for every individual in that society. How does one go from being an infant to being a teacher? There are closely coordinated, gradually shifting roles in which the prospective teacher will participate, a sequence extending from infant to toddler to child to student and, beyond that (depending on the family situation) to older sibling, adolescent, older student, adult. This role sequence intersects with others, for example, the one that extends from peer group member to citizen, voter, and activist and the sequence tutor, graduate student, teaching assistant, apprentice, scholar, teacher. Each of these roles is a source of personal identity, and each must be finely tuned to meet psychological needs at each sequence. Yet roles cannot only be sources of self-identity, for they must also be related to the social system. The growing person internalizes distinctive social capabilities with each new stage of personal identity.

[4] Parsons and Shils, p. 147.

Role sequencing must be coordinated at the levels of society, personality, and culture. The roles a single person assumes are offered by different parts of the social system at different times. Early roles are offered by family, later roles by friendship groups over which the family has little control and by institutions often far removed from both family and friendship groups, institutions like schools and governments. Yet these different roles must be carefully sequenced and coordinated; in as much as they are experienced as contradictory and abrupt, the individual will not be able to internalize them. At first glance such coordination seems inconceivable. We are not, after all, talking merely about one or two people for whom sequences must be established but about the simultaneous performance of an extraordinary number of different roles. The overwhelming quality of the coordination which is needed demonstrates, in Parsons' view, how ludicrously inadequate individualistic views of order must be. The coordination of such intricate role sequencing can only go on "over our heads." It is the product of a system, more precisely the social system. Social controls, while resting on individual decisions, aggregate these decisions through processes of coordination which no single individual can comprehend, much less direct.

To be effective, this role sequencing must, in turn, be coordinated with the development of need dispositions in the personality. To provide a simple and rather crude example, you cannot be asked to engage in abstract intellectual work, like studying for several hours at a time, unless your infantile oral needs are overcome! Similarly, young people cannot be asked to perform important leadership roles in the society until they have gone through the final Oedipal stage, which means that their psychological conflicts with authority are at least partly resolved. Social system inducements for marriage and family-rearing cannot be "phased in" before the psychological capacity for genital sexuality is provided. These requirements seem at first glance utterly mundane and simple—I have chosen the easiest illustrations I can imagine. But if one considers the enormous coordination required if psychosexual development is to coincide with role sequencing, one can certainly appreciate how this constitutes overwhelming evidence for the extra-individual, "systemic" ordering of social life.

Finally, this role sequencing and need-disposition coordination will obviously be facilitated if there are widespread common values and an internally consistent culture. If our earlier role participations and our present ones can be referred to a common culture, then the meanings that we attach to our life experience will be more coherent, reinforcing our commitment to the role we are expected to perform now. This, again, is not as easy as it seems, for an individual passes through roles in a wide range of economically, politically, and geographically separated institutions. For the cultural system to work most effectively, all of these participations should be capable of being understood as deriving from a common culture. To the degree they cannot, the meanings attached to sequential obligations will be conflicting and it will be harder for people to maintain their role commitments. This will be true, moreover, even if there is objectively coordinated role sequencing (the integration of roles with the social system) and perfect complementarity between roles and psychosexual needs (integration with the personality). The lack of shared culture will create conflict because it means that subjective orientations to roles may not correspond effectively with objective demands. To consider a concrete example, the process of social mobility requires significant movement among people who begin their life in one part of the stratification system, in one class or status group, and rise or fall to another. If culture is significantly different in one part of the stratification system as compared to another, this social mobility will cause serious disruption in effective role participation.

In the social system of advanced industrial societies there are a vast number of social roles which must be "produced" and "coordinated." At a large university, for example, there may be 2,000 teachers. These teachers may have come from all corners of the earth, yet they must have experienced sufficiently similar socialization experiences for them to have initially accepted the same social role. Yet this is only the beginning of the role coordination demanded by a large and complex institution. There must, further, be processes which allow these teaching roles to be specialized and interrelated. Teachers, moreover, must interact with others in substantially different roles, with secretaries, staff, custodians, with publishers, editors, salesmen, and, not least of all, with students.

Each of these other roles depends, in its turn, on precise role sequencing if it is to be satisfactorily performed. Finally, whether or not it is satisfying to its occupants, the social system of the university must provide ways of coordinating each one of these roles with every other.

To take just one small slice of this enormous role complex, think for a moment about what is required for a consistent and mutually satisfactory relationship between student and teacher to take place. First, the preparation for each of our roles must be coordinated, preparation which, I have indicated, involves the personality, culture, and social systems. Then, in the particular institution of which these roles are a part, the university, we need available to us a wide range of complementary resources, options, and sanctions. There are wide ranges of options to choose from: large classes or small, tight or loose grading systems, exams versus papers, to name only a few. These choices and their coordination are certainly made easier if there are strongly institutionalized cultural expectations in the university, so that no matter what our backgrounds and no matter what the resources provided we will expect much the same kind of thing. This issue of socialization into the local intellectual culture is, of course, completely separate from the other kinds of socialization involved, socialization which produces commitments, for example, to the occupational and student roles as such and to broad cultural patterns, like language, which are not role specific.

Clearly, Parsons sees the social world as an enormously complicated place. But there is still more in store! Parsons places his analysis of this complexity under the rubric of a simple question which became extremely controversial. How can all this be coordinated so that it works "perfectly"? By working perfectly, Parsons refers to smoothness of operation, to the possibility that social life could be in a state of perfect equilibrium and cooperation, like a frictionless machine. Parsons uses this equilibrium, or harmony, as an abstract standard by which to judge the requirements of society. Critics have suggested that this criterion creates an illegitimate bias in his work. Parsons maintained, to the contrary, that the equilibrium concept simply makes it easier to see what "went wrong" when we study a situation of empirical conflict. He insisted that he was postulating equilibrium only as an abstract model, not as a set of more specific commitments which actually describe the nature of empirical reality. The model of a frictionless machine, of course, can indeed be used to study the resistances and eventual breakdowns caused by friction in the real world.

The image of a perfectly coordinated two-person interaction, the "dyad" is, indeed, an extremely important one in Parsons' middle period work. He argues that if such a dyad is to be in equilibrium the expectations which each actor has for the interaction must perfectly complement the expectations of the other. What I wish to do in front of this classroom, for example, should fit in perfectly with what you would like to do as a student. Parsons refers to this as the theorem of the "complementarity of expectations," and this theorem is what Parsons has in mind when he writes about institutionalization. Perfect institutionalization occurs when role demands from the social system complement cultural ideals and when both, in turn, meet the needs of the personality. In other words, what the personality needs, in the ideal case, should be the same as what the culture views as meaningfully significant, and these in turn should be matched by the resources the social system has provided for what it defines as appropriate role obligations. If there is this perfect harmony between the different levels of society, individual interaction will be complementary and conflict will not occur. Parsons and Shils put the situation in this way: "The same systems of value standards are institutionalized in social systems and internalized in personalities, and these in turn guide the actors in terms of orientations to ends and regulation of means."[5]

I should add, finally, that in addition to all of these structural prerequisites for equilibrium—the nature of role preparation and sequencing, the coordination of roles within an institution, the significance of common culture, and the compatibility or institutionalization of different levels—Parsons devotes some attention to the nature of actual role performance itself, to the empirical processes of interaction and individuality. He recognizes that "contingency" is a major issue here, that there is an open and unpredictable character to any particular interaction. Another way of saying this (which refers back to Parsons' writing in *The Structure of Social*

[5] Parsons and Shils, p. 56.

Action) is simply to note that actors have free will and that action is inevitably temporal. This contingency opens up new sources of instability. How can it be dealt with by the actors involved? Parsons insists that much can be done during the actual course of interaction itself. Participants make conscious and unconscious efforts to maintain a satisfying course of interaction. In order to achieve this satisfaction, they use negative sanctions and positive rewards to bring other people into line with their own needs. Any ongoing interaction between two people, or between a person and a group or institution, involves continuous sanctions and rewards. If there is perfect institutionalization, a fundamental complementarity of expectations and resources, this mutual sanctioning and rewarding will allow equilibrium to be maintained in the face of contingency. On the other hand, to the degree there is the lack of complementarity between resources or expectations this continuous sanctioning and rewarding can lead to serious and disruptive social conflict, for it will serve to reinforce antiinstitutional behavior.

From this model of equilibrium and its maintenance emerges Parsons' theory of deviance and conflict.

Deviance refers to the theoretical possibility—which is an empirical probability—that relationships between people will depart from equilibrium. To define deviance, we must go back to the notion of role complementarity, the hypothetical good match between the actor's self-image and the role definitions offered by the social system. We must also recall how this applies to the ideal-typical dyad: my expectations will be your desires, your desires my expectations. Parsons' and Shils' definition of deviance as "the disjunction between role expectations and need-dispositions" now makes perfect sense.[6] Deviance occurs when the interaction between you and another, be that other a person, group, or institution, is unsatisfying to either party. This dissatisfaction can be caused by problems at any level of the institutionalization process. That there are so many facets of institutionalization demonstrates why deviance is so omnipresent, why complementarity in its fullest sense so rarely occurs.

Once dissatisfaction has occurred, what is the result? In Parsons' view, two things happen simultaneously. First, there is the internal

[6] Parsons and Shils, p. 152.

reaction on the part of the dissatisfied personality. Because there is not enough satisfaction provided by alter, ego experiences a sense of object loss, to use (as Parsons did) Freudian terms, a loss of love which results in depression or anger. This reaction is mediated by the socialized personality through defense mechanisms like adaptation, denial, and projection. This internal reaction often results in the withdrawal from role obligations, via either a passive unresponsiveness or an angry and rebellious attack. Yet, alongside this internal personality response there is an "external" reaction on the social system level itself, for the actor's withdrawal means that a role has not been fulfilled. In the first instance, this leads to a breakdown in social functioning, for the resources upon which other roles depend will not have been supplied. This, of course, sets off further instability and conflict, as other role obligations are not performed. No wonder that deviance usually provokes a whole range of "social control" mechanisms whose aim is to bring the deviant actor, group, or institution back into line and, thereby, to restore equilibrium to the system. The details of such social control, and a more complex view of the social system itself, will be the topics of the lecture which follows.

Let me conclude the present talk by making some initial evaluation of the structural-functional model which Parsons provided in this middle period of his work. In principle, this model promised to resolve the warring schools of classical sociology, to find a way of integrating cultural and material order, to find a way of attending to the individual without underestimating the role of society. I emphasize "in principle" because in practice it was difficult for Parsons to keep all the factors in his theoretical scheme both in balance and in perspective. Obviously, such a complicated conceptual scheme supplies numerous opportunities for theoretical distortion and strain; if your general perspective inclines you to any one-sidedness, this conceptual apparatus gives you ample space to do so.

The "interpenetrating" quality of this structural-functional model, for example, makes it tempting to underemphasize the significance of instrumental, situational control. True, Parsons explicitly emphasizes the independent role of society as compared to culture, but he believes that in an equilibrium situation these systems will

"line up" and overlap. If one were at all inclined toward idealism—
and we know from our earlier discussion that Parsons is—this
proposed overlap between cultural expectations and social institutions could lead one to underplay the external, objective aspects
of role resources and interaction. Parsons does, indeed, talk more
about the need for social system demands to mesh with culture
and personality than about the need for the latter to meet the
demands of objective conditions. It may well be true that much
social system structure, like the distribution of material resources
and the sanctions and rewards of others, coincides with cultural
values and socialized expectations. At the same time, it is extremely
unlikely that there will ever be a perfect fit. There will always be
some "objective world" which remains "uncovered" by common
cultural obligations; this will create "scarcity" which is unmediated
by subjective meanings and, therefore, coercive.

If one were to analyze the sources of deviance from this structural-
functional perspective, for example, one would have to be very
careful to examine the objective resources provided by social system
roles, not simply variations in common culture and socialization.
It is true, of course, that no matter what the objective allocation
of resources there can still be complementarity between actors if
the cultural system defines these existing resources as desirable. In
terms of equilibrium questions, the actual distribution of wealth is
irrelevant. If culture is internally coherent and widely shared, and
if socialization links culture to resources in any effective way, any
objective distribution may be considered just. Yet no matter how
personalities and cultures are initially structured, changing objective
resources can still create disequilibrium. Common need dispositions
and cultural values can create conflict. As soon as gaps appear
between the distribution of role obligations and socialized need
dispositions and values, the very consensus over the latter can
create sharp conflict and upheaval.

There is another possible problem, one that relates not to Parsons'
tendency for idealizing his scheme but to the problem of concrete
interaction and contingency. We might agree with Parsons that to
look for the sources of equilibrium or deviance one would want
to examine the process of institutionalization. Yet, given what
Parsons has said about individuality—that every concrete person

is different, that each has a unique personality—one would also want to study in depth the specific patterns of contingent interaction. One might wish, in other words, to examine in much more detail than Parsons does the strategies which actors use to sanction and reward one another. It seems quite likely that there are definite sequences and ways of "keeping people in line," and that different ways of sanctioning and rewarding provide fundamental resources for successful and unsuccessful institutionalization. If this is so, then the individual's capacities for regulating contingent interaction should become an object of investigation in their own right. While Parsons' theory leaves open the possibility for such analysis, it never engages it.

LECTURE FOUR
STRUCTURAL-
FUNCTIONALISM IN
ITS MIDDLE PHASE

I N THE BEGINNING of my lectures on Parsons I discussed
The Structure of Social Action in terms of the abstract definitions
of action and order, and I showed how Parsons sought to use
this presuppositional position to reconcile materialism and idealism
through a "voluntaristic theory" to which he was only ambivalently
committed himself. In my last lecture, on structural-functionalism
in its early phase, I talked about some of the most general qualities
of Parsons' structural-functional model of social life, the model
with which he began to specify the abstract assumptions of his
earliest work. I mentioned first the importance of Freud, then I
discussed the "three system" model of personality-society-culture.
After that, I turned to Parsons' conception of social roles and tried
to give you some idea of the elaborate processes involved in their
institutionalization. From there I moved to the paradigm of concrete
interaction, in which each actor is conceived as sanctioning and
rewarding the other. This, in turn, led to the final discussion of
deviance and social control, the analysis of what allows people to
step outside of roles and what happens to them when they do.

These theoretical elements gradually came into place in the years
between 1937 and 1950. Toward the latter part of this period,
Parsons' structural-functional model took on an increasingly detailed and systematic cast, a tendency which culminated, as I mentioned earlier, in the publication of *The Social System* and *Toward
a General Theory of Action* in 1950. Today I want to look in more
detail at this social system model. After doing so, I will move down

the scientific continuum and discuss a few of the case studies by which Parsons fleshed this general model out.

Social systems, Parsons argues, are concerned with two things, allocation and integration. Allocative processes distribute facilities, personnel, rewards. Integrative processes keep these distributive processes under control. Allocation is concerned with production, integration with providing production a cushion and framework. Allocation focuses on means and inevitably produces conflict; integration is concerned with ends and with the interpenetration of ends which, according to Parsons, creates stability. We will see later that there are some problems with this particular way of slicing up the theoretical pie; nevertheless, it is important first to see that there are distinctive advantages as well.

Societies must be concerned with allocation because of the intrinsic nature of the social-system level. Interaction occurs in social systems, and interaction means that there are at least two people involved. With more than one person, there arises the primordial fact of scarcity: there must always be some division of goods. This division produces competitive and evaluative mechanisms to see who gets what. Although specialized roles are developed to carry allocation out—to handle competition and perform evaluation—it is probably more interesting to see allocation as producing important dimensions of every social role. Since roles are the basic components of institutions, we can say that allocation and integration provide two basic sets of instructions around which every institution and organization form.

The first thing that must be allocated, Parsons suggests, is facilities, the "means" to control the situation in his technical sense. Such facilities are inherently scarce. Food, clothing, housing, transportation, communication, tools—all these may be allocated through institutional mechanisms. Parsons calls money and power the most generalized means of exchange and control and, therefore, the central foci of the allocative process. Money and power have a "generalized instrumental status," they are intrinsically scarce. The allocation of facilities, then, is fundamentally a matter of who gets money and power, questions influenced both by the moral, or normative, criteria which are established for distribution and by the external constraints which exist as barriers to their achievement.

It is clear, therefore, that allocative processes are not by any means simply "material," despite the fact they are organized around the problem of instrumental means. The allocation of facilities involves fundamental rules about distributing these means. Money, for example, can be distributed by a collective agency in exchange for public services performed, as in state socialism, or it can be distributed by a competition which allows individuals to keep everything they earn, as dictated by the rules of private property. Similarly, there are various ways of organizing the distribution of power. Power can be given to people on the basis of particularistic qualities like age, religious qualification, race, or personal charisma. It can also be allocated according to standardized rules, as in bureaucracies, and even, on occasion, according to the agreement of all those who are affected by power, which is the case in those few systems which have democratized power allocation.

Now the facilities which are so allocated must be used. People must be brought together with facilities. This is what Parsons calls "personnel allocation." It involves both establishing rules for the positions which handle facilities and elaborating systems which allow people to move smoothly between different positions. Parsons is talking here about training, selection, and appointment. Education is an early phase of personnel allocation. The labor market—the phase in which those educated people are actually "out there" looking for appropriate positions and salaries—is the phase that usually follows.

As with the allocation of facilities, basic rules must be established for personnel allocation to be carried out. Norms about age and sex seem always to be unwritten criteria for these processes, though their importance certainly diminishes with modernization. In more general terms, personnel allocation involves disputes over universalism versus particularism and achievement versus ascription. Should people be judged according to standards that apply equally to everybody (universalism), or should standards be tailor-made for particular groups (particularism)? Should positions be given according to demonstrated accomplishment (achievement) or according to qualities that seem unique to a particular person, like family background, religion, or race (ascription)? Clearly, there must be a fairly close relation between the rules that govern personnel processes and those that have been established to govern the allocation of facilities. If power is wielded according to bureaucratic rules, it would be unlikely that people will be allowed to assume positions of power on the basis of personalistic traits like family position or religion. If a political system distributes power democratically, it will cause problems if the labor markets for political jobs are strongly affected by ascriptive criteria like inherited wealth or if the educational system socializes people in elitist and deferential ways.

The third and final dimension of allocation Parsons describes is "rewards." He has in mind here mainly a special kind of reward, the symbolic element of prestige. Every activity, role, and achievement in society is evaluated in terms of prestige; for this reason, one can say that prestige is "allocated" and that systematic criteria are involved. The same object can serve both as symbolic reward and facility. As a generalized means, for example, money can be a valuable instrument to control the situation, yet at the same time "simply having money" may be considered prestigious no matter what it buys. Money, then, can be both a means (facility) and an end in itself (reward). The case of money shows, once again, how different dimensions of allocation interrelate. If money is central to facilities allocation but for cultural reasons not valued as symbolic reward, there will probably be far fewer facilities produced for basic societal needs. Or again, if power as a facility is allocated according to impersonal, bureaucratic rules, and the personnel distribution for power plays down ascriptive criteria like family connections and personal qualities like good looks, "who you know" and how good looking you are should not become significant bases of symbolic rewards. To the contrary, bureaucratic criteria like "doing a good job" and "objectivity" should become more prestigious and highly rewarded relative to personal qualities like innovation and imagination.

The issue of rewards allocation clearly pushes us toward the consideration of ends and away from means, toward the realms of values, culture, and personality. In Parsons' sense, prestige is the internal, voluntary element that reconciles or alienates people from the more objective allocative processes concerned with facilities and personnel. At the same time, Parsons connects the problems of ends and values with the major social task that parallels allocation, namely integration. It is, in fact, precisely with the relation of rewards to the allocation of facilities and personnel that the core of Parsons' theory of social integration is concerned. I will try to explain this apparently contradictory, and potentially confusing, situation in the latter part of the lecture; at this point, however, I am concerned primarily with explaining the theory itself. I begin with a striking paradox: there are aspects of social integration that are scarcely concerned with subjective evaluation and symbolic rewards at all. Let us consider these before moving on to more subjective concerns.

Parsons introduces the problem of integration by asking what the consequences of allocation are for the ideal-typical model of a stable system? This in itself is perfectly legitimate, for an equilibrium model does not commit a theorist to equilibrium in the empirical sense. Yet we have seen that from the very beginning of his career Parsons often confused empirical stability with the existence of the cultural level as such, an equation that reinforced his tendency to reduce his multidimensional position to a more idealist one. When we look at Parsons' treatment of integrative processes we find much the same thing. There is an amplified and complex treatment of how the interplay between symbolic rewards, personnel, and facilities produces integration, but there is hardly any consideration of the integrative problems that can arise when the more "objective" processes of facilities and personnel allocation come up against value postulates which pattern the distribution of rewards. Yet, as with so much of Parsons' work, the theoretical potential of his writing exceeds his own particular application of it. I will elaborate (in my own terms) some elements in the theory of "objective" integration below. When I do, I think it will be clear that Parsons' differentiation of facilities from personnel allocation represents a considerable advance over other theories of objective allocation. Combined with the reference to rewards, it opens up new, more systematic possibilities for explaining social disintegration.

There are two different ways in which the integrative problems raised by facilities and personnel allocation can be understood. First, there is the simple problem of the effectiveness of each system. How well are facilities being allocated? Are there enough facilities being produced to supply a given population's needs? In its most obvious sense, this issue refers to economic consumption, the provision of food, clothes, and housing. But it also applies to facilities in the sense of tools. Are tools distributed in a way that allows the division of labor to work efficiently? Are the people who make nails supplied with enough iron and steel and the right nail-punching machines? Is there sufficient manpower for the builders in a society to construct the necessary schools and factories? Moreover, is this economic production efficient? Is scientific research linked correctly to productive demands? In terms of the production of power, are political parties organized so that they can effectively generate legitimacy and responsiveness? Electoral rules, for example, may tie up the power-generating process; they may encourage a plethora of small parties which undermine consensus-building, or, to the contrary, by discouraging small parties they may undermine the possibility for grass roots responsiveness to incipient problems.

Intra-system issues can also generate integrative problems in the allocation of personnel. Are people being properly educated? Is enough money allocated for education so that basic facilities can be used? Is there the right sequencing between phases of education, the best combination of emotional and technical training? What is the relation between family life and schooling, and between these earlier phases and labor markets in turn? If schools interfere with families, for example, personnel allocation may be damaged. Social problems like divorce, alcoholism, even suicide might result. These are just a few examples of the integrative problems that ineffective personnel allocation can pose.

The second level of such "objective" integrative problems—those posed by allocating facilities and personnel—concerns the problem of coordination between these allocative processes. Here the question is not whether people are well trained per se, but whether the training system provides the right people for existing facilities. If the economy demands more and more technically trained people while educators have neither the money nor the desire to pursue technical education, severe allocative conflict can result. This is the case in the United States today. The international economy demands an increasing allocation of science-based tools, yet American labor

markets so discourage prospective high school and college teachers
that few competent science and math instructors can be found.
Another example of malintegration between facilities and personnel
concerns the way gender becomes a normative criterion for personnel
allocation. The United States economy needs highly trained women,
but the personnel allocation system assigns the care of young
children to mothers. Some of the most highly trained women are
siphoned off from the economy into such caretaker positions, while
those who remain in the facilities realm are often cut off from
effective participation in the socialization of children. Institutionalized day care might be one obvious solution for this disequilibrium,
yet, in the United States, there are not effective processes to
encourage the assumption of this role. Many other examples of
the uncoordinated relation between facilities and personnel could
be cited. To cite one more illustration, while American society
provides significant personnel incentives for lawyers, the production
of facilities might proceed far more efficiently if many of these
would-be lawyers were trained for administration, engineering, or
education.

Most social theory focuses precisely on these kinds of "objective"
threats to social integration. Marx described the growing conflict
between the reproduction of labor (personnel, in Parson's terms)
and economic production (facilities). He argued that there was a
basic contradiction between the capitalistic forces of production,
which demand increased inputs of capital and scientific technique,
and the capitalist relations of production. In terms of the latter,
capitalist laws of private accumulation and competition, he believed,
force increasing numbers of pauperized workers and bankrupted
capitalists out of production altogether, so that the reproduction
of labor power (the allocation of personnel) becomes finally impossible. Marx is perhaps the greatest example of this theoretical
focus on the objective causes of instability, but he is hardly the
only one. Because sociology is a problem-solving discipline, its
concerns have always tended to focus on the objective and practical.
It is to Parsons' great credit that, despite his tendency to idealize
integration, his structural-functional theory conceptualizes these
objective aspects of allocation in a more precise and systematic way.
Still, it is in the area of cultural integration that Parsons' most
interesting theoretical advances were made.

The problem with most social theory is that it seeks to locate disequilibrium merely at the instrumental level. It is at this level that the tensions I have just described within each allocative system and between them are located: these allocative pressures do not directly involve values and they produce pressures which—taken by themselves—have an external, objective force. Yet if it is people who are reacting to these pressures, these more "structural" allocative problems must, inevitably, be interpreted by norms. Thus, while Parsons' own application of his integration theory certainly slighted the instrumental sides, he was perfectly right to insist on the importance of the third, more subjective allocative process, the process of rewards. Parsons insisted that the deepest needs of people are not for instrumental objects but for love and respect and that, for this reason, people want symbolic rewards. Rewards contribute to stable allocation because they tie objective distribution to the ultimate values of human beings. An idealistic reading of this proposition would suggest that rewards can, therefore, successfully mediate—reconcile people to—any allocation of objective resources. A more multidimensional reading would suggest simply that prestige allocation is always a factor in integration. While Parsons himself often favors an idealist reading, his theory of reward allocation is, in principle, no more than the further elaboration of the multidimensional position.

Let's consider first the relation between symbolic rewards and the allocation of facilities. There must be an "experienced reciprocity" between them: individuals must feel as if the relation of facilities and rewards is "right." The positions which supply society with vital goods, either economic or political ones, must receive enough respect—in prestige or in symbols of prestige like money—to ensure that their tasks are efficiently performed. In capitalist societies, however, there is often a wide gap between rewards and allocation. Productive expertise, for example, is often controlled by professionals who, while highly educated, do not control the sources of money. As a result, the experts who are central to the production of facilities often feel they are not sufficiently rewarded. Roles like factory and sanitation worker, of course, receive much less money and respect, and their experience of dissatisfaction is often comparably great. Yet, while the occupants of these roles contribute to allocation in basic ways, as individual workers they exercise significantly less power and responsibility than do professionals. Only when they aggregate their allocative power through collective organizations like unions can their functional importance manifest itself. After unionization, the tension between the allocation of facilities and rewards for unskilled groups begins to be addressed.

We can also look at functional reciprocity in terms of the allocation of power. This asymmetry, in fact, often makes it difficult to recruit talented persons to Congress, a failure, in turn, that makes the production of power much less efficient. Yet the lack of reciprocity between facilities and rewards can suffer from the other side. Prestige is often far in excess of productive tasks performed. Movie stars, athletes, and the "idle rich" receive great rewards but, in terms of the facilities produced, do very little for the society at large—though it could be argued that the first two professions play an important role in the allocation of personnel by providing role models.

If rewards cannot effectively coordinate the production and distribution of facilities, disequilibrium results. What does a social system do to prevent such conflict, to maintain the integration of facilities and rewards? Since it is culture which establishes standards about what is desirable behavior, this is really a question about the relation between culture and social system. Culture produces expectations about prestige distribution, and the most central of these expectations are, in turn, concretized into laws. Property laws, for example, are crucial factors in deciding the relationship between different productive activities and monetary reward. Pure private property systems allow a vast distance between money and expertise; through inheritance one can own the means of production and the profit it produces without any particular achievement oneself. In such a system artists, writers, and scientists may produce great value for a society but, if they are unable to turn their products into property, they will not receive appropriate monetary reward.

Such pure private property systems are based upon a culture of extreme individualism. Insofar as a culture develops in a more egalitarian or collectivistic direction rewards will be distributed in different ways. Progressive income tax laws, for example, seek to assure a more integrative relation between rewards and achievement. By taxing higher incomes more heavily, they ensure that inherited wealth will be reduced more sharply than wealth which is related to achievements. Inheritance laws go even further in this direction. Laws concerning property, tax, and inheritance can, of course, be viewed from both an integrative and an allocative point of view. If your concern is purely with allocative efficiency, you may want to offer very high rewards for innovative achievement, regardless of the inegalitarian consequences. You might, in other words, wish to reduce the level of taxation on great wealth insofar as that wealth is earned by productive achievement. If, on the other hand, your concern is with social integration, you might be willing to reduce allocative production for the sake of achieving more equality and less social conflict. The debate between conservatives and liberals over the welfare state revolves precisely over this issue of integration versus allocation. History has shown that exclusive concentration on the production of means (facilities) at the expense of ends (rewards) will not only create conflict but, eventually, undermine the allocation of means itself. At the same time, capitalist countries which have taxed entrepreneurs at rates of 60 percent and more (like the social democracy of Sweden) have found that this, too, has its drawbacks. The integration achieved may have a deleterious effect on production, an allocative problem which often reacts back on social integration in turn.

I should add, of course, that money and the laws pertaining to money are far from being the only forms that reward allocation takes. Prestige manifests itself in more ephemeral but equally effective ways. Over the last century, for example, the growth of more egalitarian values has taken prestige away from the "idle rich" much more rapidly and effectively than it has taken away their property. This shift in prestige allocation has certainly been as important in reequilibrating the capitalist system as have changes in income distribution per se.

The relation between rewards and personnel allocation is similarly subject to cultural mediation and control. Insofar as cultural values become more oriented to achievement and less subject to aristocratic ideas of ascribed, or inborn, qualities, processes that seek to subordinate personnel selection to particularistic concerns—like religious or racial quotas—are increasingly thrown into doubt. Ascriptive considerations in personnel allocation are, of course, virtually impossible completely to erase. For example, being born to an upper- or a lower-class family will always have some effect no matter how open adult or student recruitment is, and birth, obviously, is a matter of luck not achievement! Still, any significant sense of disproportion between the criteria employed in personnel selection and reward distribution creates a sense of injustice, and those who feel they have been unjustly rewarded often withdraw from allocative processes or even actively oppose them. The negative consequences for integration are potentially enormous, revolution by an oppressed, discriminated against group being the proverbial case in point.

Two caveats are worth mentioning here. First, any personnel process can usually be seen from both allocative and integrative points of view, a fact which enormously complicates the resolution of social strains. Tracking in education, for example, was initiated in part to satisy the *end* of equality; the idea was to allow more social mobility for intelligent and industrious but underprivileged people by allowing higher achieving children to receive special attention. But tracking was also initiated because it provided a *means* of training the most capable personnel in efficient and effective ways. Efforts to eliminate tracking in the name of more radically egalitarian values must cope with this double-sided constraint, for its elimination may undermine the most efficient training of society's personnel. Much the same ambiguity exists in relation to "affirmative action" in hiring. Recruitment criteria in hiring are affected by both allocative and integrative concerns. Affirmative action was initiated as a vehicle for social justice in the wake of racial unrest in the 1960s. By the end of the 1970s, this "integrative" support for affirmative action began to fade; cultural values had changed, and in a time of increased economic constraint, allocative issues became much more important. In the Supreme Court's Bakke decision, affirmative action came to be justified in terms of allocative criteria alone. The court argued that education would be more "effective" if it were more racially equal—not that it would be more just. They suggested, for example, that professional education needs a wide ethnic base if professional services are to cope effectively with the problems of a diverse society.

My second caveat about the allocation/integration relation concerns the proverbial luck of the draw. Good looks, physical coordination, height, weight, inherited intelligence—all these tend to be randomly distributed. Yet each of these attributes comes into play in allocative processes. It is probably true, therefore, that even the most just social system cannot entirely eliminate the sense of injustice from society.

Parsons does not, however, write about integration only in terms of these kinds of automatic "equilibriating processes" which occur between the three allocative dimensions themselves. He also conceptualizes integration as the background against which such processes function and as the court of last resort when they fail. Childhood socialization, he believes, creates an all-important limiting framework of expectations. Parsons and Shils put this idea in a way that, once again, may discourage the hopes of radical egalitarianism.

> The process of socialization in the family, school, and play groups and in the community focuses need-dispositions in such a way that the degree of incompatibility of the active aspirations and claims for social and nonsocial objects is reduced, in "normal conditions," to the usually executable task of making allocations among sectors of the population most of whose claims will not too greatly exceed what they are receiving.[1]

Socialization, in other words, forms personalities before they enter into tension-filled allocative processes and integrative disputes. It forms the background to these processes in two ways. First, it supplies the basic categories of identification and communication without which these specific social processes would be chaotic and even incomprehensible, categories of human and nonhuman objects like good and evil, male and female. Second, it supplies a kind of feedback loop from malintegration back to social behavior that may reconcile people to role strains after they occur. Unequal class

---

1. Parsons and Shils, "Values, Motives, and Systems of Action," in Parsons and Shils, eds., *Towards a General Theory of Action* (New York: Harper and Row, 1951), p. 197.

positions, for example, can themselves become the source of socialization, supplying the expected frameworks of interpretation rather than the external objects which interpretation attacks. In this way, stratification may become so normalized that the advocacy of interclass justice can become a source of disequilibration and deviance!

Often, of course, functional reciprocity breaks down and socialization fails in its fate-inducing task. In such cases disintegration is met, in Parsons' words, by the organs of "authoritative interpretation and enforcement." The reference here is to the legal system and the coercive forces of police and state. If a society is to stay together, disputatious persons and institutions must be forced to submit their conflicts to the rules upheld by officially designated agencies of control, and whether the contending parties agree or not these rules must ultimately be enforced. Every society reserves the right to exile, imprison, and even to murder those in whom it cannot instill "cooperation." In this final discussion of social system process, incidentally, we can see, once again, how empirically intermixed Parsons' analytic concepts are. The legal system, it is clear, operates simultaneously in each of the realms which Parsons has analytically differentiated. Administrative and business law addresses itself to facilities allocation; property law has allocative aspects but also is crucial for the distribution of rewards; criminal law regulates the state's opportunity for final redress. In the final analysis, moreover, every law has a coercive dimension, for it is designed to operate whether or not cultural rewards make integration a voluntary, intrinsically appealing process.

Before turning to some case studies in which Parsons applies this formidable scheme of theoretical abstraction, it might be well to return to a simple consideration I suggested at the outset of today's lecture. One way to look at Parsons' detailed conceptualization of social system processes is to view it as elaborating the components of an ideal, typically institutionalized social role. Rather than saying simply that every role involves norms, sanctions, and rewards, we are now in a position, given the detailed structural-functional theory, to say more specifically to just what these categories refer. Every role, for example, is defined in relation to its part in the allocation of facilities: it must articulate with the "tools" its status provides.

The competence a role requires for the use of its facilities, moreover, must be coordinated with the requirements it stipulates for entering its status in the first place. Every role must, in addition, set into place prestige symbols which will reward these processes of successful assumption and competence, and it must define sanctions that will be brought into play if success is not achieved. Each such complexly defined role must, finally, mesh with the entire range of the other roles with which the social system places it in interaction. It is no wonder that, in any society, the chances for full role compliance seem so extraordinarily slim and the sources of deviance so omnipresent.

This picture of a demanding, even harsh and imperious social system is in accord with the critical ideological overtones which informed Parsons' early and middle work. We saw earlier that Parsons was sensitive to the serious imbalances in contemporary society and that he was committed to finding a nonindividualistic way to explain (and resolve) them. He wished to do so, moreover, not simply for theoretical, scientific reasons but because he believed that radical individualism and unrestrained competition—considered as norms of practical conduct rather than as scientific presuppositions—were the primary sources of disorder in Western societies (see, for example, my discussion of the disintegrating consequences that individualism has for the reciprocity between facilities and rewards). Just as anti-individualistic theory could rectify the scientific problem, less individualistic, more collectivity oriented behavior might eventually help to rectify the social one. Indeed, in the discussion of two of Parsons' case studies which follows, you can see how Parsons uses his collectivist theory not only to explain but also covertly to attack the competitive individualism of twentieth-century Western life. In the lecture following, you will see, ironically, that Parsons eventually came to believe that his new anti-individualist theory, along with the distinctive developments of postwar society, actually allowed these social problems to be superseded.

For our purposes the two most important empirical essays that Parsons published between 1937 and 1950 are "Democracy and Social Structure in Pre-Nazi Germany" (1942) and "Certain Primary Sources and Patterns of Aggression in the Social Structure of the

Western World."[2] Both have long been regarded as seminal empirical works, studied for their particular insights into the specific problems at hand. I would like to consider them here, however, in relation to the broader theoretical and ideological issues I have discussed thus far. I will show, first, how they can be understood in terms of the detailed structural-functional model presented above—despite the fact that Parsons himself never made this relation explicit. I will show, in addition, that it is possible to relate these essays to the broader theoretical and ideological developments in Parsons' work I have earlier discussed.

Because the essay on aggression supplies a general framework within which to consider Parsons' discussion of Germany, I will consider it first. Parsons wrote this essay after World War II, the devastating conflict which brought to a head the pathological tendencies that had spurred his theorizing in the interwar period. His aim was to explain why this pathology occurred, why Western society had been brought to the brink of massive destruction. Here was a true challenge for his social system theory. Could it explain the problems which had motivated its creation?

Parsons first describes the tremendous allocative strains of Western societies. For the production of facilities Western nations have developed enormously specialized and differentiated mechanisms which emphasize efficiency, expertise, and technology. Yet to achieve this extraordinary adaptive capacity, the organization of productive institutions, like the industrial factory and the bureaucratic state, must be made resolutely impersonal. Parsons suggests that this has had profound consequences for the allocation of personnel. Demands for impersonal efficiency can be met only if the intimate sphere of love and affection is radically separated from the sphere of work. The family becomes "specialized" in emotions, and the "office" assumes an afamilial, often antagonistic role. To maximize efficiency, the normative regulation of work life becomes purely universalistic and achievement oriented. Criteria for personnel recruitment must also become radically depersonalized if they are to fit with these new allocative demands. If personnel are to be trained

2. Talcott Parsons, "Democracy and Social Structure in Pre-Nazi Germany" (1942) pp. 104–123, and "Certain Primary Sources and Patterns of Aggression" (1947) pp. 298–322, in Parsons, *Essays in Sociological Theory* (New York: Free Press, 1954).

to assume impersonal work orientations, there must at some point in the training and socialization process be a sharp rejection of family life, which is diffuse and emotional. To effectuate this radical break seems to be one latent function of formal schooling and the informal schooling of "hard knocks," both of which draw children increasingly outside of the home. It is this emotionally difficult break, Parsons suggests, that makes adolescence such a difficult time. Thus, while personnel training may effectively allocate facilities, there is great cost in personality terms. The demands for emotional repression and depersonalization create frustration which may eventually have negative effects on personnel allocation itself.

The allocation of rewards, Parsons believes, cannot really overcome these strains. First, the primordial scarcity of rewards actually increases insecurity even while it effectively channels facilities and recruitment. Equally important, however, is the fact that a system which emphasizes allocative efficiency can give rewards only for achievement. The question must always be, "what have you done lately?" Thus, while rewards may reinforce allocative processes they serve to increase insecurity and frustration at the level of the individual personality. The fact that positions are awarded competitively means that no matter what rewards a person has previously acquired, he is always in danger of losing them. The emphasis of the facilities system on technology and cognitive skills, moreover, means that the abilities a person has developed to earn certain rewards are in constant danger of becoming obsolete.

Faced with such strains the integrative challenge for Western societies is clear. Parsons has demonstrated that their allocative processes have established intrinsically frustrating role relationships. The personality system of "ego" simply cannot get what it needs from "alter"—in systemic terms, from the role opportunities institutionalized in Western societies. We know from our earlier discussions that if role participation is unsatisfying, deviance results. In Western societies, Parsons believes, this institutionalized deviance occurs as follows. The anxiety and frustration built into their allocative processes are handled by the personality through the defense mechanisms of projection and externalization. Instead of allowing the actor to understand the roots of his frustration, these defense mechanisms allow the personality to place the "blame" on erroneous sources. The Western personality scapegoats unpopular social groups, blaming them for creating its real anxiety. To "explain" their problems, people create ideologies that assert the unjustified aggression of forces which they can potentially control, the "rational" response to which is aggression in turn. Aggression, Parsons believes, has become a dominant mode of interaction in Western societies. The malintegration of Western social systems produces what he calls "free floating aggression."

How can integrative processes cope with this situation? As I have already mentioned, Parsons is rather pessimistic about the system of rewards. It is very often the case, of course, that reward seeking can provide a relatively harmless outlet for free-floating aggression, from chasing footballs to running after the almighty dollar. Yet each of these activities results as often in deprivation as gratification. For every folk belief about money buying happiness there is the equally persistent recognition that "money can't buy you love." Parsons believes that cultural systems have, however, discovered a way to skew rewards which allows aggression to be redirected even if it is not eliminated. Family loyalty and community morality prevent people from unleashing their aggression against groups and institutions with whom they have established close relations. But those who are outside of this community—those which social morality does not explicitly designate as "friend"—are by this very process legitimated as subjects for aggression's full force. These external objects of aggression are the proverbial "other," the class, ethnic, racial, or national group which is seen as different and, hence, despised.

To find out precisely which groups these will be is to discover the structure of modern social conflict. To do so, Parsons argues, we must return to the allocative system. What kind of rational interest groupings have been structured by the allocation of facilities, personnel, and rewards? Whatever these lines of interest conflict are, they will be overlaid by the powerful, unconscious engines of aggressive emotions.

But what about the background for integration, socialization, and its court of last resort, the bodies of authoritative interpretation and enforcement? Clearly, socialization allows some conflict reduction simply by providing the basic and minimal "categories of identification" within which every interaction occurs. Beyond this, however, socialization may not contribute much. Parsons has described the difficult discontinuities that socialization faces when home and family become sharply divided, and, indeed, how socialization produces emotional conflicts that contribute to disintegration rather than ameliorate it. This is exacerbated, he believes, by the way in which gender is brought into play. The masculine emphasis of premodern societies meant that when the modern split emerged between family and work it was males who assumed the impersonal, highly rewarded work of facilities production, while females took exclusive control over emotions and the home. This more radical sexual division of labor increases the strains which discontinuous socialization involves. For boys the early objects of intense identification are almost exclusively female. When these males reach adolescence, therefore, they have not only to develop more impersonal and repressive need-dispositions (which is accomplished through identifying with the adult of their sexual type) but to do so they must repress a major sex-role identification from earlier life.

The common difficulties faced by other aspects of the modern integrative system make enforcement institutions such as the courts and the police more important. Parsons does not deny, prima facie, their ability to handle the destabilizing situation, but he evaluates their effectiveness by paying more attention to specific time and place. Just as the interest group target for free-floating aggression is dependent on the particular social formation, so too, Parsons argues, the authority and power of social control institutions can be decided only by looking at the particular structural and cultural situation in a given social system. With this in mind, we turn to his discussion of pre-Nazi Germany.

In discussing the allocative problems of Germany before World War II, Parsons deepens his systemic analysis of the causes of aggression and makes them historically specific. He discusses the development of the bureaucratic state, the rise of large-scale capitalist markets, the growing complexity of social relations and the growth of modern science. Each of these factors, Parsons believes, increases the efficient production and allocation of facilities enormously, but each also contributes to the growing impersonality of work and to the split between office and home. Parsons' most important innovation in this essay, however, is his focus on the polarization that these allocative processes produce. He believes that there developed in Germany a more extreme version of what happened throughout the West: the society became divided between, on the one hand, a "modern" sector which was deeply implicated in newly emerging, impersonal and rationalized structures and, on the other, a "traditional" sector which was fundamentally opposed to them. The traditionalistic groups experienced great anxiety about the loss of the old patterns slipping away, focusing on the end of religious certainty, the destruction of rural simplicity, the loss of economic stability. The modernist sector experienced anxiety because of its vulnerable position on rationalization's cutting edge. This polarization made rewards relatively ineffective, for rewards themselves appeared to be skewed along the fault lines produced by this allocative division. A new group like the German industrial working class felt it had not yet received its due; an older group like small farmers felt, to the contrary, that it was losing prestige and economic security compared to this working class group. Parsons suggests, further, that the German reward system was skewed in an exaggerated hierarchical way. Despite the decline in their objective position, the old German aristocracy maintained much of its control over the symbols of prestige and privileges. As a result its members felt superior and deprived at the same time. Members of the industrialist class, on the other hand, experienced an increase in their control over facilities but felt deprived of anything like equal access to the symbols of prestige.

No group in German society was satisfied with its lot. These unusually great strains between modernizing and traditional sectors made intergroup scapegoating relatively easy. Every group was frustrated, and each externalized its frustration as aggression against those it defined as "criminal outsiders." For the modernizing left— the workers, intellectuals, scientists, communists—the scapegoats were the groups of old Germany, the aristocracy, lower middle class, religious leaders, and segments of the new upper class who had made alliance with them. For the traditionalistic right, the scapegoats were socialists, intellectuals, scientists, and Jews. The stage was set for a battle to the death.

In the German situation, moreover, this battle could not be averted by socialization or social control. German families were even more privatized and female-centered than those of other Western nations. The compensating cult of masculinity which asserted itself in allocative institutions was, therefore, even more pronounced. This exaggerated sex linkage, in turn, made socialization even more discontinuous. These results can be found in the familiar ideologies of German reaction: the fantasy configurations of romanticism, the escapist yearnings for the old ways. Other patterns in the German cultural system undermined its integrative potential even further. The traditional emphasis on hierarchy created, in the face of modernization, a pattern of interpersonal formalism which, while providing a semblance of continuity, further encouraged a rigid resistance to egalitarian developments. By giving this formal authority its complete support, German Lutheranism certainly supported "integration" in the short-run sense, but its passive adjustment to this-worldly authority encouraged the dogmatic morality that made social reform and long-run integration impossible.

If social control were to work in this situation, the lawyers, judges, and police would have to be seen as thoroughly legitimate neutral parties. The problem, of course, was that the same pressures which polarized the allocative system undermined the neutrality of Germany's system of social control. Before World War I, the Prussian aristocracy maintained a reactionary political system that was accorded neither respect nor obedience from modernist groups. In the interwar period, during the democratic Weimar Republic, traditionalist groups felt that the tables were turned. Because they would not accept the legitimate authority of the "modernist" legal establishment, there was no way that the social control system could adjudicate, or even repress, the increasingly aggressive conflicts within German society. The result is history: the rupture of equilibrium and a revolution from the right. Revolutions can be seen as radical efforts to restore equilibrium, to establish allocative and integrative structures more accurately geared to the real conditions of a society's life. The Nazi revolution restored, at great cost, some vestige of German unity and integration. With internal enemies forcibly eliminated, the remilitarized German nation turned its aggression to the Western nations it considered responsible for the modern order it so despised. The internal stability of the Third Reich was intricately tied to the success of this scapegoating foreign struggle.

LECTURE FIVE
THE THEORY OF
SUCCESSFUL MODERNITY

IN THE MIDDLE period of his career Parsons developed a structural-functional theory of the way social systems work; for him, this meant a theory of the requirements for systems to be in equilibrium. I want to stress that to an important extent this theory takes the form of a model. It is a simplified picture of society; it must be simplified, for it seeks to talk about the precise relation of a number of factors simultaneously. Although it relies on a vast repertoire of concepts and definitions and is informed throughout by a deeply informed empirical sensibility, it is not a factual or empirical description of society as such. In principle, such a model biases the observer neither toward empirical stability nor change, neither toward a positive and approving view of a particular society nor toward a negative and critical one. This insistence on the abstractness of Parsons' model does not contradict my suggestion, toward the end of my last lecture, that Parsons sought to concretize his model by making a range of more specific commitments.

In the essays of 1937–1950, Parsons did, indeed, articulate a fairly well-developed, comparative account of twentieth-century capitalist society. This historically specific theory revealed itself to be a deeply pessimistic one, conceptualizing Western nations as systems whose basic structural processes inexorably produced self-destructive strains. From the perspective of this middle period analysis, pre-Nazi Germany was less an anomalous, deviant case than an all too typical outcome. Parsons had certainly achieved the ambition he set forth in *The Structure of Social Action*. He had overcome nineteenth-century liberal theory with its assumptions about automatic self-adjusting mechanisms.

But Parsons' ambition had not been simply to produce a theory better able to explain social breakdown and conflict. He wished also to produce a theory that would be able to conceptualize, and therefore contribute to, a society which would not be at such constant risk. The other side of his theoretical ambition, then, was a positive one. He wished to replace Utilitarianism and Idealism not just because their easy assumptions about individualism and rationality failed to explain social breakdown, but also because they could not sustain a convincing picture of social harmony. Parsons' structural-functional theory, he hoped, would not only be able to paint a more realistic picture of the destruction of reason and individuality but a more compelling and durable model of how they could be maintained. A theory like Utilitarianism, which simply assumed rational action and voluntary order, was incapable of explaining their demise. Only if a theory understood that individuality and reason were social products could their breakdown be explained and their survival understood. If Parsons' theory could face the world in all its complexity—recognizing the interplay of subjectivity and objectivity, individuality and social control—then perhaps the liberal hopes Parsons held about social progress based on reason and individual integrity could be realized.

In terms of this more positive ambition Parsons' middle period work did not fully measure up. He had not used his theory to explain how rationality and autonomy actually could be sustained. The post-World War II period in Western society gave him an opportunity to do so. This was an unusually stable and optimistic period in twentieth-century history, and the United States emerged from the war as the most democratic and stable industrial society in the world. Parsons' theorizing responded to this new situation. He did not, it must be said, suddenly become Mary Poppins; his equilibrium model continued to sensitize him to deep and continuing sourcs of social-system strain. Still, in this postwar period his theory underwent profound alterations. Before 1950, he had spoken about the "West" in critical terms, taking Germany as its leading if most depressing representative. After 1950 he spoke about "modern" society and identified it with the vigor and stability he sensed in America itself. America, not Germany, became the "prototype" for any social analysis of Western modernization. Fascist nations were deviant cases, the societies which had emerged from the war as communist industrial states almost equally so.

In ideological terms, this shift in perspective represents a transition from a critical to a relatively complacent liberalism. America and other democratic capitalist societies had entered the Cold War, and their citizens earnestly held up their particular patterns of capitalist and democratic social development as universal and right. The euphoria of the immediate postwar period seems also to have had a major impact, sweeping away the doubt and negativism of the prewar and depression years. But there were also more legitimate, scientific reasons for this change in Parsons' work. A stable and rational social order may in fact be possible, and one cannot begrudge Parsons the ambition, which he shared with all his great classical predecessors, to explore just how this possibility might actually come about. Western societies had not, in the end, self-destructed. Despite the second world war and the carnage it wrought, certain basic institutional patterns had survived, and some in particular seemed to have demonstrated great resilience and strength. Certainly any compelling theory of the social system must show the resilience which allowed some capitlist democracies to survive as well as the pathologies which threatened their destruction.

There is, then, a delicate balance in Parsons' later theoretical work. Insofar as he is simply "filling in" his general model with a new empirical analysis of Western development, his theorizing cannot be faulted. This, after all, is the virtue of general theory and model building: it applies to different contexts and can be specified in different ways. Insofar, however, as the optimistic turn in Parsons' later work actually introduces a naive bias toward "progress" and stability into the abstract model itself, this marks a disastrous development. We will see, indeed, that both these "readings" of Parsons' later work are possible. He introduces, in this later work, a more amplified and balanced account of Western development; at the same time, the work reveals an ideological tilt that exacerbates some of the reductionist tendencies we have noted already.

The best way to give you some sense of these developments is to discuss Parsons' later theory of social change. This change theory tried to explain how individuality could be realized without sacrificing "socialization"—the collective character of individuals and institutions. It promised, in other words, to explain independence and interdependence at the same time. The same is true for the new theory's perspective on rationality. While it continues to maintain that there is no "natural" rationality and that situational efficiency is only one component of action, it by no means abandons the possibility of institutionalizing rationality as a dominant form. Parsons' later theory suggests that substantively rational action can result from particular arrangements of situational structures and from particular normative guidelines regulating this situation. These possibilities are realized because modern social change develops in certain distinctive ways.

The master concept that Parsons uses to describe modern change is differentiation. In his middle period, Parsons stressed the negative consequences of institutional separation, emphasizing the psychological difficulties of strictly dividing expressive from instrumental behavior, the social difficulties of providing consistent regulation of independent institutions, the cultural problems that emerge when weakened religious institutions and cognitively specialized thought try to address the vital problems of human existence. The theory which emerges after 1950 is strikingly different.[1] Parsons stresses the positive side of institutional separation, pointing out that it allows individuals freedom from external and dictatorial control. With modernizing social change, he believes, there is increasing differentiation in every institutional sphere. Family, work, law, education, religion, intellectual life, government—all have an increasing autonomy from one another. He acknowledges there are problems which go along with such differentiation, but he emphasizes its empowering advantages. When he speaks in these later writings about societies in which modernizing social change produces destabilization, Germany, for example, he describes them as victimized by insufficient differentiation rather than by too much. According to this later analysis it was the all-embracing German

---

[1]See, for example, "Social Strains in America" (1955) in Parsons, *Politics and Social Structure* (New York: Free Press, 1969), pp. 163–178; "Durkheim's Contribution to the Theory of Integration of Social Systems" (1960) in Parsons, *Sociological Theory and Modern Society* (New York: Free Press, 1967), pp. 3–34; *Societies: Evolutionary and Comparative Perspectives* (Englewood Cliffs, N.J: Prentice Hall, 1966); *The System of Modern Societies* (Englewood Cliffs, N.J: Prentice Hall, 1971).

aristocracy that created its problems, preventing, for example, the most effective allocation of bureaucratic personnel and the just distribution of rewards. This destabilizing corruption was reinforced by the compromised interpenetration which opposed the differentiation of Church and state. These were certainly significant references in his earlier analysis, but they were combined, in that earlier treatment, with the destabilizing consequences of differentiation as such.

Parsons emphasizes in this later work on change that in a good society institutional separation does not mean that the different spheres simply go off on their own in an uncoordinated, antisocial way. Indeed, he insists that the process of differentiation produces new forms of wider, and often more binding, mutual interdependence. In the first place, differentiation does not mean that institutions become completely autonomous but rather that they become more specialized, their goals more clearly separated from the goals of other institutions. This allows one to see that differentiated institutions can actually interrelate more closely than the institutional groupings of earlier societies. Since they have become specialized, they cannot supply themselves with the resources they need. Increasingly they must rely on a wide range of inputs from other institutions, and their specialized outputs are relied upon in turn. This new social division of labor involves intricate processes of social exchange and reciprocity.

But there are also, Parsons now believes, distinctly moral consequences of differentiation. Not only is there increasing institutional interpenetration but also moral inclusion. This happens because one of the most significant things that becomes differentiated and autonomous in the course of modernization is the criterion of community membership. Full membership in the community becomes defined in terms which are more general and humanistic than specific and particularistic. People are increasingly defined as full members of the community simply because they are competent "individuals"; they do not have to possess "special qualities," like membership in particular religious, racial, familial, or economic groups. This is Parsons' conception of sociological citizenship: it is open to all those who fulfill minimum competency requirements. With the acceptance of citizenship, moreover, there is an acceptance by the individual of certain oblgations on behalf of the community as a whole. Differentiated institutions, and the autonomous individuals which now comprise them, can thus be seen as encompassed by a more inclusive community. They are protected by, and must themselves uphold, universal normative obligations, most obviously the law. The history of Western development extends "inclusion" to previously excluded groups, to racial and ethnic minorities, economically oppressed classes, and to other groups like the old, the young, the handicapped, which have formerly been excluded on particularistic grounds. In his earlier essays Parsons stressed the competitiveness and impersonality that universalism engendered. While not completely ignoring these problems, he now emphasizes the equality and opportunities it creates.

Differentiation and inclusion are two major parts of Parsons' later theory of social change. Value generalization is the third.[2] What happens to strongly held values in such a diversified and tolerant setting as the one Parsons has described? Does such pluralistic development mean that values no longer control anything at all? Parsons disagrees. Values are still important; it is merely their nature and function which has changed. Those values about which consensus exists have become very general and abstract. If a society is going to be democratic and individualistic, there must be a great deal of "generalization," for there can be no direct relation between a value and a specific activity. If a direct relationship did exist, if consensual values directly controlled action, there would be no room for diversity, rationality, and change. General values provide sources for some agreement but they do not regulate the details of everyday life.

Take the case of America, Parsons' favorite example in his later writings. If America is to remain a democratic society, its citizens must agree upon the general values of liberty and (to a lesser extent) equality. We need not, however, all agree on values that are more specific, that is, on values that connote specific forms of institutionalizing these general commitments (see my discussion of these more specific alternatives in lecture 4, above). We do not

---

[2]Actually, Parsons identifies four major processes of change, the last being something he called "adaptive upgrading." Because I regard this as merely another way of describing the effects of the other three, I will not talk about it further.

have to agree, in other words, about whether socialism or capitalism is the best way to realize liberty or equality, let alone about whether our present economy works most effectively through deficit spending or through a balanced budget. With modernization, value generalization affects the value commitments that inform every institutional sphere. In religious life it is no longer considered a moral obligation to follow the Catholic, Protestant, or Jewish version of God; one is accepted as a "religious person" if one simply believes in God per se and leads one's life in a manner that is consistent with this general moral obligation. (There seems not yet to have been sufficient value generalization in the United States so that spiritual commitments are accepted as legitimate which give up the belief in God altogether.)

Parsons believes that generalization has deeply affected our most fundamental value commitments, so much so that by the middle of the twentieth century the most basic American value has become "instrumental activism." The emphasis on activism means that Americans experience a general duty to control their environments, both natural and social, and to achieve practical results in a disciplined way. The instrumental emphasis means that Americans feel this activism must be in the service of some moral and social obligation. The value "instrumental activism," however, mandates nothing about what the particular nature of this guiding norm might be. By defining the dominant American value pattern in this way, Parsons suggests that Americans can be committed to the same general value even while they carry out widely different activities in conflicting institutional contexts.

Parsons has described the realization of rationality and individuality in a normative and collectivist way. The three fundamental processes he has described allow modern society to embody what he calls "institutionalized individualism." The differentiated, inclusive, and value-generalized society is individualistic in the sense that the initiative for the action of its units—whether individuals or collectivities—comes in large part from the units themselves. In this kind of society, in contrast to communist or traditional societies, there is no overall directing agency responsible for making ultimate decisions, nor is there a specific value that society can be said to embody which seeks to impart to social development an overall design. In this society, Parsons insists, "choices are open," social change is continuous, and the interpretation and meaning of emerging situations is contingent. There is indeterminacy in the metaphysical sense: what is good or bad is not, and should not be, firmly codified in advance. Yet there remains a strongly "institutionalized" element in this opening toward individual choice. Most importantly, of course, this individualism is itself the result of social processes which no single individual can control. Individual choice in a specific historical moment is relatively free because of value generalization, but the acting individual who chooses has neither created value generalization nor is particularly aware of its existence. The institutionalization of individuality, Parsons believes, also creates certain obligations. Individuals must agree to work cooperatively and to be responsible to norms, just as they must reconcile themselves to a relatively small role in determining the overall course of social life.

In his later theory of social change Parsons has painted a different but in certain respects even more sophisticated post-Utilitarian picture of society. It is a picture that is neither materialist nor idealist, neither individualist nor anti-individual in turn. Social control exists in abundance, but it relies heavily on individuality and individual choice. Indeed, as we will see in the second part of this lecture, social control is confined in great degree to the production of active and socially responsible individuals.

Does this picture resemble Western or even American society in the postwar period? The answer seems to be "yes and no." Certainly it captures something that is absolutely vital to this more recent phase of modernity. In the postwar period we have experienced more stable and more democratic societies than at any other time in the industrial era. Yet it is clear, at the same time, that this picture has certain one-dimensional features; there is a tendency— not always carried through—to convert every vice into a virtue and every strain into a source of stability. There is, in fact, a deep ambiguity in Parsons' later model of modern life. On the one hand, he presents it as a general model denoting an abstract social type. On the other, he presents it as an empirical description of postwar America. For empirical, ideological, and even presuppositional reasons, Parsons often generalizes from American society to his model of modern society as such. Insofar as this has occurred, the model becomes idealized and overly one-sided, failing to cover all the different possibilities for modern change. Yet for all its faults it is still wonderfully revealing, not only of certain important processes in American society but of crucial dimensions of modern societies as such. Let us turn now to Parsons' more specific discussion of how such quintessentially "voluntaristic" social systems actually work.

We will do this by returning to our old friends, allocation and integration. These, you will remember, are the social system processes which Parsons first set forth in his middle-period theory. In a subsequent lecture I will discuss his later thinking on the allocation of facilities; here I want to focus on his later theorizing about the allocation of personnel and rewards.

In the later writings Parsons' understanding of personnel allocation focuses more than anything else on socialization. The socialization process, we recall, is involved in both allocation and integration. In terms of allocation, it must produce the best trained personnel for the jobs at hand. In terms of integration, it should work in such a way that the unequal rewards which inevitably result from efficient allocation will be accepted with equanimity, that is, will be seen by the role occupant as consistent with his internalized values. Both aspects of socialization—its allocative and its integrative sides—are essential contributions to the institutionalization of adult roles; they are essential to the acceptance of a stable, effective occupational position after youth and education are completed. "Acceptance" means that the role is considered to be complementary with the motivational complex of earlier roles; "effective" means that the facilities attached to the role mesh with the person's earlier technical training. We are aware from our earlier discussions how fragile Parsons considers such institutionalization to be. If personnel and, particularly, socialization processes are not operating well, the delicate relationship between efficiency demands and rewards will certainly break down, with deviance and conflict the result. In view of the changes I have traced in the post-1950 work, you might expect that in these later writings Parsons will find that socialization does not, in fact, usually break down. You will not be disappointed in this prediction, nor will you be surprised at the complexity and elegance of the model for equilibrium which Parsons actually presents.

I want to begin by emphasizing the unusually significant role that socialization plays in the kind of "voluntaristic society" Parsons envisions in his later theory of modernity. For a society to exhibit what Parsons calls "institutionalized individualism," for it to be both highly differentiated and broadly inclusive, the individuals who are its members must adhere to high levels of self-control. If society is structured so that its ultimate direction is open to individual action, then it is individual action itself—people's ability to motivate themselves—that will determine their social position. This ability depends upon individual value internalization. In a voluntaristic society, internalization "produces" the allocation of personnel and facilities; it does not depend primarily on external coercion and control. The importance of childhood socialization and education now becomes clear. They are crucial because they provide the major processes against which value internalization takes place. It is clear, as well, that in this "modern" situation value internalization is hardly the same as conformity. The values internalized are the highly generalized ones of instrumental activism. They emphasize rationality, independence, and self-control. Their internalization develops highly abstract and sophisticated cognitive and moral capacities.

School is the intermediate point between family and occupational world. As such it is the prototypically modern milieu for socialization in both the allocative and integrative sense. In a well-known essay entitled "The School Class as a Social System,"[3] Parsons shows how the character of the elementary school classroom, and the whole sequencing of the elementary school experience, is geared to these functional tasks. The really significant learning that goes on in an elementary school classroom, he suggests, is not factual but social. Socialization succeeds to the degree that a student manages to identify with and internalize the values of the teacher. For such identification to be possible and productive, the teacher role must be defined in a way that is consistent with its intermediate

---

[3] Parsons, "The School Class as a Social System: Some of Its Functions in American Society" (1959), in Parsons, *Social Structure and Personality* (New York: Free Press, 1964), pp. 129–154.

position. On the one hand, the teacher resembles the female head of the family and promotes familial values like diffuse affect, personalism, informality, and play. At the same time, the teacher must embody the values demanded by the occupational world—abstraction, rationality, mastery, independence, and cooperation. The first set of values facilitates identification; the second set directs identification to the adult role.

In terms of explicit demands, "teaching" is governed by the adult-oriented code. The teacher not only insists upon effective intellectual performance, upon rationality and mastery, but she or he also demands cooperation, the acceptance of authority, and good citizenship. One of the most striking facts about formal achievement in the elementary grades, Parsons suggests, is that "these two primary components are not clearly differentiated from each other. Rather, the pupil is evaluated in diffusely general terms; a *good* pupil is defined in terms of a fusion of the cognitive and moral components . . . The 'high achievers' of the elementary school are both the 'bright' pupils, who catch on easily to their more strictly intellectual tasks, and the 'responsible' pupils, who 'behave well' and on whom the teacher can 'count' in her difficult problems of managing the class."[4] Elementary school grading is influenced by both these criteria, which taken together indicate the degree to which the child has succeeded in learning the mixed set of values required for institutionalized individualism.

The success of this internalization—and, therefore, the explanation for whether or not a student receives high grades—depends to a large degree on the independence training a child has already received in his family. This helps to explain the relatively bad school performance of working-class and disadvantaged children, for, Parsons suggests, the lower one goes in the class structure the less independence is stressed in family life. This impact of family on school performance clearly represents a closed, supra-individualistic element in even the most modern social systems, since it places tremendous importance on the group qualities outside of an actor's control. Yet Parsons insists that schooling as such remains an open competition that embodies institutionalized individualism

[4] Parsons, "The School Class," p. 137.

in the purest sense. The competition is informed by the general values of rationality and freedom. Grades reflect the child's capacity for performance during school, nothing else. While this performance capacity is partly the result of inherited intelligence, over which individuals have no control, it is more dependent upon the student's ability to internalize the school's generalized values. It is the capacity to become "value-generalized" which is at issue, and it is clearly the lower-class/high ability child who is subject to the most cross-pressure and has the most at stake.

The crucial threat to the successful internalization of schooling values is the peer group, which also presents a fallback once internalization has failed. Peer groups, Parsons believes, are an inevitable source of "temptation" in modern societies, the product of strain between office and family. In his middle period work Parsons described this differentiation as producing frustration which led to anti-social aggression. Here he describes it as leading to the peer group, a much more closely bounded and controlled arena which, nonetheless, embodies similarly "diffuse" impulses. On the one hand, peer groups are places for continuing activism and achievement, for demonstrating prowess in the skills of independence and cooperation. At the same time, peer groups let children and adolescents (and others!) get away with all the things that schooling seeks to socialize them away from: compulsive conformity, overweening personal loyalty, romantic and simplistic ways of looking at the world. True, schools themselves, especially elementary schools, must embody some of these peer group values if they are to earn the early identification of the initially family-centered child, yet these peer values must always be in a secondary position. Peer groups threaten schooling by reversing its value priorities. Children seek out peer groups partly to escape schooling values.

As children enter into their teenage years, peer group life blossoms into youth culture, the mixture of eros, art, physical prowess, and political nonconformity that provides a transitional, "softening" millieu through late high school and college years. Youth culture emphasizes the search for meaning and the problem of identity, not impersonal achievement and universalism. Parsons described this "dropping out" institution long before it had become an internationally acclaimed social "problem" in the late nineteen-sixties.[5] His description of youth culture is continuous with his earlier concern for such escapist phenomena as romanticism, which he also described as a stopgap between family and work. It is, however, a much more muted and optimistic treatment of this earlier theme. Parsons stresses, for example, that contemporary youth culture is effectively restrained by the culture of institutionalized individualism, so much so that it allows youth to continue to play a "socially responsible" role. The possibilities of aggression it feeds, and the deep frustration it represents, are now largely ignored.

Yet even for the later Parsons peer groups and youth culture are serious sources of deviance from the "modern adult role." If this deviance is too strong, youth will not want to assume adult roles. Committed to the diffuseness of youth and peers, they will not wish to engage in the affectively neutral, instrumental activism that is required. Whether personnel allocation is successful or not depends on where the primary identification of youth lies: with the peer group and youth culture or with the teacher and the school. Lower-class children have special problems in this regard. Trained in homes that do not emphasize these "middle-class" success values, they are not as well prepared to make the necessary identifications in school life. They are caught between the values of the school and the values of the home, between the values of the teacher and the anti-authoritarian value of the peer group. This cross-pressuring may lead to withdrawal and deviance. It is no accident, according to Parsons' theory, that the violent culture of street gangs is so much more pervasive in lower-class than in middle-class youth. The tragedy of this situation, Parsons notes, is that successful value internalization is the only legitimate hope that lower-class children have. If middle- and upper-class children have not internalized success values in a strong and forceful way, they have the safety net of family connections and inherited wealth to fall back on.

These are some of the pressures which undermine the effective allocation of personnel. They also contribute, Parsons points out,

[5] See "Youth in the Context of American Society" (1962), in Parsons, *Social Structure and Personality*, pp. 155–182.

to the ineffective allocation of rewards. In principal, we recall, reward allocation should play an integrating role by harmonizing the unequal results of the allocation of facilities and personnel.

In many respects schooling is a perfect vehicle for fulfilling this function because it distributes personnel by a criterion which is also a highly sought after reward, namely grades. High grades are the means to attain powerful position and great facilities, but grades are also symbolic rewards for performing in a culturally valued way, symbolizing as they do universalistic achievement. Because grade allocation tends to be accepted as a fair evaluation of individual capacity, positions and facilities which follow from grades are effectively legitimated. There is only one danger that this apparently neatly integrative reward system faces: people must accept the legitimacy of achievement values if they are going to accept the validity of the unequal rewards. They must, in other words, feel they have "only themselves to blame" if they receive bad grades, recognizing that their own lack of performance brings them unequal facilities and reward. Yet according to Parsons' own analysis of the sources for school socialization, it is precisely for low achievers that this "rewarding" quality of grades is put to the sharpest strain. It is the very people who are less committed to these achievement values who tend to receive the lower grades.

The stratification system, then, undermines the desired duality of grades. The criterion which distributes positions and facilities may gradually become separated—especially among less privileged groups—from the criterion that determines rewards. If children do not aspire to universalism and achievement, lower grades will not seem like a legitimate punishment (reward deprivation); since they have not deeply internalized school values, they may well feel that they have continued to act in a proper and deserving way according to their own lights. This "deviant" transvaluation of values will be rewarded by any extensive peer group participation, which is in turn more likely if a child experiences punishment, or simply the lack of reward, in school. To the degree this occurs, the particularistic "loyalty standards" of youth culture can become an institutionalized basis for challenging the just distribution of social rewards. If this happens, the reward system has failed in its task of integrating dominant values and allocation, and serious disruption can result.

Parsons assumes in this model that the allocation of facilities and personnel is, in fact, guided by universalism and is responsive to the individual's achievement. This is the reason for his optimistic prediction that, while individual rebellion against these school standards can be profound, no basis exists for continuous, group-based alienation from societal processes. Such a prediction assumes, however, certain empirical facts, like social mobility and institutional fairness, which may not exist. One can, in fact, employ this same model of deviant youth to understand how in quite different empirical situations anti-integrative revolutionary process might arise. If the allocation of positions and facilities is not based on universalism and achievement, if it is, in fact, biased and distorted in the interests of a dominant group, then those who experience the inevitable frustration of inequality will eventually see the game as "fixed." To the degree they realize that achievement values do not govern allocation, then the alienation which invariably accompanies socialization will be supported by "fact." Thus, revolutionary communist and fascist movements appeal to many of the same diffuse value commitments as peer and youth culture, and in truly malintegrated situations they offer a natural continuation. Right-wing movements make anti-rational values their rallying cry; left-wing movements, while relying on "irrational" emotions and cultural alienation often make the renewal of "achievement" and "universalism" their militant demands.

Parsons' analysis of personnel and reward allocation in schooling demonstrates both the theoretical sophistication and the political and empirical ambiguity of his later work. While the model is a complex and powerful one, it is often compromised by the way in which Parsons' postwar "Americanism" narrows his empirical reference and flattens his sense of ideological possibility. Qua model, the theory does not necessarily assume successful personnel allocation and rewards; still, it never refers to a situation in which opposition to this success would have the final say. In important respects, of course, Parsons seems to have been right, but this seems to be as much the result of empirical conditions in a certain unique historical period as the result of anything inherent about "modern" allocation per se.

These conflationary tendencies in Parsons' later writings—which sometimes reduce model to ideology and even empirical proposition—reinforce (and are reinforced by) the tendency toward ideal-ism we already noticed in his earlier work. It is this idealist tendency, the tendency toward a "pure" voluntarism rather than a multidi-mensional one, which leads Parsons in the later work to focus much more on personnel allocation than on the allocation of facilities. Because of this choice he can focus on socialization, the most internally directed and voluntaristic of all social system pro-cesses, the one which, if successful, ties such social process intimately to culture and personality. We have just seen how this idealization comes back to haunt Parsons. It was the failure to consider the possibilities of systematic class-based inequality in the allocation of facilities that allowed him to underestimate the destabilizing po-tential of personnel allocation in schools. If these processes are more systematically considered, the model can begin to explain the sources of even revolutionary instability in a sophisticated, even penetrating way. Only if Parsons' model is purged of its presup-positional, ideological, and empirical reductions can it retain its independent status; only by doing so can Parsons' initial political-cum-intellectual ambitions be achieved.

This is the great paradox that haunts Parsons' later work. Even as the theory grew more supple and sophisticated its generalized status became more open to doubt. This paradox created great problems in Parsons' own work but even more for the theorizing which followed it. Indeed, I will suggest in my later lectures that this explains much about the character of sociological theory in the entire period after the second world war. But I am getting ahead of myself. I am not yet finished with the theoretical upheaval that transformed Parsons' later work. The transformation which I will describe confirms, to my mind, Parsons' status as a revolutionary theorist, despite the fact that the advances of this later work were obscured by the ambiguities I have described, ambiguities which have been highlighted by recent theoretical movements which have taken up explicitly "anti-Parsonian" themes.

LECTURE SIX

PARSONS' LATER THEORY

ALTHOUGH PARSONS' theorizing about education and youth extended into the 1960s, it seems to have been constructed with the structural-functional framework of his middle period very much in mind. By the time this work was completed, however, a major transition in Parsons' theorizing was well under way. Many have mistaken this shift for a fundamental break not only with form but with the substance of his earlier work. It seems clear, to the contrary, that an essential continuity remained. Still, a change there certainly was.

Before I outline what this new phase was like, you should know something about why it occurred. Parsons, incidently, gives us little help in this task. Like all "grand theorists" (a somewhat derogatory term invented by C. Wright Mills), Parsons regarded every change in his work as merely the logical unfolding of its basic structure. Each new aspect, every new phase, was an advance, and every advance was perceived as having been dictated by increasingly clear insight into the structure of the real world. You will see that, while I agree with Parsons that his later phase was "better" in many ways, I do not see it as an unequivocal improvement, nor do I think it can be explained in such exclusively empirical, as opposed to theoretical, terms.

In my view there is no gainsaying the permanent accomplishment of the middle period work. No general theory since has matched its potential for analytic precision and its capacity for detailed reference to the empirical world. Still, the model was confusing in certain strategically important ways.

An ironic but nonetheless illuminating way to sum up these problems is by suggesting that there remained in this middle period work too much of Marxist and Utilitarian thought. It was Marx, of course, who used the rationalistic assumptions of Utilitarian theory to develop a "base/superstructure" model of society, arguing that the material, economic forces form a base upon which all moral and ideological—superstructural—elements are built. In Parsons' middle period theory we find, ironically, much of this same ambience. One part of the social system, allocation, is designated as primary; it is the sphere of instrumental activity, the "first actor." Another part, integration, is treated mainly as a reactive sphere which "mops up" the spillover from this first sphere by getting people to believe in moral scruples and, if that fails, by applying social controls. By differentiating allocation from integration in this way, Parsons seems to attach them to means and ends respectively. He implies, moreover, that a society's concern with allocating means comes first, that integration deals mainly with the problems created by allocation, and that ideal things like values exist because material things like money and power need to be controlled. But the parallel with Marx's base/superstructure theory extends still further, for Parsons superimposes upon this material-ideal split the antithesis between conflict and order. Allocation not only concerns means but creates conflicts; integration not only concerns ends but is devoted to the restoration of equilibrium. This raises a very "Marxist" kind of question: would there *be* any values if equilibrium could be sustained through allocative processes alone? In his middle period work Parsons, the great critic of materialism, would ironically have been forced to answer "no."

How would Parsons have got himself into such a fix? Because, it seems to me, he tried to use his conceptual vocabulary to do two different things at the same time. On the one hand, he used it to describe the fundamental social system processes that produce the different "elements" of the unit act—means, ends, norms, and conditions. This marked the "presupppositional" reference of his model. On the other hand, Parsons tried to use this same conceptual vocabulary to differentiate specific empirical tasks, for example, the economic production of facilities from the processes of social control. This marked the "propositional" reference of his model. It is true, of course, that models must always face both ways, toward specific empirical concerns and basic meta-empirical ones as well (see diagram 1.2 in my first lecture). Still, models cannot actually encompass both at the same time. In fact, if you look closely at what Parsons says about how allocation and integration actually work, you can see that because he tries doing both these tasks he ends up fully doing neither. When he speaks about the allocation of facilities, he is forced to talk about the production of certain ideal elements like norms, and when he speaks about integrative rewards he is led to speak about the strategic allocation of material sanctions like money. Just so, Parsons could never really confine conflict to allocative tasks and order to integrative ones. His social control agencies are rife with the potential for conflict, and his producers of facilities are critical if often unreliable sources of social order.

The most revealing evidence of the problems in this middle period scheme is the ambiguous status of "rewards." Rewards are explicitly defined as products of the third kind of allocation, the allocation that distributes prestige. Yet they are never spoken of in terms of the "means" problem alone, which is certainly the case for the first two allocative processes, facilities and personnel. Instead, Parsons describes rewards primarily as related to values, phenomena fundamentally structured by the system of ends. Further, prestige allocation is pictured as the main integrating force in society, despite the fact that it is often in marked tension with the allocation of facilities and personnel. This tension is a very real one, and I am not criticizing Parsons for acknowledging it. What I am pointing to, rather, is the fact that to describe it he must cannibalize one conceptual sphere with another. If reward allocation primarily reflects values, then it is fundamentally implicated in the very processes which are supposed to be conceptually antithetical to it—the integrative processes which deal not with allocation but with its consequences. That Parsons smuggles values into allocation demonstrates, of course, that he is by no means prepared to accept the implications of his base/superstructure model. He has done so to demonstrate the interpenetration of ends and means, stability and conflict. It is this gap between his substantive theoretical insight and his formal conceptualization that Parsons' later innovations are intended to address.

In this later work Parsons develops a theoretical model which sticks more closely to presuppositional concerns. Though conceived as providing access to empirical issues, the later theory models these issues from the point of view of much more generalized ones. The new model does not describe detailed empirical tasks; it deals almost exclusively with the fundamental social processes which produce the different elements of the unit act. The new model, then, is couched at a much higher level of abstraction. We will see that this abstraction is a great advantage. It allows more elegance and simplicity, and it also allows Parsons to resolve points that once had confused him. At the same time, this abstraction is not without disadvantages. Its elaboration draws Parsons away from the details of the real world. Once he has discovered his new model, we will see, he rarely returns to the dense specificity of his middle period work.

Parsons called his new discovery the "interchange model."[1] His students nicknamed it the AGIL model, an acronym based on the first letter of each subsystem which when read as "agile" also communicates the new model's greater flexibility! This AGIL model describes the social system as divided into four different dimensions, none of which corresponds completely to any given institution and each of which relates both to stability and change. The four dimensions represent different degrees of proximity to ideal and material concerns, and the model's intention is to synthesize the idealist and materialist traditions in the most effective possible way.

"Adaptation" (A) is a dimension that represents the forces in the social system closest to the material world, i.e., the coercive, "conditional" forces which must be faced and adapted to whether people like it or not. The economy is the sphere most closely connected to the adaptive sphere. "Goal-attainment" (G) represents forces which while still heavily influenced by material, adaptive concerns are more subject to ideal control. Organization is the key to this subsystem; it seeks to control the impact of external forces in order to achieve carefully delimited goals. Politics and government are the spheres of society most clearly associated with "G." "Integration" (I) represents forces that emerge from the inherent thrust toward solidarity. Solidarity is the feeling of we-ness which

---

[1] First presented as a model of the social system in Parsons and Neil J. Smelser, *Economy and Society* (New York: Free Press, 1956).

develops within groups. Because it is group specific, it is regulated by norms rather than broader values. Thus, though much less influenced by objective and material considerations than either adaptation or goal attainment, integration is governed less by purely subjective considerations than one might initially conceive. "Pattern maintenance" ("latency" or "L") represents the most purely subjective forces in society. It is the sphere of general values, though these are values which bear sufficient relation to objective concerns to be institutionalized. Even "L," after all, is a dimension of the social rather than the cultural system, so it is still subject to material constraints.

None of these spheres, or subsystems, is completely ideal or completely material, a point which is forcefully articulated by the diagram which Parsons employed to represent their interrelation (see diagram 6.1).

The whole point of drawing the subsystems in this way is to be able to focus on the phenomenon of "boundary relations." Each sphere of activity is a subsystem whose boundaries are composed

Diagram 6.1.

Adaptation (A)	Goal attainment (G)
Economic facilities	Political goals
Pattern maintenance (L)	Integration (I)
Values	Norms

of other subsystems with more material or more ideal concerns. From this fact of intermediacy, Parsons draws the conclusion of interdependency. Each subsystem engages in interchanges across its boundaries, each needs what the subsystems on its boundaries can provide, each of its adjoining subsystems needs what it can provide in turn (diagram 6.2).

Each level of ideal and material interest, then, depends on the support, or the "input," from subsystems with more material and more ideal concerns. Parsons uses an economic analogy to stress this point about interpenetration. Each subsystem, he writes, is produced from a combination of the inputs it receives from the subsystems on its boundaries. Each of the four subsystems produces a distinctive output or product—money, power, norms, values. This product is created from inputs, or "factors of production," that come into the subsystem from those around it. The product, in turn, becomes a new factor of production, an input, in the creation of the output or product of adjoining subsystems.

Diagram 6.2.

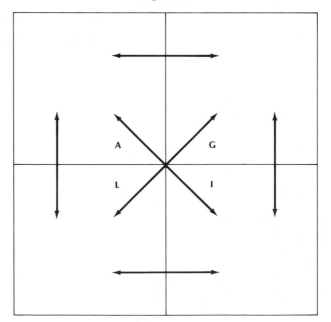

The economy, for example (see diagram 6.3), is composed of factors of production derived from the "G" subsystem (the internal organization of business is political, in Parsons' sense, as is the external support from the state); from the "I" subsystem (legal norms regulating contracts and the solidarity of economic actors); and from the "L" subsystem (general value commitments internalized in the personalities of economic actors.) These inputs interact with the specific exigencies of material adaptation ("A" problems) to produce economic goods and services, often represented by outputs of monetary wealth.

Let us consider a very different example, like the church (diagram 6.4). Here is the prototypical institution of cultural life, but in Parsons' scheme it is hardly treated as an emanation of the cultural system. True, it is rooted more in value commitments than in economic life, but it is also affected by inputs from the material exigencies of the economy, from the organization (support or antagonism) of the state, and from the nature of the norms and solidary relations in the society.

Diagram 6.3.

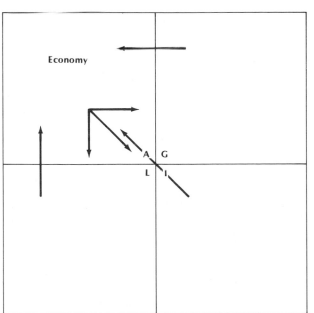

By the way, though modern institutions tend to specialize in producing different kinds of products—religious institutions, for example, are usually clearly separated from organizations specializing in material production or in political power—every institution, no matter what its specialization, can be internally divided into each of the four functional dimensions as well. Within a church, Parsons suggests, there are adaptive, political, integrative, and pattern maintenance forces at work, just as within a corporation there are positions specializing in the internal regulation of values, the promulgation of norms and solidarity, political organization, and adaptation to the external enviroment (see diagram 6.5).

It is clear, I hope, that this interchange model solves one of the major problems that muddied Parsons' middle period work. It makes it impossible to think that any of the basic social system processes is, by itself, either material or ideal. The continuous operation of any institution can be analyzed only through its boundary relations with different subsystems. Confronted with this interdependent model, the social scientist cannot minimize the role

Diagram 6.4.

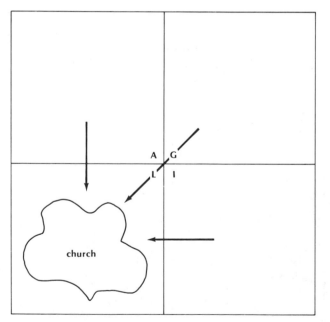

Diagram 6.5.

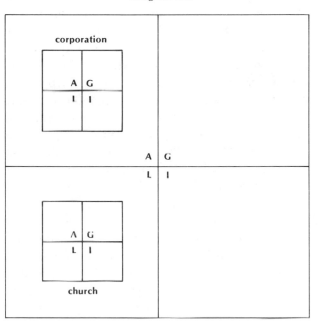

of any of the different components of complex social systems. I believe that this kind of interpenetrating, inclusive model is always what Parsons had in mind. One could go back to the early descriptions of aggression and Nazism, or to the processes modeled in the middle period, and reconceptualize them in terms of the boundary exchanges he has now described. With the interchange model, Parsons found an elegant, precise, and sophisticated model to articulate his long-standing ambition to synthesize ideal and material forms.

It should also be evident that, in principle at least, this interchange model can also resolve the second major problem of the middle period work, namely the tendency for that work to separate the analysis of stability from conflict. According to interchange theory, no subsystem specializes in stability or change; both processes, rather, are ever present empirical possibilities. Equilibrium depends on a general reciprocity between inputs and outputs throughout the social system. Each subsystem must get a certain amount of support from its environing systems, and this support is far from an automatic thing: it depends on whether the subsystem can supply its environing systems with the resources they need. If a sector or institution cannot command the resources it needs to continue operation, its production will falter. If its output falls, so do its contributions to other systems, which will feel cheated and withdraw their inputs in turn. Conflict will result, not just between different subsystems but within them as well. The conflicts Parsons so often described in his earlier work can be reconceptualized in such interchange terms. Education, for example, may be seen as an output from "L" to "A" and "G". Children are taught appropriate values, they enter the labor market (the boundary between "L" and the organizations of "A" and "G") and eventually they assume adult positions of organizational responsibility. The more differentiated and autonomous the institutions in "L", "A", and "G", however, the longer and more difficult this transition from socialization to adult position becomes. Inputs from families and schools remain crucial, but they become more difficult to make.

The forces produced by each subsystem in the interchange model often exert themselves in an "invisible" way. The norms which "I" produces, for example, are not concrete things that people consciously confront, nor are the "organizational problems" (the product of "G") which a group faces always concretely embodied in the form of an actual person or state. But Parsons suggests that there are many times when these subsystem forces do, in fact, assume a very concrete and specific form. He calls the concrete forms of subsystem products "generalized media of exchange."[2] The medium for the adaptive subsystem is money, for the goal attainment system power, for the integrative system influence, and for pattern maintenance value commitments. Each of these media is a concrete sanction or reward; it is wielded by people and institutions trying to get results in interaction with others. States and politicians wield power to commit people to their goals, corporations and entrepreneurs use money to get cooperation, universities and churches invoke hallowed values (like God or rationality)

---

[2] "On the Concept of Influence" (1963), pp. 355-382; and "On the Concept of Political Power" (1963), in pp.297–354, in Parsons, *Sociological Theory and Modern Society;* "On the Concept of Value Commitments" (1968) in Parsons, *Politics and Social Structure* (New York: Free Press, 1969), pp. 439–472.

to gain adherents, and representatives of solidary groups use influence to get people to join with them.

Behind each medium, of course, stands the interchange process. In the course of a particular action, individuals, groups, or institutions "represent" a particular subsystem; they act in their own interest within the confines of exchange. They wield a medium, hoping to exchange some of it for the media of adjoining subsystems; in so doing, they hope to gain the "factors of production" needed to produce more of their own. One need only listen to the appeals of a public radio or television station during a funding drive to know the kind of bargaining that the use of even such a subjective medium as value commitments involves! Invoking cultural ideals and playing upon guilt feelings, fund raisers try to "trade" some of their station's value commitments for the more conditional factors necessary for the station's continued production. To produce more of the value medium, they need more money, power, and organization, and solidary support from the community.

It is because he viewed media as caught up in the vicissitudes of exchange that Parsons conceptualized the form of each medium in a flexible way. He described each medium as having a kind of split personality. On the one hand, it can be generalized and symbolic, a form which corresponds to being accepted by others on the basis of trust. Dollar bills, for example, are a mere symbol of goods and services, yet people will accept this flimsy piece of paper for real goods because they trust its promissory value. Such a medium has "generalized" status; it is a general thing which stands for a wide range of specific goods. But this generalized, symbolic form is not automatically maintained; its "backup system," the system of economic "production," must be in good working order. Why? Because the "real goods" must be there when the consumer decides to "make good" on the promise of the generalized medium.

If the backup production system falters, if people learn that money is not easily redeemable for real goods, people will no longer accept the product of economic production in its symbolic form. They will demand not generalized promises but the concrete goods themselves. Parsons calls this concrete form the medium's "base." While each medium consists of base and symbol, social systems work much more smoothly if the symbolic form is widely accepted. If economic actors all demanded real goods in exchange for services, we would be back to a barter economy. Such restricted exchange would undermine the division of labor and, eventually, the wealth of society. Banking, for example, would be eliminated because people would not trust the symbolic status of promissory notes, and without banking it would be impossible to aggregate capital for large-scale production. A society's resort to the base form and barter does not occur arbitrarily. It is only when a social system actually begins to break down and production falters that generalization is reduced and the "base" form demanded. This demand contributes to the vicious circle of distrust which makes production that much more difficult.

The same kind of dynamics I have outlined for money applies to the other media as well. Influence, you remember, is the medium of the integrative system, whose "product" is solidarity and norms. In its generalized form, influence works because a person trusts that the wielder of influence "really" is what he or she says they are, that they really are friendly, i.e., solidary with, the same groups and communities to which the person who is influenced belongs. The person assumes, in other words, that the symbolic medium, influence, can be redeemed for the "real thing," communal solidarity. To allow yourself to be influenced means, in fact, that you do not try to "look behind" the influential person in order to force him to show us his solidary ties. Instead, you allow yourself to be influenced by the person on the basis of his personal demeanor, by his "presence" alone.

One can see from this example how efficient the generalized status of influence is. Influential people can organize new groups quickly, responding to contingencies in a flexible way. But the generalized status of influence depends on effective integrative "production." If integrative production fails, social solidarity breaks down, and influence will not be so easily accepted. Rather than being inclined to trust a stranger as a potential friend, you will be inclined to see those trying to influence you as potential enemies. If you feel this way, you will try to get them to "prove" their solidarity with you by trying to establish their ties in irrefutable ways. In highly unstable situations, where integration has really broken down, people may allow themselves to be influenced only by those in their immediate region or their neighborhood, or only by those in their own religious, political, or ethnic group. The "base" of influence is felt, or experienced, solidarity. As the integrative system fails and symbolic influence is increasingly rejected, the basis for experienced solidarity becomes so narrow that the ability to influence can come to be circumscribed by familial, blood connections alone. This introduces a "barter system" for influence which would make it almost impossible to form wider associations.

Of all the social system media it is power that draws Parsons' most concentrated attention, and it is upon his discussion of power that I propose to spend the rest of this talk. But there is another reason for my decision, for the topic of power also provides a concentrated comparison of the middle and later phases of Parsons' work. When Parsons discusses power and its "production," he is continuing in another form his earlier concern with allocative processes. If we analyze this later treatment of power, therefore, we will be able to offer one final evaluation of the strengths and weaknesses of the later work.

Parsons emphasizes that power has two levels. Its base, what Parsons calls its "intrinsic persuader," is force pure and simple. The state with its monopoly on physical coercion, or an individual with physical superiority, can make people do what they themselves may not wish to do. Yet while this is one form of power, Parsons stresses that it is not its only form. As we know from his earlier work, he believes social systems work much better if people want to do what they must do. Power possesses this voluntary component in its generalized, symbolic form. People want to do what power has the objective capacity to force them to do if they believe in its legitimacy. If power is legitimate, people trust it, and if they have trust they will follow the orders of powerful actors without demanding proof of his actual control!

This is the essence of Parsons' later model of power as a generalized medium of exchange. Whether power actually operates as a generalized element, however, depends on concrete empirical considerations, for it is the nature of the actual social system within which it functions that determines the resources the power system can draw on and the interchanges it conducts. It is characteristic

of Parsons in his later phase that for an elaboration of these more
empirical considerations he turns to postwar American society. By
far the best example of such work can be found in his article,
" 'Voting' and the Equilibrium of the American Political System."[3]
The detailed theorizing in this essay brilliantly fulfills Parsons'
analytic ambition to construct a post-Utilitarian theory and his
ideological ambition to understand how reason and individuality
can be socially sustained. You can also find in this essay all the
characteristic faults of Parsons' theorizing, his tendency to emphasize the normative over the material aspects of his model and his
inclination to portray the American system as the fulfillment of
every progressive ideological goal.

Parsons maintains, to be sure, his model of power as the product
of a multidimensional production process. Power, the capacity for
goal-attainment ("G"), is the product of inputs from adaptation,
integration, and pattern maintenance. Political leadership is the
capacity to combine these ingredients into effective system goals.
Power needs economic facilities ("A"), cultural legitimation ("L"),
loyalty and support ("I"). If power is to gain a generalized status,
if it is to be legitimate, it needs inputs from each of these sources.
To receive such inputs it needs to give valued outputs in turn.
The process sounds circular, and it is meant to be. The "health"
of power—whether it remains symbolic and generalized—depends
on the effectiveness of exchange, and vice versa.

The focus of Parsons' essay on voting is on the input to power
production from the integrative subsystem. If power is to be generalized, it must receive solidary support. The "G"-"I" interchange
goes like this: solidary groups in the public offer support and loyalty
to the polity in exchange for leadership. In a democracy, Parsons
believes, the most crucial aspect of support is voting, or, to put it
another way, voting is the act through which solidarity is politically
channelled. Why does voting necessarily involve the generalization
of support? In a large and complex society, a leader cannot possibly
represent every single interest or constitutency. The voter cannot
"barter" his power; he cannot act in an instrumentally rational

---

[3] Parsons, " 'Voting' and the Equilibrium of the American Political System,"
(1959) in Parsons, *Politics and Social Structure*, pp. 223–263.

way, guided by the motto, "I give you my vote, you give me what I want in return." If you vote for someone, you assume that, eventually, your instrumentally rational interests will be met, but it may take a long time and in the meantime it is quite possible that only the general interests to which you are indirectly committed will be served. If this is a fact of modern political life, and Parsons believes it is, then the voter must generalize his support from the candidate's interest position to "what he stands for." The voter must, in effect, give his trust to a generally accepted leader. This trust, aggregated through millions of votes, is an input to the production of power which makes the elected official legitimate. If power is legitimate, it will be accepted even if in the short run the voter's specific interests are not served.

This reasoning process is presented in a completely abstract way, from the viewpoint, as it were, of the social system itself. But how does the generalization which voting produces really come about, in a concrete and specifically empirical sense? In Parsons' explanation we can see the familiar confrontation with Utilitarianism with which he began his career. The first point he makes is that the voter cannot act in a completely rational way. The issues the voter must address are too complicated to understand empirically; even experts who have studied the issues often disagree about their meaning. The impossibility of exercising absolute rationality means that the interpretations of individual voters will inevitably be guided by normative standards. Here is how Parsons put this point: "When a rational decision is not possible, but at the same time, there is pressure to make commitments, there has to be some stable set of reference points so that beliefs can give meaning to the commitment and pople can feel 'comfortable' about it."[4]

Voting, then, is an act of faith, a supposedly rational act that is actually guided by normative commitments which precede the act itself. From this critique of the Utilitarian approach to action Parsons moves on to the problem of order. The normative reference points of voting, he suggests, are rooted in stable subjective structures, the solidary groupings which are products of the integrative subsystem. Rather than "for what?", the crucial question which

---

[4] Parsons, " 'Voting'," p. 218.

actually guides a person's vote is "with whom?" The most stable group with whom people vote is their own family, and voting statistics show that most family members do, indeed, vote the same. In the form of empirical propositions about voting Parsons has restated the critique of Utilitarian individualism which he first made in *The Structure of Social Action*.

How does the political process in a democratic society transfer the solidarity generated by the family to the vote and, eventually, to the candidate himself? Parsons believes there exists a sequence of solidary groups, groups which "borrow" from primordial family solidarity and extend it in turn. Solidarity extends from the family to informal primary groups, like friendship networks and cliques, and from there to ethnic, religious, occupational, class, and regional groupings. Each of these solidary communities draws on the "we-ness" experienced in family life and, taken together, they extend this we-ness all the way to the political candidate himself.

The crucial mechanism for turning this solidary network in a political direction is the political party. Parties are intermediaries between solidarity and power, for they are both solidary groups and arenas for power struggles between candidates for objective power. Simply belonging to a political party focuses solidarity in a sharply political way, though this commitment remains at such a general level that it cannot, in itself, decide the nature of any particular vote. It is the cultural aspects of the party's political campaign that provide a more specific, candidate-centered focus. It is the "style" of the campaign—in the vernacular, the "hot air" rather than the nuts and bolts issues—that extends solidarity to the candidates and that is crucial in determining the vote. Through campaigns, the generalized solidarity which extends from the family through intermediate groups to political parties is attached to generalized political promises like "efficiency," "fair taxes," "cutting back big government," and the like. These promises are accepted because of influence, because they are generated by political figures who seem, to the voter, representative of familiar solidary groups. Once the candidate is elected, this normative commitment to generalized issues becomes the basis for legitimacy, for maintaining the generalized status of the political medium.

Even if a candidate wins, however, it is quite possible that he will not be able to produce truly generalized power. Specific political mechanisms can neutralize the input of political trust. Much depends, for example, on the nature of political parties. If there are many small parties, rather than a couple of big ones, the solidarity invested in individual votes cannot extend in a smooth line to the victorious candidate. Small parties must form coalitions, and the candidate who is actually elected never has the complete trust of the factions that are not his own. Because there does not exist full generalization and trust, factions in the coalition will be quick to demand the fulfillment of specific interests, the immediate payment of their promissory notes. In this way the coalition candidate may be denied the possibility of exercising true leadership, which consists in directing the country in new directions which have not yet been conceived. This is bad for the country because its collective goals are much less likely to be achieved. It is also bad for the leader's tenure in office because it is bound to be unstable. Since the leader cannot fulfill all interests at once, his supporters are bound to become frustrated; they will withdraw their support for him at the first opportunity. This loss of generalized status makes power, in Parsons' words, "deflated." The leader whose power is deflated will have to engage in bargaining and barter if his goals are to be achieved. Sometimes he will even be compelled to rely upon brute force. Deflation through overzealous demands, of course, is not limited to coalition governments. It also presents a danger to candidates who are elected by an informal coalition the members of which feel no real solidarity.

Yet even if power is fully "legitimate," even if the persons voting for the candidate have really generalized their support, a significant problem remains. What about the losers? They have ended up with no power at all, except the power they indirectly possess as members of the social system for whom goal-attainment activities are formally conducted, i.e., their power as citizens. We are reminded that, though Parsons focuses on solidarity, voting is a means of allocating and distributing scarce resources. The value of the goods distributed makes it all the more important to understand what forces might lead the losers to stay in the system rather than opting out and starting their own. Obviously, there must be some grounds for consensus and agreement outside of the party system, beyond the issues which the parties have made visible and decisive for holding power.

Parsons' model of the social system, with its insistence on multidimensional exchanges, prepares us to consider all sorts of inputs
to power, both subjective and objective, as significant for creating
supra-party agreement. He himself, however, discusses primarily
the supra-party role of normative and solidary concerns. These
sources of agreement, he points out, can come from "above" and
"below" the party as well as from within the party itself. First,
there must be normative consensus about political rules and cultural
agreement about central political concerns. The former issue refers
to the proverbial "rules of the game." All parties must acknowledge
the existence of rules about political selection procedures—rules
about how campaigns should be run, how many votes it takes to
elect, how authority is transferred, and so forth. If such procedural
rules are accepted, and power is fought according to its terms,
then losers must accept the winner's power as legitimate and accord
it some measure of generalization. These rules of the game, of
course, are inscribed in constitutions, elaborate sets of rules governing not simply elections but the whole range of political social
interactions. In back of both procedural rules and constitutions,
however, there stands, in Parsons' words, "a common framework
. . . of cognitive definition of the situation."[5] Parsons is referring
here to the need for a common political culture. Given such
common understanding, there will be agreement across party lines
on the characteristics of the candidates, the relevant criteria upon
which to judge their performance, the crucial issues facing political
society. Such common perceptions serve to console and integrate
the losers.

But there must be extensive agreement "below" the party as
well. To describe this Parsons refers to the conception of cross-
cutting loyalties. Losers in a campaign will remain integrated if
they belong to nonpolitical solidary groups which include members
from the other major parties. Modern societies tend to produce
such cross-cutting solidarities because their complexity makes any
neat political alignment next to impossible. You usually find yourself
in voluntary associations, neighborhood groups, occupational associations with all sorts of different people, many of whom have

[5] Parsons, " 'Voting'," p. 222.

sharply differing political affiliations. Parsons suggests that such overlapping solidarity leads to feelings of solidarity with members of other parties and to some nonpolitical trust in the candidate they elect.

There is, finally, one other, rather mundane factor which Parsons cites to explain the integration of losers into the political system. This is the simple alternation of ins and outs. If you know you will never be allowed to come back into power, you are much less likely to support the candidate who beat you out. If you know that your own chance will come again, you are more likely to give the newly elected incumbent a little rope.

What Parsons has discussed here are problems which develop from the "distribution" of power, even after its successful "production" has been assured. Severe distributive problems arise, in his view, in sharply divided societies. Sharp divisions mean that losers (1) may not share supra-party consensus on rules or culture, (2) may not have cross-cutting party ties, (3) may not have the institutional opportunity for getting back into power. If you look back to Parsons' discussion of pre-Nazi Germany, you will see that these are precisely the sources of instability he pointed to there; his later work, then, produces a conceptual reworking of this earlier theorizing but produces no fundamental empirical or presuppositional departures.

I hope you will agree that in this later effort Parsons has produced an intricate, often compelling analytical framework, and, in addition, that this later interchange model can be specified in an empirical way. Yet it is precisely in this empirical specification that the familiar problems of Parsons' theorizing surface, problems which even in these final minutes of our discussion of his work we can hardly fail to explore. These are the same problems we earlier observed in the middle period work and, before that, in *The Structure of Social Action* itself: an overemphasis on the normative, the equation of normative control with the maintenance of empirical equilibrium, and, finally, the equation of normative equilibrium with the realization of a good society.

Although power is clearly one of the principal means of social allocation, Parsons actually is much less concerned with the production and distribution of power than with the problems these processes create for integration. Parsons does, of course, write about power's production, but he is concerned only with the facet of production, the "I" input, which is keyed to normative integration. He focuses almost exclusively on the solidary support for power and the problem of its generalization, and the generalization of a medium, we must recall, implies for Parsons the relation to common values which he considers decisive for social integration. You might note here how similar this ambiguity is to the lacunae we discovered in Parsons' earlier treatment of rewards. While rewards were nominally defined as elements of allocation—as keyed, therefore, to efficient production of money and power—they were treated by Parsons much more in terms of their capacity, as carriers of prestige, to bring values to bear on political and economic power. In that earlier case too, in other words, central aspects of allocation and production were treated as manifestations of integrative demands.

This is not to say that Parsons' normative treatment of political production is unimportant. To the contrary, it is vital and interesting. Still, this treatment is weakened by Parsons' failure to consider more conditional inputs to power production, for example, the crucial issue of power's access to money and the contribution to its production of efficiency and coercion. Moreover, Parsons' treatment of the solidary input itself suffers from an unwarranted empirical assumption: he optimistically describes this input as resting on consensus and he underevaluates how often it is skewed by the unequal distribution of ideal and material goods. To the degree that such typical bases of solidarity as class, race, region, and religion involve inequality, there will be more than one "line" of extended solidarity. True, there must in every case exist an extended solidary sequence from family to larger association to political vote, but to the degree that inequality exists, this sequencing occurs in separated lines. If this is true, then the solidary support for candidates will be a source of distrust and conflict rather than order and agreement. It is because of such divergent lines of support that political parties in many countries "specify" solidarity in fundamentally conflictual ways.

In much the same way, the force of material arrangements and the fragmentation between and within empirical subsystems can undermine the consensus building processes that Parsons has described as coping with problems of unequal distribution. Inequality and discrimination weaken a dominated group's commitment to common rules of the game and common definitions of the situation. They also make it less likely that political winners will ever let the defeated parties return to power. While Parsons has sorely neglected these empirical possibilities, it is precisely his multidimensional analytical model which allows us to work them out. Once again we confront the paradox that haunts his entire work.

Parsons' analytic reductionism, however, is only one element in this paradox; there is also the moral or ideological one. Parsons began his great system-building effort to demonstrate not simply that reason depended on nonrational processes but that, in a modern society, such nonrational processes could form the basis for reasonable action more broadly defined. He wished, further, to demonstrate that the failure of analytical individualism did not mean that individuality could not be sustained in a supra-individual, more "societal" way. In his early empirical essays he was very affected by a sense of this moral side of his calling. Even in his later work— for example, the writing on education—some explicitly moral attention remains, even though the social achievement of individuality and rationality is often made too easy by half. In much of his later work, however, as the discussion of voting indicates, Parsons loses sight of his critical ideological ambition altogether. Having proved that rational voting in the Utilitarian sense is impossible, he leaves the question of substantive rationality aside. But surely, within the confines of complexity and cultural determination, the question of the relative rationality of voting remains significant. Societies can do much to increase the education and insight of voters, to maintain their rationality in a nonreductionistic sense. Much the same can be said for Parsons' later argument against individualistic theory, which suggests that political leaders cannot be held accountable in a direct, one-to-one way. One can grant the truth of this proposition and still believe that efforts to increase political accountability are viable. Laws which demand parliamentary review of presidential actions or extend public access to information are examples of institutional structures upon which such efforts can be based.

Finally, there is in Parsons' later work on politics a disturbing and, in light of his earlier work, a perplexing lack of concern for the relative universalism or particularism of political culture itself. Granted, the degree of common culture is central to stability and instability. Once stability is achieved, however, the moral status of the state remains in doubt. It is not simply whether or not culture is shared and consensual but whether it is universalistic which decides whether the political system can sustain individual liberty and allow for the rational challenge to political authority.

The irony of Parsons' later work is apparent. While he becomes increasingly successful in his effort to identify the social conditions within which reason and individuality can be achieved, he became less excited by the critical ideology which would make their institutionalization possible. This is not to say that Parsons actually gives up his democratic concerns. It was rather that in the optimism of the postwar world he became convinced (much as Hegel once had been) that reason and individuality were in the process of being realized in the political system of his own country. Less conscious of the distance between the ideal and real, he became more content to describe this system than to evaluate the possiblilities for its critique and transcendence.

The consequences of this double reduction were fateful. Not only was Parsons' later theorizing less lively, but it was much more vulnerable to attack. Once the hegemonic prestige of American society wavered, once the bloom of the postwar world began to fade, Parsons' commitment to "the American Century" made him seem to many ideologically obsolete. A moralistic attack began on his work, an attack which could seize on real explanatory problems. Inevitably, in the process of establishing these criticisms, anti-Parsonian theorists obscured the real ideological and explanatory achievements of Parsons' work.

LECTURE SEVEN
THE REVOLT AGAINST THE PARSONIAN SYNTHESIS

PARSONS CERTAINLY was not the only significant sociological theorist of the postwar era. In France, George Gurvitch pursued an influential phenomenological program and Raymond Aron developed a Weberian political sociology of the modern world. Prewar social critics like Theordor Adorno and Max Horkheimer remained influential in Germany, and C. Wright Mills carried out empirical investigations of these critical themes in America in the 1950s. Parsons' former student, Robert Merton, presented a series of power theoretical formulations of a more middle range, empirical kind.

It seems unquestionable, however, that in this postwar era Parsons was the most important theorist by far. There were "social," or extrinsic reasons for his relative predominance, and I will note these below. But there were intrinsic, intellectual reasons as well. No theorist in this period could match the scope of Parsons' work, the fundamental character of his concerns, the complexity of his analysis or the rigor with which it was carried out. Nor were there any other efforts at grand theory so centrally informed by, and directed to, centers of empirical research in sociology. But whatever the scientific or institutional explanation, the empirical fact of Parsons' theoretical hegemony remains. In postwar sociology, his work became the central point of theoretical reference. How this postwar theoretical period came to a close, and what succeeded it and why, are topics we must now try to understand.

While Parsons preeminence lasted well into the mid-1960s, the seeds of the rebellion against Parsonian, or "functionalist" theorizing had begun by the end of the decade before. The story of

Parsons' fall, the reasons behind it and the theoretical alternatives which emerged, is what the rest of these lectures are about. Only by telling this story in all its intricacy and detail can the real history of sociological theory since World War II be understood. Only in this way, moreover, can we gain the theoretical perspective to essay the possibilities for sociological theory today. This latter concern, in my view, is the only real justification for a historical enterprise. To see where we go from here, we must see how we came to be here in the first place.

Throughout my discussion of Parsons I insisted that there were important ideological motives for the creation of his theory and important ideological reasons for its eventual success. This in no way undermines the theory's intellectual significance. It simply underscores a point I made at the very beginning of these lectures, namely, that every element on the scientific continuum has its own autonomy. Though interpenetrated with one another, each level contributes to the contours of a given theory in an independent way. Thus, I have suggested that while Parsons' theory of society was by no means simply ideological, his general theoretical proposals were, indeed, linked to his political hopes for the revitalization of the postwar world. Parsons himself, of course, would not have admitted this ideological connection—few self-respecting "scientific" theorists would link a theory to anything other than empirical facts! Yet whatever Parsons' own self-consciousness, it is clear, I think, that he believed that his new and improved sociological theory could accomplish important ideological, not just explanatory tasks. Not only would the theory better explain social instability but it would, he hoped, itself contribute to the process by which political consensus and social equilibrium were achieved. Similarly, Parsons believed his new theory could better explain the irrationality of twentieth-century society, but he hoped, in addition, that this theory would indicate how a new kind of ethical rationality could be achieved. Finally, Parsons believed that his new theory avoided the individualistic bias that made Utilitarian theory unable to explain collective order; at the same time, he hoped that this new theory would show that individual autonomy could be maintained in a more social way.

Only by seeing this ideological dimension of Parsons' ambition can it be understood how closely the fate of his theory has been tied to social changes in the Western world. Though it was initiated to explain the crisis Western society faced in the 1930s, it became truly popular and important only as the prospects for Western society dramatically improved after World War II. In this period, moreover, there occurred a subtle but significant shift in the empirical and ideological focus of Parsons' work. Earlier, his synthetic theory had focused on negative data and had primarily been oriented to critique, a critique which largely submerged Parsons' positive program for ideological renewal. By the 1950s, the positive side of his ideological ambition came to predominate. Now he used theory to illuminate the stabilizing features of Western society, to argue that they formed the basis of a "good" society, the leading model for which, he believed, was the contemporary United States.

You can easily understand, in light of these strong ideological links, that any significant change in the social environment of the postwar period would greatly affect the reception of Parsons' work. To put the connection crudely and simply, if the prestige of the United States were fundamentally challenged, if it looked less like the model for a good society, then the prestige of Parsons' own theorizing would falter. More generally, Parsons' theory of modern social evolution depended on the possibility of creating a post-capitalist, post-socialist "welfare state." This modern social system would be capable of combining individualism and equality, and it would transcend the conflicts of earlier industrial society by integrating within a broad societal community groups formerly oppressed on the basis of religion, race, and social class. If changes in Western societies made the achievement of such a welfare state either less likely or less attractive, this would have broad repercussions for the reception of Parsons' work. Of course, changes in the reception of his work are not, it should be said, intrinsically related to its scientific validity. A theory may well be unpopular even if it is empirically true, and, vice versa, a theory may achieve great popularity even if it is scientifically dubious. Parsons' theory, moreover, is internally complex and sometimes actually contradictory. We have seen how the possibilities of his abstract model were often narrowed by the ways he put it to use in the postwar period, and such internal conflicts extended even to the general presuppositions of his theory themselves. Yet, while the validity of Parsons' work must be assessed independently of its postwar reception, it clearly contained significant weaknesses. Insofar as the social background of scientific theorizing changed, the ideological rebellion against Parsons' theorizing would seize on them.

To understand the background for the transition away from Parsonian theory we must put ourselves back into the milieu of the immediate postwar period. In the years following the war's conclusion there was the fervent hope—and widespread belief—that a new world was dawning, that the bloody sacrifice had created the conditions for a modern society unsullied by the contradictions and conflicts of the past. The scourge of Nazism had been defeated by an alliance of capitalist and communist nations, a unity which held out the exhilarating promise of a future world without strife. Even after this alliance broke up, moreover, fundamental shifts away from conflict seemed to be underway. In capitalist nations, the glaring economic inequalities of the earlier period were being softened by redistributive welfare legislation, legislation that had grown out of the interclass unity experienced by capitalist nations during the wartime period. With the exception of several sharp skirmishes in the late 1940s, there was remarkably little class conflict in the fifteen years that followed the war, particularly in comparison with the Depression years.

On the world scene, of course, communist and capitalist countries had embarked on the gigantic conflict called the Cold War. Yet, ironically, this also contributed to the sense of stability and renewal. The Western political parties which were most critical of capitalist development muted their critiques out of fear that they would become aligned—either in reality or in the public mind—with international communism. Russia itself, moreover, retained a positive image in the minds of many Western "progressives," intellectuals and activists who had fought throughout the interwar period for increased equality and class integration. In the immediate postwar years, Soviet Russia greatly expanded its influence, not only into Eastern Europe but into Asia as well. This advance allowed the communist intelligentsia which remained active in Western nations to share the optimism of their anticommunist fellow progressives: the good society was obviously coming into being through the expanding influence of the Soviet state.

By the end of the 1950s these high hopes had begun to fade. In part this was simply due to the continuing stability and progress of Western nations themselves, for this stability allayed the anxiety that had fueled the utopianism of the immediate postwar period. "Reality" began to set in, and with it the sense that Western social organization had not, perhaps, been altered in an unprecedented history-shattering way. The simple passing of time also eroded the inspiring intra-national solidarity which had developed during the crisis of the war. But fundamentally new developments also occurred in the postwar situation, objective changes which altered the perception of citizens and intellectuals about the vitality of the postwar world.

By the end of the 1950s, Western societies were, once again, beset by class and racial conflicts. In the United States, for example, the civil rights movement had begun to disrupt the Southern states. The renewal of such conflicts led many observers to question the basic contours of postwar society. A good example of such questioning can be found in the shift in thinking of the English socialist intellectual T. H. Marshall. In the immediate postwar period Marshall had written a series of influential essays which hailed the welfare state as a viable alternative to Marxian, class-bassed socialism. By the end of the 1950s, however, his sense of an unprecedented historical opportunity had waned, and he could be found speaking out against the new forms of inequality and conflict generated by the "affluent society." Perhaps the conflicts which Marx had predicted would destroy capitalist society—and which Parsons had insisted modern society would overcome—were still there?

Another fundamental shift in the social situation of Western societies concerned the orientations of left-wing intellectuals. In 1956, at the twentieth Party congress of the Soviet Union, Nikita Kruschev spoke openly for the first time about the horrors of Stalin's dictatorship. Revelations about this dark night of Soviet communism continued in the years following. These revelations were severely disappointing, indeed were traumatic, for the communist intelligentsia in Western nations. They experienced a sense of despair about whether a new and really just society could ever be created, a despair summed up in the title of an important book of that period, *The God that Failed*. Once the Soviet Union had been exposed as a "fraud," the radical hopes of critical intellectuals could no longer be invested in any actual society. What resulted was a kind of transcendentalization. Displaced from existing society, radical hopes became more radical and utopian. Rather than investing hope in the future of Russian expansion, radicals focused, once again, on transforming their own societies. Especially among radical youth, revolution in Western capitalism once again became the order of the day.

Another factor which weighed heavily on the minds of citizens and intellectuals was the growth of instability in the underdeveloped nations. In the years following the war these nations had undergone rapid decolonization, and Western confidence in their successful development was very high. By 1960, however, it had become clear that development would not be easy, and certainly was not an inevitable process. Moreover, the "third world" (as it had come to be called) was increasingly viewed more as a source of instability and revolution than as an arena for democratic progress and the fulfillment of Western values.

New conflicts also emerged within Western nations themselves. On the level of intellectual life, philosophies like existentialism crystallized the sense of insecurity which individuals experienced in a complex, differentiated society and the challenges to individual autonomy which even a democratic industrial society entailed. Beatnick and bohemian movements, enlivened by these broader philosophies, developed a critique of postwar society as demanding conformity rather than allowing individualism. Spurred by these elite movements, increasingly strident and self-confident "anti-establishment" movements emerged in Western societies. This new romanticism was nowhere more clearly articulated than in the youth culture. The relative affluence and independence of postwar youth made them an ideal carrier for the sensual, rebellious culture of rock-and-roll music; this culture made youth an increasingly potent critical force in the postwar world.

All these developments—the shifts in subjective sensibility and the objective changes in politics and social structure—contributed to the creation of a more pessimistic and critical ideological atmosphere by the end of the 1950s. That individuality and rationality were in the process of finally being realized was increasingly open to doubt, as was the assumption that social stability, the rock upon which these ideological hopes ultimately rested, was finally secured. This deflation of ideological hope made the acceptance of Parsonian functionalism more difficult. Parsons had implicitly tied his new theory to a positive outcome for postwar society; if this outcome seemed in doubt, so too would the accuracy of his theory.

This new ideological sensibility motivated theoretical critiques of functionalism because it arose alongside significant changes in the institutional framework of Western sociology itself. In my opening lectures I discussed how significant the institutional barriers against sociology had been in prewar Europe. Not only had there been great initial resistance to the establishment of sociology departments within universities, but the instability of the post-1914 period made the creation of any new forms of intellectual life organizationally impossible. All this changed in the period after World War II. In the first decade after the war European sociologists and students came to the United States to study what was increasingly perceived as an "American science." But with the renewed stability and affluence of Europe, which included the spread of mass education, new academic institutions developed which gave sociology unprecedented support. These new sociology departments became one important institutional basis for the anti-functionalist movement.

The other institutional basis was the creation of new sociology departments within the United States. The immediate postwar period was dominated by the old and established departments of Harvard and Columbia. It was in these departments, as I indicated earlier, that Parsons and his students held most sway. Even in the former haven of pragmatist sociology, the University of Chicago, functionalist sociology—under the influence of Parsons' co-author, Edward Shils—began to exert a dominant influence. Yet with the spread of mass education in the 1950s a number of other influential sociology departments emerged. These new departments—Wisconsin, Berkeley, UCLA, Stanford, to name a few of the most prominent—provided organizational resources for the young sociology Ph.D.'s who were being affected by the more pessimistic ideological climate of the later postwar period. It was from within these departments that the critical American challenges to Parsons emerged.

Fueled by renewed ideological pessimism and supported by an autonomous institutional base, a new generation of theorists confronted head on postwar functionalist sociology. Many of these intellectuals felt that the world simply was not developing as Parsons' empirical predictions had led them to expect, and they wondered, quite naturally, whether his more general theory was correct. Even if the theory was not considered to have been falsified, the very existence of such doubts undermined the aura of legitimacy that had surrounded and protected Parsons' work, much as, today, the failure of revolutionary movements has undermined the surface plausibility of Marxist theories. But more than ideological and empirical issues were involved; fundamental theoretical issues were at stake, and in the minds of Parsons' critics these were inseparable from their ideological and empirical concerns. In many instances these theoretical disagreements responded to genuine ambiguities and failures in Parsons' general theory, problems that I have tried to identify in my previous discussions. In other instances, however, Parsons' critics fell into repeating theoretical mistakes which Parsons had, in fact, already "figured out." Sometimes, in my view, they seemed unable to learn from the theory they were in the process of criticizing. For this reason, it is impossible for me to say that theoretical development in the post-Parsonian period has been unequivocally progressive. It has advanced our theoretical understanding on many points; on many others, it has been deeply regressive.

I should point out, in this regard, that even if one accepted Parsons' theory in its most abstract form, the new empirical conflicts of the postwar world and the new ideological themes might well have led one to question the more concrete framework in which Parsons had imbedded his later theory. Even if you accepted functionalist theory, in other words, the development of new economic and racial conflicts, the instability of the third world, the rise of existentialism and critiques of conformity, and the emergence of revolutionary youth culture might have forced you to develop new kinds of theories of the "middle range."[1]

---

[1] I have argued elsewhere that, in fact, many of Parsons' most important students sought to make exactly these kinds of revisions in his general theory. See Alexander, *The Modern Reconstruction of Classical Thought: Talcott Parsons* (Berkeley and Los Angeles: University of California Press, 1983), pp. 282–289.

The complexity of the challenge to Parsons recalls the point I made earlier in this lecture, namely, that we must never forget the distinction between the general levels of presuppositions and models and the more particular and concrete empirical insights through which a theorist fills these in. There is always, moreover, the inevitable mediation of ideology. Parsons' theory could be challenged at a number of different levels and in a number of different ways. Critics could argue that it was irrevocably and thoroughly wrong, demanding new "anti-Parsonian" formulations at every level of the scientific continuum (presuppositions, ideology, models, methods, and empirical propositions). They could, on the other hand, challenge one or another particular level of Parsons' theory, focusing on the error of his empirical understanding, his model, his ideology, his presuppositions, or his methods. I will argue that one of the principal problems of post-Parsonian theory has been its confusion over which level of analysis it is taking on. On the one hand, problems which emerge from a very specific level of Parsons' work have been treated as if they had a generalized status. On the other hand, problems of a very general, presuppositional kind have been identified with particular models and empirical concerns. Critics have often purported to challenge the entire length and breadth of Parsons' theory when in fact they are challenging one or two levels alone. These critical strategies, then, illegitimately "conflate" the antonomous levels of sociological theory. Much of my discussion in the following lectures will, accordingly, seek to clarify just what the critics' objections are. I will try to differentiate the issues upon which post-Parsonian criticism rests.

Whatever its substantive claims, however, the "form" of post-Parsonian criticism has been relatively constant. It has made its criticisms by demanding the revival of pre-Parsonian modes of "classical" theorizing. One continuing critical reference, therefore, has been Parsons' first great work, *The Structure of Social Action*. In this work, you may recall, Parsons presented his initial theory through an interpretation of significant classical figures, particularly Weber and Durkheim. It was only natural that when critics came to challenge Parsons' theory they would challenge his readings of the classics in turn. This challenge was fueled by a perplexing fact: despite his deep encounter with his classical predecessors, Parsons' relationship to them was never made completely clear. On the level of analytic theory, it was plain, he intended to supersede them. He believed that he had either solved fundamental problems in their work or else that he had developed their initial insights in a much more sophisticated way. One thinks here of Parsons' solution to the dichotomy of idealism versus materialism which had dogged the theorizing of earlier periods. On these purely analytical grounds, then, Parsons believed that his theories should replace those of earlier theorists, and that only "Parsonian" theory need henceforth be read. At the same time, however, Parsons was aware that the very abstractness of his formal theorizing meant that it could not be sustained or even fully understood without utilizing the work of his classical predecessors. His models and developmental generalizations, for example, rested upon the factual material provided by Weber's comparative sociology and Durkheim's studies of modern integration. Despite his feeling of analytic superiority, therefore, Parsons encouraged his students to read and study the classics and to make use of their substantive formulations.

For all these reasons, it was logical that Parsons critics would initially challenge him through a revival and reinterpretation of the classics. By invoking the classics, they could, in the first place, challenge Parsons' authority by pointing to earlier sociologists who were equal or even greater than he. More substantively, they could challenge Parsons' theory by bringing to bear the great authority of alternative classical approaches. These disputes with Parsons, then, involved major arguments over how to interpret the classical theorists and, indeed, over just who the major classical figures acutally were. Parsons had offered what seemed to many of his critics tendentious readings of Weber, Durkheim, and Freud. Equally important, he had left out of the classical pantheon Marx, Simmel, and Mead, not to mention philosophers like Hegel and Husserl. While the critics challenged Parsons' theories on the analytic grounds of scientific validity, their arguments were almost always accompanied by attack on his interpretations of Weber and Durkheim and by briefs for the historical importance of other classical figures.

In light of what I have just said it might seem peculiar that the post-Parsonian theorizing which emerged around 1960 did not explicitly present itself in a classical guise, as, for example, "Weberian," "Marxist," or "Simmelian" sociology. In fact, these new theoretical variations cannot be explained simply as revivals of earlier forms. That the classical names were not adopted and these new forms were not mere revivals reveals a crucial fact about theoretical development over the last twenty-five years. The theories which have challenged Parsons have not been simply post-Parsonian but *anti*-Parsonian. Between contemporary and classical theorizing there lay the formidable corpus of Parsons' work. Any attempt to come to grips with social issues in a new and different way could do so only in relation to this imposing, post-classical figure. By the end of the immediate postwar period Parsons' dominance was so great, the acknowledgement of his brilliance and originality so widespread even among those who questioned his work, that every attempt to create a new theory could establish itself only by challenging aspects of the theory Parsons had sought to establish. The challengers could not simply step outside the Parsonian tradition and start anew—even if they were taking their critical bearings from classical traditions which, they believed, were entirely outside the scope of Parsons' work.

Here is the great irony of contemporary sociological theory. Though relying on the classics for guidance and critical inspiration, these challenging theories have been able to define themselves only in close relation to Parsons' work. Parsons' theory continued to exercise its tremendous influence even in the process of its "defeat." Because the attempts to supersede his work could, apparently, be defined only in relation to a negative, "Parsonian" pole, the challenges formed one side of the dialectic from which they could never escape. This dialectic guaranteed that the defects in Parsons' social theory would indirectly be passed on by his challengers, since their critical starting points were defined by the stance of Parsonian work. It also meant that, rather than learning from Parsons, his challengers felt compelled to supersede him in a purely negative way. Hegel called this kind of process an abstract negation and he suggested that such purely abstract opposition end up only by creating a dialectic of unfruitful, one-sided antagonisms. What was preferable, Hegel believed, was a concrete negation, a supersession that included central elements of the opposition, rather than simply suppressing it. I agree with Hegel. In the course of the lectures which follow I will suggest that contemporary sociological theory must escape from the unfruitful dialectic between Parsons and his challengers. If this is to be a concrete negation, the substance and validity of these challenges must be fully understood. My discussion, indeed, will seek to show the interrelation between Parsons and his critics, not simply their self-conscious antagonism.

The first of the theoretical challenges we will consider called itself "conflict theory." This tradition defined itself in opposition to Parsons' focus on "the problem of order," identifying what it believed to be his ideological justification of stability with his insistence on the importance of cultural systems and the "nonrational" phenomenon of cathexis and internalization. There were English, German, and American variants of conflict theory, which took their classical inspirations, respectively, from Marx, Weber, and Simmel. The second challenge we will discuss, "exchange theory," followed the criticism by conflict theorists of Parsons' emphasis on normative action and psychological internalization, but it differed sharply by criticizing his focus on collective order as such. At least in its earliest and most influential form, exchange theory argued for individual negotiation as the sole basis of institutional life. Initially an American phenomenon, it drew heavily upon classical economics and Utilitarianism, on Simmel, and in its later versions upon Marx. "Symbolic interactionism"—the third movement I will discuss—followed the individualistic emphasis of exchange theory, though it also accepted Parsons' own tendency to emphasize normative over instrumental elements of the individual act. Inspired by American pragmatism and especially by Herbert Blumer's interpretation of Mead, symbolic interactionism portrayed individual negotiation as a vehicle for self-expression and sharply played down the instrumental elements of manipulation and control.

Ethnomethodology and phenomenology, which we will also consider, had a profoundly ambivalent character, and in its German and early American forms actually emphasized the individual contribution to "cultural system" processes in a nonreductionist way. The reliance on Husserl, however, and the necessity to confront Parsons in an increasingly antagonistic way, led eventually to its radical underplaying of the instrumental and economic elements of life and of the collective level as such. Hermeneutical, "cultural sociology," which I will discuss after ethnomethodology, finally breaks away from this individualistic anti-Parsonian turn. Drawing upon Dilthey and German Idealism it forthrightly embraced the determinism of collective cultural constraints. Its own version of anti-Parsonianism manifests itself in an attack not on Parsons' alleged idealism but on his very lack of it, on the way he insistently emphasized the autonomy of social system problems and the independence of personality. When we finally turn to "critical theory," the most important postwar version of neo-Marxism, we will see, ironically, that it accepts more of the original Parsonian corpus than any of the earlier, "bourgeois" challengers. What distinguishes it sharply from Parsons is its ideological transcendentalism and its radically different view of imminent social development.

These challengers tried and in many cases succeeded in setting new agenda for the relevant topics of sociology: that conflict is more important than order; that the relative equality of exchange is a more significant topic of analysis than the norms which regulate it; that individual processes of meaning-formation are more critical than supraindividual cultural themes; that—conversely—structured cultural codes are more critical than contingency and necessity; finally, that the only significant mode of social theorizing is that which makes moral criticism, not scientific explanation, its principal goal. Yet while significant new themes were established, the overall theoretical accomplishment of these post-Parsonian developments remains, in my view, open to doubt. The reason for this doubt can be traced to the fact that they never fully clarified their relationship to Parsons himself. On the one hand, they challenged legitimate weaknesses in his work. On the other, they mirrored his own misunderstandings and, because they sought negation in an abstract rather than concrete sense, they usually developed one-sided explanations which denied synthesis as a theoretical possibility. As a result, the theoretical claims they raised were often invalid, even while the substance of their challenge was often correct. Finally, almost all these critical theories refused, because of an empiricist bias, to join Parsons' work on the most generalized, nonempirical level of all, the level of presuppositions.

I will, therefore, evaluate these challenges in several different ways. First, I will examine them in terms of the criteria they themselves have established. What is their conscious and explicit challenge to Parsons' work? Does it hold up? Were they right? Do they accurately challenge positions that Parsons really maintained? I will often answer these questions in the affirmative, though perhaps just as often I will not. The positive and negative elements of these challenges are usually thoroughly intertwined. My second line of evaluation will concentrate on the unacknowledged dimensions of these post-Parsonian theories. Here I will try to expose the distorted communication they have produced, the way they have constructed unnecessary antitheses, the manner in which they have often (following the lead of Parsons himself) conflated and reduced the relationship between various levels of sociological work. Finally, I will be interested in the implicit, presuppositional challenge these theories make, and I will evaluate this aspect of their confrontation with Parsons from a point of view that embraces— as the best of Parsons' own theory did—the goal of presuppositional synthesis. Insofar as these critical theories take up presuppositional challenges, they often go beyond Parsons' work in important ways, for, as I have pointed out, Parsons' own work is often one-sided in an idealist way. Insofar as they themselves are manifestly one-sided, however, these challenges create a sterile dialectic with the worst of Parsons, and they mark a regressive departure from the theoretical standards set by Parsons at his best.

As the discussion proceeds, the rest of my interpretive strategy will become apparent. I start from the understanding of presuppositional logic I laid out in my opening lectures, the basic notions of action and order and the implications for substantive theorizing of every presuppositional position. I also start with a definition of sociology as a complex continuum composed of independent but interpenetrating levels. Each level has certain properties, some of which I have described in my earlier analyses of Parsons' work. The dynamic element in this conceptualization comes from the notion of conflation, from my understanding of the dangers and confusions which develop when the autonomy of different levels is reduced, when a single element on the continuum is said to determine all the others.

Finally, I will rely heavily in what follows on the notion, which I also described earlier, of residual categories. When unresolved tensions develop in general theories, theorists will resort to ad hoc ways to resolve them. To cope with these tensions they will introduce, in what is usually an unthought-out way, theoretical categories which are residual to, or outside of, the logically developed, systematic strands of their argument. Such tensions are produced in at least two ways, by one-sided reductions in a theory's presuppositional stance and by conflation or inconsistency between the various levels of the broader continuum.

While residual categories are the result of theoretical tensions, for the sake of interpretation it is often more useful to move backwards, from one's discovery of residual categories back to the basic tensions which they have been developed to obscure. I will try to show how the discovery of residual categories in post-Parsonian theories can lead us to central tensions in these works. I will suggest, further, that it is only by working through these residual categories that one can transcend these theories—and Parsons'—in a concrete rather than abstract way. I will suggest, in fact, that the major followers within each post-Parsonian tradition made real headway only by taking up the originating tensions revealed by the residual categories of the original theory, and I will argue that insofar as they failed to resolve these initial tensions their own work ends up by producing new residual categories in turn.

What I hope to end up with is not simply critique but reconstruction. Parsons began his famous theoretical quest with spirit of theoretical ecumenicism. He would provide a way to "end the warring schools" and in the process contribute to the renewal of a fundamentally liberal social order. Today, the spirit of ecumenicism has broken down, and the schools which Parsons (ambivalently) sought to reconcile have come to war again. It does not seem coincidental that this theoretical breakdown has coincided with a growing pessimism about the prospects for the postwar world and, indeed, with the breakdown of many aspects of modern social systems themselves. It is my hope that the reconstruction of our postwar sociological tradition will contribute to a new ecumenicism and to a new level of theoretical synthesis. Though I am less optimistic than Parsons, it is possible that such a theoretical renewal can, in addition, contribute to the intellectual clarification upon which any future ideological and social renewal would have to be based.

LECTURE EIGHT
CONFLICT THEORY (1): JOHN REX'S STRATEGY

I F YOU PICK up any sociological textbook today you will see an account of how the field of sociology is divided into two opposing camps, the "functionalists" and the "conflict" theorists. These textbooks will probably inform you, moreover, that this gigantic opposition is not just a matter of general theory but that it informs and divides some of the most crucial subfields of empirical sociology. While all of this is true, I will argue in the course of these next two lectures that it is regrettable as well. Once a challenge to Parsonian theory on the level of abstract generality, the perspective of "conflict theory" has seeped into the pores of empirical work. Political sociology, race and ethnic relations, stratification, collective behavior—all these and many other areas are deeply affected by the challenge conflict theory posed to functionalism. Conflict theory, then, was not simply the first major challenge to Parsons; it has also, in the long run, been the most influential.

Theories which emphasize the significance of conflict go back, of course, to the very beginning of social theory itself. What we are interested in here, however, is precisely how this theme re-emerged as a conspicuous and influential feature of postwar debate. The term "conflict theory"—as a systematic alternative to the "order theory" of Parsons—first appeared in 1956 in Lewis Coser's book, *The Functions of Social Conflict*.[1] Shortly thereafter, it was raised again by Ralf Dahrendorf in *Class and Class Conflict in Industrial Society*.[2] Both of these were influential arguments, but

[1] Lewis A. Coser, *The Functions of Social Conflict* (New York: Free Press, 1956).
[2] Ralf Dahrendorf, *Class and Class Conflict in Industrial Society* (Stanford: Stanford University Press, 1959).

neither, in my view, represents "conflict theory" in its purest form. Coser's book is a critique of Parsonian theory "from within," arguing that even from a perspective which emphasizes the prerequisites of functioning systems social conflict can be considered positive and valuable. While Coser explicitly drew for this argument on Simmel and Freud, the work remains an effective example of a point I made at the end of my last lecture: even Parsons' critics took over his theory in some significant part. Coser's conflict theory is written more or less from a functionalist perspective. Dahrendorf's work poses different problems. His justification for a conflict theory is derived from Marx and Weber, and he spends a good part of his book on exegetical and interpretive arguments which sort out and demonstrate the "conflict" relevance of these two classic authors. Much of the rest of the work, moreover, argues that the special conditions of postwar society make only a non-Marxist theory of conflict tenable. The space Dahrendorf devotes to "conflict theory" per se, then, is relatively small.

The book which I will take as the prototypical model of conflict theory in its purest form—*Key Problems in Sociological Theory*, by John Rex—was not, in fact, published until 1961.[3] Though clearly sharing common interests with the two earlier works, Rex's book represented still a third, independent effort to challenge Parsons as a theorist of order. Before taking up this theory in its abstract form, I will speak a bit about the social and ideological background not only of Rex's contribution but of conflict theory in general.

If you look at the theorists who initiated this conflict challenge (and there were more conflict theorists than the major ones I have just mentioned), it is clear that they all shared an ideological antagonism to functionalist theory. In one way or another they stood outside the relatively optimistic American experience of the postwar period; they did not see, as Parsons did, the imminent possibility for realizing rationality and liberty in the postwar world. C. Wright Mills, whose *Power Elite*,[4] though not explicitly "conflict theory" certainly provided ample support for it, came out of Texan radical populism and studied at the University of Wisconsin with

---

[3] John Rex, *Key Problems in Sociological Theory* (London: Routledge and Kegan Paul, 1961).
[4] C. Wright Mills, *The Power Elite* (New York: Oxford, 1956).

emigrant German intellectuals of a Marxist and critical bent. Coser, the other major American figure, was himself an emigrant from Europe and an active participant in the labor and socialist struggles of the late 1940s and 1950s. Rex and David Lockwood, both writing in England, identified themselves with the British labor movement and with the interests of the working against the capitalist class.[5] Dahrendorf, too, was part of this Social Democrat tradition. A German who had experienced Nazism first hand, he also closely followed the rebellions by eastern European workers against their Stalinist rulers. Rather then seeing the strife-torn decades of the 1930s and 1940s as a deviant case which had to be explained, the view to which Parsons had come by 1950, these theorists viewed this period as paradigmatic of Western social life, indeed of all social life in general. They stressed the continuity between this earlier period and postwar life, generalizing from it to develop a theory of society as such.

These ideological concerns are expressed by Rex in the preface to his 1961 work, and we can find here, as well, reference to some of the other institutional and social factors involved in the anti-Parsonian movement. When Rex notes, for example, that "sociology is becoming an increasingly popular subject in Britain" and that "there has been an increasing tendency when public issues are being discussed to give weight to the opinions of men calling themselves sociologists," we see the impact both of the renewal of European universities and of the more positive image in European intellectual life of the sociological discipline as such. We also see how Rex differs from Parsons by insisting that sociology has a public and political rather than private and academic function. Rex shares, moreover, the renewal of postwar critical idealism, suggesting that "sociology may be thought of as a radical critical discipline."[6] Yet he has also been chastened by the failure of Marxism in its Communist form, and he warns that "embracing a new political radicalism" may betray the sociologist's responsibility to both students and public. These groups, he believes, have the

---

[5] David Lockwood, "Some Notes on 'The Social System'," *British Journal of Sociology* (1956), 7:134-146.
[6] Rex, *Key Problems*, pp. vii and viii. Page references to Rex will hereafter be given parenthetically in the text.

right to expect the sociologist "to expose more sharply the real, as distinct from the utopian, value choices which face them." We can see, finally, the direct effect on Rex of his experience of a social order radically different from that of postwar Western societies. "The line of argument which has been developed in this book," he writes, emerged in part through "my attempts to relate sociological theory to the understanding of the turbulent time and place in which I first studied it." Rex first studied sociology in South Africa, a society of sharp inequality, brutal domination, and intense social conflict. It is from these social and ideological facts that "conflict theory" was nourished.

In my last lecture I talked about the kind of polarizing effect Parsons' postwar domination had on the post-Parsonian debate. I suggested that the force of his theorizing made subsequent theorists define their work in relation to his own, and that the process of doing so led these critics to adopt more sharply antagonistic, either/or positions than they might otherwise have done. This pattern, I should add, is only a more pronounced version of a process inherent to intellectual development itself. Hegel taught us that the construction of a new concept depends on the prior perception of its very opposite, for every idea must define itself in opposition to some other. This is a purely logical argument, but it helps illuminate the course of social scientific development as well, in particular the extraordinarily significant role played by what often seems to be irrational polemic. A new argument in social theory is always made in relation to a previous theory. More to the point, theorists feel compelled to argue *against* another theory and, most likely, in the name of some already articulated alternative. In the history of post-Parsonian theorizing it has usually been a classical author who has provided the "in the name of"; it has always been Parsons who has provided the name to be "against."

It seems inevitable that this "against" argument is going to involve caricature. Rather than presenting the adversary in a balanced way, the theory which hopes to supersede it will "set it up." This distortion, of course, remains implicit, and it is usually done without conscious intent. In *The Structure of Social Action* Parsons certainly set up his illustrious predecessors, Durkheim and Weber, even while praising them to the skies. Because of his unusually dominating

position, much more exaggerated caricature was often the fate of
Parsons himself. For twenty years, indeed, he has existed as something of a straw man. It has been vital for each strand of contemporary theory to "read" Parsons in a specific way, for only by
revealing particular weaknesses in his work can the challenging
theory be legitimated as true. To the degree that these challenging
theories present only one-sided visions, Parsons' theory must be
presented as one-sided as well. Successful theories, of course, are
not simply rhetorical arguments: they must illuminate some aspect
of empirical reality that has not yet been sufficiently exposed. The
important challengers to Parsons found real weaknesses in his work;
they exposed one-sided elements in his work and emphasized areas
which were, correspondingly, underplayed.

   This digression allows us to understand how Rex set about
transforming his ideological dissatisfaction with Parsons into a theoretical alternative and critique. To successfully claim his work as
conflict theory, you see, Rex had to create an opposition called
order theory. He does so by establishing what I will call the "myth
of functionalism." First, he developed an ideal type of functionalism
as it appeared in earlier, anthropological thought, then he described
Parsons' theory as if it were merely an extension and elaboration
of it. Functionalism, Rex suggested, is inevitably a theory that takes
human physiology as its referent; it has, he insisted, a literal biological model in mind. Now the body is a system which cannot
undergo fundamental change after maturity is reached; it either
maintains equilibrium or breaks down. Rex holds, therefore, that
in functionalist theory the "system" is considered given and un-
changeable, that it is viewed as possessing an innate, taken for
granted stability.

   To complete the transition from this general perspective on
functionalist theory to Parsons' work Rex makes two additional
claims. He suggests that while every real social system varies according to whether the interaction is cooperative, conflictual, or
anomic, "Parsons is quite explicit about the fact that he is concentrating on the first case" (p. 89). At another point he puts this
in the more technical language of Parsons himself. Parsons is
concerned, he tells us, only "with the case of the completely
institutionalized social relation" (p. 108). This, then, is Rex's first

claim, that Parsons is concerned only with order in the sense of stability. His second claim emerges from the first. Not only is Parsons said to concern himself exclusively with order but, Rex insists, he conceives of this order as depending completely on the internalization of values. In Parsons' view, according to Rex, "the interests which can be pursued and the faciles which are available for use by particular individuals and classes are dependent upon the value system in operation" (p. 110). These values, moreover, themselves become effective in a thoroughly idealist way. In Parsons' view, Rex tells us, authority "springs spontaneously from the normative consensus of a society" (p. 125).

Now there is no doubt that Parsons' real position on these issues is fundamentally ambiguous. On the one hand, he employs equilibrium models in a rigorously analytic sense, as an abstraction against which the actual course of empirical reality can be measured and judged. On the other hand, we saw repeatedly that Parsons was more interested in the processes which restored stability than in those which created conflict and that particularly in his later work he viewed history as proceeding toward stability rather than conflict. This conflation of model with empirical concerns is exacerbated by Parsons' tendency to define "the problem of order" in a contradictory way. On the one hand, he considered it a strictly presuppositional problem: it concerned whether one allowed for collective patterning or took a more individualistic approach. In these terms, the opposite of order is randomness, not instability or conflict. At the same time, Parsons placed alongside this presuppositional understanding of order a much different idea. He suggests that individualistic theories don't address the order problem because they do not understand the sources of stability; he even claims, further, that materialist theories can't solve the order problem because stability cannot be maintained through coercion alone. What about Rex's claim that Parsons presents an exclusively normative theory? Certainly there can be no more explicit argument for a multidimensional synthesis of idealism and materialism than that which Parsons constructed in *The Structure of Social Action* and in his later, more systematic models. To accomplish this synthesis, I have argued, was Parsons' major ambition and it played a central part in his ideological hopes as well. Yet it is true, nonetheless, that Parsons violated this synthetic ambition at every turn, that from the very beginning of his career he created a parallel argument for the greater relative weight of ideational forms. He argued values' greater importance on the grounds that they alone allowed for control to be reconciled with freedom and, at other points, because they alone supplied the resources for stability. In the later, more systematic work he overemphasizes integrative rewards, even while he lays out more clearly than ever before the interplay between rewards and the allocation of facilities and personnel.

There is no denying, then, that Parsons' theory presents Rex with a complex and difficult interpretive task. Yet rather than clarifying its protean character, Rex reduces a complex ambiguous picture to a simplistic, often vulgar distortion. Rex, in other words, sees only the conflationary and reductionist sides of Parsons' development. For him, Parsons is concerned only with stability, conformity, and norms—he is a theorist of order. The multilayered quality of Parsons' work is lost. This is a shame, since this eliminates some of its very best parts.

Why has this interpretive brutalization been carried out? I believe it is to justify the theory that Rex himself would like to pursue. Parsons must be pictured simply as an order theorist if there is to be room for a theory that identifies itself with social conflict. He must be pictured as an idealist to gain legitimacy for a theory that emphasizes instrumental motives and material concerns. He must be seen as maintaining a rigid and consensual functional model if the very use of functional models is to be open to doubt. Parsons must be portrayed as having chosen only one side of every important theoretical dilemma because Rex himself insists that a choice must be made, that action is either instrumental or normative, that order is either coercive or voluntary, that empirical life is either conflictual or cooperative. This reading of Parsons, in other words, is intended to justify Rex's model of a "conflict society," the model upon which his conflict theory is based.

I will consider Rex's model of society in terms of three issues: his discussion of allocation, his approach to integration, and his understanding of social change. These points are systematically interrelated in Rex's theory as they were in Parsons'. Indeed, Rex works within a structure that is parallel to Parsons' own; this formal similarity makes the substantive differences between them more visible and significant.

Parsons assumes that allocation always occurs within the limits established by socialization, since it is adults brought up within families and schools who are the objects and directors of allocation. Socialization, however, establishes very wide limits, and allocation may operate in some tension with the institutionalized values which influence (though do not determine) the distribution of rewards. The key to the flexibility of Parsons' schema is the way he differentiates between different kinds of allocative goods. Facilities, personnel, and even rewards themselves are subject to allocative pressures which derive from demands for efficiency and the maintenance of power, but, while facilities retain a primary instrumental status, personnel and rewards intrude upon the domain of the nonrational, upon culture and norms.

Rex adopts for his own model of society a very different point of view. In the first place, he makes explicit and unequivocal a position which, I earlier suggested, lurks (confusingly) just below the surface of Parsons' own conceptual schema: he insists that allocation precedes integration and that the latter is an "effect" of the former. This explicit prioritizing of the allocation/integration relation has profound implications for Rex's model of social life, for it puts the more instrumental and more objective process into the driver's seat and makes value-related process merely reactive. But the second step which Rex takes is even more important. He limits his conception of allocative elements to purely instrumental objects, to what he calls "the means of life" (p. 123). This reduces still further the possibility that values or norms can affect the social system. With these two initial steps Rex can present the following causal sequence for any pattern of behavior. The system of economic allocation assigns to different parties appropriate facilities; the system of political power distributes authority in a way "to prevent any violation of the system of economic allocation"; the system of ultimate values asserts "the legitimacy of this system of power distribution"; finally, religious beliefs and rituals have "the effect of causing adherence to this system of ultimate values" (p. 94). This materialistic and deterministic sequence is made even more pronounced by Rex's empirical assumptions. Even for Parsons the allocation of facilities involves hierarchy. For Rex it involves sharp hierarchy and great inequality. Since he regards the allocation of facilities as the first and most influential process, it is no wonder that in light of this empirical assumption, he sees the sequence money→ power→ values→ ritual as serving the interest of class domination.

This viewpoint on allocation leads, quite naturally, to Rex's "conflict" approach to integration. Parsons, you recall, sees the multilevel strains produced by allocation as subject to mediation by a number of different integrative forms, ranging from the possibility for voluntary self-control to the exercise of purely coercive power. The capacity for voluntary integration exists because the cultural system is always a background to allocative struggles; since the understandings of these struggles are never simply the creation of the groups involved, the possibility for collective understanding through social consensus exists. Parsons acknowledges that the domination by a single social unit, a class, for example, is empirically possible, but he sees this as only one possibility among many others. The complexity of his model indicates that such a situation would depend upon the outcomes of a wide array of independently variable empirical processes.

Rex's views on integration could not be more different. The prominence of facilities allocation in his scheme, and his empirical understanding of its radically inegalitarian thrust, indicate from the very beginning a much more hierarchical, less voluntaristic thrust. He insists that integration cannot be understood in terms of the properties of "systems." Integration does not occur because instability triggers independent mechanisms of control which function by virtue of their institutional position rather than their personal interest; neither does it happen through informal processes which occur outside the conscious intentions of the parties involved. Social order, in Rex's view, is the conscious result of the assertion of power by a single group, and this group is the same one that exercises control over allocation.

Social systems, then, are directed by independent, self-interested units. Each unit functions as the "means or conditions" for the action of every other (p. 93). Each unit, then, must be studied in terms of its "use" to every other, the role it "plays in terms of the scheme of action of the hypothetical actors with which the model starts" (p. 94). His model starts with a hypothetical actor (person or group) which controls the allocation of facilities; the control of the second actor is explained by the way in which it fits the needs of the first, and so on down the line.

> The model may further be used to explain the behavior of still further persons C, which serves as means for the action of B, whose behavior is an essential means for the hypothetical actor A. It also serves to explain the various norms, controls and sanctions which induce B or C to behavior in the required ways. (p. 94)

As this last sentence indicates, integration for Rex is only residually a matter of values or norms. Primarily, it is a question of domination and interest. "A conflict of interests or ends," Rex writes, "is put at the centre of the mode of the system as a whole" (p. 102). Since a social system is normally divided into hostile factions, norms are relevant only insofar as they provide internal integration for fighting groups: "The relevance of emphasizing normative elements then lies in the fact that they help us to explain how individuals subordinate their own private interests to those of the group or class" (p. 102). Norms cannot negotiate, let alone eliminate, conflict between groups. Each class will try "to ensure its own position by trying to convince members of other classes that its position [is] 'legitimate.' Equally the leaders of the subject class will seek to deny this claim" (p. 144).

This discussion of integration is inseparable from Rex's model of how systems change, for it is through his understanding of change that he produces variations on the common theme of integration through power. He is trying, he suggests, to develop a model of "the basic conflict situations" (p. 123). "In its simplest form," he suggests, "this model starts by assuming two parties with conflicting aspirations or aims" (p. 122). Any change in this situation is determined by the power at the disposal of different groups. Certain shifts in the distribution of power may prevent the dominant group from carrying through its aims. We are a long way here from the idea, so important to Parsons' model, that in a democratic society most social change results from group conflicts which are channelled by institutionally differentiated authorities and norms! Indeed, Rex begins his theory of change from what he describes as the "ruling class situation," a social system in which a dominant group exercises total control over every institutional dimension of social life. Yet while ruling classes always try to legitimate themselves normatively, long term voluntary subordination to their rule is impossible. Why? Because, Rex believes, the unequal allocation of facilities will inevitably make discontent rational and, for this reason, will eventually lead to rebellion.

The thrust for progressive change, then, is omnipresent. Parsons, you recall, was not nearly so sanguine. The mere objective presence of strain must, in his view, always be mediated by the structured expectations of personality. Cathexis to the established order will overcome "rational" frustrations; if not, cathexis not only directs the course of any response but fuels it with aggressive fantasy. Rex disputes the role of personality systems: "Parsons fails to consider the alternative that ego might persist quite rationally in his original demands without developing any pathological symptoms or ambivalences" (p. 119). But even for Rex the rebellion against existing conditions, though inevitable, is in most instances doomed to fail, at least this is true as long as the structures of allocation, which set the initial limits on group relations, remain unchanged. If changes in the balance of power are forthcoming, however, the society moves from a ruling class to a "revolutionary situation." It does so because of transformations in technology, organization, means of communication, or leadership, for it is these factors which are "involved in the power situation of the dominated group" (p. 126). Changes in these factors may provide the means for the dominated group to overthrow its rulers, and it is means, of course, that Rex considers crucial to the course of change. Because the ends of his constituent units are rational and rebellious by assumption, he can describe their response to shifts in their situational environments as if it were unaffected by their cultural situation. Parsons, by contrast, felt compelled to indicate the very different forms of rebellion that different cultural orientations might produce. He believed that overarching symbolic definitions defined the objects of anger for rebellious actors, an anger that had been generated in systematic psychological ways.

But even if the "integration" produced through ruling class control has broken down sufficiently to allow revolution, there still is no guarantee that this revolution will succeed. By adjusting itself quickly to the changing balance of power the old ruling class can produce new conditions more satisfactory to the subject classes. There will follow "a truce situation" in which equilibrium is established. Whether this will occur depends, once again, on purely rational and efficient calculations: "The gain of not having to pursue the conflict to its most drastic extremes would outweigh the cost of giving up the possibility of completely attaining the group's goals" (p. 127). Yet even if the two parties are in some sort of uneasy equilibrium, they still have nothing subjective, or internal, in common. The logic governing their interaction—the structure of this new integration—is one of least cost: "Each side [has] recognized that compliance to a certain degree was more profitable than a continuance of the conflict" (p. 113). Such an equilibrium is extremely precarious, for it depends on the distribution of power being balanced in a finely tuned way. Since the truce is never taken as an end in itself, each party continues to search for ways of garnering unilateral advantage. If such a means is found, the balance of power will be destroyed, and conflict replaces the fleeting period of transition.

Once again, the contrast with Parsons is dramatic and direct. He believed that the power systems of postwar Western societies were relatively differentiated and pluralistic and that, for this reason, there was a good chance that challenges by outgroups would lead to genuine inclusion rather than a simple truce. Inclusion is, for Parsons, a statement about solidarity; it means a broadening of the *feeling* of commonality to formerly excluded others, not merely the extension to them of economic bribe. Inclusion, moreover, is usually accompanied by value generalization, the abstraction of the common culture which stretches its capacity for cross-class regulation. All of this, naturally, leads Parsons to predict much more permanence to reformist kinds of change than Rex allows.

At one point in his systematic discussion Rex suggests that he is creating another "branch of sociological theory," one that is directed to the study of conflict rather than order. Yet this broad claim is, ironically, too modest. Rex is contesting Parsons in a more direct and even more ambitious way. He is insisting that conflict is the center of every society; even when order exists it must be seen as the result either of victorious conflict or its frustration. Rex has constructed this "conflict model" in three stages. First, he reduced allocative processes to facilities alone, and he gave to this allocation temporal pride of place. Second, he conceptualized integration as the rationalization of domination, denying the impact of common culture as a basis for informal social control. Finally, he described social change as the product of a series of power conflicts between discrete groups, conflicts over which neither differentiated social institutions nor meaning systems exercised control. Behind this conflict model stands Rex's interpretation of Parsons as a one-sided theorist of order and stasis. This interpretation legitimates the one-sidedness of Rex's model, in turn, for the model can be presented as solving the problems of Parsons' analysis.

In the lecture that follows I will look at some of the empirical and ideological justifications for this conflict theory and the support they lend to Rex's anti-Parsonian challenge. I will go on, however, to critically examine Rex's presuppositional stance, and I will suggest that it is here that his fundamental difficulties really lie. I will show that these presuppositional problems lead to significant residual categories in his work and I will argue, in conclusion, that these residual categories are endemic not only to every attempt to establish a conflict theory but any empirical study which adopts a "conflict" position as well.

LECTURE NINE
CONFLICT THEORY (2): REX AND THE PROBLEM OF COERCION

WHETHER OR NOT Rex's conflict model of society is a good one must, in the first instance, be a matter of empirical judgment. To be seen as a successful contemporary theory it is not enough simply to challenge Parsons, it is necessary to illuminate new things in the factual world. The challenge to every post-Parsonian theory is clear. It must address itself to real weaknesses in the original theory, and it also must go beyond these weaknesses through positive conceptual development of its own.

Despite the problems in Rex's work, it is indisputable, it seems to me, that his conflict theory has succeeded in accomplishing both these tasks. It raises significant empirical problems which Parsons either played down or ignored, and it does so through an often penetrating textual critique. Despite the possibilities Parsons outlined for a truly general and inclusive theory, his work moved toward particularism, after all, on a number of different levels. In part this reflected his tilt toward normative concerns on the presuppositional level; in part it reflected his conflation of this idealism with an over-commitment to empirical stability and an ideological commitment (at least at a later point in his career) to the social structure of the United States.

Writing from the vantage point of England in 1960, Rex saw through many of these mistakes. Rex saw that Parsons had unfairly associated the Hobbesian, antinormative position on collective order with the randomizing effects of the "the war of all against all."

"Is this really the only alternative?" he asks. "Is the problem posed correctly by Parsons in the first place?"[1] What Parsons called Hobbesian or "factual" order may, after all, not necessarily lead to unpatterned behavior. "Short of a war of all against all, there is the possibility that the ends which men pursue in a social system may not be fully integrated." This lack of full inegration is not the randomness produced by individualistic theory, rather it indicates that "the society is divided into two or more groups with conflicting aspirations." The very prototype of this nonnormative but nonetheless very real order is the model of ruling class domination that Rex puts forth.

In his discussion of allocation, Rex attacks this theoretical weakness by establishing his empirical superiority on a more specific level. Quoting Parsons to the effect that every social system, because of the primordial fact of limited supply, must have mechanisms for the allocation of facilities, he makes the following, very reasonable deduction: "We might expect this to lead to a discussion of the struggle for power in social systems" (p. 110). He is right in suggesting that such a discussion did not really occur. Instead, according to Rex, Parsons treats "the scarcity of facilities imposed by the unequal distribution of power [as] something to which the social system has to be adapted." By the social system, in this context, Parsons often means simply institutionalized value patterns, in his technical terms the distribution of rewards or the normative aspects of integration. Rex catches this reduction very well: it is "the value patterns [which] ensure the perpetuation of a particular system of allocation of facilities and power." It is in this way, Rex suggests, that the "discussion of power drops into the background and the system [of allocation] is discussed as though it were integration purely in terms of value-patterns." While I argued in the proceeding lecture that Rex is certainly wrong to suggest that this critique exhausts the theoretical significance of Parsons' allocative model, we can find in this critique more than a grain of truth.

It is in the context of his attack on Parsons' allocative theory that Rex raises another important interpretive issue and a corre-

---

[1] Rex, *Key Problems in Sociological Theory* (London: Routledge and Kegan Paul, 1961), p. 102. Hereafter page references to *Key Problems* will be given parenthetically in the text.

sponding empirical point. He reminds us of a possibility that Parsons would certainly acknowledge "in principal" but which he definitely underplayed, namely that individuals can share a common "cultural pattern" producing a "common idiom" even while "their actions will [not] necessarily be integrated with one another" (p. 86). The fact of a common idiom may, in this situation, mean nothing more than the fact that two enemies are accosting each other in a common language. Language, after all, is a terribly significant element of the cultural system, even though it does not, by itself, provide "institutionalized values" that coordinate social action in such a detailed way that cooperation is the result. Parsons carefully separated culture from the norms which inform social system and role relationships, but he associated only the latter with the agreement which occurs in the belief systems of interacting actors. Rex is suggesting that Parsons was not careful enough to distinguish the various levels at which agreement can occur.

Rex puts this criticism in a slightly different way when he says that while Parsons identified three dimensions of cultural life—the cognitive, expressive, and moral—he really preferred to discuss the moral alone. But it is the cognitive strand which guides action which is rational in an instrumental sense. Once again, Rex suggests, Parsons "sets out a range of possibilities but he goes on to develop a particular one of them only" (p. 106). The moral strand of culture is emphasized because it relates to integration; the other two types, especially the cognitive, "tend to drop into the background" (p. 106). Why? Perhaps it is because cognitive standards can be agreed upon even while the actions they inform are radically in conflict. Parsons demonstrated that instrumentally rational action, like economic behavior, must be understood in a post-Utilitarian way as depending upon values like universalism and impersonality and the self-discipline of complex socialization. Yet even if two actors share these internalizations and personality traits, there may still not be sufficient complementarity between their other expectations—their moral or expressive ones—to ameliorate conflict between them. Even if complementarity between these other cultural modes exists, moreover, there may be such inequality in facilities or rewards that this common preceptual scheme may lead, in the end, only to sharper conflict.

These are the very real empirical questions that Rex raises in response to Parsons' work. He asked some worthwhile ideological questions as well. Parsons had begun his theorizing with a critical edge. In the postwar situation, however, his liberalism had become rather complacent, accepting the domestic tranquility of this period as a structural quality of postcapitalist systems per se. Rex will have none of this. He supports not some postwar "system" but the working class. "The proletariat," he writes, "have not behaved as so many 'alters' in a sociological scheme. They have pursued their own ends and produced the socialist movement" (p. 109). Here, indeed, is the ideological impetus behind Rex's conflict theory, an unabashed identification with the interests of one particular group of actors. For Rex, the postwar quiet was not produced by an entirely new social structure but merely by a "truce" between parties still formally at war. Because allocation had not really changed, this truce was bound to break down. Whether or not Rex was wrong to ignore developments which actually were undermining any simple two-class model is beside the point. With the renewal of social conflict in the late 1950s his more critical ideological position looked more realistic than Parsons', and it certainly was more attractive to liberal partisans in the new ideological debates. These debates marked the beginning of what turned out to be twenty years of renewed social conflict, conflicts in which many sociologists actively participated. The postwar social structure was challenged and changed, and for those who participated in this process only a critically edged sociological theory would do.

In light of what I have suggested you well might ask why, if he made such valid criticisms and established such significant empirical and ideological points, did Rex go on to develop his "conflict theory" instead of something more subtle and complex? If he understood that Parsons often underplayed the significance of the Hobbesian solution to order, why did he himself have to go all the way over to the other side and make this solution preeminent in turn? Realizing that allocation involved conflict and power, why did he need to make these the main point of allocation and to identify allocation with facilities alone? While he was right that instrumental action and cognitive culture were underplayed in Parsons' scheme, why did he himself emphasize instrumental action at the expense of moral and expressive standards and, indeed, at the expense of any independent control exercised by common culture itself? The answers to these questions can be found in the presuppositions which constrained Rex's work. He was bound to certain narrow perspectives on action and order. These postions created pressures which, given his empirical and ideological positions, gave him very little theoretical choice. It is to these presuppositional issues that we now turn.

Let us begin with Rex's assumptions about the nature of action. It shows his mettle as a theorist that he is aware of the distinctiveness of this question and its vast empirical consequences. "The 'hypothetical actor'," he writes, "is a theoretical construction, and statements about his motivations have empirical implications" (p. 78). Now what, in light of this concern, does Rex choose to say about the hypothetical actor? Simply that most action, in the context of modern society at least, is instrumentally rational. Rex insists on the "purposiveness" of all action, and he believes that this purposiveness implies that actors are concerned primarily with finding efficient means for ends which are taken as givens. Actors seek to attain their ends through a proto-scientific evaluation of their situation; they decide what is rationally necessary and they go out and get it. Each of the three basic social situations he has described—conflict, truce, and revolution—assumed, he acknowledges, that "interaction process was of the rational type." (p. 79).

On what grounds does Rex make this fateful assumption about action's rationality? His principal justification is derived from his view that Western societies have developed in a rational, "modern" way. Marx and Weber laid out the classical reasoning behind this historicization of action. Different types of action, they suggested, belong to different periods of history. From this kind of reasoning there emerges a sharp dichotomy between "traditional" and "modern" life. In modern societies the average mentality is dominated by empirical sciences. Even if norms are still relevant to action, they are norms of an exclusively rational type: "Our own culture places the major emphasis on the norms of empirical science" (p. 84). In effect, this scientizing of norms eliminates their relevance, for if one assumes that action is guided only by rational norms the very issue of cultural mediation is unimportant; rationality is assumed to exist, and it ends up appearing to have a "natural" force.

In this historicized framework, Rex transforms the difference between rational and normative action into a confrontation of rational action versus ritual. For action to have a normative, non-rational reference, it must assume the form of ritual. Ritual is the very embodiment of completely unthinking, only quasi-purposive action, and, as such, it is consigned to premodern periods. It is rational, not ritual action which is "directly applicable to the kind of social system which we find in industrial society" (p. 102). Rex finds descriptions of ritual action to be "rather exotic accounts" (p. 81). Throwing up his hands, he confesses that rituals are mysterious and notoriously difficult to explain (p. 84). But Rex has forgotten what was perhaps the primary lesson of Parsons' work. Rational and nonrational are not, Parsons stressed, two different types of behavior. Rather, they are analytic dimensions of every act, of every historical period, of every temporal moment. What Rex presupposes about action, then, marks a regression in sociological theory, a movement back to the dichotomous, warring schools of classical thought.

It is much more difficult for Rex to articulate his presuppositions about social order, at least in an unambiguous way. His search to do so, indeed, is a highly revealing one. The instrumentalist, rational tradition assumes that people do not internalize the world and that, as a result, individuals treat one another as autonomous, discrete means to their own independent ends. Given his rationalist orientation, it is not surprising that Rex entertains this stance in a serious way. He suggests that society may really be composed of totally independent individuals. Thus, while maintaining Parsons' notion of the unit act, he uses the term in a concrete rather than analytical way: society is composed of concrete units and concrete acts, of real individuals acting in an independent way (p. 93). Rex is aware, however, that this highly individualistic perspective raises the problem of randomness. He worries about the "infinite complexity" of the patterns created by such individualized actors. "It leaves open," he suggests, "the possibility of an infinite number of different accounts of social systems varying according to their starting point." (p. 89).

Why does Rex hesitate before this spectre? Other post-Parsonian theorists, we will see, view it with equanimity. Rex hesitates because

he is not satisfied with such an individual-centered view. He has a
commitment to rationalism and an inclination to the atomism it
implies, but at the same time he is clearly committed to a more
explicitly "social," collective theory. Does this difficulty sound familiar to you? Twenty-five years after Parsons articulated the notion,
Rex finds himself caught on the horns of what Parsons called the
"Utilitarian dilemma." If Rex is to maintain his commitment to
the autonomous individual, he risks exposing his theory to the
randomness of "an infinite number of starting points," with the
result that social order could not be understood. But what is the
alternative to randomness if the commitment to rationalistic action
is to be maintained? It is to adopt a coercive, external, anti-
voluntaristic perspective on order, one in which motive, subjectivity,
and freedom have been pushed from the theoretical scene.

   This, of course, is exactly what Rex actually did in his conflict
model of society. His "ruling class situation" is the correlate on
the level of model to his presuppositions about rationalism and
collectivism. Given his denial of significant cultural internalization,
it is only through this or some equally coercive model that he can
explain social order in a supra-individual, collectivist way. It is,
therefore, presuppositions, not just empirical insight and ideological
vision, which lead Rex to insist that differences in coercive power
are the main factors that explain order and change, that allocation
is primary and linked to material things rather than to ideas, that
integration works through external force rather than normative,
internal control. Rex begins his conflict theory with a humanistic,
radical critique of power and with a commitment to the ability of
rational actors to create social change. It is ironic that his presuppositions force him to reinstitute the overwhelming power of external conditions in a systematic way.

   But, you might well respond, Rex has not simply theorized about
ruling class domination. In his model of the revolutionary and truce
situations he had developed a theory about voluntary and eman-
cipatory action as well. On the face of it this is true, and it leads
us to an important question: what does a theorist do when he
confronts a "logical bind" which contradicts some of his most
important theoretical ambitions? I will consider this problem first
in relation to Rex's discussion of the revolutionary situation. It is
a simpler case and the strategy he pursues is easier to see.

Revolution occurs, Rex has suggested, only when there is a change in the power situation of the dominated group. This should follow, in his theory, only from a change in the material process of facilities allocation. Now Rex does, in fact, suggest that rebellion depends in part on the simple number of oppressed people and on their economic indispensability to the ruling class, elements which change, he rightly insists, in relation to changes in technology. What is perplexing, however, is that he also suggests that the power situation of the dominated group depends on their aspirations and on their capacity for corporate action. How does he define aspirations? The strength of a group's aspirations, he writes, depends upon "the effectiveness of indoctrination and the quality of leadership, upon the intensity of their exploitation and upon the example of similar groups in other societies" (p.126). As for a group's capacity for corporate action, it depends on "leadership and organizing ability as well as on the organizational examples coming from outside the group, including the example of the ruling class" (p. 126).

Nothing much more is said by Rex about these conditions for revolution, but the mere fact that they are noted leads us to an important insight. On the one hand, Rex has listed external factors over which no one has control. Factors like technology, indoctrination, and exploitation are perfectly consistent with an instrumentalist argument which concentrates on the allocation of facilities. Other factors Rex cites, however, point to a much more normative and voluntaristic framework: leadership, organizing ability, and the example of other groups (this latter, presumably, functions as an ideal after which dominated groups model rebellious action). By including these factors Rex has reached for elements which are outside the boundaries of his systematic theory. It is not surprising that he can say nothing much about them, for to elaborate on them would surely involve a theoretical logic more amenable to nonrational action and cultural controls. But because Rex cannot elaborate them, these categories remain ad hoc and unsystematic. They are residual to his central argument, suggesting the randomness he has sought to overcome.

Rex faces what I will call the "conflict dilemma." The horns of this dilemma are "coercion" and "residual category," and if Rex wishes to remain within conflict theory he is bound by this dilemma to choose one of these alternatives. If Rex wishes to articulate a truly voluntaristic theory of revolution, he will have to become explicitly multidimensional, allowing the very elements he has systematically denied to reenter theoretical play. If he wants to maintain his conflict theory, he cannot embrace voluntarism; he must maintain an explicit commitment to the coercive approach. Is there any way that coercion can be maintained and voluntary behavior simultaneously allowed? In a certain sense there is. Rex can introduce residual categories, concepts that are ad hoc, unsystematic, sub rosa, concepts which have an oblique rather than direct relation to the theory he systematically and explicitly expounds. The resort to residual categories marks a discrete turning away from the explicit theory, a turning away never explicitly acknowledged. This hidden, ad hoc quality is unfortunate, for it introduces contradiction and confusion. Yet the only way to avoid these consequences would be to step outside the conflict dilemma itself. To avoid both coercion and residual category, the presupposition of rational action would have to be transcended.

Let us turn now to Rex's consideration of the "truce situation." Since "truce" comes closer than either revolutionary or ruling class situation to characterizing the postwar period which stimulated Rex's theorizing, what he has to say about its inner workings is of particular interest. The very concept of truce, of course, presents him with another apparent anomaly, for it is defined as a period without conflict which is maintained without domination. Could it be that the subjectivity intimated by his theory of the revolutionary situation has, in his theory of the truce, finally become explicit and forthright? Is he acknowledging that issues of aspiration, normative models, and socialization are central to controlling conflict? This is certainly not how he describes equilibrium in his systematic theory, where the cessation of conflict is attributed solely to rational calculation about the impact of changing external conditions. Conflict will end, he writes, only if "each side recognized that compliance to a certain degree was more profitable than continuance of the conflict" (p.113). This instrumental thinking refers to the origins of truce; to say anthing different would risk an explicit normative linkage with the implicit subjectivity of the revolutionary situation out of which the truce proceeds. Yet in his description of the phenomenon of the truce—as distinct from its origins—significant normative residual categories occur. If Rex cannot transcend the conflict dilemma, neither can he avoid it.

What Rex seems to suggest is that while the institutions of the truce may have been initiated for instrumental reasons, eventually they form a "system" which has the cultural potential to control selfish motives in the interest of society at large. The initial class compromise, he writes, makes "possible the emergence of a value system and social institutions which are the social institutions of neither class" (p. 128). This nonclass situation, he emphasizes, has the property of an integrated social order: "The new institutions of welfare belong neither to the working class nor bourgeoisie but to the social system of the truce itself. (p. 128). This sounds suspiciously like Parsons' own vision of the postcapitalist postwar world. While Rex has abandoned a functionalist model in principle, he seems to have adopted the model of a functioning system in fact, that is, in his empirical understanding of postwar society.

This model, however, might still be conceived as indicating the neutrality of postwar states and organizations, while remaining inside Rex's presuppositions about instrumental action and coercive order. The social system of the postwar world, then, would represent an empirical departure, not a generalized challenge. Coercion could remain as the source of order, but it would now be under the control of an egalitarian state rather than a dominating social class. This is not, however, what Rex intends. The very notion of coercion must be stripped away. Whether the "new unitary society" comes about, he writes, depends on "how long the prevailing balance of power lasts." Is this merely because the longer the supra-class state remains in existence, the more likely its power is to be respected? Not at all. It is because if a balanced power situation is "prolonged" a "new generation will arise for whom conflict is only a folk-memory." This latter, subjective recollection, moreover, will be completely overpowered by another normative fact. Rather than class values, "the institutions and values of truce will be the ones which [are] internalized." As a result, the institutions of the truce will "acquire a legitimacy in the eyes of the whole population which the old ruling-class institutions never enjoyed." The truce system maintains itself through internalization! Power balance allows an initial lull in fighting; autonomous institutions and values develop in this lull; these values are subsequently internalized. The post-domination system socializes people into neutral values which integrate the system by producing their voluntary consent.

It would seem that Rex has traveled full circle. To describe the crucial postwar period of truce he has relied on Parsons' normative theory of systemic integration rather than on his own propositions about conflict. Since he recongnizes this was not a period of conflict, he is bound, ironically, by the conflationary logic of his instrumental theory—which identifies empirical conflict with instrumental collectivism—to step outside of a coercion explanation. But to avoid coercion, he must introduce an extraordinary residual category, the phenomenon of normative integration itself. If resources are balanced and the members of the system have internalized the same values, the prospects of future conflict seem slight. Indeed, we can find a number of central institutions in contemporary society which have led just such a prolonged existence. The eight-hour working day, unemployment insurance, social security, trade unions, and universal suffrage are pivotal institutions which have been around for more than half a century. If we take Rex at his word, these are institutions of the truce; they represent the workings of a new, postcapitalist system, and they ensure the internalization of universalistic values like inclusion and cooperation. To find out what the strains in such a postcapitalist society might be, we would have to study in detail how this system relates the distribution of personnel to the allocation of subjective rewards, and how this interrelation affects the central process of socialization itself. We would be led back, in other words, to considerations which were at the very center of Parsons' later work.

Rex, not surprisingly, certainly is not prepared to jettison the presuppositions of his systematic theory. His points about internalization as the fulcrum of a new stability are left dangling. Moving from one horn of the conflict dilemma to the other, from residual category back to coercion, he develops a line of reasoning that suggests it is not really necessary to face such (theoretically) troubling consequences of the truce. He does so by introducing what he presents as an important qualification: "If the ruling classes have made concessions simply in the face of the countervailing power of the masses, then the weakening of this power due to the collapse of [lower-class] morale during the truce may lead to the old ruling class returning to its old behavior" (p. 128). Yet such an instrumental motive for ruling-class concessions—fear in the face of countervailing power—is precisely what Rex had always proposed; he had simply proceeded from this initial, instrumentally motivated compromise to suggest that the institutions of this truce would appear in a neutral form which, if prolonged, would lead to the internalization of cooperative values. Now, if the ruling class itself has begun to internalize neutral values, something which Rex has given us no reason to doubt, high morale in the dominated group is unnecessary, for it need no longer fight against class domination.

But if Rex's new qualification is logically superfluous, it is theoretically necessary: it makes reference to the phenomenon of internalization unnecessary because it makes the prolongation of the truce impossible. Since initially concessions are bound to be instrumental, the collapse of morale within the dominated group is inevitable. Since Rex now apparently assumes that the motives which initiated truce—the instrumental assessment of cost—will continue to motivate each group when the truce ensues, this collapse of morale becomes pivotal. With an increase in its power the dominated class may lose its fighting spirit, but the ruling class, whose power is decreasing, certainly will not. Determination by external conditions remains the name of this game. With his crucial qualification, Rex has moved away from residual category and back to the coercive emphasis of his systematic work. His references to the normative implications of a prolonged truce now seem like an irritating source of confusion. This, of course, is exactly what Rex set out to accomplish. Ad hoc and unsystematic in themselves, his residual categories are pushed further from the center of Rex's work.

In my first lecture on conflict theory I indicated the systematic quality of Rex's analysis. In this lecture, while I have indicated what I regard as the legitimate elements in his empirical and ideological program, I have also described how his presuppositional commitments, in light of these elements, pushed Rex onto the horns of the conflict dilemma. This dilemma, I believe, is endemic to any conflict theory. The residual categories it produces invariably lead even the most effective conflict theory to assume a contradictory and often confusing form.

The same equivocations and residual categories, for example, can be discovered in the work of the two other founders of conflict theory, Lewis Coser and Ralf Dahrendorf. Each, for example, introduced "extenuating empirical considerations" to explain why postwar society was not, in fact, in a particularly conflictual form. In *The Functions of Social Conflict* Coser talked about the "safety valve" of reform and the integrative effects of the kinds of conflicts which follow the rules of the game. Yet he never explained why neutral, supra-conflict institutions existed to allow reform in the first place, or from what (integrative?) sources such binding, constitutional rules could emerge. Similarly, after outlining a theory of omnipresent, instrumental conflict in *Class and Class Conflict in Industrial Society*, Dahrendorf suggested toward the end of this work that the pluralization of modern societies has undermined the authority structure upon which serious conflict depends. Pluralization has made much less likely the superimposition of the hierarchy in one institution with the hierarchy in another (in Rex's terms, a situation in which the same class "rules" in every institutional sphere). Yet, while instrumental factors like technology and anti-authoritarian structures could certainly explain the origins of such pluralization, the effects of this new system, one of which Dahrendorf calls the extension of the realm of the "social" to formerly excluded groups, seem to go well beyond the confines of conflict theory itself.

These empirical explanations of stability seem, for these theorists as for Rex, to constitute a kind of implicit return to the "differentiation" model of Parsons' later work. As with Rex, these empirical departures in the work of these other conflict theorists are accompanied by efforts at normative theorizing which seem residual and ad hoc. Thus, while Coser's macrotheory of conflict relies on Simmel's exchange model, he insists that Freudian theories of irrational motivation must replace any notion of the rational weighing of costs. This allows him, for example, to explain why conflict might lessen rather than intensify aggression: it provides a release, a safety valve, for repressed hostility. Further, as I suggested at the very beginning of these lectures on conflict theory, Coser's model of society remains, in crucial though often hidden respects, within the parameters of functionalism itself. While taking his explicit point of departure from conflict theory, he borrows the normative elements of functionalism to explain what otherwise would be difficult facts. Coser writes, for example, that "a flexible society benefits from conflict because such behavior, by helping to create and modify norms, assures its continuance under changed conditions."[2] This tendency continues in his later work, which is even less paradigmatic of conflict theory in a pure form. In *Books*, his recent analysis of the publishing industry, he takes as a key explanatory variable the social control provided by the impartial refereeing system of university presses.[3] Because of their commitment to the impartial norms of intellectual excellence, Coser believes, these small presses act as "gate-keepers" which have succeeded in maintaining high quality despite the onslaught of the profit criterion of corporate publishing.

Dahrendorf's early work is more consistently instrumental, though his digression about extending the "social" to excluded groups clearly converges with Parsons' idea of inclusion. This reference, ironically, becomes explicit in Dahrendorf's later work, *Society and Democracy in Germany*, where he takes over Parsons' early emphasis on Lutheranism as a significant source of the explosive conflicts of pre-Nazi Germany.[4] In Dahrendorf's subsequent work, this normative reference becomes even more pronounced. In an essay seeking to explain the lack of serious terrorism in contemporary England, for example, he linked this lack of divisive conflict to the long-standing English moral tradition of civility and constraint.

When we look at the most recent exponents of conflict theory, we find this turn toward the normative has become self-conscious and explicit. Randall Collins, whose *Conflict Sociology* represents the most systematic, second-generation rendering of the tradition, has tried to weld an instrumental emphasis on the omnipresence of conflict and antagonism with a "micro" theory of individual relations governed by ritual and stimulated by needs for emotional

---

[2] Coser, *The Functions of Social Conflict* (New York: Free Press, 1956), p. 154.
[3] Coser et al., *Books* (New York: Basic Books, 1982).
[4] Ralf Dahrendorf, *Society and Democrcy in Germany* (New York: Doubleday 1967).

release.[5] He can accomplish this awkward marriage only by insisting that ritualized encounters are sharply bounded by external economic and political conditions, indeed, that the former provide "translations" of the latter. On the basis of this contention he can continue to maintain an ostensibly anti-cultural and anti-Parsonian "conflict" position, as he did when he argued in a recent article that the concept of "norm" should be struck from the language of sociology.[6] Surely, however, this very suggestion demonstrates the residual, contradictory qualitites in Collins' argument. How can the rituals of interperson behavior avoid normative standards that "socially" mediate emotion and perception? In many ways, then, Collins too has moved back to Parsons, and while his insights are often superior his work has also suffered from its failure to appreciate the problems Parsons addressed. This appreciation is not forthcoming because an abstract antagonism to Parsons is at the very basis of the conflict tradition. Only if a more "concrete negation" is attempted can a general theory be established which sees conflict and order for what they actually are, specific and variable empirical conditions rather than generalized theoretical assumptions. If such a general theory were proposed, the residual categories which mar the work of these conflict theorists could be systematically included as elements within a larger whole.[7]

None of the post-Parsonian theories we have considered here, anymore than Parsons' original theory, are simply theories for theory's sake. True, they present models at a high level of generality; they are not attempts to explain specific empirical cases. Yet the models are oriented to explanatory concerns and their ambition is to reorient empirical sociology in turn. In the thirty years since its articulation, conflict theory has had an enormous impact on the practice of empirical sociology, producing a "conflict perspective" in every empirical field. Deviance has been reconcep-

---

[5] Randall Collins, *Conflict Sociology* (New York: Academic Press, 1975).

[6] Collins, "On the Microfoundations of Macrosociology," *American Journal of Sociology* (1981), 86:991, n. 3.

[7] I will suggest in my concluding lecture, indeed, that in his latest work Collins may, in fact, be moving in precisely this direction. One can find in his work increasing reference to Durkheim's cultural theory and even to Parsons'. See, e.g., Collins, "The Durkheimian Tradition in Conflict Theory," in Jeffrey C. Alexander, ed., *Durkheimian Sociology* (New York: Cambridge University Press, 1987).

tualized as the product of a ruling group's control over definitions of powerless behavior. Professions are explained on the basis of a monopoly of expert knowledge and as the result of successful power struggles by practitioners against patients. Racial discrimination is portrayed as internal colonialism, as resulting from power conflicts between initial settlers and newcomers. The status differences creating stratification are conceived as power differences dependent on the control of material facilities or information, and group inequality has been linked to the capitalist class. Politics is linked to resource mobilization and group struggles, and revolution is portrayed as an "anti-voluntaristic" response to shifting material conditions. Underdevelopment is conceived as the product of a world system dominated by Western capitalist states. Conversations between men and women are explained as a struggle situation which, in principle, is not different from the conflict of rape.

Much more could be said along these lines, but let me conclude by suggesting this outpouring of empirical work cannot by any means be equated with scientific progress. The errors of the postwar generations haunt the work of contempories. While conflict theory has provided a crude, if sometimes incisive, model for empirical research, its restricted scope has set strict limits which have forced this empirical work to introduce yawning residual categories and frustrating ad hoc explanations. None of these empirical studies has fully avoided the issues of consciousness and moral control, nor have these studies ever completely avoided some reference to systems as such. They have merely been forced to sneak such issues in by the back door, leaving logical inconsistencies in their work of an often embarrassing kind. Nor will further empirical research be able to vitiate these errors—an old sociological saw. They are located in theoretical logic. To correct them, we must engage more general levels of analysis. This is precisely the task in which these last two lectures have been engaged.

LECTURE TEN
EXCHANGE THEORY (1):
GEORGE HOMANS' INSIGHTS

THE BREACH WITH Parsons' functionalism established by conflict theory indicates how theoretical change proceeds along both scientific and social tracks. The growing disappointment with the performance of Western societies after World War II provided ideological motive for conflict theory's dissent, and the presuppositional disagreement with Parsons' multidimensional, sometimes normative bent provided the theoretical rationale for an intellectual challenge. Contrasting empirical "findings," of course, also played a role, though I am inclined to see these more as the product of ideological and presuppositional shifts than as independent factors in their own right. After all, Parsons was himself exposed to the same changing empirical milieu, and he came up with very different empirical descriptions. In back of these immediate, initiating factors there stood the theoretical traditions which the dominance of Parsons' structural-functional theory had effectively denied, the traditions whose classical status allowed them to be crucial legitimating resources for the construction of alternative, anti-Parsonian theories. In the case of Rex's conflict approach, the critically significant traditions were Marxism and an instrumentalized form of Weberian theory.

Shortly after conflict theory challenged Parsons' hegemony there emerged an equally determined critical movement which emphasized rational exchange. At first the work primarily of one man, George Homans, and the book he published in 1961, *Social Behavior: Its Elementary Forms*,[1] "exchange theory" soon became a widespread

---

[1] George Caspar Homans, *Social Behavior: Its Elementary Forms* (New York: Harcourt, Brace, and World, 1961).

movement throughout the social sciences. It gained not only major adherents but influential revisers—some of whom we will consider later in this set of lectures—and it deeply affected sociological work in virtually every empirical field. One reason for this success, it seems to me, is that exchange theory closely resembles the commonsense perspective on everyday life in Western society. But there are other factors as well, and it is these intellectual and sociological issues which will occupy us today.

When Homans first presented exchange theory, in an article in the *American Journal of Sociology* in 1958,[2] it was in the context of an anniversary issue devoted to one of the great doyens of classical sociology, Georg Simmel. Yet while Homans claimed Simmel's patronage, and while he drew substantially on the more contemporary tradition of Skinner's behaviorist psychology, the real tradition that Homans reclaimed for post-Parsonian sociology was classical economics. Classical economic theory was born in the seventeenth century in the work of John Locke and formalized by the work of the Scottish moral philosophers, especially Adam Smith, who formulated the famous notion of "laissez faire." It reached a high point in the work of the nineteenth-century Utilitarians, Bentham, Ricardo, and Mill.

You may remember that I talked in my introductory lectures about the critical role played by classical economics in the rationalistic and individualistic theorizing of the nineteenth century. The theory described social life as the exchange of more or less equal commodities between more or less rational individuals. The rise of this mode of analysis, therefore, can certainly be seen as tied very strongly to progressive developments in Western cultural and social history. It viewed institutions as built upon the conscious interests of inherently rational individuals. Not only economics but politics, too, can be viewed in this light, for at the heart of classical economic theory stands the notion of contract. Just as economic life is conceived as based on contracts between individuals, political life is viewed as one great contract between citizens and their government. This political contract theory formed one of the most important

---

[2] Homans, "Social Behavior as Exchange," *American Journal of Sociology* (1958), 62:597–606.

intellectual justifications for the development of democratic societies. It argued that, because society is composed of free and unconstrained individuals, governing political forms should be arranged to respect this "natural" freedom.

But classical economic theory was not simply a philosophy, an articulation of general presuppositions about action and order. It was also an explanatory, highly specific empirical theory. Indeed, it produced the first body of social scientific theory which could be mathematically articulated, developing equations that predicted things like prices, value, profit, and costs. This specificity allowed it to have great practical effect, and it was deeply involved in both the successes and the failures of nineteenth-century capitalist economies. Behind its explanatory propositions there stood a critically important model of interest relations in the empirical world. According to this model, economic actors were rational, to be sure, but they could act only as individuals. How, then, could their actions be coordinated? This occurs, the classical model proposed, through the "invisible hand" of the market. Individuals make their choices on the basis of efficient self-interest, but the market arranges the context of each decision so that it results in the best interest of all. The market makes sure that prices go down, for example, when goods are over supplied. Since a lower price for a good makes its purchase attractive, the potential surplus in that good, which could create problems for the seller, will soon be overcome. In this way rational individual exchange will lead, inevitably, to equilibrium and harmony. The model posits what one great commentator on this tradition, Elie Halevy, called the natural identity of interests.[3]

Yet for many participants in, and observers of, this early capitalist system, the proposal that there was a natural identity of interests seemed ideological and absurd. Faced with the instability and conflict of early capitalism they took the individualism of economic exchange theory severely to task. They argued, against the classical model, that the sources of social order lay outside individual control, that such collective forces usually made the partners in exchange

[3] See Halévy's *The Growth of Philosophic Radicalism* (1901–1904; New York: Kelley, 1972).

unequal, and that this inequality explained the conflict and instability of the time. Utilitarian reformers like Bentham argued that
a strong English state should redistribute power so that an "artificial
identity of interest" (Halévy's term again) could be formed between
economically and politically contesting groups. Marx, though more
radical, agreed with Bentham's attack on the natural identity theorem of classical economics. He differed by insisting that such an
artificial identity of interests could be achieved only through socialist
revolution.

Stimulated by political and ideological concerns, then, these challengers to classical economic exchange theory raised profound
theoretical—in my terms, presuppositional—issues. It is important
to see, however, that while criticizing the reigning conception of
order as too individualistic, they did not challenge its perception
of action. Bentham and Marx both viewed people as behaving in
a rational and efficient way. Cultural constraints, good or bad, were
not for them sources of instability, nor could they become the
grounds for renewed cooperation. In fact, reformist Utilitarians
and Marxian socialists both associated the influence of norms and
ideals with the conservative forces they opposed. For the Utilitarian,
they were associated with the customs and honors of the aristocracy
and the superstitions of the Church; for the Marxists they implied
the false liberal ideals of the bourgeoisie. Normative factors, in
other words, implied irrational and antirational, not simply nonrational action. They stood in the way of the equality these critics
of laissez-faire exchange wanted to create.

If you see in this nineteenth-century challenge to classical economics the outlines of "conflict theory," you are certainly right to
do so. Bentham and Marx laid the basis for Rex's work. It was by
drawing on these traditions that Rex equated material inequality
with conflict, and reform with changes in external conditions.
Moreover, just as Marx's well intentioned theories often led to the
coercive imposition of "equality from above," so, we have seen,
did conflict theory end up supporting a coercive understanding of
the nature of social control.

Now where does all this leave Homans, the man who revived
classical economic theorizing in the late twentieth century? It seems
to me that by reviving exchange theory Homans sought to reverse

this historical process. Despite its elegance and often penetrating insight, Homans' work must, in the end, be viewed as an effort to turn back the clock, theoretically and ideologically. Let me develop this point a little further by drawing on Homans' own statements about his work.

Homans' theory, despite its positivist search for explanation, is still a form of self-reflection. Like Parsons and Rex before him, Homans' was responding to what he viewed as the crisis of Western society. The formative years for him, as for Parsons, were the Depression years of the 1930s. His mature exchange theory, and its popularization, coincided with the breakdown of postwar consensus in the late 1950s and early 1960s. I have suggested earlier that the renewal of ideological pessimism in this period meant a break with the optimism of Parsons' liberal faith. Only now, as we turn to Homans, is it clear that the alternative to this optimistic faith did not necessarily have to come from the left. Homans is a man of the American right. He offered a conservative challenge to a liberal, reformist understanding of the social system in our time.

Homans' intention is to restore the notion that a natural identity of interests exists between men. No great external impediments stand in the way of equality and cooperation, he believes, and no complicated theory of human motivation is necessary to explain how men may act to bring this about. Common sense will prevail, against the perceptions and often the interests of dissatisfied groups. Ideological and theoretical motives, then, were involved in the development of exchange theory, a fact clearly acknowledged in a remarkable autobiographical passage which appears in the introduction Homans made to the collection of his essays. Homans begins his recollection by establishing the link between the Depression experience and his search for a new, more viable sociological theory.

> Someone has said that much modern sociology is an effort to answer the arguments of the revolutionaries. As a Republican Bostonian who had not rejected his comparatively wealthy family, I felt during the thirties that I was under personal attack, above all from Marxists.

Homans goes on to describe his encounter with Pareto, a theorist who opposed Marxian economics while agreeing with Marx that interests determined action.

> I was ready to believe Pareto because he provided me with a defense. His was an answer to Marx because an amplification of him. Marx had taught that the economic and political theories of the bourgeoisie—and I was clearly a bourgeois— were rationalizations of their interests. Pareto amplified Marx by showing that this was true of most theories of human behavior. . . . At least the proletariat had no more intellectual justification in demanding my money or my life—and it looked as if they were demanding both, and my liberties to boot— than I had for defending myself. Emotional justification was something else again. . . . If we could only meet as honest men—or honest rationalizers—we might divide up the take without fighting. It was the intellectual guff talked about by the alleged leaders of the proletariat that put one's back up and got in the way of a settlement.[4]

One sees clearly from this forthright statement how Homans' renewal of rationalistic and individualist theory provided, simultaneously, an understanding of, a defense against, and a solution for the instability of the day. It provided an understanding because it frankly acknowledged the clash of interests which were at stake in the class war. Such recognition could be made with a clean conscience, moreover, because the tenets of exchange theory held that no party to negotiation is more rational or more powerful than any other. Herein lies Homans' defense, for this theory cannot envision either side as having access to a higher, more legitimate "reason"; all such claims can, then, be denigrated as irrational, emotional rationalizations of interest. As Homans wrote in his systematic presentation of exchange theory: "Some of the greatest profiteers we know are altruists."[5] How, finally, does such a theory of exchange provide a solution? Since its individualistic assumptions recognize no fundamental differences in power, the parties engaged in conflict are said to be able to meet "as honest men." Honest

[4] George C. Homans, *Sentiments and Activities* (New York: Free Press, 1962), p. 4.
[5] George C. Homans, *Social Behavior*, p. 79.

men will readily admit that greed is their motive, and harmony will be restored once the spoils are divided.

The ideology behind Homans' exchange theory, then, sharply departs from Parsons' liberal and essentially humanistic vision. It acknowledges no possibility that higher reason or ultimate good can be realized in social life, that actors might transcend their self-interest for the greater welfare, that society might be able to institutionalize collective justice. From the perspective of Homans' exchange theory, the ideal of a community of brotherhood is a delusion. Cooperation, not community, is the intended model, something which can be achieved through individuals acting on the principle of "I'll scratch your back if you'll scratch mine." Faced with the exploitation and reckless power that systems inspired by this philosophy have often legitimated, you might be inclined to condemn Homans as an irresponsible conservative. But one consideration should give pause: Homans is himself fiercely committed to political liberty and to the autonomy of the individual conscience. In the course of introducing his systematic theory, he says at one point that if people are "Yankees—white Anglo-Saxon Protestants living in New England—they hold a taste for the fruits of conscience as dearly won as a taste for olives."[6] He himself is the quintessential Yankee, so he speaks here from self-knowledge. Homans, then, has no personal wish to justify the elimination of human ideals, least of all the commitment to voluntarism and individual will. Like most individualistic and rationalistic theorists, however, he seems unable to appreciate how difficult such freedoms are to realize in the modern world.

Still, ideology is not the exclusive determinant of sociological theory. Ideology inclines a theorist toward one position or another, but it is the range of other commitments which, taken together, finally determine in which direction theorizing will go. Let us examine now the process of specifically theoretical reasoning by which Homans arrives at his post-Parsonian thinking about exchange.

To begin, we must recall that every challenging theory in the postwar period had to create its own Parsons. Each had to develop

[6] *Ibid.*, p. 46.

a negative target which would justify its own positive theoretical claims. This straw man, however, was never made up of straw alone. The challenger could be successful only if his polemic was directed at real weaknesses in Parsons' thought, the resolution of which would be welcomed by significant members of the sociological community. For Homans, this construction of a straw man was more than a mere academic exercise. It was redolent with personal meaning. He and Parsons had been colleagues in the Harvard department for many years. He had been a student when Parsons had been a young instructor in the 1930s. Parsons was always "just ahead" of Homans throughout his scientific career.

Homans' "Parsons" resembles the Parsons of conflict theory. Because both theories insist that action has an exclusively instrumental hue, they find Parsons to be an exclusively normative theorist. Yet Homans' Parsons also differs from conflict theory's in critical ways. First, because Homans insists on the superiority of individualistic theories he must paint Parsons in a much more anti-individualistic way. Second, because Homans is committed to a very different form of scientific theorizing he must bring in an issue which never existed in the conflict debate, the methodological question of the proper mode of explanation.

While Homans' objections to Parsons' mode of explanation were not, in my view, central to his substantive theoretical claims, they did become central to later developments in post-Parsonian theory. Homans claimed that structural-functional theory is not truly scientific. It is much too general and abstract, too concerned with producing concepts and definitions, too focused on the formulation of general models. As a result, Homans suggests, functionalist theory cannot be really explanatory. Because there is a great distance between its generalized level and the processes of any specific society, functionalism cannot name the precise cause of any specific effect. Homans put it this way in his presidential address to the American Sociological Association in 1964, a speech which became a central element in post-Parsonian developments: "I take it that what sociology has to explain are the actual features of actual societies and not just the generalized features of a generalized society."[7] To achieve the desirable specificity, Homans insists, the-

---

[7] Homans, "Bringing Men Back In," *American Sociological Review* (1964), 29:813.

orists must work on the propositional level. Propositions are if/
then statements which leave no doubt about precise predictions or
about the suggested cause of predicted effects.

It is my view that Homans is wrong in this explanatory dispute,
though not necessarily wrong in his more general critique of Parsons. I mentioned in an earlier lecture that Parsons' theory has an
uncomfortably abstract quality and that especially in the later work
he had great trouble moving from general models to propositions
about specific societies. Furthermore, propositions are, indeed, central to sociological theorizing, since it is only in its "empirical
payoff" that theorizing (in contrast, for example, with philosophy)
ultimately makes any sense. This said, theory which claims to consist
entirely of propositions is self-deceiving, and to the degree that
Homans helped to lead sociology down this path he helped spread
a sterilizing illusion. A body of simple propositions may look as if
it is standing alone, but in fact it can emerge only from more
complex comceptual schemes. Propositions depend on general and
widely ramifying models, and they are always undergirded by presuppositions about action and order. Whether a theorist is aware
that these other levels inform his propositional work, and whether
these levels are latent or explicit, is irrelevant. While Homans
himself insists that his theory is simply propositional, we will see
in the following discussion that his apparently simple statements
carry heavier and more general theoretical baggage.

In fact, it is precisely such general considerations which lay behind
the other parts of the straw man Homans constructs. Like conflict
theory, exchange theory insists that the chief characteristic of
functionalism is its focus on norms, that norms are the principal
resources for the definition of social roles, and that roles are the
basis of a functionalist view of society. Unlike a conflict theorist,
however, Homans does not complain that this normative focus
eliminates social conflict. Homans himself, after all, is committed
to the natural (i.e., harmonious) identity of interests. What Homans
complains about is something entirely different, something which
is much more closely connected to the nature of the theory he
seeks to propose. Norms and roles, he complains, refer only to the
collective, institutional framework of action, not to action itself.
To really explain action you need a theory of "subinstitutional"

behavior.[8] Because functionalists focused on norms and roles, he insists, "they took conformity to norms for granted."[9] Homans suggests, by contrast, that rules cannot spell everything out in advance, that the concrete reality of interaction means that things are always changing. As he writes in his introduction to *Social Behavior:* "It takes time for rules to get formulated, and once formulated they tend to stay on the books for relatively, though not absolutely, long stretches of time. In the mean time the actual behavior of individuals goes on, changing with changing circumstances." If, therefore, sociology is to be truly explanatory, it must focus on these changing circumstances. These changing circumstances, the new or changing elements in action, are the "contingent" elements. Since "no rule can spell out in enough detail how persons should behave in every contingency,"[10] it is behavior and not rules which sociology should describe. Homans' sociology will, in the words of his presidential address, "bring men back in."

With this claim that Parsonian theory ignores the actual behavior of real individuals Homans opened up a vein which theorists would mine for years to come. It revealed real weakness in Parsons' theorizing, and it certainly spoke to deep-rooted theoretical discontent. The focus on behavior over against norms—in the name of interaction, individuality, intentionality, or microsociology—has been one of the central disputes in the field since Homans' time. It is also a dispute, however, which can never be carried out in the name of the individual alone. While the individual versus collectivity dispute refers to the problem of order, there remains the other presuppositional problem, the problem of action. Homans' "subinstitutional" behavior is, inevitably, behavior of a specific type, and the men he brings back in are men with certain particular (in my view quite limited) capacities. Exchange theory is not simply individualism, it is rationalistic individualism. Homans' individuals are economizers, exchangists, men who act in the name of efficiency. This insistence on a certain type of action is camouflaged by Homans' individualistic objection to norms, but it is equally responsible for the most notable characteristics of his work.

[8] Homans, *Social Behavior*, pp. 391–398.
[9] "Bringing Men Back In," p. 814.
[10] *Social Behavior*, p. 3.

The model Homans proposes for subinstitutional behavior is derived from economics. According to this tradition, individual interaction consists in sanctioning and rewarding, and the response of each individual to the other is geared to the "payoff" each receives. What you do, and how much you do of it, depends on the amount and kind of reward you get. Since this is just as true of the person with whom you interact, interaction amounts to nothing more than an exchange of rewards. The more often an action is rewarded, and the more valuable this reward is, the more often you will repeat it. The value of a reward is determined by its supply: how much have you had of it lately and how much more do you need? Your supply determines whether a reward will be valuable to you, your partner's determines how much he is willing to give. The quantity and nature of your reward, however, are not the only factors determining your profit from interaction. There is also the element of cost. To pursue an action you must spend certain resources; most importantly, you must forgo other potentially fruitful lines of action. Profit is reward minus cost. Action must be mutually profitable to proceed. Homans call this "the open secret of human exchange."[11] The secret is to give up something that is more valuable to the other person than it is costly to you, and to find a way of persuading him or her to give you things that are more valuable to you than costly to them.

This perception of behavior as calibrated exchange leads to a vision of social order as depending on continuous negotiation. If you do not get the response you want, you will try to increase the reward you offer. For example, people "can make each unit of approval they give to others a warmer kind of approval."[12] You may also try to increase the value of each "unit of reward" by making it more scarce. Homans believes that continuous profit from interaction requires just such constant calculation and ingenuity, for he sees no extra-individual structures, neither norms nor conditions, which have any binding effect. Continuous activity, moreover, leads to continuous comparison with others. Is another person getting more for his activity toward me than I am getting

[11] *Ibid.*, p. 62.
[12] *Ibid.*, p. 66.

for this same activity toward him? Given his low costs, is he receiving too much? This is the problem of distributive justice. Homans says this is also vital to every exchange, for it determines just what amount of reward is actually enough.

Homans has provided a simple and elegant model of action and order. Let us consider some of its achievements before exploring the problems it raises.

Exchange theory challenges functionalism on both action and order. Since I have suggested earlier that there are critical respects in which Parsons' positions on both issues are problematic, it should not be particularly surprising when I tell you that there are important areas where exchange theory makes significant and welcome contributions. I considered the problem of action at some length in my lectures on conflict theory, for this was also a point of challenge for Rex, and I spoke about Parsons' ambivalent position on action in earlier discussions of his work. Formally, Parsons produced a multidimensional approach to action; substantively, he often emphasized its normative over its instrumental forms. His conception of the unit act includes ends, means, and norms, and his analysis of the social system includes allocation and integration (in the middle period) and AGIL (in the later). Yet Parsons chose to identify his early unit act theorizing as "voluntaristic," and he often used it to negate instrumental perspectives in an abstract way. In his later work, the centrality of reward allocation and the uneven application of the AGIL interchange model often biased Parsons' systematic models. There were times when Parsons presented society as if norms would be followed and social order ensured if only socialization were strong enough. In fact, however, the more multidimensional strands of his theory lead to a very different conclusion, namely that external conditions, calculations of efficiency, and self-interest always mediate subjective expectations. By underplaying the cognitive dimension of action and overplaying the moral and emotional, Parsons underemphasized the means/ends calculations about efficiency which Homans puts at the center of his work.

Homans' presuppositional critique relates to order as well. Parsons clearly is wedded to a collectivist account. He maintains that individualistic theories imply randomness and that for this reason they cannot "solve" the problem of order. Does this mean, however, that Parsons believed sociology should not talk about individual action or the process of interaction between individuals? In principle, it does not mean this at all. Parsons himself spent a good deal of *The Structure of Social Action* detailing the components of individual acts. He emphasized that every act involves an element of "effort," a contingent, temporal quality that refers to free will. In the middle period work, furthermore, Parsons outlined a paradigm of interaction which he called the "dyad," in which ego and alter sanction and reward one another within the context of established norms and conditions. This dyad, you may recall, was crucial for Parsons' attempt to explain how dissatisfaction with norms can lead to deviance. Parsons emphasized, in this regard, the "double contingency" of interaction. One can even find several points in Parsons' work where he emphasized the significance of individual, contingent responses and the importance of the manipulation of instrumental means. In his analysis of socialization, for example, he recounts how the withdrawal of parental reward leads children to alter the means they employ to gain their ends—the cries, the sounds, the facial expressions, the mode of pleasure-seeking behavior they employ. It is the creation of new means, Parsons insists, which allows new norms to develop in the parent-child interaction and only then are different understandings internalized and the transition to different phases of socialization completed.[13]

A collectivist theory, then, even a functionalist one, certainly can acknowledge and even highlight the role of individual, contingent activity. A crucial distinction must be made here between empirical level of analysis and presuppositional approach to order. In his discussions of individual interaction Parsons focused on a particular empirical process, a level of analysis. He was doing so, however, within a presuppositional context that was decidedly collectivist, since he emphasized that such contingent action occurs in relationship to (internally and externally) socially structured constraints. It is one thing to focus on the individual as the point of one's

---

[13] See, for example, Talcott Parsons, "Family Structure and the Socialization of the Child," pp. 35–132, in Parsons and Robert F. Bales, eds., *Family, Socialization, and Interaction Process* (New York: Free Press, 1955).

empirical analysis and quite another to adopt, as Homans proposes, an individualistic position in terms of one's presuppositions about the sources of patterned action in general. A collectivist theorist may, indeed, focus empirically on the level of individual interaction or even on the level of the personality itself. Likewise, an individualistic theorist may try to explain not the isolated individual but a group or even a nation-state. The point at issue is the more general analytical assumptions which are made about such empirical processes, i.e., how relatively important are a priori socialized attitudes or coercive structures as compared with historically specific, contingent, individual signals and responses?

Yet, once again, while it is true that Parsons' functionalist theory can, in principle, include the element that Homans made the point of his challenge, it is equally certain that Parsons' particular application of this theory gives Homans' challenge legitimate grounds. Collectivist theory need not ignore the individual level of analysis, and Parsons does not always do so. Still, he usually does. His is a systems theory. It focuses almost exlusively on levels larger than the individual, on groups, institutions, subsystems, value patterns. To conceptualize these larger-than-life units Parsons assumes that there is, of course, a level of individual interaction. While he does not deny the fact of contingency, however, he assumes that there is a probability that contingent action will conform with normative patterns and the institutional balance of punishments and rewards. How systemic processes actually articulate with individual capacities and interactions is not something that Parsons ever spells out or even seems particularly concerned about. This leaves in functionalist theory a gaping empirical hole, for the individual and the dyad constitute a critical level of empirical life. They are not more important than a group, an institution, or a system, but neither are they less important either. Larger processes always involve smaller, micro units; if the workings of these smaller units are not explicated we can never fully account for equilibrium in social systems nor for their change.

Exchange theory, then, supplies a significant corrective to functionalist work. Its focus on contingency illuminates a new level of analysis, its emphasis on rational action counterbalances a dangerous presuppositional tilt. By acknowledging exchange the vocabulary of functionalist thoery can be expanded in significant ways. Thus, while institutionalized norms provide standards for choosing appropriate means, specific means still must *be* chosen. Normative standards must be put to use, and within the context of these normative standards considerations about the efficiency of means is an important criterion of choice. Since norms are more general than any particular case, we usually have a choice between several legitimate means. One way we make a choice is by testing a line of action for its cost and reward. We compare the rewards which are available for different actions and the profitability and relative justice of each.

But the "uses of contingency" go even deeper than this. How do we know what is a means and what a condition? How, in other words, do we know what in our material situation is possible to change and make our own (i.e., a means) and what we must take as unalterable (i.e., as a condition)? Simply to state the matter in this way demonstrates how contingency and calculation are involved. While the conditions of action appear in systems analysis as unalterable parameters, in terms of individual interaction this appearance is contingently arrived at. It is the individuals who separate, in the course of each action, what is unalterable from what can be put to their use, what must be acknowledged as a condition from what can be used as a means. They do so by testing their environments. They decide, given their current priorities and resources, what part of that environment would simply be too expensive to alter. If it is too costly, they treat it as out of reach—a "condition" for that particular act. It is through this same kind of trial and error process that individuals set new goals in response to their changing external environments. We establish new goals according to what we conceive to be contingently possible, not simply in accord with what is consistent with previous goals and with general norms. What is efficient depends on what other means are available to us, what rewards are forthcoming, what our costs are, and how we compare these to what is available to other actors.

Exchange theory, moreover, demonstrates how such contingent considerations of efficiency affect even the operation of norms themselves. For example, in the course of interaction within a role, how do we know whether role definitions—the relevant institutionalized norms—are actually being shared, whether the person with whom we are acting is behaving consistently or contrarily to our role expectations? In part, we know this simply by interpreting his action in relation to our internalized expectations. But something else is involved. We are also very sensitive to whether the rewards he is providing us are too costly for us to reciprocate. Can we afford to cooperate, given our own expenses and supplies? Can we afford the means to respond effectively to our partner's acts? Do we feel that the rewards we are giving are morally appropriate relative to the rewards he is giving us in return? Finally, if we decide that our partner's actions do not conform to our expectations, how do we carry out the sanctions involved in social control? We begin to withdraw our rewards. To do so, however, we must carefully calibrate their effectiveness in making more costly the course of the other's acts.

What I have done here is to insert the conceptual vocabulary of exchange into the broader framework of functionalism. I am suggesting that this revised neofunctionalist theory may be preferable to Parsons' original. It is certainly also different from Homans' own. Homans was not trying to fill out functionalist theory, to add a new level of analysis, or to keep it from being biased in one way or another. Homans sought to replace functionalism completely and to put in its place a theory which had no use for broader frameworks or for anything other than rational individual acts. For Homans, action is simply exchange, and individual negotiation is not an empirical level of analysis but the presupposition of order itself. Exchange theory focuses on contingent elements *as opposed to* structured ones and on quantitative, calculable motives *rather than* subjective, interpretable ones. While we may recognize the broader significance of Homans' theory, and the fundamental correctives it offers to Parsons' work, this does not amount to an evaluation of Homans' theory as such. I will get to this in the next lecture.

LECTURE ELEVEN
EXCHANGE THEORY (2): HOMANS AND THE INDIVIDUALIST DILEMMA

W E ENDED the last lecture with a problem. Granted that exchange theory generates strong insights about particular aspects of social behavior and the construction of social order, is it, in fact, a general theory of action and order as such? How might we answer this question? Well, one thing we might do is to turn to the theory's empirical claims. If we find there descriptions or propositions which do not seem empirically valid the theory's universality is thrown into doubt. This criticism would have the same status as the question I raised about Rex's claim that postwar capitalist society remained a two-class system.

Let us, then, accept for the sake of argument Homans' presuppositions and models and look, rather, at some of his specific predictions. Evaluating the cost of a typical action, he suggests at one point that asking for help is "expensive" because it is humiliating.

> [A] person can either do his own work or get help from and give approval to Other. If he does his own work he forgoes the value of getting help. But if he chooses to get help what value does he forgo? We believe that under these circumstances he, like many men, forgoes the value that we ordinarily call self-respect, the feeling that he is good enough to do his own work without help.[1]

[1] Homans, *Social Behavior: Its Elementary Forms* (New York: Harcourt, Brace, and World, 1961), p. 61. Page references to Homans' *Social Behavior* will hereafter be given parenthetically in the text.

But is asking for help inherently a cost? Is self-respect always based on maintaining the kind of absolute independence that this proposition implies? How, indeed, can a subjective concept like "self-respect" enter into an exchange theory in the first place? Similar empirical questions are raised by another proposition Homans makes, this time about the exchange of punishment. "The more one hits," he states, "the more the other hits back, for it is rewarding to hurt someone that hurts you" (p. 57). Perhaps, but certainly not in religious orders or utopian societies! Like his proposition about help, this seems a clearly culture-bound statement. In strictly empirical terms we have to wonder whether Homans has based his generalizations on data too narrow to support them. This suspicion seems justified by the frank aside, early in his book, which allows that he has relied almost purely on American sources: "Though I believe that the general features of elementary social behavior are shared by all mankind, I believe it as a matter of faith only, and the evidence that I shall in fact adduce is almost wholly American" (p. 7).

Yet however such empirical issues raise questions about the generality of Homans' work, they are not sufficient, in themselves, to undermine his theory. Other data can be found and, given Homans' theoretical power, there is little doubt he could construe such data as giving more support. It is exactly this kind of "mopping up" operation which occupies the followers of a theoretical master. What we must do, then, is to examine Homans' general framework itself. It is this general framework that presupposes Homans' perception of the empirical data and sharply constrains every attempt at empirical reconstruction. If I criticize Homans' empirical statements it is merely my word against his. If, however, I find contradictions and strains inside his theorizing, I may be able to gain Homans' support, as it were, against himself. If Homans must introduce significant residual categories into his thinking, this amounts to an implicit acknowledgment that significant weaknesses exist and points the way, in spite of itself, to theoretical alternatives.[2] If ad hoc statements made by Homans himself contradict his own

---

[2] I discussed this interpretive strategy of looking at residual categories in lecture 1, above.

theory's systematic intent, we are on firmer ground in questioning the theory ourselves. Let us consider, then, Homans' presuppositions about action and order, and let us see whether he can maintain the principles of exchange theory in a consistent way.

Homans insists on the complete rationality of action. His actor is concerned only with efficiency and profit. Into these objective calculations feelings and subjective value inclinations never intrude or, to state the issue in terms of exchange, feelings and subjective inclinations follow and are formed by calculations about profit. The actor's ability to calculate, his capacity for rationality, is never problematic; it is not something that has to be learned. Because it is an innate capacity, the theorist's (and the actor's) attention is always directed outside the self to visible, concrete things. Profit, you recall, is reward minus cost, and reward is based on the external stimulus received. The first question to ask about reward is a quantitative one: how much is received? The second is qualitative: what kind of stimulus is it, how much is it valued? Value is also objectively calculable, for it is a matter of external supply: how much of this stimuli has been received in the past? Cost, for its part, refers to resources lost, either through outright expenditure or through objective opportunities foregone.

If we know the external situation of the actor, then we must know how he will act. Since the rationality of his action is taken for granted, the environment of this action will determine its course. Since it is rational calculation of material, visible factors—basically, of quantity and supply—which determines profitability, determination of the course of action can be made as easily by the scientist-observer as by the actor himself. Such behavior is predictable for the social scientist, and it is predictability and precise explanation which, according to Homans, one strives for in sociological theory. This predictability would be impossible if subjective, internal states of mind were allowed into theoretical play, for in this case the actor's (and the scientist's) calculations about external conditions would be mediated by nonrational, less easily visible facts.

It is for all these reasons, presuppositional as well as methodological, that Homans is led to make the radical claim that internal states do not actually exist, at least not independently of externally observable acts.

> Sentiments are not internal states of an individual any more
> than words are. They are not inferred from overt behavior:
> they *are* overt behavior and so are directly observable. They
> are, accordingly, activities (and) we need no special proposi-
> tions to describe their effects. (p. 34)

In theory, therefore, Homans' actors do not have an internal
consciousness which is differentiated from their external activity.
Taken to its logical conclusion this means they have no memory,
for memory would allow the sentiments attached to past acts to
accumulate independently and to intrude on present ones. Because
Homans links sentiments to present activities, he feels compelled
to eliminate memories about "options foregone" from his formulations about cost. Opportunities can refer only to present options, options which are objectively observable: "For an activity to
incur cost," he writes, "an alternative and rewarding activity must
be there to be foregone."

> We shall consider as costs only those forgone rewards that
> remain available throughout the period in which a particular
> activity is being emitted, as the reward of escaping from fatigue
> is open to the pigeon throughout the time it is pecking. If I
> am offered two jobs, only one of which I can take, no doubt
> I shall find it painful to make up my mind; but as soon as I
> have taken one and turned down the other, which is then no
> longer open to me because someone else has gotten it, then
> the rewards of the job I let go are no longer a cost to me
> in doing the job I took. (p. 59)

If the ability for memory to affect cost has disappeared, then
Homans may be right in likening men to pigeons. If memory exists,
however, this analogy breaks down, for while pigeons may respond
only to present opportunities, men with sensibilities certainly do
not.

Homans has presented a systematic and consistently rationalistic
perspective, even if it has been at the cost of impoverishing his
perspective on human beings. The sign of truly distinguished theorists, however, is that they sense the limitations of even their most
systematic work. They know where it will be vulnerable, and they
move, consciously or unconsciously, to shore it up. This shoring

up, however, can be done only in an ad hoc way; to do anything else would be to undermine his theory's systematic integrity. It is clear, indeed, that Homans is acutely aware of the limiting character of exchange. Contradictions and residual categories abound.

In his very first general proposition about exchange, for example, he suggests that the subjective capacity for discrimination is vital for calculating profit. "The more similar the present stimulus situation is to the past one," he writes in regard to his prototypical actor, "the more likely he is to emit the activity, or some similar activity, now" (p. 53). What Homans is saying here is that actors must compare the external stimuli they are currently receiving with their experiences of stimuli in the past. But if this is true, the analogy between men and pigeons is lost. In fact, Homans goes on to suggest that "whatever establishes the similarities and differences in question—whatever makes men discriminate between stimuli—may be exceedingly complicated. It is far more complicated for men than it is for pigeons" (p. 53). It is so complicated precisely because the ability to discriminate depends entirely upon the subjective capacity to recollect the past—upon the "memory" which Homans is so intent on leaving out. "With a man the discrimination may be the result not only of his everyday experience but also of his formal education, his reading, and the verbal arguments he may have listened to. They may be unconscious or the result of conscious reasoning" (p. 53). Since the past is carried by sentiments, the tight link between a person's sentiments and his contemporary activities has been lost. It is, moreover, much more difficult to predict—objectively—the behavior of a person if we must compare the stimulus he is now receiving and that which long preceded it. We would have to know whether the actor himself feels that a similiarity exists. Memories and sentiments differ from person to person. We are pushed back from a theory of observable realities to an interpretive theory about states of mind.

Discrimination also implies standards. We compare things to one another by comparing both to a more general standard of what such types of things should be. Once again, this leads us back to the past, a fact which Homans seems to acknowledge when he writes that it is through "processes of past learning" that patterns of contemporary stimuli have the effect they do (p. 74). Are such

learned standards of discrimination, however, in any way different
from Parsons' norms? Has not Homans' reference to discrimination
led him implicitly to recognize—to note in an ad hoc way—the
reality of nonrational action and of extra-individual constraints on
experience?

These reservations about a purely instrumental perspective on
action also surface in the contradictory definitions Homans offers
for "value." Value is absolutely vital to any theory of exchange:
it is the qualitative element which, with the quantitative, determines
reward. Homans' second general proposition about exchange has
two parts. The first is quantitative, referring simply to number:
"The more often within a given period of time a man's activity
rewards the activity of another, the more often the other will emit
the activity" (p. 54). The second is qualitative, focusing on value:
"The more valuable to a man a unit of the activity another gives
him, the more often he will emit activity rewarded by the activity
of the other" (p. 55). But we can also find in Homans' work a
very different approach to value. "The value of the unit [an actor]
receives," he writes, "is the degree of reinforcement or punishment
he gets from that unit" (p. 40). Why is this different? Whereas in
the former proposition, value is described as an independent mediator of stimuli, in the latter it is seen as determined by the stimuli.
In the latter case it is the behavior of the actor which tells the
value of the stimuli, in the former, the independent assessment of
value predicts what the behavior of that actor will be, i.e., whether
the stimuli will reinforce or punish him.

Why is Homans so ambiguous about this central concept? We
have seen that he is perfectly capable of developing an objectivist
definition of value, namely, that value is determined by the recip-
ient's previous supply of the object. Since this definition succeeds
in turning quality into quantity, why would Homans want to avoid
placing value in an independent position? Because, I believe, he
has misgivings about the actor's ability objectively to calculate the
meaning of "previous supply." We have seen how he feels compelled
to acknowledge the role of discrimination, and how he links discrimination to the role of memories about past rewards. The
problem, then, is that if value is determined by past supply, then
it is surely dependent upon discrimination. To allow value to be

an independent mediator of stimuli is, therefore, to tie exchange to internal, even irrational things. Value would become something imputed to stimuli by (stored up reservoirs of) sentiment and sensibility. Far better to reduce value to an epiphenomenon of stimulus, forcing the observer to examine the specific course of observable action if value is to be ascertained. Is this a case of the tail wagging the dog? I will argue that it is.

My discussion of Homans' problems with action has been guided by my conviction that presuppositions establish a "theoretical logic" which sharply limits the possibilities for empirical descriptions of the "real world." Homans clearly wants very much to talk about discrimination and accumulated memory, but his commitment to instrumental presuppositions about action makes it extremely difficult for him to do so. Certain references can be smuggled in by the back door, but if his theory is to remain recognizably an "exchange theory" any analysis which links discrimination to states of mind, and value to both, would have to remain occasional and ad hoc. Homans must directly contradict such analysis in his systematic work.

In this particular sense one can say that theoretical logic meets empirical reality head on. "Reality," I believe, is multidimensional: there are norms and interests, individual negotiation and collective force. A theorist may ignore significant parts of this complex reality, but he can not make them go away, and one indication of an important theorist is that he senses they are still there. Thinking both from "inside" and from "outside" his conceptual framework, he makes efforts to find these neglected elements some place in the theoretical whole. No empirical reality, of course, is ever sensed "in itself." If a theorist is aware of other variables it is because he has been exposed to—and at some earlier point may even have adopted—other presuppositions.

I have described just this sort of problem in my earlier discussions. Parsons' idealist tendency led him to introduce one-sided normative reductions that threatened to negate the multidimensional model he strived so hard to produce. Rex, for his part, faced what I called the conflict dilemma. His commitment to rationalism and collective order forced him to choose between coercion and residual category. To avoid both he would have had to step outside his rationalist framework and to acknowledge that collective force, and conflict and order, could be built upon normative foundations. Thus, even while Rex chose coercion, he insinuated normative ideas about supra-class consensus into his theory of the postwar capital/labor truce. To continue theorizing about supra-class values, however, would have meant approaching order from assumptions about action very different than the instrumentalist ones he held. It is precisely this possibility that creates the dilemma for theory of the conflict type. I want to return now to my critique of Homans' exchange theory, moving from my analysis of action to a discussion of his treatment of order.

Instrumental rationality is central to exchange theory, as it is to conflict theory. What distinguishes exchange from conflict theory (on the presuppositional level) is its forcefully individualistic position on the problem of order. Homans claims that "elementary behavior" is behavior rewarded by another concrete, living, breathing person. While acknowledging the existence of "silent third parties," he will not directly write about them. He theorizes only about dyadic relations. He is not just trying to illuminate a level of empirical analysis but insisting on a fundamental theoretical—more precisely presuppositional—position.[3] Homans insists that collective order, the level of institutions in empirical terms, derives from "subinstitutional" behavior. Collective patterns result from individual, face-to-face interaction. This individual interaction is exchange.

But Homans faces a problem. It is the problem of order. Since he rejects the collectivist position, is he not tied to the infinite complexity of individual negotiation? Infinite complexity is simply another way of talking about randomness. Of course, Homans seems to accept randomness; what other way to explain his discussion of individual action as guided only by calculations about the profitability of exchange? But he also wants to relate these actions to supra-individual order, the existence of which he never denies. As a result, Homans faces what I will call the "individualist dilemma." To maintain an approach to order that is individualistic in a clear,

---

[3] For the distinction between empirical level of analysis and presuppositional position, see discussion in the preceding lecture.

consistent, and honest way, a theorist must introduce into his construction a level of openness to contingency that makes his explanation of order approximate randomness and unpredictability. But whatever the theorist's formal commitment, and whether or not this contingency is seen eventually to lead to collective order, few individualistic theorists are, in the end, fully satisfied with such randomness. Their dissatisfaction may derive from "the pressure of reality" or from the pressure of competing, more collectivist social theories. After all, even the most individualistic theorist is a sociologist, not a psychologist or an existentialist philosopher. But whatever its sources, this dissatisfaction pushes individualist theorists toward more collective ideas, for despite their formal commitments they try, in one way or another, to embrace some aspect of supra-individual order.

The individualist dilemma is a choice between randomness and residual category. It is created because this "theorist with second thoughts" will not—indeed, cannot—give up on his formal claims to a thoroughgoing individualism. For this reason, the "collectivist moment" he introduces must be hidden inside residual categories. Because it cannot be part of the systematic, forthright argument of the theory itself, this collectivist reference will be indeterminate and vague. For this problem to be resolved the dilemma itself would have to be transcended. This could come about only if the formal adherence to individualism were abandoned, for only then could the sui generis autonomy of social order be stated clearly rather than camouflaged in ambiguity. The contingent and individualistic element of social order could then be inserted into a collectivist theory as a significant level of empirical analysis rather than as a theoretical presupposition as such.

In principle there are two paths by which Homans could introduce residual categories asserting collective order. He could describe this supra-individual force in a rationalist form, pointing to the kinds of material controls over individual behavior that preoccupy conflict theorists like Rex. Since Homans shares Rex's perspective on action, this strategy would seem to make perfect sense. It is significant, then, that Homans does not avail himself of this opportunity. Though he is caught within the individualist dilemma, we can see no evidence of his resort to residual categories in a rationalistic form. Why not? Because, I believe, Homans is so committed to individualism not simply in a presuppositional but in an ideological sense. Remember this self-confessed Yankee insisting that the "fruits of conscience [are] as dearly won as a taste for olives"? On some levels Homans must have realized that any movement to material collectivism involves coercion, and he is too committed to individual liberty to allow this to happen. But there is another side to this ideological resistance. Homans' liberalism is of the conservative, laissez-faire kind. To move toward collectivism within an instrumental mode would acknowledge material constraints on the proto-economic actor. It would allow that a "natural identity of interests" might not exist, and that, faced with a breakdown in social order, the solution lay in the reform of political-economic institutions. Conservative laissez-faire would then give way to progressive reformism, even to the kind of socialism and Marxism which inspired Rex.

Homans' ideological-cum-presuppositional refusal to acknowledge material constraints, however, has debilitating empirical consequences, even if it allows him to avoid the problems that Rex's work suggests. Homans maintains, for example, that we must "assume, by whatever process of trial and error you please, [that] the two [partners to an exchange] have struck a bargain as to the *kind* of service each will provide, and that for the time being neither will provide another kind" (p. 54). But is the kind of service different actors provide a matter actually decided by individual trial and error? Is it entirely the result of bargains decided by the contingencies of the immediate situation? Surely not. Kind of service refers to the allocation of facilities, and Rex and Parsons both have shown how such allocation is structured by collective demands. For Parsons it is a matter of role definitions and the exigencies created by scarce resources. For Rex it is determined by the power differential of dominant groups, which is itself related to supra-individual factors like technological conditions and party organization. Homans, by contrast, insists that the power of bargaining parties is basically equivalent. He acknowledges the possibility that monopoly can affect supply and demand, but he insists that "either party may break off the exchange" at any time (p. 67). Punishing, disadvantageous exchange, he believes, will continue "only if for some reason neither of the two men can avoid hostilities, or if the other aspects of exchange are rewarding in themselves and the chances of successive victories falling to one side or the other are about equal (p. 57). To me this seems like an outlandish distortion of empirical reality. If bargaining power is unequal, if one side has a monopoly on goods which the other side absolutely needs, then the weaker party cannot simply break off the exchange when it becomes punishing or unrewarding. To suggest that it is simply equality that ensures continuing punishment is bizarre. Surely we should also look to inequality and the inability to bargain successfully with others.

It should not be surprising, then, that Homans insists, in the end, that exchange takes place in what economists call a perfect market. "The sort of market we are dealing with in this book," he writes, "holds no absolute monopolists—for our people are always free not to enter into exchange at all." Neither, he adds, "does it offer a man many alternative sources of reward." Because of this, he reasons, "exchanges between two persons tend to continue" (p. 78). We are back to the pre-Marxist ideology of Locke and Adam Smith, to the insistence that there is an inherent, natural identity of interests between individuals which makes collective control unnecessary. Homans' exchange theory is utopian in just the kind of conservative way developed by laissez-faire. Unequal facilities, the oppression and exploitation of others, do not exist. Homans' empirical assumptions reinforce his ideological position. Together, they allow him to ignore an entire complex of problems engendered by the individualist-rationalist position.

Yet while Homans has avoided, for good reasons and bad, the problems of rationalistic conflict theory, he has avoided facing the problem of collective order only in one of its forms, not collective order as such. The problem of order still hangs over his head like the proverbial sword of Damocles. For Locke, the inventor of classical economic theory, the natural identity of interest could be maintained by making certain empirical assumptions about the state of nature, namely that men are naturally friendly and potentially cooperative and that they have due regard for one another's rights. Yet while Homans accepts Locke's ideological emphasis on natural identity and the freedom of conscience, as a twentieth-century sociologist even he cannot really accept Locke's notion of inherent sociability and individual respect. In spite of himself, then, Homans is forced to move outside the purely individualistic framework he has systematically established. Since he rules out the possibility of doing so within an instrumentalist framework, only one possibility remains. To move toward collectivism while maintaining voluntarism he must alter his understanding of action. By doing so he can introduce residual categories about collective order in a nonrational form. Earlier we have observed that Homans is occasionally inclined to doubt the complete instrumentality of action, namely, in his references to discrimination and its links to the subjective past. At the end of that discussion, however, Homans threw up his hands at this unwelcome complexity, much as Rex threw up his hands at the prospect of explaining ritual behavior.[4] "Obviously the problem between stimuli, past activities, and present ones is of the first importance," Homans wrote, "but we shall state no further general propositions about it, and accordingly this book falls far short of being a complete psychology" (p. 53). But in the end Homans has very little choice. Ineluctably, by virture of the instability of his limited presuppositional stance, he is forced to root values and discrimination in collective, noncontingent, and normative sources of reward.

Let us begin with his treatment of the thorny problem of values. I talked with you earlier about the central equivocation in Homans' definition of value. On the one hand, he sees value as an independent mediator of stimulus, the element which decides the qualitative *kind* of stimulus which, along with the quantity of stimulus, determines "reward." On the other hand, Homans backs away from making value so central, suggesting that we can define the value of a stimulus only after we know that reinforcement has occurred. This central equivocation, I suggested, relates to the potentially embarrassing recognition by Homans that the perception of rewards involves discrimination, and that discrimination, far from being related only to external, objectively observable acts, is rooted in memories of past associations and feelings. This problem is

---

[4] For Rex's expression of theoretical helplessness before the problem of ritual, see p. 145, above.

magnified when Homans turns from action to order, from discrimination to values as such. "Values like pride, altruism, aggression," he writes, "are just the ones that give us most trouble in predicting and explaining the behavior of men." The reason they are the source of such trouble is that the value they provide to the actor cannot be tied directly to observable actions: they are "values that are, as we sometimes say, their own reward" (p. 45).

What did Homans mean by this? He means that general values like pride, altruism, and aggression tend to remain sources of commitment whether or not they are reinforced by the responses of others. People who are prideful or aggressive feel rewarded simply because they have acted in accordance with these values—no matter how others respond. Where, then, does their reward come from? Obviously it can come only from within themselves. If you have internalized previous rewarders, the actions they valued become your own values. Acting in accordance with these values then becomes a reward in itself. Such action is independent of present, observable, external sanctions, the very kind of sanctions which define action as exchange.

For Homans even to suggest the possibility of such internalization turns out, not surprisingly, to be a tremendous source of trouble. If value involves past internalization, the scientific observer cannot focus simply on exchange. Because Homans acknowledges that "a man's past is where we must look for enlightenment" in this regard, he goes on to suggest that "the past offers in principle the information we need to assess values independently of the amount of activity a man puts out to get values at present" (p. 45). To explain response, which involves the actor's calculation of profit, the analysis of present interaction must be supplemented by the study of the past, for it is not simply rewards but "the same special tastes for rewards" that decides if actors will respond similarly to the same quantity of stimulus (p. 45). But the past leads Homans to seek help from the very theoretical traditions he deplores. First he turns to Freud, the rock upon which Parsons built his later theory of cultural order. "If there is one thing we have learned from Freud," Homans writes, "it is that a man's past history, sometimes so long past that he has trouble talking about it, is a powerful determinant of his present behavior" (p. 45). Freud wrote about nonrational action; Parsons tied this conceptualization of action to nonrational sources of order. Homans seems here to follow Parsons' lead. "Members of a particular society," he writes, "are apt to have acquired the same special tastes for the rewards they received at the hands of their mothers, fathers, and other members of their community" (p. 45). He discusses the different effects of national communities and regional subcultures. Finally, he is led to acknowledge that the heart of value is the conformity to norms.

> When we get down to particular groups of people, a special kind of reward, the reward obtained by conformity to a norm becomes important. A norm is a statement made by a number of members of a group . . . that the members ought to behave in a certain way in certain circumstances. The members find it rewarding that their own actual behavior and that of the others should conform to some degree to the ideal behavior described by the norm. (p. 46)

It was Homans, of course, who had argued against just this kind of norm-centered thinking in functionalist sociology. His systematic theory is built on the proposition that conformity to norms is an illusion, that actors respond only to the immediate contingencies of rewards and punishments.

Nobody, least of all a sociological theorist, likes to admit that he has contradicted himself. Do you remember how fast Rex backtracked after introducing residual categories into his analysis of the truce?[5] Homans does the same thing. After introducing one residual category after another, he reverses his field by introducing a second line of ad hoc reasoning. Value, he now suggests, is divided into two parts, constant and variable. This is how he puts the issue: "[A] person values help highly if, first, he is the kind of man that needs help, and if, second, he has gotten little help in the recent past" (p. 48). The "kind of man" a person is refers to value's constant element, and this, Homans suggests, changes very slowly. It is not, in other words, much affected by exchange. Whether or not a person has received much help "in the recent past" refers to the second element in value, the variable part.

[5] See my discussion of this on pp. 148–151, above.

Variable value is quantitative and related to the visible here and now. It, and only it, can be directly related to exchange.

What are we to make of this new development? On the one hand, Homans seems to have acknowledged that a significant determinant of profit stands outside exchange, that it is linked through the process of discrimination to norms, communities, and socialization. At the same time, however, he has introduced a conceptual distinction which allows his theory not to confront this recognition. "This book," he writes, "is concerned with current, face-to-face behavior and its changes within rather short spans of time" (p. 48). At every other point in his book Homans defines his topic as "elementary behavior," which in his terms is always face-to-face. Here, however, he has introduced the crucial qualification, "changes within short spans of time." But if he has just acknowledged that constant, long-term factors are a major component of valuation, must they not also be part of elementary behavior as well? Logically the answer is yes, strategically the answer is no. Homans has introduced the constant/variable distinction to avoid cultural analysis, not to embrace it. With it he can claim that it is only behavior that changes over short spans of time which is of interest. "Since variation, not constancy, is what we undertake to explain, we treat the first [constant] component of value as simply given . . . and do not feel that we must always explain it. Within the limits we set for ourselves, whatever varies we explain and whatever stays constant we take as given" (p. 48). Perhaps Homans should have changed the subtitle of his book to "Elementary Behavior in Short Spans of Time!"

I have tried to convince you that Homans' discussion of value is extraordinarily important, for I believe it demonstrates the impossible limitations faced by a theory which conceptualizes society as exchange. Even if I have succeeded, however, you might respond that the whole of this equivocal discussion occupies only a few brief pages of Homans' book. You would be quite right to do so. I think, however, that I can find in Homans' work a much more substantial section which is just as revealing and ad hoc. This is his twelfth chapter, entitled "Justice."

To understand what Homans is about in this crucial chapter, we must remember that he would like to present exchange as if it were governed by the purely contingent, pragmatic standard of "rough equivalence." If I am bound to give you back something roughly equivalent in value to what you have given me, then my response can be predicted on the basis of looking at your stimulus (and, of course, at my relative supply of it). This kind of objective equivalence, however, is difficult to ascertain. Because the goods (the stimuli) I am giving back to you are bound to differ in some way from the goods (the response) you are giving me, they cannot be exactly compared. Moreover, while our relative supplies seem fairly easy to establish, our relative costs—what each of us gives up by proceeding with the exchange—similarly involve comparison between different kinds of good. How, then, can we decide whether stimulus and response actually are equal? We must engage in comparison, comparison between your goods and mine, your expectations and mine, your alternatives and mine. But we will no doubt also compare our own situation with that of others in society to see what they have been getting in similar situations.

Homans is aware of all this. Indeed it is he who brings the issue of comparison up and who sees immediately its implications. In making comparisons, he writes, we are involving ourselves in the issue of fairness, and the fairness of exchange raises the problem of distributive justice. But if exchange involves distributive justice, and distributive justice hinges on comparison, are we not, ineluctably, led back to the problem of interpretation and to the existence of standards for interaction which stands outside any particular act? Homans is caught, once again, on the horns of the individualist dilemma. Faced with the problem of randomness (pure individual contingency), he moves toward residual category.

The very first sentence of chapter 12 indicates Homans' awareness that he is entering the cloudy world of the ad hoc: "We must now begin to tuck in some loose ends that in earlier chapters we deliberately left dangling" (p. 232). The loose end he tries to tuck in is distributive justice. To deal with it—remember his strategy in regard to value—he introduces a distinction between two different principles. The first is that the value a person receives from a group in one area of activity must be consistent with his rewards in other areas. This principle of consistency sounds at first perfectly all right, since it seems to be quantitative and instrumental. The problem is that to explicate it Homans must return to a normative understanding of collective order which sounds, once again, very much like what was proposed by Durkheim and Parsons.

To illustrate the principle he chooses a case study about Alex. Alex was a member of a teenage youth group, a bunch of boys who hung around together and did a lot of different things. One of the things they did was bowl. Alex bowled well and in doing so he lived up to group expectations. This good bowling constituted a stimulus, and according to exchange theory Alex should have received in return for it an equivalent reward. He did not, however, receive such a reward from his group. The reason, according to Homans, was that in other areas of group activity "he violated important group norms" (p. 234). In offering this explanation, Homans implies that group solidarity is critical to the allocation of rewards. Yet Parsons himself insists on exactly the same thing when he defines social integration as of equal importance as social allocation. Because the members of Alex's group held dearly to group values, they placed, it seems, a value on conformity as such. As Homans put it earlier, the group's values were regarded as ends in themselves. But if rewards are, indeed, distributed not just in response to a specific activity but also in relation to a person's overall performance as a member of a group, then it would seem that the interests of distributive justice subordinate exchange to moral solidarity.

In his second principle of distributive justice Homans brings in the residual category of morality in a different way. The reward a person gets for his activity, he suggests, must be equivalent to his "investments" (p. 237) Again, on the face of it this reference seems to have a quantitative and economic cast, which would make it consistent with an instrumentalist perspective on exchange. But Homans actually does not define investment in an economic way. He uses it to refer to sociologically relevant elements in a person's character. Your investments refer to things like skill, age, race, sex, and family of birth. Investments, in other words, have nothing directly to do with the stimulus to which you are exposed or your immediate cost. Rather, they are the residues from earlier activities which have given you your "status." This status defines, culturally, to what extent you are regarded as a "good" or "deserving" person.

The reward you receive for any stimulus you provide is mediated by your status outside the particular transaction.

Any calculations that an outside observer makes about profit, therefore, must be crucially mediated by considerations about what investments a given society thinks are important. For the sense of having made a profit depends not on the objective equivalence of rewards and costs but on the calculation of these objective qualities in relation to what an actor thinks he deserves. Mutual satisfaction depends, then, upon cultural consensus about investments. Should high birth count as a valid investment? If it does, then clipping stock coupons will be considered sufficient stimulus to be rewarded with wealth. Should race or sex count as an investment? If so, then equal work by persons of different sex or race can legitimately result in unequal pay. This is the reward system in a conservative or aristocratic society. If, by contrast, simple "personhood" or "citizenship" is deemed the principal investment, then rewards may be equalized even in the case of unequal work. This is the definition of investment, the norm of distributive justice, under utopian socialism.

These, of course, are precisely the normative issues which conflict theory sought to reduce to an outcome of mere power struggles, since conflict theory depends on utilitarian exchange. In Homans' reconstructed theory of exchange, however, it is just these normative expectations which determine perceptions about the distribution of rewards. When Homans observes that cooperation between social actors seems always to be breaking down, he points to objective disagreements, not objective inequalities. "The trouble," he writes, "is that [people] differ in their ideas of what legitimately constitutes investment, reward, and cost, and how these things are to be ranked. They differ from society to society, from group to group, and from time to time in any one society or group" (p. 246).

It seems to me that in this discussion of his second principle Homans has illuminated processes on the level of individual interaction which correspond to critical problems Parsons approached from the level of the social system. For both theorists the issue is how can rewards mediate between institutionalized values and the allocation of facilities and personnel? They do so, Homans has explained, because the individual desire for distributive justice relates the objective profits from exchange to group expectations about the worth of individual qualities. Parsons' answer, by contrast, referred to equilibrium pressures on allocative and integrative systems. The explanations are complementary. In contributing to such a theoretical "advance," Homans has stepped far outside his systematic theory of exchange.

Very early in *Social Behavior* Homans acknowledges that there may be significant elements of social behavior which are determined by role requirements as distinct from interactional exigencies of exchange. "But my student of elementary social behavior would leave to other social scientists," he writes, "the task of explaining why the role got to be what it is, and take upon himself [only] the job of explaining the variations in actual behavior once the role is given" (p. 5). This notion of leaving the explanation of certain key dimensions of action and order to others is a sure danger signal. It is an alarm which rings when objectively limiting theoretical assumptions are about to be wished away. We saw how Parsons announced a division of analytic labor within the social sciences—with sociology assuming the job of explaing norms—just after he had introduced a drastically idealistic foreshortening of his multidimensional approach. In much the same way, certain conflict theorists, like Dahrendorf, proposed that the normative and harmonious (as opposed to conflictual) elements in society should be handled by other theorists who specialize in "integration." But such diplomacy between general theorists is sleight of hand. Proposals for an analytic divison of labor are oblique signals that a theory cannot handle fundamental aspects of social life. What follows such signals are confusing residual categories, not diplomatic recognition.

I have taken the position that Parsons' ambition to create a multidimensional and synthetic theory was a laudable one. I tried first to demonstrate how Parsons himself fell far short of these goals, by introducing an idealist reduction, by conflating presuppositional and empirical questions, by being unable to separate ideological applications from more general concerns. Conflict theory, I then tried to show, addressed each of these failings in significant ways, and in doing so allowed us to move beyond Parsons' narrow application to a fuller exploration of the multidimensionality of social life. At the same time, I suggested, conflict theory itself was conceptually flawed; its own instrumental reductions led to lines of ad hoc reasoning which were often mirror images of Parsons' own. I hope it is clear to you that I have treated exchange theory in much the same way. Homans initially conceptualized a theoretical arena which Parsons barely had touched, the level of concrete interaction which assumes a rationalistic form. By taking these analytical emphases for general theory itself, however, Homans restricted his theory in a manner which made it impossible for him systematically to embrace the full range of social life. Rather than demonstrating his theory's superiority to Parsons', the residual categories he was led to introduce actually revealed a convergence between his theorizing and the multidimensional thread in functionalist work.

I have discussed Homans' theory not simply as the work of a talented individual—though its individual flavor is clearly apparent—but as the prototype of "exchange theory" itself. The theoretical logic it exemplifies, and the constraints which this logic entails, hold good, in my view, for every attempt to develop a strictly individualist and rationalist perspective on social life. Any theorist who takes exchange as the primordial form of sociality will run into the problems which permeate Homans' work. The exchange perspective leaves theorists with a dilemma: they must choose between randomness and residual category. If they are not satisfied with either, they must step completely outside the boundaries of their work. This dilemma has a "structural" status: it exists no matter what the personal intentions, the ideological ambitions, the empirical commitments of the particular theorist are.

In an important early development in exchange theory, for example, James Coleman indicated great sensitivity to the conservative and individualistic drawbacks of Homans' original formulations.[6] He insisted, by contrast, that all exchanges occur within collective frameworks which establish distributions of power, and he went on to say that these frameworks are held in place by constitutional

---

[6] Coleman, "Foundations for a Theory of Collective Decisions," *American Journal of Sociology* (1966), 71:615–627.

systems that normatively limit the abuse of uneven power. But Coleman never offered a way of theorizing about normative, constitutional rules themselves. While intending his theory to represent simply an "amendment" to individualistic exchange, in so amending it he was led to introduce the same residual categories he had meant to overcome. Peter Blau tried to amend Homans in much the same way.[7] He insisted upon the uneven distribution of supra-individual power, and he acknowledged the independent mediation of norms about just desserts. In considering the origins of such norms, however, Blau was forced to describe them merely as "emergent from exchange," a description which left them little more explained than the individualistic theory Blau had set out to overcome. It was perhaps because of this incongruity that later in his career Blau dispensed with exchange analysis altogether, on the grounds that it was irredeemably individualistic. He turned, instead, to a "structural" theory which looked at extra-individual constraints in a completely materialist way.[8] Alvin Gouldner, in a well-known article which appeared at about the same time as Blau's and Coleman's early work, developed an exchange critique of functionalist theory by arguing for the centrality of the "norm of reciprocity."[9] But as still another revision of exchange theory this attempt also suffered from the residual status of its concept of "norm." Where did such a norm come from? Was it generated by exchange, in which case it was redundant, or did it come from outside exchange itself, in which case this revision converges with the functionalism it was trying to replace.

In my view more recent work in the exchange tradition makes such implicit contradictions only more apparent. In 1974 Peter Ekeh made a systematic, frontal attack on Homans' work.[10] He argued that the notion of direct, face-to-face exchange has to be complemented by notions of indirect exchange, according to which each particular exchange is affected by the needs or costs of some

[7] Blau, *Exchange and Power in Social Life* (New York: Free Press, 1964).
[8] Blau, *Inequality and Heterogeneity* (New York: Free Press, 1977).
[9] Alvin W. Gouldner, "The Norm of Reciprocity: A Preliminary Statement," *American Sociological Review* (1960), 25:161–178.
[10] Ekeh, *Social Exchange Theory: The Two Traditions* (Cambridge, Mass.: Harvard University Press, 1974).

"silent" third party. This indirect third party, however, seems no different than the solidary group which Homans pointed to in his first principle of distributive justice. To make exchange normative by making it "indirect" is equally ad hoc. It violates the principle of parsimony—let alone the fundamental criterion of consistency— to suggest that issues like solidarity and system integration should be forced to fit into the constricting and theoretically discordant language of social exchange. Charles Kadushin's later writing on indirect exchange suffers from the same surplus complexity, as does William Goode's attempt to make exchange theory the basis for his systematic explanation of the distribution of prestige in social life.[11] Goode "corrects" exchange theory by reminding his readers that the exchange of symbolic resources—a subset of the "rewards" mentioned in Homans' and Parsons' work—must be regulated by what Durkheim called the noncontractual elements of contract, and that for this reason any analysis of prestige must deal with cultural bases which are outside of exchange itself. Buy why start from a theory of the primordiality of exchange in the first place? Why not state from the outset that while exchange is an analytical dimension of action it cannot come close to explaining action by itself? The answer, perhaps, is that to do so would be to step outside the theory of exchange as a unique tradition.

Rationalistic and individualistic assumptions permeate the empirical study of social life; they are not limited to analyses which formally announce themselves as part of the "theory of exchange." Studies of collective behavior as resource mobilization often emphasize rational choice, as do discussions of revolution. Political sociology employs such assumptions routinely. Many theories of race and ethnic relations depend on them. Explanations of international relations use proto-exchange theories to model the behavior of nations, family sociologists use them to explain the development of emotional pathologies. Conflict theories rely upon exchange to explain the actions of individual parts of complex

---

[11] Charles Kadushin, "Cast Thy Bread Upon the Waters for Thou Shalt Find It After Many Days: Notes on Motivation in Network Behavior" (unpublished paper, 1978), William Goode, *The Celebration of Heros: Prestige as a Social Control System* (Berkeley and Los Angeles: University of California Press, 1979).

systems. Marxists use exchange to explain the logic of alienated individuals and groups in capitalist society.[12]

Though few of these efforts push their theoretical assumptions in a systematic way, the limits of their empirical explanations follow the fault lines we have discovered in the more explicit and generalized logic of Homans' work. This, after all, is the rationale for pursuing general theory. It is a microcosm of sociology. By considering general theoretical problems we are engaged in an abstract and concentrated consideration of sociology itself.

---

[12] John Elster formalizes this tendency in the "rational choice Marxism" he has recently offered in Marx's name: "Marxism, Functionalism, and Game Theory," *Theory and Society* (1982), 11:453–482.

LECTURE TWELVE
SYMBOLIC INTERACTIONISM (1): PRAGMATISM AND THE LEGACY OF GEORGE HERBERT MEAD

T HE EXCHANGE and conflict challenges to functionalist hegemony emerged on the postwar scene at specific times. They were formulated in the late 1950s and early 1960s. They appeared as new theories, though of course they had classical roots. The case is much different for the next theoretical challenge we will consider, the tradition which has come to be called symbolic interactionism. It has been around in one form or another for most of this century, and its intellectual origins go even further back. Even if we limit ourselves to its modern form, which emerged in the writings of Herbert Blumer, we must go back to the 1940s. Modern interactionism, then, appeared long before Parsons' intellectual dominance began to wane. Indeed, it emerged at about the same time as Parsons' own functionalist theory. Yet in the immediate postwar period it was Parsons, not Blumer, who assumed a position of theoretical leadership. To understand why you might recall some of my earlier discussion of the history of sociology.

I noted in an earlier lecture that the sociology departments at Harvard and Columbia, and Parsons' functionalist sociology in particular, came into prominence by "defeating" the more pragmatic, individualistic, and empirical sociology of the Chicago school. The latter was very much influenced by Pragmatism, the precursor of symbolic interactionism. The early phases of this tradition, however, were not recognized as constituting a major theoretical school; they were, rather, viewed as significant approaches to sociological research. In that early period, German and French sociologists made Europe the center of theoretical work. Only later, in the interwar period when these great European traditions began to disintegrate, did some of the most important theoretical contributions to interactionism by Mead appear, as did the critical reformulations by Blumer. These works certainly were known and discussed in the post-World War II period, but the "migration of sociological theory to America" was associated not with the emergence of a theoretically more sophisticated interactionism but with Parsons' functionalist theorizing. Only in the process of challenging Parsons' dominance did interactionism come to be regarded as a major theoretical tradition. It was in the 1960s that Blumer's theoretical essays were first brought together, and it was in this decade that younger theorists seriously took up Blumer's challenge to develop "interactionist" approaches in various empirical subfields.

I will discuss this contemporary, post-Parsonian challenge in my next lecture. Today I will try to explain the historical background from which it emerged.

With symbolic interactionism we encounter the same kind of individualistic response to functionalism that we found in Homans' exchange theory. We will see, in fact, that it has much the same ideological background, since it is inspired by the belief, or at least hope, that society can be organized around a natural identity of interests. The roots of exchange theory can be traced to the individualism of seventeenth- and eighteenth-century contract theory and to the classical political economy of the nineteenth century. The individualism of symbolic interactionism, however, is linked to very different intellectual traditions. These traditions are deeply rooted in American history. Indeed, interactionism is the only theoretical challenge to Parsons that rests entirely within the American tradition. It is the only theoretical tradition in Western sociology that is almost entirely "American" in its outlook. If we are to understand the possibilities and limits of interactionist theory we would do well, therefore, to know something about the intellectual history of America itself.

While all societies have manifest tensions between the freedom they allow to individuals and the obligations they demand of their communities, this tension has been more striking in America than anywhere else. Perhaps this is because from its beginning, almost 400 years ago, America has been as much an area of the imagination as a geographical entity. It has been the place where "everything is possible," where there are supposed to be no limits to achievement. It has been the land of opportunity, invention, and liberty. Perhaps because of this faith America has been the only Western country without any real socialist tradition. There has simply not been enough communalism for that. Left and right in American history have never embraced collective ideologies; they have always presented themselves as variations on individualistic thought.

This emphasis on the individual is, in my view, the source of the best and the worst in American history. It is easy, I'm sure, for all of you to see the good parts. It is natural for those of us living in American society to see freedom positively, that is, as the elimination of constraint. But individualism has also been an ideology in American society. It has often hidden the effects of unfair institutional barriers. It has often inspired brutal competition and restless dissatisfaction. Homans' social theory neatly embodies these contradictory qualities. Though he expresses a personal concern with individual conscience and a commitment to the ideal of freedom, he portrays people as individual "capitalists" with no irrational feelings, consciences, or ties to their pasts. He also ignores, or at least cannot explain, the collective, social barriers to individual rewards. When he is forced to recognize the background characteristics of individuals which affect the rewards they receive, he calls them investments rather than limitations!

Homans exemplifies the rationalistic individualism of the American marketplace. But American individualism is rooted in non-economic spheres as well. There is, after all, a presuppositional alternative to such rationalistic individualism. This is individualism of a nonrational, normative, subjective sort. Moral individualism has also been a major force in American history, and in this lecture I will be more concerned with this strain than with its economic counterpart.

The moral individualism of American society comes, above all, from the religious heritage of Puritanism and evangelical Protestantism. It is directed not toward the desire for material acquisition but to questions of meaning and evaluation, relying on the capacity that Homans called discrimination. The Puritans closely scrutinized their internal motives; they looked for salvation to the conditions of their souls not, in the first instance, to their objective environments. But this introspective religion, especially as it became more evangelical in the nineteenth century, was extremely individualistic. People were conceived as having a direct relationship with God which was unmediated by formal rules and institutional hierarchies. It was for this reason that American evangelical Protestantism posed such a severe challenge to institutional religious communities.

In the early and middle nineteenth century, this religious tradition achieved a secular form in the first major American social theory— the "Transcendentalism" of New England intellectuals like Ralph Waldo Emerson and Henry Thoreau. The link between these secular theorists and Puritanism is clear. The Transcendentalists were spiritually, not materially directed; they were concerned with the salvation of men's souls. They were also highly individualistic, picturing man as isolated from his social environment and advocating the liberation of actors from social constraint. Emphasizing individual will over against social determinism, they proposed to reinvigorate American society by putting individuals back into the "natural" state. This natural state would be good for the soul. It would demand discipline, introspection, and hard work if the individual were to survive. This ethic was a kind of secularized Puritan response to a rapidly changing society. Remember, Thoreau escaped to Walden Pond from the bustling society of mercantile greater Boston.

I want to emphasize, however, that the attitudes these religious and secular individualists took toward community were not entirely of a piece. They did not, for example, give up on the hope that a cohesive social order could be constructed. Religious individualists lived with the fervent hope that religious organizations and even the American nation could be reconstructed as a community of voluntary believers. If religious faith were sufficient there could be a "self-controlling" community which would do away with the need for overbearing institutions. Such a community, it was believed, would still provide powerful social control, but this control would be of an informal type. In the secular thought of the first half of the nineteenth century, Transcendentalists expressed a similar belief that social relations and ethics would grow out of the intuition, or conscience, which all people possess and which allowed them to know the good.

Yet both these groups approached community and society in a rather ad hoc and residual way. Collectivities larger than the individual were usually viewed with alarm; laws, values, religions, states, and customs were usually seen as reflecting the interests of reaction and conservatism. America, after all, was a revolutionary country. It should not be surprising that the first truly "organic," institutionally oriented social thought in America was written by Southern racist intellectuals in the two decades before the Civil War, in good part as an apologia for the coercive institution of slavery. By contrast, the liberal and radical movements of the early nineteenth century, for example, Jacksonian democracy and Abolitionism, were aggressively individualistic. Among major Western societies of this time, the United States was the only nation where radicialism never assumed a conspicuously collectivist form.

This tension between individualism and a latent, residual communalism continued in the latter half of the nineteenth century. In most respects individualism continued to be the dominant stream. Economic life provides the best example. This was the era of the "robber barons," who created the first great, and brutal, phase of industrial capitalism. The economic opportunity this transformation implied was reflected in deeply held popular beliefs. In the Horatio Algier myth Americans enshrined the story of rags to riches commercial success. In the myth of the "yeoman farmer," which played such an important part in American expansion, a vision of hard work as yielding unlimited opportunity stimulated expansion in the agricultural West. The great social theorist for post-Civil War Americans was the English Utilitarian Herbert Spencer, who proposed the individualistic notion of the "survivial of the fittest." Spencer's Social Darwinism proclaimed the benefits of the dog-eat-dog individualism espoused by the newly emerging capitalists, while conveniently overlooking the barriers to opportunity capitalism established and its costs for human community.

By the end of the nineteenth century, however, the problems with such individualistic social theory and self-help ideologies became increasingly apparent. An American reaction developed which paralleled the anti-individualistic movement which was fuelling the birth of sociology in Europe. The notion of unlimited opportunity for individual action, many Americans began to feel, could not explain the disorder and instability which began to overtake industrializing America. The rugged individual, it seemed, was also the rapacious capitalist, who in transforming and industrializing society initiated class war and pitted group against group. In the countryside, the yeoman farmer discovered he could not control the very markets through which his individuality was supposed to be expressed. America was beset by depression, urbanization, and often quite desperate rural blight. The flood of European immigrants entering the country only increased sensitivity to group forces as against individual ones.

While the intellectual response to this crisis sometimes took on a collectivist hue, more frequently it emerged as a new form of critical, socially sensitive individualism. Rather than conceptualizing the collective causes of this crisis, American intellectuals were inclined to respond to the constriction of individual opportunity which was its result. Reacting against the narrowing of freedom, they demanded more freedom in turn. They referred, in other words, to the constriction of freedom as itself the cause of their predicament. They attacked the "formalism" of American thought and institutions. They found formalism and rigidity in corporate economic consolidation, in the centralization of wealth and power, and in the Victorian conventions of America's European-oriented upper classes. They also found it in the increasingly hierarchical character of American society which they associated with the end of the American frontier. All of these social reactions were echoed for them in the world of thought. American intellectuals saw European intellectual life as riddled by formalism and fatalism. In Kant there was too much apriorism, in Hegel too much formal and deductive metaphysics. The grand systems of Spencer were criticized as divorced from the experience of the real world. All these systems seemed mechanistic. They made formal what was, after all, the product of human experience. It was wrong, these American intellectuals believed, to treat markets, laws, and institutions as if they were automatic self-regulating mechanisms which were not affected by concrete human experience. What was needed, then, was a turn from formalism to experience.

It was out of this social climate, and these intellectual criticisms, that the uniquely American philosophy of Pragmatism arose. Pragmatism can be viewed both as a general intellectual movement in late nineteenth-century America and as a technical philosophical and theoretical system which informed the first phase of "interactionist" sociological theory. I will begin by taking the first route and talk about Pragmatism as a general orientation.

Pragmatism challenged the formalism of American society by emphasizing protean experience. Against Hegel it insisted that experience was the source of growth; against Kant it insisted that experience was the source of people's knowledge of the good. It may seem a bit ironic—given the anxiety about disorder which had been created by individualism—but this emphasis on experience gave individualism a new birth. It helped create a new, more optimistic, reforming kind of liberalism, a brash and crusading renaissance of faith in the richness and creativity of individual action in the world. It promoted the notion that a new social order could be created by force of will. Abstractions and traditions about right and wrong were not considered to be relevant to such creation, nor were institutional barriers which might appear to resist it. Ethics, laws, and habits would be upheld only if they "fit" experience. Institutions do not continue by themselves; they must be felt to be right by the individual's life in the world.

Yet to portray Pragmatism as completely individualistic would be wrong. It responded to the felt breakdown of order and to the anger about excessive individualism in a familiarly American way. It demanded that social order be reconstructed as a voluntary community. This pragmatic approach to community was called a theory of "social control." It held that through interactions with others people would naturally want to adhere to social obligations, obligations which themselves would arise through this same process of interaction. People are considered to be naturally of good will, and institutions constructed through the interaction of such good-willed actors were viewed as sufficient to keep them in line. If a society does move to conflict and disequilibrium, this negative movement will inevitably be counteracted by efforts at re-equilibration. Because the consequences of disequilibrium will be directly experienced, people will naturally wish to initiate reform. This process of change is not formal or ideological. Rather, it occurs pragmatically, through trial and error. Here is the American version of the "natural identity of interests" which underlay Europe's laissez-faire economic theory.

This optimistic pragmatism affected every area of American intellectual life. Veblen, Commons, and Ely created a discipline called "institutional economics" which countered the formalistic, classical variety. They argued that if the institutional and social context of economic processes were changed the economy would be different. This new economic context would emerge from experience and it would fit the common needs of individuals. It would not result from new formal systems, either from the laws of economics or the axioms of socialist ideology. In political philosophy, theorists like Royce and Croly and more empirical thinkers like Wilson and Ford conceptualized politics as closely related to experience and reform. They talked about relating formal government to subjective value; and in place of rigid contract theories, notions of abstract rights, and mechanistic legal formulations, they substituted fluid, action-oriented theories. In history, the generation of "progressive historians," like Turner, Beard, and Parrington, moved away from "scientific" and deductive schemes to studying the actual experience of social groups and the open-ended structure of history. In law, there arose a legal realism quite antithetical to the formal legal philosophies of the continent, an appproach exemplified by Oliver Wendell Holmes' oft-quoted remark, made in 1881, that "the life of the law has not been logic but experience." Finally, there were the philosophers of pragmatism themselves, people like Peirce, James, Dewey, and Mead, who sought to give to this vast intellectual movement a more precise analytic form.

As a general outlook, then, pragmatism was dynamic, naturalistic, anti-formal, and voluntaristic. It was linked to social reform and activism. It had a theory of community, though this was more a vision of results than an understanding of cause: the residue of right-thinking individual experience and expression. If you sense in this Pragmatic movement an unresolved tension between collectivist desire and individualist commitment, you would be right.

We can see this tension in its technical philosophy as well, and in the sociological theory it eventually informed.

As a technical philosophy Pragmatism reflected and perfected the thrusts of this general intellectual movement. In presuppositional terms, it tended toward the normative and individualistic. Actors are in search of value; they want to infuse "purpose" into their situations. They pursue value and purpose in the course of their experience. They adapt to the world, but in adapting they also interpret and evaluate it. Practice is more important than theory, experiment more significant than abstraction, process more important than form. Darwinism had a powerful impact: the emphasis on growth and adaptation through experience was crucial for the Pragmatists. Darwin had emphasized that structures depend on experience and that for this reason there is no preordained shape to the structures of life. Intelligence, for Darwin, was problem-solving. The most famous maxims of Pragmatic philosophy sound perfectly Darwinian—"truth is synonymous with the solution of the problem" and "process will determine form."

Yet, Pragmatic philosophy did not entirely eschew community and constraint, any more than did the other traditions of American individualism I mentioned earlier or, indeed, the Pragmatic movement as a whole. If we look closely at Pragmatic philosophy we can see within it a critical tension. We find that some Pragmatists were more willing and able to recognize the extra-individual, social sources of control than others.[1]

It is from James and Dewey that the epigrammatic individualism of pragmatic philosophy emerges. James developed a personalized theory of meaning which claimed that a concept *means* the experience to which it leads. The mandate of the pragmatic method is, from this perspective, to test all abstract conceptual beliefs against practical individual experience. As James put it, one must "determine the meaning of all differences of opinion by making the discussion hinge as soon as possible upon some practical issue."[2]

---

[1] See, for an elaboration of this point, the far-reaching work by J. David Lewis and Richard L. Smith, *American Sociology and Pragmatism* (Chicago: University of Chicago Press, 1980).

[2] William James, *Essays on Radical Empiricism and a Pluralistic Universe*, Ralph Barton Perry, ed. (New York: E. P. Dutton, 1971), p. 83.

Despite his much more communally sensitive political bent, Dewey was similarly oriented to the here and now and opposed to any conception of overarching tradition and idealized, a priori commitments. His "American" individualism fairly burst forth. Subjectivity, he wrote, is "initiative, inventiveness, varied resourcefulness, and the assumption of responsibility in choice of belief and conduct." Individuals are not simply morally responsible for their choices of beliefs; they are theoretically conceptualized as the major source of them. Dewey saw social order not as a constraint on individuals but as something which individuals start over ever anew: "Society is one word, but infinitely many things." In this way Dewey precluded the symbolic generalization—the normative, or value, element—upon which any notion of a subjective supra-individual order must rest. The Pragmatic social scientist must concentrate on the particular, concrete, contingent situation of action, not on some normative order within which it rests. "The new pragmatic method," Dewey wrote, "takes effect by substituting inquiry into these specific, changing and relative facts for solemn manipulation of general notions."[3]

Against this individualist strand of Pragmatism stands a more collectivist and synthesizing approach developed by Charles Peirce and George Herbert Mead. Peirce's work has not yet been given its due, yet it was he who actually founded Pragmatic philosophy and who was acknowledged by his contemporaries as its most original and systematic thinker. I cannot consider Peirce's complex work in any detail here, but I think the fundamental point of his thinking can be described in relatively simple terms. Peirce strove mightily to reconcile the need for a community of ethics and obligation—and the empirical existence of such communities—with a Pragmatic emphasis on individual experience in the real world. To pursue this synthesis, he developed the first elaborate theory of symbols, or signs—a theory which since his time has usually been associated with work in much more collectivist traditions. Pcirce argucd that systems of signs exist prior to an individual's experience. Yet while they provide the context for every act of experience, it is experience and practical action which provides the

[3] John Dewey, *Reconstruction in Philosophy* (Boston: Beacon, 1957), p. 200.

criteria for truth. If this strikes you as a bit contradictory, you are not alone. I do not believe that Peirce was wholly successful in this synthetic effort. Still, even while he reproduced the tension in American intellectual thought, there can be no doubt about the nature of his ambition or the synthesizing thrust of his work. Far from separating the symbolic meaning of individual acts from the "real" referents—the problem we will find in contemporary interactionism and later in ethnomethodolgy—Peirce developed a theory of symbols to inform his account of practical reason.

We can understand more about the nature of this accomplishment by examining the thought of Mead, for while Mead was only indirectly affected by Peirce (particularly via Royce), his relationship to individualistic pragmatism was much the same. Like Peirce, Mead sought to force Pragmatism into a more collective mode. Equally important, he pushed Pragmatic philosophy in an explicitly sociological direction.

When Herbert Blumer coined the term "symbolic interactionism" in 1937, he believed that he was faithfully summarizing Mead's social philosophy. I will contend, in the lecture following, that Blumer did nothing of the kind. I will suggest that Blumer and contemporary interactionism have followed the much more individualistic strand of Pragmatism, while Mead, like Peirce, sought a more synthetic blend of individualism and community. We would do well, then, to examine Mead's social theory in more depth. You will see, I think, that it provides a fitting conclusion to our discussion of the tension between individualism and community in American thought.

In my lectures on exchange theory I described the difference between individualism as a presuppositional commitment and individualism as a level of empirical analysis. If it is a presuppositional commitment, individualism—which can also be called, as Homans and others have termed it, "contingency"—is considered to define the nature of social order. Order is pictured as irredeemably negotiated, as emergent from individual interaction, as having no collectivist roots. If, by contrast, contingency is not taken as a presupposition, it may be seen as referring to one level of empirical analysis, to the open, nondetermined element which is part of every individual act. Pragmatic social theory, and American thought more generally, have usually taken individualism as a presupposition; it is for this reason that community and collective order have usually been accorded only a residual place. Mead is distinguished by the fact that he takes just the opposite tack: he tries to explain contingency as one moment in collectively structured social action.

In individualistic theory, an actor is conceived as himself defining the meaning of the objects with which he interacts. Mead argued, by contrast, for the autonomy of meaning vis-à-vis action. Meaning is found in symbols, not acts. Mead believed that supra-individual symbolic systems are the most important creators of the meaning of an individual's objects. It is "symbolization," he wrote, not the individual per se, which "constitutes objects not constituted before." He insisted that "objects . . . would not exist except for the context of social relationships wherein symbolization occurs." In opposition to what would be the traditional individualist position, he argues that the most common symbol system, language, does not follow from action but precedes it:

> Language does not simply symbolize a situation or object which is already there in advance; it makes possible the existence or the appearance of that situation or object, for it is part of the mechanism whereby that situation or object was created. . . . Objects [are] dependent upon or constituted by these meanings.[4]

At the same time, however, Mead was a Pragmatist. He emphasized much more than those in other traditions the significance of concrete individual interaction. He called interaction the "conversation of gestures." Gestures refer to the manifold movements and expressions in which people engage, including language. With his notion of gestures, Mead enters the Pragmatists' world of experience and activism, but he does so in a distinctive, synthesizing way.

Gestures can be treated as dependent for their meaning either on an individual stratagem or on more generalized symbolic frame-

---

[4] George Herbert Mead, "Selections from Mind, Self, and Society," in Anselm Strauss, ed., *George Herbert Mead on Social Psychology* (Chicago: University of Chicago Press, 1964), p. 165. Page references to Mead will hereafter be given parenthetically in the text.

works. It is the latter position that Mead takes, though we will see that he by no means abandons individual strategy as a significant empirical component. The meaning of gestures, Mead insists, does not rest upon individual manipulation. Gestures "are significant symbols," he writes, "because they have the same meanings for all individual members of a given society or social group, that is, they respectively arouse the same attitudes in the individuals making them that they arouse in the individuals responding" (p. 159). Far from providing the rationale for a return to individualism, then, Mead views his theory of gestures as a means of understanding how the contingency of individual action becomes enmeshed inside symbolic structure. Gestures, he believes, make possible "the symbolization of experience" within the broader field of meaning (p. 128). They allow people to link ongoing, new experience with social categories, to represent the world to themselves in the process of throwing themselves into the world. It was to emphasize and elaborate the social character of gestures that Mead developed the notion of the "generalized other." Every person acts in reference not just to the immediate other but to a more generalized social other. This generalized other is internal to the actor, the product of his long socialization into collective life. Individualism, then, is quite deceptive: "The individual experiences himself as such, not directly but only indirectly, from the particular standpoints of other individual members of the same social group or from the generalized standpoint of the social group as a whole to which he belongs" (p. 202).

The collective, or socializing impact of this generalized other is critically elaborated in Mead's theory of the game, a notion that makes a profound contribution to integrating empirical contingency and collective order. When children are very young, Mead believes, their sense of other individuals has not yet become generalized; as a result, children engage in play rather than in games. They take the role of other children, moving from one kind of behavior to another in a discrete, sequential way. At this early point in their development, then, children can only put themselves in place of the other. With further development, however, children can actually incorporate into themselves an abstract understanding of the roles which significant others assume. By such incorporation there is constituted the "rules" of the game, for there is a "generalized other" which can now invisibly regulate the behavior of individuals in the interest of all. Only with rules are real games possible, for only with the rules provided by a generalized other can indivi- dualized interests and goals be pursued in a social way. When an older, game-playing child gestures, Mead insists, he is certainly gesturing for himself, but he is also gesturing for others. Because this internalized generalization affects his personal identity and even his very perceptions, he automatically takes into account the positions and obligations of his fellow players.

This is how Mead applies his abstraction to the game which has been called America's pastime. I refer, of course, to baseball.

> The baseball player who makes a brilliant play is making the play called for by the nine to which he belongs. He is playing for his side. A man may, of course, play the gallery, be more interested in making a brilliant play than in helping his team to win, just as a surgeon may carry out a brilliant operation and sacrifice the patient. But under normal conditions, *the contribution of the individual gets its expression in the social processes that are involved in the act, so that the attachment of the values to the self does not involve egoism or selfishness.* (p. 239, italics mine)

A ballplayer, in other words, is certainly playing for himself. He has his own position, and it is he and he alone who must field a ball hit to his area of the park. If he fails it will be his error, and if he makes a brilliant play it will be his gain. Yet this individually interested action is thoroughly defined by the social situation of the act. How a man plays his position is decided by the interests and locations of the other eight players; every act of egoism is simultaneously a social loss or gain. He is only a baseball player because he is a member of a team.

> The taking of all of those organized sets of attitudes gives him . . . the self he is aware of. He can throw the ball to some other members because of the demand made upon him from other members of the team. That is the self that im- mediately exists for him in his consciousness. He has their attitudes, knows what they want and what the consequences

of any act of his will be, and he has assumed responsibility for the situation. (p. 230)

The game for Mead is an analogy, a microcosm, of all social systems and groups. His understanding of gesturing in games allows him to maintain that individual gestures *are* social institutions. According to conflict theory, institutions are structured and objective orders. Mead has shown, by contrast, that collective order corresponds to the generalized experience of its members. "An institution," he suggests, "is, after all, nothing but an organization of attitudes which we all carry in us" (p. 239).

Yet the contingent and individualizing aspect of action has not yet been expressed. Mead is interested in gestures not simply because they show how the social is specified by individual situations. He uses them also to show how the social is changed. The gesture involves an element of individuality and freedom. Why? Because it involves the passage of time. For Mead, temporality is the essence of contingency. It is the "temporary inhibition of action," in his view, that allows thinking. In the course of carrying out an action, the individual is presented in his consciousness with "different alternative ways of completing [what] he has already initiated" (p. 169). Because gestures occur in time, they involve the consideration of various courses of action. For this reason, every new gesture has an emergent property that distinguishes it from those preceding.

That which takes place in present organic behavior is always in some sense an emergent from the past and never could have been precisely predicted in advance—never could have been predicted on the basis of a knowledge, however complete, of the past, and of the conditions in the past which are relevant to its emergence. (p. 177)

As part of his effort to conceptualize the properties which are emergent from action, Mead differentiates the "I" of an actor from his "me." The "I" is the novel element, the "me" the social element corresponding to the generalized other. Mead calls the "I" and the "me" "two distinguishable phases" of the same act. In describing the genesis and constitution of acts, he suggests an alternation of contingent and determined phases. The "attitude," in Mead's terms, constitutes the first part of the response to another's gesture, and he insists that one's "attitude" is socially determined by the me, by the nature of the internalized symbolic order. The meaning you give to my gesture is immediately given, in a thoroughly unconscious way. Yet, Mead cautions, this does not constitute your total "response" to my gesture. Within the context of your responsive act—unconsciously, preconsciously, or consciously—you perform various rehearsals, feeling and seeing imagery of various kinds, exploring the ramification of this or that response. Only after such rehearsals do you complete your response. Subsequently, you will evaluate the relation between the meaning you have given to the other's gesture and the effect of your response on the immediate and generalized others involved.

In my lectures on exchange theory, I defined the individualist dilemma as the unhappy choice between randomness (which comes from a consistent individualism) and indeterminacy (the residual status of "collective references" which cannot be introduced in a direct way). To the degree that Mead has successfully brought together "attitude" and "response" he has avoided giving community the residual status it assumes in most individualist work. By doing so he has shown how contingency becomes incorporated in the moment-to-moment specification of collective order. Yet Mead did not entirely escape the individualist dilemma altogether. There are significant places in his work where the autonomy of attitude and response is collapsed. He proclaims, in these instances, that the meaning of a gesture is determined not by a prior symbolic system but by the respondent's gesture itself, that is, by contingent and purely "pragmatic" individual considerations. He writes at one point, for example, that

> The response of one organism to the gesture of another in any given social act is the meaning of that gesture and also is in a sense responsible for the appearance or coming into being of the new object. . . . The act or adjustive response of the second organism [therefore] gives to the gesture of the first organism the meaning which it has. (p. 165)

This individualistic strand in Mead's work is, in part, the result of problems which in my view are inherent in the philosophy of

Pragmatism itself. This philosophy is too anti-Kantian and anti-Hegelian to allow any of its practitioners to transcend fully an individualistic point of view. Mead certainly was part of the Pragmatist movement, and it should not be surprising that he was affected by the tensions within it. Whatever its source, this individualism came home to roost in a way that eventually undermined Mead's synthetic accomplishment. It did so because the interpreter of Mead's thought for contemporary interactionists has been a Pragmatist much more exclusively individualistic then he. This man was Herbert Blumer, and I will take up his theory and contemporary interactionism more generally in my next lecture.

Before doing so, however, I would like us to reflect, for a moment, on Mead's contribution not to classical sociology but to theoretical thinking in the contemporary period. Is it possible that Mead can be conceived as contributing to the debate which has developed in the post-Parsonian period? This, after all, is the same challenge against which I measured the contributions and promise of the contemporary, post-Parsonian theories of conflict and exchange.

This seems a rather strange question to ask of a theory whose author died fifty years ago. Why bother with Mead, when we have his successors, the contemporary theorists of symbolic interactionism, so closely at hand? You will certainly be able to answer this question better at the end of my next lecture than you can right now, for it is the contemporary theorists whom we will consider next. For now, you must take something on trust: to see just what is at stake in these modern developments, we must think first about the possible contemporary relevance of Mead.

Mead left an ambiguous but extremely significant legacy to modern sociological theory. The ambiguity revolves around the distinction between empirical level of analysis and presuppositional approach. This same distinction, I have shown, is relevant for post-Parsonian theories as well. Should we take exchange, for example, as referring to one empirical dimension of social action or as identifying a presupposition about action itself? In the case of Pragmatic social theory the question refers to order not action. Should we take the individualistic reference as referring to the contingent element within an empirical social arrangement or to a presupposition about order as such? In Mead's technical terminology, the problem can be put in terms of the relation between attitude and response. Response is that segment of an action, or gesture, which includes the "I," the unpredictable, contingent part of the self. Attitude, by contrast, refers to the culturally determined segment of the responding gesture, which Mead described as preceding the more strategic and open-ended response. Should we view the response to an action as one empirical phase of gesture, or the "theory" of gesture itself? Are the I and me different levels of an empirical actor, or do we presuppose the actor either as an I or a me?

Now to the degree that Mead successfully separated the phases of attitude and response analytically while interrelating them empirically, he made a fundamental contribution to our understanding of how a voluntaristic theory of action actually gets "played out" on the level of concrete empirical reality. He allows us to go way beyond Parsons' theory, but in a synthetic and multidimensional direction which was pointed to by Parsons' himself. In Parsons' original formulation of voluntaristic theory, he described "effort" as central to the prototypical unit act, the other parts of which were means, ends, norms, and conditions. "Effort" brought free will and contingency into Parsons' action theory. Yet in the course of his subsequent sociological work, and even in *The Structure of Social Action* itself, Parsons had very little to say about this element.

Mead's theory, by contrast, allows us to see just how effort can be brought in. The norms of the unit act become represented through the actor's "me"; they are his social self. The "I" is the engine which allows more specific goals or ends to emerge. The conditions and means of the actor's situation, whether material or human, are "objects" to the actor in a particular action, often presenting themselves as gestures to which the actor must respond. Because his response is initially defined by the attitude he takes up, the norms which stand outside a particular act are necesarily brought into play. But response involves much more than this phase. The actor must answer this gesture, once its meaning has been defined, in a specific and concrete way. It is impossible to predict precisely what this final response will be, but the goal which is eventually chosen will produce a definite, if slight, new direction for the overarching normative framework. This particular response becomes one of the gestures to which others henceforth respond, to which their own normative frameworks must take up an attitude and adapt in a specific way. It seems clear to me that this much more elaborate understanding of "effort" allows us to understand, in a much better way than we could in Parsons' work, how the moral constraints on action are in a continuous process of adaptation and change. Mead's investigation of this empirical element makes it much more difficult to confuse normative order with empirical stability in the way that Parsons did so often in his more general theoretical work.

I want to stress that even if we understand Mead's contribution in this way we must still conclude that he left a great deal out. He is concerned primarily with phases of interpretive process. While this may illuminate a framework within which the kinds of instrumental calculations which are the primary focus of exchange theory may be understood, it certainly does not take any direct account of such processes themselves. Mead can help us understand how we naturally interpret others' gestures in terms of broader conceptions of value and justice; these inputs define our attitudes toward stimulus or reward. But about the costs, supply, and demand of stimulus and reward, knowledge of which provides some sense of the "objective" profit from gesturing, Mead has nothing to say. Nor, of course, does he describe in any detail the collective constraints, cultural or material, within which gesturing proceeds. There is an important sense, however, in which these considerations do not really matter. Insofar as Mead was producing insight into various levels of empirical analysis he naturally contributed more to our understanding of some areas of social life than to others. We do not ask an analysis of one element of empirical life to answer for every other at the same time.

Yet Mead does not in every instance accept this self-limitation. We have seen that there is an element in his work which does take his emphasis on contingency as suggesting a theory of order rather than a level of empirical analysis. He sometimes collapses the attitude and response phases of action, and in doing so presents meaning as if it were merely the product of specific interactions. If the "I" becomes so dominant, then meaning is completely contingent, and there can be no collective sources of order at all. This tendency seems quite contrary to the main thrust of Mead's work, which aimed precisely at demonstrating how institutions were part of the self. This internal view of institutions allowed social control to be conceived as a variation on mutual self-control and it envisioned, as did the Pragmatic movement more generally, a decentralized, informal society instead of a bureaucratic and coercive one. In this respect, Mead's theoretical hopes and ideological ambitions converged with Parsons', who sought to make internalization serve much the same political purpose.

Would we not be right in concluding, then, that Mead's early theory of interaction had the potential to make a considerable contribution to theoretical debate in the post-Parsons period? Unfortunately, this is not what has happened at all. Why not? Because, I believe, contemporary interactionism has moved away from Mead's own institutional and collective thrust. Mead's most important successors have emphasized his indeterminacy, the strain in his work which emphasized individualism in a presuppositional way. They tend to collapse attitude and response, and to identify individuality with the "I" in a manner which Mead would thoroughly have disapproved. The result is a rather one-sided misunderstanding of society, especially of how within a social framework individual action can proceed. How this has happened is my topic in the lecture that follows.

LECTURE THIRTEEN
SYMBOLIC INTERACTIONISM (2): INDIVIDUALISM AND THE WORK OF BLUMER AND GOFFMAN

THE CONTEMPORY TRADITION of pragmatic social theory was "officially" created in 1937, when Herbert Blumer wrote an article identifying Mead as a "symbolic interactionist."[1] In retrospect this date of publication seems filled with irony, for it was in that same year that Parsons published *The Structure of Social Action,* a work which created an approach to symbols, action, and freedom which more closely resembled Mead's own! But his historical coincidence was not quite so accidental as it first appears. Parsons was part of a younger group of American sociologists who were breaking away from the institutional and intellectual hegemony of the Chicago school, from the Pragmatic sociological tradition which—in their eyes at least—has been relatively untheoretical and individualistic. It was in 1936 that this rump group of mostly Harvard and Columbia trained sociologists had set up the *American Sociological Review* in opposition to the Chicago journal, the *American Journal of Sociology.* Blumer had been a graduate student of Mead's, a professor in the Chicago department and, until this anti-Chicago group deposed him in 1935, the secretary of the national sociological association. Blumer came to

---

[1] Herbert Blumer, "Social Psychology," in E. D. Schmidt, ed., *Man and Society* (New York: Prentice-Hall, 1937), pp. 144–198.

intellectual maturity, in other words, in a period when interactionism was declining in influence. Yet he was also writing just after major works of Mead had posthumously appeared, and during the years 1941–45 he went on to become editor of the *American Journal of Sociology.* It is easy to imagine how—faced with the challenge of Parsons and these other Eastern-trained "young Turks"—Blumer may have been led to define a more individualistic form of interactionism. This definition maintained the distinctiveness of the Chicago tradition and in doing so may have kept it alive.

In the postwar period, as Parsons' influence grew into a kind of intellectual domination, Blumer wrote a series of essays attacking the "established" sociological position. These were finally collected in 1969 in a book called simply *Symbolic Interactionism: Perspective and Method.* In the course of these essays Blumer laid out a positive course for his students to follow. He also established a position which they were to fight against. His formulation of the established position is a scarcely concealed polemic against Parsons. With this polemic Blumer, like Rex and Homans, establishes a negative straw man to justify his positive program for sociology.

Blumer argues that Parsons, and functionalists generally, treat human behavior as if it were merely the product of factors which "play upon" human beings. For these theorists actions are "mere expressions or products of what people bring to their interaction or of conditions that are antecedent to their interaction."[2] Because people's actions are left out, Blumer says, social systems are conceived as operating "automatically," without any reference to real human beings. The Parsonian tradition, in other words, ignores meaning as a topic for sociology.

Like Homans, then, and like every individualistic tradition in contemporary theory, Blumer objects to Parsons on quite different grounds than do the theorists of the conflict school. Rex, you may remember, argued that Parsons was too voluntaristic and subjective in his understanding of order. Blumer argues that Parsons is not nearly individualistic and voluntaristic enough. Now it is true, as

---

[2] Blumer, "The Methodological Position of Symbolic Interactionism," in Blumer, *Symbolic Interactionism* (Englewood Cliffs, N.J.: Prentice-Hall, 1969), p. 10.

I suggested in my earlier discussion of Mead, that Parsons had definite problems conceptualizing the open element of order in an empirical way. If you are interested in contingency you must develop the kind of concrete and detailed understanding of the process of interpretation which Blumer lays out. At the same time, however, it seems scarcely credible to suggest that Parsons viewed factors as playing upon persons from the outside, even less so to claim that he viewed systems as functioning without reference to people and that meaning was not a problem for his sociology. Negative straw men are set up to justify particular positive positions. They are weapons in the never-ending theoretical war.

If Blumer's caricature does not tell us much about Parsons' theory, it may tell us much about his own. Social factors can be construed merely as playing upon human beings to the degree that human actors are pictured in asocial and acultural ways, that is, as sharply separated from the society in which they live. Systems can be seen as operating over the heads of real people if the personalities of real people are seen as developing quite apart from their experience in society. Functionalist sociology can be pictured as unconcerned with meaning only if meaning is viewed as emerging from completely personal decisions and feelings. To understand Blumer's straw man, we must turn to the theory which he used it to justify.

What is Blumer's approach to action? In contrast to Homans' it is not at all instrumental. Quite the opposite. Blumer is concerned with communication, not exchange. He insists that people insert interpretation between stimulus and response, their interpretation corresponding to the "discrimination" which Homans noted but usually ignored. While this recognition of interpretation is certainly something which can be said for Blumer's theory, there are some drawbacks to this insistence as well. In the first place, it is the other side of his normative, idealist bias. Just as Homans emphasizes exchange at the expense of discrimination, Blumer emphasizes interpretation at the expense of exchange. This idealism can reach highly unrealistic extremes. "The nature of an object," Blumer actually suggests at one point, "consists of the meaning that it has for the person for whom it is an object" (p. 10). To equate nature with meaning is a serious mistake.

The other drawback to Blumer's interpretive theory of action has to do with the fact that he ties it resolutely to experience. If in Mead's terms we can say that Homans' mistake was collapsing attitude and response to stimulus, Blumer's mistake is reducing attitude and stimulus to response. Blumer veers back to the individualistic side of pragmatism and away from Peirce and Mead; his insistence on anti-formalism and experience amounts to an individualistic position opposed to social force. He suggests at one point, for example, that "culture is clearly derived from what people do" (p. 6). This is pure Darwin. Peirce and Mead would not have gone nearly so far in their pragmatic method. Indeed, they would have argued that what people do is just as much derived from culture! But Blumer wants to tie interpretation to concete, individual interaction. He insists that "meaning is derived from or arises out of the social interaction that one has with one's fellows" (p. 2). It is gesture that determines attitude, not vice versa: "The meaning of a thing grows out of the ways in which other persons act toward the person with regard to the thing" (p. 4). Blumer is turning the individualism of exchange theory inside out. He and Homans both focus exclusively on the individual in his or her interactive environment. Unlike Homans' individual, however, Blumer's is a discriminator before he is anything else. "The human individual confronts a world that he must interpret in order to act instead of an environment to which he responds . . . He has to construct and guide his action instead of merely releasing it in response to factors playing on him" (p. 15).

Symbolic interactionism, then, gives the actor complete sovereignty. It is a lot like good old American ideology. The actor is protean, the completely undetermined determiner, the mysterious, romantic, spontaneous creator of everything in the world. Here is the yeoman farmer, Horatio Algier, and Thoreau in Walden all rolled up into one: "The actor selects, checks, suspends, regroups, and transforms the meanings in the light of the situation in which he is placed and the direction of his action" (p. 5). Mead's formulation would have the actor referring to symbolic systems. The continuing refrain in Blumer's account, by contrast, is "self-indication." To find the meaning in a situation the actor refers back to himself. Through self-indication, Blumer claims, "the human makes an object of what it notes, gives it a meaning, and uses the meaning as the basis for directing its actions" (p. 14). This attributes to the actor an incredible power, almost an omniscience. He has complete control. He can choose, with complete presence of mind, among a fantastic range of conscious, unconscious, and symbolic things.

> Action on the part of a human being consists of taking account of various things that he notes and forging a line of conduct on the basis of how he interprets them. The things taken into account cover such matters as his wishes and wants, his objectives, and available means for their achievement, the actions and anticipated actions of others, his image of himself, and the likely result of a given line of action. (p. 15)

Mead allowed that the temporality of gesture means that response involves temporary inhibition, which gives actors split seconds to consider alternatives. For the most part, however, he insisted that such self consciousness takes place within the parameters of culturally determined attitudes. For Blumer precisely the opposite is true. It is the self-conscious response of the individual qua individual that determines the attitude he will take. Blumer's statement on this is worth quoting at length.

> Self-indication is a moving communicative process in which the individual notes things, assesses them, gives them a meaning, and decides to act on the basis of the meaning . . . Environmental pressures, external stimuli, organic drives, wishes, attitudes, feelings, ideas, and their like do not cover or explain the process of self-indication. The process of self-indication stands over against them in that the individual points out to himself and interprets the appearance or expression of such things, noting a given social demand that is made on him, recognizing a command, observing that he is hungry, realizing that he wishes to buy something, aware that he has a given feeling, conscious that he dislikes eating with someone he despises, or aware that he is thinking of doing some given thing. By virtue of indicating such things to himself, he places himself over against them and is able to act back against them,

accepting them, rejecting them, or transforming them in accordance with how he defines and interprets them.[3] (pp. 81–82)

This normative individualism defines Blumer's general theoretical position, the position which has come to be regarded, as the publisher notes on the back cover of Blumer's collected essays, as "the most authoritative statement of the point of view of symbolic interactionism." We might question this theory in several different ways. It seems, for example, to raise immediate empirical problems. In Blumer's approach to meaning as self-indication we see the Pragmatist and Puritan interest in practicality and use. Interpretation is subordinate to purpose and to the need for acting confidently in this world. As Blumer says, "interpretation is a formative process in which meanings are used and revised as instruments for the guidance and formation of action."[4] This holds that any interpretation is tested and retested in the world of practical experience, and discarded if it does not fit. But can an actor compare an attitude he has taken to a reality which is itself naked of any subjective disposition? Can perception of discrete objects be made without any generalized context? Blumer believes it can, so it follows that for him meaning can be understood simply by looking at the local interactional setting. "The sets of meanings that lead participants to act as they do," he writes, "have their own setting in a localized process of social interaction" (pp. 19–20). This is the same kind of entirely presentist perspective I questioned in Homans. It asks us to envision an actor without significant memory of past events, an actor who—at the very least—has never built up from early attitudes to generalized beliefs. This seems to me an unlikely state of human affairs.

We might also query Blumer's theory from an ideological point of view. Can such a vision of contingency and self-control do justice to the alienation and coercion that seem so immanent in the modern world? Individualistic theory does not logically imply blind optimism about the individual's fate in the modern world. It does, however, often lead to such optimism in practice. There is no better example

[3] Blumer, "Society as Symbolic Interactionism," *Symbolic Interactionism* (pp. 78–79), pp. 81–82.
[4] "Methodological Position," p. 5.

of such a link than Blumer's article "Sociological Theory in Industrial Relations," which he published in 1947. This article illustrates how Blumer models his political evaluation of postwar society on the open, individualistic, antistructural qualities of interactionist theory. He lauds "the dynamic character of modern life" in general; more specifically, he suggests that "we live in a dynamic, democratic, competitive society." The problem with existing theories of industrial relations, he argues, is precisely that "sociological thinking has not been shaped from [such] empirical consideration[s]."[5]

Blumer begins by criticizing the approach that takes industrial relations as "cultural data," as "organized practices and customary routines." This theory misses the central point, he claims, for rather than culturally ordered and routinized, industrial relations are "intrinsically tense, mobile, and unstable." Blumer also objects to the approach which sees industrial relations in terms of stratified status relationships. This premise, he writes, "does not seem to me to have much sense," and he confesses that "I am unable to see how such local status relations either occasion, govern or explain the mobile industrial relations" of today. Finally, he challenges the perspective which tries to place worker/management relations in a historical perspective emphasizing the long-range trends of social development. While acknowledging that such constraints exist, he suggests that their effect on action is severely limited. Rather than predicting conflicts on the basis of long-term trends, one must look at the "constant striving of opposed parties" and the mutual adjustment this necessitates. It is not long-range trends that determine industrial actions. What occurs, rather, "is forged from countless and varied discussions, from judgments of complicated situations, from calculations of the timeliness of action, from the threats and opportunities yielded by the play of events."[6]

When Blumer finally characterizes his own approach to industrial relations it is hardly surprising that he sees scarcely any controlling structure at all. While he acknowledges the obvious collective factors which "initiate" worker/management conflict, he insists that none of these factors in any way determines it: "The new activities are

---

[5] Blumer, "Sociological Theory in Industrial Relations," *American Journal of Sociology* (1947), 12:277–778.
[6] "Sociological Theory," pp. 274–275.

not ordered by the structure they are rebelling against." He believes, in fact, that "the most noteworthy feature of the relations between workers and management in American industry is that the relations are dynamic, uncrystallized and changing." Labor relations, in his words, "is an unsettled area which is not structured or governed by a structure."[7] For conflict theory and even for Parsons (in his middle period essays), industrial relations present a complex of power, property, and solidarity which has been at the very center of conflict and instability in the modern world. Blumer passes such negative qualities over with bland references to "a moving pattern of accommodative adjustments." Rather than unequal power and entrenched rules about allocation and integration, Blumer finds "a vast, confused game evolving without the benefit of fixed rules and frequently without the benefit of any rules" at all.[8] Even Mead viewed games as deeply structured processes, while insisting on their reciprocal, mutually satisfying quality. But Blumer stretches the traditionally upbeat ideology of American Pragmatism to its breaking point. In the wake of a devastating war which revealed the accumulating power differentials and dangers of class and political conflict throughout Western society he paints a naive picture of freedom and self-realization in an essentially stable world.

But my focus throughout these lectures has been more on presuppositional than on empirical or ideological issues. Blumer himself is much more concerned with "orienting" issues than with specific, middle-range work. What kinds of problems, then, can we find in the most general level of Blumer's "theoretical logic," in the way he conceptualizes action and social order? I have already mentioned the issue of his very one-sided, idealist understanding of action. Certainly, interpretation and discrimination are elements of action which must never be ignored, as they are, for example, by the instrumentalist traditions of conflict and exchange. But neither can they constitute the sole focus for understanding action. As a student once asked me in regard to Mead's theory of the baseball game as a cooperative, purely gestural activity, how can Mead explain why managers get fired? Material conditions and instrumental mo-

---

[7] "Sociological Theory," pp. 275, 272, and 275 respectively.
[8] "Sociological Theory," p. 277.

tivations exist, and it is a mistake to presuppose action in a way that makes it impossible to study them.

At this point, however, I am more interested in Blumer's presuppositions about order than action. I believe that his individualistic assumptions about the construction of social order are the most important barriers to his attempt to build a successful theory of individual interaction. These barriers exist on the level of thinking itself. Though they produce confusions about the empirical world, they are not produced by theoretically independent empirical observations themselves. Indeed, they establish a general "logic" from which empirical analysis finds it impossible to break. As I suggested in my lectures on Homans, individualistic theories face an inherent dilemma, an essentially irresolvable set of choices. On the one hand, they want to maintain absolute contingency. In doing so, however, they must embrace the randomness that such a contingent approach to social order entails. If they are not entirely satisfied with the unpredictability that randomness implies—and few social theorists are—they will seek to introduce into their work more collective and constraining forces by the back door. But this back door entrance ensures that these references are doomed to a residual, ad hoc status. The individualist dilemma is a choice between the indeterminacy of residual categories and the randomness of pure contingency.

If you read Blumer's work with an eye toward this logical tension, I think you will agree with me that it leads him into a great deal of trouble. More than any major theorist in the post-Parsonian period Blumer forthrightly embraces randomness. He seems to revel in the unpredictability that his position entails. It is not so much that he fails to recognize that structural, collective factors exist. He acknowledges a social order. The problem for him is, how can it be explained? How do we understand the manner in which it comes into being? In his 1947 essay on industrial relations, Blumer says structural factors may "initiate" action, and he repeats this suggestion in his later theoretical essays. He also warns, however, that "this initiating factor does not embrace or explain *how* it and other matters are taken into account in the situation which calls for action"[9] (p. 16, italics mine).

[9] "Methodological Position," p. 16, italics added.

The question is, does Blumer himself explain this "how"? The answer, I think, is that he does not. He asserts merely that it is there, that there is a "how," and he contents himself with suggesting the method by which you might go about studying it. "One has to get inside of the defining process," he tells his fellow sociologists. Instructing his readers in a manner that even more clearly expresses the evanescence of "attitude"—remember in what a structural way Mead himself approached attitude?—Blumer writes that you have "to catch the process of interpretation through which actors construct their actions"[10] What he is getting at here is the notion that there simply is no way to explain order in a systematic way. It is unpredictable, and because of this unpredictability you must be resigned—or satisfied—with describing order as it unfolds. "The process of self-indication exists in its own right and must be accepted and studied as such." You cannot explain order, you can only get inside it and watch it happen.

In this line of his thought Blumer clearly embraces randomness. But even he cannot be entirely satisfied with it. While he cannot let himself explain order in collectivist terms, he would like to explain it in a less individualistic way. What is the solution? Blumer must introduce collective explanations residually. In this way, while suggesting them, he can also act as if in some way they are really not there. In so doing he moves from one horn of the individualist dilemma to the other, from randomness to indeterminacy. You might well ask at this point why I use the term indeterminacy? Because the role played by a concept that is logically contradictory to—residual or outside of—the systematic part of a theory is never very clear. It has an ad hoc quality, appearing casual, unthought out, hasty. For these reasons I say it has an indeterminate, or undetermined, relation to the theory as a whole.

Let's see how Blumer gets into this trap. As I have mentioned already, he often feels compelled to recognize the existence of collective structures. When he does so he tries to avoid giving them causal power. He suggests that they merely initiate action and that they may be taken into account by the actor in different ways. The problem, of course, is that even to initiate action is to have some

---

[10] "Society as Symbolic Interactionism, p. 82."

determinate effect. To present something which must be taken into account is to constrain the actor in a rather significant way, no matter what he eventually makes of it.

Sometimes Blumer himself seems to recognize this problem. He writes, for example, that "from the standpoint of symbolic inter- action the organization of a human society is the framework inside of which social action takes place and is not the determinant of that action."[11] What is the difference between a framework and a determinant? Perhaps by the latter Blumer means the exclusive cause of action, but even if a framework may not be the exclusive cause it offers some collective constraint. This problematic distinc- tion illustrates Blumer's indeterminacy. To acknowledge that social forces constitute a framework is to suggest collective presupposi- tions. To distinguish this, in the second part of the same sentence, from something called a determinant is to try to deny that a collective reference has just occurred. The result is a muddle which leaves the collective reference in an indeterminate state. To deny collective determinants is to embrace randomness. To deny collec- tive determinants and to acknowledge collective frameworks is to embrace indeterminacy. Blumer is caught on the horns of the individualist dilemma. He is continually introducing, and then seek- ing to modify, factors which condition and constrain individual choice. Another typical statement in this regard occurs at the beginning of the book. "Ongoing activity," Blumer suggests, "es- tablishes and portrays structure or organization."[12] (p. 7). But you cannot have it both ways. To "portray" structure is to describe something which is already there; to "establish" structure is to create something which is not.

Sometimes Blumer manifests this dilemma in a more roundabout way. Thinking about the significance of collective order, he remarks at one point that "the preponderant portion of social action in a human society, particularly in a settled society, exists in the form of recurrent patterns of joint action."

In most situations in which people act toward one another they have in advance a firm understanding of how to act and

11 "Society," p. 87.
12 "Methodological Position," p. 7.

of how other people will act. They share common and pre-
established meanings of what is expected in the action of the
participants, and accordingly each participant is able to guide
his own behavior by such meanings.[13]

This is a revealing passage, for Blumer seems to acknowledge here
the crucial significance of structured meanings, what Parsons called
norms and values. To read such a passage is to be reminded of
how Homans surprised us by relating discrimination to value and
distributive justice to community standards and social solidarity. I
think I suggested, at that point, that Homans was giving with one
hand what he had taken away with the other, and I will suggest
here much the same thing. Blumer is acknowledging the centrality
of the very supra-individual structures he has endeavored to deny.

But a passage does not an argument make! As we read on we
see that Blumer clearly has second thoughts. Slowly but surely his
reference to structured meanings becomes hedged with conditions
and eventually assumes a residual status. Even in the passage I
quoted above he inserted the phrase "particularly in a settled
society," thus leaving open the possibility that in certain societies—
the unsettled ones—meaning is not really structured at all. Blumer
soon makes this reservation explicit, insisting on the page following
that it is "not true that the *full expanse* of life in a human society,
in any human society, is but an expression of pre-established meanings." He now moves to establish parity between periods of structured and unstructured meaning. "Such areas of unprescribed conduct," he writes, "are just as . . . recurrent . . . as those covered
by pre-established meanings." Finally he undermines the structured
dimension entirely. "We have to recognize," he warns, "that even
in the case of pre-established and repetitive action each instance
of such joint action has to be formed anew."[14]

But if joint action is formed "anew" at "each instant," how can
it be seen as pre-established and repetitive? Only if contingent effort
is always directed to institutionalizing pre-established meanings. To
vitiate this apparent contradiction, Blumer suggests that repetitive
action and established meaning are determinate only if interpre-

---

[13] "Methodological Position," p. 17.
[14] "Methodological Position," pp. 17–18, italics mine.

tation is ignored. "The participants still have to build up their lines of action and fit them to one another through the dual process of designation and interpretation," he says. But for repetitive joint action, he goes on to say, this dual process proceeds in reference to "recurrent and constant meanings"! Blumer seems to be extremely uncomfortable. With each new sentence and phrase he moves forth and back inside the individualist dilemma. He does not want to choose between individual and group. But the only way to avoid choosing is to embrace contingency as a level of empirical analysis, not as a presuppositional fact. Yet such a moderated position is exactly what Blumer designed his contemporary interactionist position to fight against. Parsons and functionalist sociology can be sharply challenged only from the radical, not the modified position. It should not be surprising, therefore, that Blumer ends the paragraph from which I have been quoting by reinstating the theoretical choice in presuppositional, either/or terms. "It is the social process in group life that creates and upholds the rules," he writes, "not the rules that create and uphold groups life."[15]

Blumer has not only been the authoritative interpreter of the contemporary symbolic interactionist tradition, but he has exemplified its strengths and weaknesses in a magnified way. Theoretical and polemical at the same time, his work boldly articulates the strains which any attempt at such a highly individualistic position entails. Yet while the individualist dilemma has kept interactionism from presenting a really satisfactory general theory of society, it has also stimulated a great deal of creative theoretical work. Reacting against Parsons and empiricists alike, anti-Parsonian theorists have been attracted by the open individualism of Blumer's approach at the same time that they have been challenged by the instability it represents.

At least four different lines of interactionist work have developed as reactions to such strain. One line follows a relatively pure "Blumerianism," insisting on negotiated meanings and sticking closely to the study of immediate, unfolding interactions. The early challenge to the functionalist theory of deviance, for example,

15 "Methodological Position," p.19.

followed this type of interactionist path. Howard Becker and other theorists in what came to be called the "labeling" tradition challenged the notion that deviance can be explained as caused by structured strains in the social system.[16] Becker argued, instead, that it is interaction that produces deviance. People become labeled "deviant" by significant actors and henceforth are regarded as such. No long-term structural forces can explain how or why this happens. Enough variation exists—there are always a number of different subcultures—so that ample opportunity for effective labeling always abounds. Values are not particularly important either; they merely present environments which individual and group actors—the labelers and the labeled—make use of. More important than the cause of deviance in this approach is the theoretical description of the typical deviant "career." This involves constructing what is called a "natural history" of how people become deviant rather than developing an explanation of the "why." This situation-specific, indeterminate approach to deviance has had an enormous influence on sociology. Insofar as it has recognized that actors are often of unequal power, moreover, it has converged with trends in conflict theory as well.

There has been another trend in interactionism which, while continuing to take the negotiation of order as its immediate topic, has recognized the significance for action of external context— even if it has necessarily left this context relatively unexplained. The theory of "collective behavior" is a good example. Interactionist theory virtually invented this approach to social change single-handed. The collective behavior approach tries to describe change not in terms of structural causes but in terms of open-ended patterns of individual and group interaction. Concentrating on things like opinion formation and consensus building strategies these theorists try to develop—much as labeling theorists do— natural histories of how change happens rather than explanations of why.[17] They give importance to social movements rather than to social forces and concentrate on emergent properties instead of

---

[16] Howard S. Becker, *Outsiders: Studies in the Sociology of Deviance* (Free Press of Glencoe: Glencoe, Illinois, 1963).

[17] Ralph Turner and Lewis Killian, *Collective Behavior* (Englewood Cliffs, N. J.: Prentice-Hall, 1972).

vested interests. In the hands of a skillful practitioner like Ralph Turner, collective behavior theory recognizes that structural environments for social movements do exist—institutional forces like laws, courts, and value systems. By not analyzing how the variable structure of this environment actively affects social movements, however, there remains an ad hoc quality to such structural reference that is never really overcome. The same ambiguity affects another major avenue of contemporary interactionist work, namely role theory. Turner, for example, has emphasized "role making" as opposed to what he considers the more passive, functionalist understanding of role acceptance.[18] His conception of the active, contingent, and individualistic element of role behavior does not actually deny the existence of socially structured role obligations as such. Where such structuring comes from, however, and how it affects what role the individual actually assumes, is left unresolved. The structural concerns are bracketed; the how becomes more important than the why.

There is a third strain within modern interactionism which has been even more careful not to reject the collectivist side of Mead's earlier work. This tradition has come to be known as the "Iowa" as opposed to the Chicago school (the Blumerian one). While Blumer took up the "I" in Mead's theory at the expense of the structured "me," the founder of the Iowa school, Manfred Kuhn, seems to have done just the opposite.[19] Kuhn's "self theory" looks to socially constructed individual identity as the source of action. This interactionism has tried to develop relatively complex and deterministic theories about how social selves operate and why they come into being. The inclination here is to adopt a thoroughly structuralist approach to individual interaction. For example, a recent theorist in this tradition, Sheldon Stryker, has presented interactionism as if it were basically a modification of social systems theory.[20] He completely incorporates collectivist concepts like system, role, and status, into his work and he presents them as if they were part of

---

[18] Turner, "Role-Taking: Process versus Conformity," in Arnold M. Rose, ed., *Human Behavior and Social Processes* (Boston: Houghton Mifflin, 1962).

[19] Manfred H. Kuhn and Thomas S. McPartland, "An Empirical Investigation of Self-Attitudes," *American Sociological Review* (1954), 19:68–75.

[20] Sheldon Stryker, *Symbolic Interactionism* (Menlo Park, Calif.: Benjamin Commings, 1980), pp. 52–54, 57–76.

interactionist theory itself. This twist on interactionism certainly presents an opportunity for pushing presuppositional individualism toward a "level of analysis" approach, but in the process, it seems to me, the unique contribution of interactionism, which has largely to do with contingency, is in danger of being lost.[21]

There is yet a fourth strain in interactionism. Here the collective dimension of social action is recognized as extremely significant, but the focus on contingent initiative is not at all given up. Systematic attempts are made to bridge the individual/society gap, attempts which, while often uneasy and sometimes contradictory, present some of the most illuminating conceptualizations of this problem ever to appear. Of all interactionist responses to the individualist dilemma, this strand seems the most exciting and productive strain. Gusfield, for example, has worked in this mode from the beginning of his career, taking values and power structures as contingently manipulable but nonetheless resilient elements that cannot be entirely overcome.[22] But the greatest theorist in this line has been Goffman. The most important "interactionist" in the generation younger than Blumer, Goffman's brilliant studies have done more than any other to legitimize this tradition as a major strain in post-Parsonian theorizing. Even Goffman, however, while extending interactionism in a fundamental way, has not entirely escaped its problems. In the last part of this lecture I want to point to some of the achievements and difficulties in his work.

The first and most influential book Goffman wrote is called *The Presentation of Self in Everyday Life.* In his short preface he tells us that while he is reporting on what transpires between individuals in the "confines of a plant or building," it is not such environments of action with which he is concerned. Rather, he is concerned with

[21] The same kind of revisionism can be seen in the recent work of Howard Becker, which earlier provided a leading example of the individualistic challenge to functionalist work. In *Art Worlds* (Berkeley and Los Angeles: University of California Press, 1984), Becker takes an emphatically systemic view of the creation and distribution of art. He devotes himself to the normative conventions and structures that organize interaction, and treats artistic deviance as a marginal status position rather than a product of interaction.

[22] See his two studies of major social problems: Joseph Gusfield, *Symbolic Crusade: Status Politics and the American Temperance Movement* (Urbana: University of Illinois Press, 1963), and *The Culture of Public Problems: Driving, Drinking, and the Symbolic Order* (Chicago: University of Chicago Press, 1981).

face to face interaction. Life is a stage where there are players and audience. One "presents a self" to "define a situation" in a way that allows one to gain some kind of control over the impressions of others.[23] In the theoretical introduction which follows, he portrays society as if it were composed of thoroughly atomized individuals, individuals who seem as though they have never seen one another before and never inhabited the same world. Still, these individuals are compelled to interact, and for this reason they seek to define the situation.

The question is how. In principle, Goffman suggests people in interaction can rely on "sign-vehicles." Signs allow an actor to understand a person with whom he is unacquainted by comparing clues about conduct and appearance with his previous experience of the ways in which other people behave. This hypothetical actor can also, in principle, rely on past experience about how people are likely to act in particular settings, or he can reason from his experience about the nature of the "typical actor's" personality. Such references to signs and to structured cultural information recalls the approaches of Peirce and Mead, and, of course, would connect Goffman's interactionist theory to significant elements in Parsonian work. Goffman insists, however, that such references are radically insufficient. "During the period in which the individual is in the immediate presence of the others," he writes, "few events may occur [i.e., signs given off] which directly provide the others with the conclusive information they will need" (p. 1). Not only are signs and symbolic references never conclusive, but Goffman contends that they actually conceal the most important social facts. The crucial facts are completely different from cultural patterns; they have to do with the unique and utterly contingent aspects of the situation. The "reality" of the situation, Goffman suggests, is a completely individual reality. No one can know the crucial facts of interaction but the individual himself.

If the crucial facts about interaction are inaccessible to actors other than the actor himself, how can interaction proceed? Total strangers must accept information on faith, Goffman reasons, and

[23] Erving Goffman, *The Presentation of Self in Everyday Life* (New York: Doubleday, 1959). Hereafter page references to *The Presentation of Self* will be given parenthetically in the text.

given these bits of information they will infer the rest (p. 2). As an inherently unique and unfamiliar actor, you must provide "the other" with material. You must create, consciously or unconsciously, impressions which allow plausible inferences to be made about your intention and identity. These impressions will, inevitably, be false and misleading because only an actor can know himself. Goffman underscores this crucial point by making an analogy to actors on the stage. To create impressions, he believes, people use techniques drawn from the artifice of drama. By engaging in "dramaturgy" they seek to "control others" by creating certain impressions. An actor may wish others to think highly of him, "or to think that he thinks highly of them, or to perceive how in fact he feels toward them, or to obtain no clear cut impression." An actor may wish to ensure harmony with others, or he may wish "to defraud, get rid of, confuse, mislead, antagonize, or insult them." The actor's interest is his own, and he engages in action as an entirely separate individual via manipulating the perceptions of others.

> Regardless of the particular objective which the individual has in mind and of his motive for having this objective, it will be in his interests to control the conduct of the others, especially their responsive treatment of him. This control is achieved largely by influencing the definition which the others come to formulate, and he can influence this definition by expressing himself in such a way as to give them the kind of impression that will lead them to act voluntarily in accordance with his own plans. (pp. 3–4)

Goffman paints a picture of social life as strategic and Machiavellian, in which individuals use stealth and false advertising to realize their will. Social order is not based on sincere motives; it does not involve solidarity; it does not reflect overarching values. To the contrary, in order to create a "veneer of consensus," there must be "suppression of heart-felt feelings." Order is sustained by "each participant concealing his own wants behind statements which assert values to which everyone present feels obliged to give lip service" (pp. 9–10). This is carried out when people utilize "defensive and protective" practices to "safeguard impressions" (p. 14).

In this strand of his argument, then, Goffman merely makes vivid and more dramaturgical the individualistic approach Blumer laid out. Goffman studied in Chicago, the ancestral home of Pragmatic social theory, and while Blumer left long before he arrived the tradition very much survived. Of course, Goffman's individualism differs sharply from Blumer's in its often jaundiced view of motive and its insistence on the omnipresence of manipulation. This reflects clear ideological contrasts: Goffman was developing his own approach when optimistic liberalism declined toward the end of the 1950s. By contrast to Blumer's, Goffman's actors are not only individuated but alienated; their true selves can never be revealed. If they act on faith, it is the "bad faith" which existentialism defines as based on insincerity and conceit. Rather than a free and relatively satisfying society, we are faced with a hopelessness which gives up society altogether.

That is a brief ideological evaluation of Goffman's position. We can also ask questions about its empirical adequacy. Is it actually possible to conceive of this extraordinarily contingent relation between person and role as typical of social relations? In Parsons' terms, Goffman has described personality as if it were completely separated from social system and cultural life. The actor's personal conception of what it means to be a "self" can find no natural or spontaneous expression in his or her social role. Parsons would call this a condition of radical disintegration highly conducive to deviance. While we may not want to go along with him entirely, we might well ask whether a society constituted on such a basis might long continue.

There are, finally, presuppositional problems which can be raised with this strain in Goffman's work. Can any sociologist, much less one so finely attuned to nuance and style, really accept the randomness that such an individualistic conception of social order implies? I suggested earlier that symbolic interactionism moves back and forth between randomness and residual category because it almost always tries to counteract individualism with a collective reference. And, indeed, as we read further in Goffman's book we find that right alongside his individualistic theory he introduces a competing, thoroughly collectivist conception of social order— ostensibly to elaborate it. When Goffman was at the University of

Chicago he did not study only with Blumer's teachers and successors. He studied also with a social anthropologist named Lloyd Warner. A more collectivist descendent of Durkheimian sociology could not be found.

If Warner was not Goffman's only teacher, he certainly taught him something he never forgot. When Goffman turns from his general theory of action as dramatic performance to his substantive analysis of its "props" and "techniques," a strikingly different kind of theory emerges. Because they are face-to-face interactions, he writes, all performances involve "fronts," the physical appearances an actor presents to the public. Do actors invent these fronts and use them according to their whims? From his earlier discussion we would say they do. Goffman's rather surprising answer is that they most certainly do not. Fronts, he writes, are "expressive equipment of a standard kind" (p. 22). They are composed of setting ("assemblages of sign-equipment"), appearance (indications of social status), and manner (personal presentation). Since manner is achieved through setting and appearance, sign-equipment and social status clearly play a very influential role. It seems that whether the actor likes it or not he or she is oriented to sets of cultural constraints.

Indeed, rather than shy away from this fact Goffman now wants to make the most of it. He describes how fronts enmesh individual performance in social control. They generalize away from the particular performance to the collective type. "However specialized and unique a routine is," he insists, "its social front, with certain exceptions, will tend to claim facts that can be equally claimed and asserted of other, somewhat different routines" (p. 26). He remarks, for example, on the tendency for a whole range of different occupations to present their performances as clean, modern, competent, and honest. Far from the unique product of a contingent individual, such a front is institutional, the product, in his words, of "abstract stereotyped expectations" (p. 27). Drawing directly on the most anti-individualistic, Durkheimian language, Goffman writes that "the front becomes a 'collective representation' and a fact in its own right." Since roles are defined by fronts, it follows that they can scarcely be the product of individual invention. To the contrary, "when an actor takes on an established social role," Goffman writes, "he finds that a particular front has already been established for it."

Whether his acquisition of the role was primarily motivated by a desire to perform the given task or by a desire to maintain the corresponding front, the actor will find that he must do both. Further, if the individual takes on a task that is not only new to him but unestablished in the society, or if he attempts to change the light in which his task is viewed, he is likely to find that there are already several well-established fronts among which he must choose. (p. 27)

If we bracket for a moment Goffman's insistence on the asocial autonomy of personality, it is easy to see this analysis as a detailed, interactionally specific elaboration of the very theory he ostensibly is writing against—of Parsons' notion that roles direct individual action through institutionalized norms and the allocation of facilities. Goffman himself suggests, for example, that the abstract and generalized character of fronts makes them ideal socializing vehicles, which was one of Parsons' central points. Through fronts, Goffman writes, performance is "molded, and modified to fit into the understanding and expectations of the society in which it is presented" (p. 35).

But Goffman is not satisfied even with this. Introducing a concept called "idealization," he begins to offer an anti-individualistic understanding of motive itself. Actors, he now suggests, have a strong desire to conform to the accredited values of society. Hence they have a tendency to "idealize" their performances, that is, "to incorporate and exemplify the officially accredited values of the society" (p. 35). Because of this idealizing motive, performance often has a ceremonial quality; it becomes "an expressive rejuvenation and reaffirmation of the moral values of the community" (p. 35). Goffman, earlier the pragmatic individualist, now wants to model social order on the lines of dogmatic ritual behavior! And he devotes the next twenty pages of his book to laying out the different ways in which such symbolically determined performances must be done. "Everyday secular performances," he writes, "must often pass a strict test of aptness, fitness, propriety, and decorem" (p. 55). Actors must strive mightily to make their behavior internally consistent, since one anomalous gesture may throw the "reality" of their performance into doubt; they must not look as though they are trying too hard or not hard enough; they must give an impression of utter infallability; they must exhibit only the end product of their performance, not the difficult rehearsals; they must segregate the audience for each performance from the audiences for their other social roles. What we have here is an impressive list of the complex "performance requirements" required for any and all social roles. These are the established techniques which actors must use if they are to succeed in exhibiting, in the open and contingent world of individual choice, their commitments to values in ways that avoid sanctions.

Reality is a "fragile thing," Goffman writes (p. 65). He has certainly gone way beyond Parsons in explaining just what the functionalist concept of "double contingency" means. It means that throughout interaction sanctions are considered, rewards are offered, internalizations are projected, and every shade of difference is subject to continuous scrutiny and interpretation. Yet while Goffman has opened up the "level of the individual" more incisively than any other contemporary theorist, there is no evidence in this more collectivist strand of his work that he wants to take a presuppositional stand supporting individualism.

What, then, are we to make of Goffman's interactionist theory? Its multivalent character can be seen, on the one hand, as expressing the empirical tension produced by a differentiated and complex society. There is an inevitable gap between personality needs and social system roles, and an inherent slippage between both and the consensual values which are "supposed to" hold good for all. In view of these gaps, Goffman is quite right to stress the calculation and symbolic strategization which allow the modern individual to navigate the difficult contingencies of everyday life. When we consider his work as a whole, however, we can see that Goffman often goes much further than this, that this picture of empirical tensions often gives way to theoretical tensions. Insofar as this occurs, he produces irreconcilable portraits of social worlds presupposed in antithetical ways. In my view, sign vehicles are either relevant or they are not. Actors either make reference, however contingently, to Durkheim's sacred things, or they are "misinformers" who try "to profit from lies."[24] Goffman cannot have it both ways, yet there

---

[24] For Goffman's suggestion that actors do make such references, see p. 70, and for the contradictory point, see p. 62.

are times when he wants to, when he simply cannot or will not decide.

Goffman's subsequent work, I might add, suffers from much the same kind of brilliant ambiguity. In *Behavior in Public Places*, for example, he claims time and time again that he is studying the norms and rules which control interaction in face-to-face groups. At the same time, he is at pains throughout his analysis to demonstrate that the attitudes an individual takes to others are determined by the concrete situational exigencies he encounters, particularly the spatial distribution and physical behavior of other people.[25] In *Asylums* this dualism is even more apparent. On the one hand, Goffman wants to demonstrate that the categories employed by doctors, orderlies, and patients is a product of their contingent jockeying for power and control, on the other that the nature of their interaction is inevitably determined by the structure of the "total institution" in which they live and work.[26]

Let me end these lectures on Pragmatism and interactionism by citing—out of context—a famous warning by Max Weber. In 1919, in the midst of Germany's postwar upheaval, he warned his students that revolutions are not "trolley cars you can get on and off at will." If they opted for revolution, he warned, they would have to live forever with the consequences, either good or bad. The individualist dilemma is not something that an individualist theorist can simply decide to give up. Once you embrace a theoretical tradition you are bound to maintain it. As long as you do not renounce your allegiance entirely, you are bound to it, warts and all. You benefit from its unusual insights, you are hurt by its blind spots. In these lectures I have tried to show how the modern interactionist tradition opens up to systematic inspection great areas of contingent individual life. These openings are purchased, however, only by submitting interactionism to the schizophrenic consequences of the individualist dilemma. I made much the same point in my earlier discussions of the theories of conflict and exchange. I will make it several more times in the lectures that follow.

[25] Erving Goffman, *Behavior in Public Places* (New York: Free Press, 1963).
[26] Erving Goffman, *Asylums* (New York: Anchor Doubleday, 1961).

LECTURE FOURTEEN
ETHNOMETHODOLOGY (1): PHENOMENOLOGY AND THE LEGACY OF EDMUND HUSSERL

W E ARE NOW in the very heart of our investigation into post-Parsonian sociology. We began with Parsons' path-breaking attempt at theoretical realignment, which created a new vocabulary for sociological theory in the postwar world. I argued that Parsons did, indeed, make fundamental advances in the conceptualization of society—in his synthesis of material and ideal traditions, in his effort to conceptualize systems without giving up on actions and personalities, in his ability to analyze stability, change, and modernity with the same general conceptual scheme. At the same time, I suggested that there were fundamental flaws in Parsons' work, and that it was scarcely (to paraphrase Woodrow Wilson's falsely idealistic hopes for another great enterprise) the "theory to end all theories" which he had hoped to produce.

It was within the intellectual context of the Parsonian conceptual scheme, and the social context of the breakdown of postwar optimism, that new intellectual traditions arose. So far we have considered three of these: conflict theory, exchange theory, and symbolic interactionism. Each can be seen, I have argued, as responding to critical ambiguities in Parsons' original theory. Each must also be understood as developing an independent theoretical position in its own right. Each position starts from a different presuppositional stance, one permutation out of the small number of logical possibilities. Conflict theory takes a rationalistic approach to action and a collectivist approach to order. Exchange theory maintains rationalism but conceives of order in an individualistic way. Symbolic interactionism keeps this individualistic position on order but, in sharp contrast to exchange and conflict theory, presupposes action in a normative, nonrational way. Because none of these positions is a multidimensional one, each leads its followers into irresolvable dilemmas. Conflict theorists must either embrace determinism or allow residual categories to undermine the systematic structure of their work. Exchange and interactionist theories, for their part, face what I have called the individualist dilemma. Their order position leads to randomness rather than determinacy, and the effort to avoid this danger leads to the equally unpalatable prospect of residual categories and ad hoc theorizing. In my later lectures I will round out this exploration of theoretical logic by discussing a challenge that is normative but also collectivistic hermeneutic, cultural sociology—and I will explore significantly more critical ideological variants of these same theoretical positions.

By now my own position should be clear to you. I see each of the challenges to Parsons as elaborating one of the possible presuppositional alternatives which are available to sociological theory. Together, they have broken Parsons' whole into distinctive and competing parts. Yet no matter how powerfully argued, these alternatives were bound to be only partial theories. The reason is that none of these alternatives takes over Parsons' goal (as distinct from his theory) as their own; none, that is, tries to be synthetic or multidimensional. Only a synthetic position can avoid the resort to residual categories which tears a theory apart; only a multidimensional position, moreover, can express the kinds of value commitments—to conditional freedom, to the mediation of material constraint by subjective volition—which, in my view, any satisfactory modern social theory must have. My own goal for theory goes back to Parsons. I want to construct a multidimensional, synthetic theory which is less ambivalent than his original attempt, which has, in other words, the courage of its convictions. What better way to accomplish this than to build upon the achievements of those challenging Parsons' work, without taking over the reductionism which made them vulnerable in turn?

The new synthesis I am trying to construct is already partly complete. I have tried to build it in two ways. First, I have converted into different levels of empirical analysis insights which were originally couched in theoretical, presuppositional terms—arguments about the significance of rational action, material constraint, conflict, interpretation, and contingency. Second, I have tried to bring these alternative presuppositional arguments together to shore up a truly synthetic position. Much more work remains to be done. Significant challenges to Parsons' theory have not yet been considered. Only if we do so can we get on with the task of building an alternative theory.

What I will be considering today is not an alternative presuppositional position but a new and in some ways more profound elaboration of one we have already considered. Ethnomethodology presupposes the same normative, individualist stance embodied in interactionism, but it specifies this commitment in an entirely different way. You will recall that when I began discussing interactionism I felt compelled to go back to its very earliest forms, to the history of Pragmatism and particularly to the social theory of Mead. This was not because of antiquarian curiosity. It was, rather, because much of contemporary interactionism seems to me peculiarly arid. Mead's early elaboration of this tradition differs from such contemporary theorizing in significant ways. I will continue this archeological bent in the present lectures on ethnomethodology and phenomenology. You will soon see why.

Ethnomethodology was started by Harold Garfinkel in the 1960s as another radical challenge to Parsons. Though I will try to show you that some of Garfinkel's early formulations were not nearly so "anti-Parsonian" as commonly believed, there is no doubt that as his theorizing developed—and he founded his ethnomethodological "school"—it increasingly became couched in a sharply individualistic form. To be sure, there is much to distinguish this ethnomethodological individualism from Blumer's interactionist one, but I will try to show you that it remains an individualistic theory nonetheless. In the course of its development, then, ethnomethodology has been individualistic in both an "empirical" and a "presuppositional" sense. I want to talk today about the source of this ambiguity. I will suggest that the theory has accepted collective order while denying it at the same time. To understand how and why this has been done, we have to go back to the very founder of phenomenology, Edmund Husserl, and we must place his thought against the background from which it emerged.

Husserl, who was German, began writing in the 1890s and finished his work in the mid-1930s, roughly the same period as the founding generation of American Pragmatists. His thought, too, developed in the midst of an acute sense of social and intellectual crisis. Europeans experienced not only instability but a stultifying sense of rigid objectivity, so much so that the period has been called "the age of anxiety." Durkheim and Weber, of course, responded to this crisis with collectivist theories which became much more widely known than Husserl's more obscure, philosophical work. They opposed the constraint of the age by developing theories of collective subjectivity. By contrast, Husserl tried, much as the American Pragmatists had, to resuscitate creativity and hope by showing how collective order actually is constructed through individual intention and experience. In the European context this was a much more unlikely response to the fin-de-siècle crisis than in the American. Only the French philosopher Henri Bergson took up a similar line of theorizing. It should not be surprising that Bergson's individualism also had a significant, if much smaller effect on the emergence of the subjectively individualistic tradition in sociology.

Husserl started the theoretical tradition called "phenomenology," which has a long pedigree in German intellectual history but which he cast in a substantially new form. What phenomenology meant for Husserl was that reality is structured by perception. Even the things whose objectivity we normally take for granted are "there" for us only because we make them, or take them to be so. Husserl, then, responded to the sense of chaos and disorder of his time by making doubt about the realness of reality central to his theory. By incorporating the uncertainty, the anxiety, and the relativism of the early twentieth century, of course, he might be seen as having actually contributed to the experience of disorder in a theoretical way. At the same time, however, Husserl believed strongly that there is a reality. What he wanted to show was that individuals contributed to the perception of reality in a crucial way. He accepted, for example, the objective truth of science. He insisted, nonetheless, that this objectivity could not itself be understood in an extra-subjective, impersonal way. In his view, you have to give up on the certainty that the world exists without subjectivity if you are to understand how the objective status of the world can be maintained.

If you think this sounds rather paradoxical, you are right. Husserl believed that there is an order and a structure to the world. This belief in supra-individual order differentiates his thought from the Pragmatists' with whom he had so much else in common. Yet, and here he is very like the Pragmatists, he combined this belief with an insistence that our knowledge about the structures of the world do not issue from the world itself.

It is not surprising to discover that Husserl was a mathematician before he became a philosopher, for it is in mathematics that we encounter the notion that objective truths which emerge from the logic of mind reflect, at the same time, the actual structure of the external world. Just as mathematics has a peculiar relation to "positivism"—the notion that a scientist's knowledge is a more or less direct reflection of the outside world—so does Husserl's phenomenology. For while phenomenology agrees that scientific knowledge mirrors the real structures of the outside world, it does not see this knowledge as having developed as a reflection of it. Rather than knowledge proceeding directly from the sensate experience of the world, it is viewed as deriving from active, constructive powers in consciousness. Husserl was a sharp critic of psychologism. He believed little could be gained by dwelling on how somebody "experienced the world." It is not experience of the world which produces knowledge; it is consciousness which creates the world which is subsequently experienced. Pragmatists, to the contrary, celebrate experience; they believe that through the intense, psychological encounter with the world the reality of structures can be directly perceived. Husserl took an individualist stance, but he saw the individual as deeply implicated in orderly patterns. This paradox is captured very well in a statement he made in a set of lectures which formed the basis for the last book published in his lifetime, *Cartesian Meditations:* "The objective world, the world that exists for me, that always has and always will exist for me, the only world that ever can exist for me—this world, with all its objects . . . derives its whole sense and its existential status . . . from me myself."[1]

The first individualistic tradition we studied, exchange theory, would have thought this position utterly absurd. For Homans, it is the objective world which shapes this "me," which is, after all, described by him as a reasonable facsimile of a calculating machine. Though Blumer understood that the individual actively interprets and constructs this reality, he treats the nature of this reality as unproblematic, conceiving of the actor as interpreting an external, noncultural situation. Mead avoided this problem, since he insisted that the basic meaning of the situation is assumed before an individual makes any assessment of the relative possibilities for strategic and interactive behavior. Yet Mead's understanding of attitude formation was itself quite mechanical. He saw it as emerging, instantaneously and automatically, from the memory of past encounters stored in the "me." Husserl has much less to say than Mead about the social and developmental origins of such collective reference—for example, the generalized other—but he has much more to say about how the subjective structuring of the situation actually proceeds.

To understand the role that individual consciousness plays in constructing the world, you must cast doubt on the "realness" of the world. You must, in other words, assume a position of doubt about whether what you see and hear outside of yourself actually exists apart from your making it appear to be so. "The world is for us," Husserl says, "something that only *claims* being" (p. 18; italics mine). Its objective being, in other words, is not automatically given; it is a claim, an ambition, that must be made good. The "sense of reality," the "sense of structure", comes from the individual person, not from the world itself: "It is given to consciousness *perceptually* . . . as it itself" (p. 19; italics mine).

But how does consciousness and/or perception actually pull this off? To find out you must develop a methodology, a technique for doing social analysis, which allows you to center the world around

---

[1] Edmund Husserl, *Cartesian Meditations* (The Hague: Martinus Nijhoff, 1960), p. 26. Hereafter page references to *Cartesian Meditations* will be given parenthetically in the text.

the individual—almost the Copernican Revolution in reverse. You must give up your "naive attitude" toward the world, which accepts the world as valid without human participation. Husserl calls "daily practical living" naive, because it is based on one's "immersion in the already-given world, whether it be experiencing, or thinking, or valuing" (p. 152). Because actors are immersed in the world, they do not realize that it is they themselves who are producing it. "All those productive intentional functions of experiencing, because of which physical things are simply there, go on anonymously. The experiencer knows nothing about them, and likewise nothing about his productive thinking" (pp. 152–153). But these intentional functions, the constitutive work of consciousness, go on nonetheless; "The numbers, the predicative complexes of affairs, the goods, the ends, the works, present themselves because of the hidden performance; they are built up, member by member." It is precisely because they are so effective that "the intentional performances from which everything ultimately originates remain unexplained" (p. 13).

Husserl sees action and order in terms of the "productive intentional functions" which, proceeding anonymously and unconsciously as "hidden performances," allow the world to appear, ironically, as if it does not need conscious at all. He calls this focus "transcendental subjectivity," for it studies the universal functions of the mind without regard to any particular mental content (p. 20). Indeed, only by "bracketing" the naive assumptions we make about the reality of the particulars of our existence can transcendental subjectivity be discovered. To do this, to shed the naive attitude, is to engage in what Husserl calls the "phenomenological reduction." The phenomenological reduction is the method by which we can study the essential structures of pure consciousness.

Phenomenology is the "a priori science." It studies the rules that consciousness follows for making things seem actual (p. 28). Perception presents the things of the world as authentic and interconnected, whereas reality, in Husserl's view, is actually an unconnected stream of atomized events. Phenomenological analysis shows how consciousness, through hidden performances, transforms this objective reality into something quite different, into an image of a transcendental, objective, authentic, and integrated thing. To find out the rules for the operation of such consciousness, Husserl sets out to discover "a mode of combination exclusively peculiar to consciousness" (p. 28).

How does consciousness combine what are actually discrete, unconnected events into an apparently integrated and orderly whole? In their desire to synthesize and combine elements of reality, Husserl suggests, people inevitably draw connections between things in their environment. Try to think, as Husserl often does, of some three-dimensional object, for instance a chair. Recall, in a completely literal way, what images your vision of such an object actually amount to. What do you see of the chair in the course of moving about the room? You certainly never see the complete, well-proportioned chair as such. Instead, you see part of one leg, a different part of another, a small slice of seat from a weird angle, and so forth. The images of objects actually presented to the mind, therefore, are random, changing, and essentially unintegrated.

Yet the mind does not accept, or even consciously see, such "incoherent sequencing" (p. 43). First, consciousness seems very insistent on making spatial connections. You almost always believe that near, far, and middle range things are part of—indeed, must be seen as composing—a whole. More generally, the mind inevitably constructs a "horizon of reference." You make an immediate, tacit connection between things you genuinely see, things you have not yet perceived but anticipate seeing, and things you believe you would be able to see if you wanted to. Husserl describes these unseen but mentally imagined things as "also meant" (p. 44).

All these constitutive abilities are based on memory, and a more anti-Homansian perspective on the past could hardly be found. Husserl believes that every new impression is seen as "evidence" of some general type of thing. Yet this can happen only if we remember things from previous experience; we use our constructive capacities to make connections between atomistic images, to make them seem like things seen in the past. "New evidences," Husserl writes, "are restituting of the first evidences" (p. 60). This appreciation of memory allows him to suggest yet another structuring mechanism that is inherent to consciousness, namely the ability to connect events temporally in order to create temporal sequences. There seems to be an internal and naive sense of the connection between past, present, and future. This capacity is one other way we make continuous connections between things which are, in objective terms, separated and unattached.

It is the mind, then, that constructs the axes of space and time which allow the world to take on spatial and temporal objectivity. Because of such ability, when the actor encounters things he senses that they are "already constituted" in advance (p. 45). The object, Husserl says, is "always meant expectantly as having a sense yet to be actualized." Or as he puts this in the metaphorical language which ethnomethodology was later to take up, "in every moment of consciousness it [the object] is an index" of prior expectations (p. 46). In conventional terms, of course, an index is an abbreviated set of indicators which point to more elaborate discussions appearing earlier in a book. Husserl is saying that objects encountered in reality have much the same status; they stand for, they signify, a host of meanings which have been learned in earlier experience. To allow newly encountered objects to achieve indexical status, specific techniques are required. Above all, there is the constant use of analogizing.

> Each everyday experience involves an analogizing transfer of an originally instituted objective sense to a new case, with its anticipative apprehension of the object as having a similar sense . . . At the same time that sense-component in further experience which proves to be actually new may function in turn as institutive and found a pregiveness that has a richer sense. (p. 111)

More specific than the technique of analogizing is "pairing." Consciousness constantly pairs things with other things, people with things, people with people, people with the actor himself. What rules pairing is the principle of identity. It is through such specific techniques and through the general constitutive mechanisms of consciousness that the "object world" can be said to be an achievement of intentional acts.

Husserl believed that the study of such techniques would usher in a new world for the social sciences, one that would establish the essential bases of social order once and for all. We must focus on the "universal phenomena of the transcendental sphere" (p.

112)—the techniques of consciousness—so that we can analyze "the transcendental constitution of any object whatever" (p. 51). By "object," Husserl meant to include the entirety of social, not just physical life. Just as phenomenology has provided "a *constitutional theory* of physical Nature," so it would provide "a constitutional theory of man, of human community, of culture." Each of these topics, Husserl believed, "points to a vast discipline with different lines of investigation." The purpose of each discipline would be to convert the investigation of "naively" held concepts like "real space" and "real property" into a study of the intentional practices which constitute each of them as "objective" social facts (pp. 63–64).

This is an extraordinarily ambitious program. If it were carried out it would, indeed, illuminate some of the most complicating problems in contemporary social theory. The question remains, however, whether such a transcendental phenomenology really could substitute for contemporary social science as such. It is my conviction that it certainly could not. While Husserl's study of consciousness points to crucial elements in the subjective construction of collective order, it offers no compelling evidence that this consciousness is any more important than the environment within which its activity unfolds.

By making the claim that phenomenology will initiate a new social science, Husserl is suggesting, in our terms, that it can explain social order as such. Rather than pointing simply to a new level of empirical analysis, he wishes to establish individualism in a presuppositional way. With this claim, the stimulating, paradoxical quality of his theory changes into a confining theoretical dilemma. If viewed as presuppositional rather than empirical discussion, Husserl's position is a one-dimensional and limited one. As far as the problem of action is concerned, his elaborate attention to consciousness can be seen as the other side of his neglect of instrumental rationality, the very type of action that relates the actor to his world "as if" it were composed only of external objects. Indeed, Husserl openly embraces this idealist position. "I . . . have objects," he writes, "solely as the intentional correlates of modes of consciousness of them" (p. 37). At one point, in fact, Husserl actually calls his method "transcendental idealism," insisting that "every imaginable sense, every imaginable being . . . falls within the domain of transcendental subjectivity, as the subjectivity that constitutes sense and being." And he argues that "the attempt to conceive the universe . . . as something lying outside the universe of possible consciousness . . . is nonsensical" (p. 84).

The idealism of Husserl's approach to action is compounded by the individualism of his approach to order. Idealism can be collective or it can be individualistic, and it would certainly be possible to focus on the constituting features of consciousness while not presupposing order as constituted by individual consciousness alone. Husserl, however, looks at the structure-producing capabilities of the individual mind *rather than* the typical structures and processes of culture. As a result, his view has some of the same weaknesses as traditional religious thought. It seems revealing to me that he closes *Cartesian Meditation* by quoting from Augustine: "Do not wish to go out; go back into yourself. Truth dwells in the inner man" (p. 157).

I should immediately add that Husserl, like so many of the other important theorists we have already discussed, was not completely unaware of the shortcomings of his work. This, by the way, has always seemed to me one indication of a theorist's stature, namely, that he senses the limits of his own theory and moves to extend them. While I have certainly criticized the ad hoc theorizing which usually results, this takes nothing away from the great insight required to introduce it. It is usually the unimaginative theorist who finds no problems with the theory within which he works and whose writing, therefore, is more internally consistent.

Toward the end of his life, in published and unpublished work, Husserl indicated a genuine desire to connect his insights into individual consciousness with a recognition of the collective status of the social. He suggested that the intentional construction of meaning gives rise to, and is carried out within, "life-worlds," which is the name he gives to collective orders like cognitive styles, symbolic patterns, and communities. As he wrote, for example, in an essay which was published only after his death: "To live as a person is to live in a social framework, wherein I and we live together in community and have the community as a horizon."[2]

[2] "Philosophy and the Crisis of European Man," in Husserl, *Phenomenology and the Crisis of Philosophy* (New York: Harper and Row, 1965), p. 150.

It is essential to see, however, that while Husserl comprehended some of the limitations of his approach, he did not succeed in reconceptualizing the presuppositions of his theory as such. Indeed, more than most great thinkers he succeeded in introducing new categories—in this case the concept of "life-world"—without resorting to residual category.

The life-world, Husserl explained, is formed by extending the techniques through which actors constitute their own individual worlds. Actors construct society through analogy, pairing, and the host of other techniques through which discrete and unfamiliar things appear integrated and "already known." Husserl writes, for example, of how "the other body there enters into a pairing association with my body here" (p. 119), and he suggests that "it is implicit in the sense of my successful apperception of others that their world, the world belonging to their appearance-systems, must be experienced forthwith as the same as the world belonging to my appearance systems" (p. 105).

But in light of the understanding of symbols, cultural systems, and socialization we have developed in this course, this approach to the relation of individual and society seems highly artificial. Husserl is still maintaining that everything starts with the irreduccable atom of the individual, that society is a mode of consciousness which begins with you yourself. All that is changed is that he now is willing to admit that "not all my own modes of consciousness are modes of my *self*-consciousness" (p. 105; italics mine). The problem is that the "others" who are described by Husserl as the objects of these socially oriented constructive techniques are left completely unexplained. Husserl begins his account in the following way: "Let us assume that another man enters our perceptual picture" (p. 110). He never provides an explanation of what motivates that man to enter in the first place or what he is actually thinking when he does so.

In my view, Husserl was not really interested in the structure of the life-world after all. Rather, he wanted to demonstrate that, whatever collective order is like and however it is internally constituted, its ability to exert collective control rests on the phenomenological techniques of consciousness. This seems precisely the point he was making in a now famous letter he wrote to the anthropologist Levi-Bruhl. He acknowledges here that a cultural analysis of collective patterns can also show sources of social life which are "beneath" the naive reality of the life-world, but he insists, nonetheless, that this social understanding of the structure of life-worlds can only be preparatory to phenomenological analysis as such. In such moments, Husserl succumbs to the temptation to transform the collective reference of his theoretical individualism into a dangling residual category.

The best students of a great thinker are bound to revise him in significant ways, for they are often much more concerned then he with the vulnerable points in his thought. Husserl's most important followers focused on this delicate issue of the "social." They tried to tranform these references in his later work, whether residual or not, into theories which related phenomenology to sociology in a systematic way. In the process, they tried to make individual "consciousness" a level of analysis rather than a presuppositional position. Maurice Merleau-Ponty, for example, wrote about Husserl's "dilemma." He analyzed this dilemma in terms of whether the life-world should remain residual to phenomenology or whether it should be conceived as significantly affecting the objects that individual consciousness helps to produce. He himself believed that intentionality can operate only in reference to the culturally given— "it is not the mere sum of expression taken in isolation."[3] Another important revisionist, Alfred Schutz, took the argument even further. "Our everyday world," he insisted, "is, from the outset, an intersubjective world of culture."[4] Schutz developed what he called a mundane rather than transcendental phenomenology. He inserts transcendental intentional activity into the context of particular cultural orders and he wants to show how both play essential roles.

Schutz and Merleau-Ponty both produced strong and perceptive programmatic statements about the need to redefine the consciousness/society relationship. Schutz, moreover, conducted several empirical studies that were so programmatically informed. Yet even Schutz's most ambitious effort remained provisional,[5] and most of

[3] Maurice Merleau-Ponty, "The Philosopher and the Sociologist" [1960], in Thomas Luckmann, ed., *Phenomenology and Sociology* (London: Penguin, 1978), p. 153.

[4] Alfred Schutz, "Phenomenology and the Social Sciences" [1940], in Luckmann, pp. 134-135.

[5] Schutz, *The Phenomenology of the Social World* (1932; Evanston, Ill.: Northwestern University Press, 1967).

his theorizing presented an "amalgamation" rather than a truly synthetic marriage of sociology and phenomenology. The relation was announced but never really consummated. Look, for example, at this statement in what probably remains the most influential theoretical statement Schutz ever made.

> The naively living person . . . automatically has in hand, so to speak, the meaningful complexes which are valid for him. From things inherited and learned, from the manifold sedimentations of traditions, habituality, and his own previous constitutions of meaning, which can be retained and reactivated, his *store of experience* of his life-world is built up as a closed meaningful complex. The experience of the life-world has its special style of verification. This style results from the process of harmonization of all single experiences. It is co-constituted last but not least, by the perspectives of relevance and by the horizons of interest which are to be explicated.[6]

The first two sentences in this statement acknowledge the collective cultural complexes that precede and influence individual action. The last three sentences refer to Husserl's techniques for "verifying" the familiarity and objectivity of the external world. Schutz is saying, quite rightly, that through spatial and temporal consistency, through analogizing from oneself to other people, through pairing, expectant meanings, and indexing the culture that is already shared is made more widely applicable to new actors and to ongoing events. This statement points in the right direction, but it does not really get us on the train.[7]

---

[6] Schutz, "Phenomenology and the Social Sciences," p. 137.

[7] The same very clear desire for synthesis combined with the inability to carry it through can be seen in Schutz's delightful essay, "Making Music Together," in *Collected Papers* (The Hague: Martinus Nijhoff, 1964), pp. 159-178. On the one hand, Schutz connects Husserl's insistence on the "typifying" nature of consciousness to the power of collective culture over the musical understanding of performers: "The player's general preknowledge of [a musical piece's] typicality becomes the scheme of reference for his interpretation of its particularity" (p. 168). At the same time, he wants to suggest a much more individualistic interpretation, saying that "such anticipations are more or less empty" (p. 168), because they are interpreted in different ways in different situations by specific performers. Later he insists, quite ambiguously, that "the social relationship prevailing among the performers" is "founded upon" their ability to cast their relationship to the composer and to one another as a simultaneous, face-to-face relationship in the "vivid present" (p. 177). Yet certainly this very presentness of individuals to one another depends equally upon the cultural structure inherited from the past.

Schutz's most important student, Harold Garfinkel, tries to take us all the way there. In the early phases of his career, Garfinkel continued the camouflaged effort to resolve the individualist dilemma in a truly synthetic way. He wanted to create a social, supraindividual reference in phenomenology which would allow it to escape both randomness and indeterminacy. I will argue that in this early phase of his career Garfinkle was able to pull this off more effectively than any of his predecessors.

Garfinkel's early success, I believe, has something to do with the intellectual background from which he emerged. Husserl's training in mathematics gave him a somewhat deceptive sense of order as just "being there." Merleau-Ponty, by contrast, was a political activist whose socialism gave him a more accurate understanding of how historically specific structures influenced action. The Marxism in his background, however, made it harder for him to understand how culture actually works. Schutz, by contrast, while studying with Husserl was influenced by Max Weber as well. He took over from Weber the notion of collectively rooted normative patterns, though he was reinforced in his own individualism by Weber's sometime tendency to make cultural patterning an appendage of individual choice, and he reacted against Weber's overemphasis on rationality by becoming even more introspectively subjectivist in turn. Garfinkel, by contrast, had the good fortune to be trained by Parsons as well as by Schutz. Parsons had worked out the individual-society-culture problem further than any before him, and what he had not been able to understand gave Garfinkle good leave. From Parsons, Garfinkel could understand that order is given and persistent and outside of any individual actor. He also understood from Parsons that because order is cultural it is internalized and that for this reason it rests upon the feelings and intentions of actors themselves. It was because of Parsons that Garfinkel came to be preoccupied with normative order in a way that was quite different from earlier theorists in the phenomenological tradition.

Though Garfinkel produced a number of different articles in the 1950s and 1960s, the most powerful statement of this early, and I believe most successful, position occurs in his long, detailed, and relatively obscure essay on trust, published in 1963 but probably written sometime before.[8] He introduced in this essay an entire conceptual schema in the context of describing a series of ingenious empirical tests about how people play games. Certainly it was not mere accident that this fundamental attempt to incorporate normative order into the analysis of individual intention occurred in a study of "games." Games, as Mead demonstrated in his by no means unrelated work, are the very prototype of institutions which link individual desires to social needs and which, by doing so, civilize rivalry by submitting it to common rules.

The first and probably most important move Garfinkel makes in this essay is to describe the games he is studying as supra-individual "normative orders" and "disciplines." You have trust between the players in a game to the degree that this normative order is maintained. But how can it be? To answer this Garfinkel brings together Parsons with Husserl and Schutz. Following Parsons, he suggests that rules are, and have to be, internalized. Following phenomenology, he warns that they must also be "worked." They must be worked at because norms and rules are effective only because they operate in conjunction with "consciousness" in a phenomenological sense. Norms and rules produce expectations for behaviors which articulate neatly with the order-creating, meaning-intending functions of consciousness. The rules of a game depend on good faith. Good faith works because the mere existence of internalized rules creates "constitutive expectancies" among the players. Rules, therefore, exhibit the following characteristics. First, players in the game (i.e., the members of a group) expect a rule to be followed unquestioningly. They see it as "objective," and assume the "natural" and "naive" attitude toward it which Husserl suggested is endemic to everyday life. Second, every player in a game expects all other participants to exhibit the same natural attitude, a proposition that follows from the phenomenological notion of pairing.

How are these expectations confirmed? How is this naive attitude maintained? The trick is that actors feel compelled to constitute reality to conform with their normative and social expectations.

---

[8] Harold Garfinkel, "A Conception of and Experiments with 'Trust' as a Condition of Concerted Stable Actions," in O. J. Harvey, ed., *Motivation and Social Interaction* (New York: Ronald Press, 1963), pp. 187-238.

Garfinkel believes that rules provide "categorical possibilities" which are viewed by the actor, unconsciously to be sure, as intended events. People then make every possible effort to bring "all actual observations . . . under the jurisdiction of intended events as particular cases of the intended event."[9] This is what following rules means. Rather than games following rules, it is equally true that rules follow games!

Here is how this phenomenological reconstruction of norms works in practice. Every situation in a game is referred for definition and interpretation to the rules. These rules are viewed as embodying past experience, while in fact they helped produce and direct prior experience much as they are doing with this new event in turn. There is, then, in every game an ongoing process of what Garfinkel calls "normalization": new events are depicted as normal and consistent with past events and with the overarching rules. To describe in what actual techniques normalization consists, Garfinkel follows Schutz and Husserl in suggesting comparability, analogy, pairing, and most interestingly of all, the "etc. clause." This last, Garfinkel's own invention, holds that no given set of rules can be expected to refer beforehand to every possible kind of event; for this reason, every given set of rules must be extended and reformed to cover new situations without seeming to be changed at all.

It is because these intentional techniques are continuously employed that a naive attitude toward rules and norms can be maintained by members of social groups. It is because of the constituting techniques of our consiousness that we think rules exist and that we believe they control behavior, not only ours but everyone else's. This belief is actually a self-fulfilling prophecy. What really happens is that we elaborate and extend rules to fit our new situation, forcing the rules to fit this objective reality as much as limiting this reality by our prior commitment to them. This is the nature of normalizing—and normativizing—action.

Social order can be threatened if constituent expectations are violated in such a drastic way that they cannot carry through with normalization. The new event in this case produces senselessness rather than sense, and radical or revolutionary norms must be

[9] *Ibid.*, p. 194.

constructed which will allow normalization in a new and different "game." Senseless events, in this subtle sociological definition, mean events that defy analogizing. There is, in Garfinkel's words, a "breaching [of] the congruency of relevances" and of the "interchangeability of standpoints." Even the plastic "etc. clause" is not supple enough. Collective memory malfunctions; it cannot traditionalize reality. Normative order breaks down. The constitutive mechanisms of consciousness have not changed; what has changed is the collective inputs on which they depend. Yet there is still an interrelationship, for the continuity of normative order depends upon these constitutive mechanisms taking place. When the latter falter, the discontinuities of the former are made much more intense.

Because of his presuppositional commitment to collective order, Garfinkel's phenomenological insights have produced remarkable results. Rather than challenging the existence of collective order, he has illuminated how much the construction of this order depends on the actor's ability to grapple with contingency. He has shown that Parsons' most important "functionalist" concept—cultural integration—cannot be fully understood without referring to processes of which Parsons was scarcely aware. For value internalization is not the whole story; the socialized personality must "act" in constitutive ways. Integration is sustained from event to event not simply through value internalization but through the normalizing process which Husserl and Garfinkel describe. Meaning consistency is not only a matter of arranging symbols coherently inside the cultural system. It is also the result of being able to construe events logically from the inside. For this reason Garfinkel can argue that sociology must pay careful attention to "accommodative work." Although from the perspective of the intentional actor collective order does indeed have the quality of a contingently emergent product, Garfinkel seems clearly to understand that accommodative work occurs only with reference to internalized rules: constitutive expectations exist, and intentions are carried out, only in relationship to an internalized culture that produces an initial cultural mapping of legitate order.

What we have seen in this early work of Garfinkel's is a strain of theorizing we found also in Goffman and to a much greater extent in Mead. I am referring to a compelling exploration of individual action that is not "individualistic." This is just the kind of thinking which is necessary if a multidimensional theory is ever to become more fully elaborated and empirically specified. The problem is that such theorizing requires remarkable intellectual discipline. You must be open to individualism without fully embracing it, and you must be able to accept order without allowing its deterministic quality to dominate your thought. Garfinkel developed this approach during the 1950s, when the challenge to Parsons' collectivist theorizing had hardly begun. When he named his theory "ethnomethodology" in the 1960s the anti-Parsonian movement was fully underway. In my next lecture I will show you how in the course of becoming ethnomethodology Garfinkel's thought underwent a subtle but profound change, and how in the course of the 1960s he became caught by the individualist dilemma—after having first transcended it.

LECTURE FIFTEEN
ETHNOMETHODOLOGY (2): HAROLD GARFINKEL'S REBELLION AGAINST NORMS

W HEN GARFINKEL WROTE the searching essay on trust which I discussed toward the end of my last lecture he was not yet an "ethnomethodologist." What I mean by this is that he had not yet started the "school" he was to lead from the 1960s on, and he had not yet invented a name to separate this school from the rest of sociology. At that relatively early point Garfinkel was simply the student of Schutz who was also the student of Parsons. Not just any student, of course! He sensed perhaps more acutely than any before him the individualist dilemma which lay at the heart of phenomenological sociology, and he had begun to find a way out.

What I will suggest in this lecture, ironically, is that as Garfinkel's phenomenological sociology became ethnomethodology he began to lose his way. As his work became caught up in the anti-Parsonian movement of the 1960s the delicate balance upon which his synthesis depended was destroyed. Taking an explicitly anticollectivist stance, he became caught up in the individualist dilemma, and this dilemma defined the school which he named. As you might imagine, this backing away was fraught with ambiguity. While I would regard it as a movement away from a theoretically superior position, Garfinkel himself (my colleague here at UCLA) views it quite differently: as a movement toward greater insight into the true contingency of the social world. Let us begin, then, by reviewing the nature of what I consider Garfinkel's great early achievement, an achievement whose momentum carried well into the transition of his middle period.

To appreciate the difficulties that Garfinkel overcame in this early work we must remind ourselves of the dilemma that individualistic thought involves. For a theorist to maintain individualism in a clear and honest way, he must introduce fantastic randomness into his picture of how the world comes to be orderly. Basically, he must deny that patterning exists outside of any specific situation. Most theorists, however, precisely because they are sociologists, will not be satisfied with such a position, and they will move, more or less hesitantly, toward embracing some element of the collectivist alternative. Yet as long as formal commitments to individualism are maintained—as long as the theorist continues to call himself an "exchange theorist," or a "symbolic interactionist," or a "phenomenologist"—this collective reference can be introduced only in a residual way. Because it must be ad hoc it will inevitably be indeterminate, hence theoretically and empirically frustrating. The dilemma, then, is produced by being confronted with the mutually unsatisfactory choices of randomness and residual category. The tension which is produced by being stranded on these horns often leads the theorist to resort to "last instance" arguments. He suggests that, while collective dimensions may exist, in the last instance individual and contingent negotiation still creates order.

I have suggested that this dilemma defines the plight of some of the most important theoretical movements in the postwar period. Homans claimed to be satisfied with his focus on "subinstitutional" behavior, but he introduced all sorts of collective references which implicitly modified this radical position in significant ways, notions like value, investment, and justice. Blumer seemed, at first glance, to be much more satisfied with a purely individualist line, but even he brought back references to collective structures, and his attempt to confine them to sharply delimited temporal periods threatened to unravel the clear and consistent threads of his general theory. Goffman, too, seemed initially to relate social order only to the presentation of the self. He soon developed, however, a much more elaborate and satisfactory version of contingent behavior, though the systematic ambiguity in his work never entirely went away. Finally, I have shown how Husserl, the founder of phenomenology, saw his task precisely as explaining firmly established order in terms of individually constituted acts. But even he, in the later stages of his work, came to acknowledge the independent structure of the actor's environment, and while he himself rarely explained this environment by stepping outside of individualist categories his followers certainly did so. Merleau-Ponty, Schutz, and others sought to bring collectivist elements into a phenomenological sociology of the "mundane" rather than transcendental sort. Yet while their work pointed in the right direction, they did not possess, I have suggested, the theoretical resources which were necessary to pull this trick off.

Because Garfinkel had studied with both Parsons and Schutz, he could, by contrast, take some truly significant steps toward theoretical resolution. He paid detailed attention to intentional practices, but this effort seemed designed to show how omnipresent collective, supra-intentional rules—Parsons' "normative order"— really were. His emphasis on the significance of such rules, on the other hand, was grist for the phenomenological mill. For he insisted that the omnipresence of culture testified merely to how ingenuous individuals were in "constituting" the appearance of reality. A priori, noncontingent trust is fundamental to the very sensicality of an individual's life; yet this trust relies completely on the normalizing actions of single individuals. What Garfinkel is able to do here is to embrace the contingent, purely individualist element as a level of empirical analysis rather than as a presupposition of social order itself.

Despite this synthetic trust of this earlier work, there are—even here—some troubling ambiguities. Though he has clearly argued that normative rules are collective, that they are not reducable to intentions and practices, he raises the possibility in several programmatic statements that exactly the opposite may be true. In the very first page of the trust article, for example, he makes the following claim: "The way a system of activities is organized *means the same thing as* the way its organizational characteristics are being produced and maintained."[1] We might translate this as follows. "The way a system of activities is organized" refers to its rules. The way these rules—the organization—are "produced and main-

---

[1] Garfinkel, "A Conception of and Experiments with 'Trust' ", in O. J. Harvey, ed., *Motivation and Social Interaction*, (New York: Ronald Press), p. 187; italics added.

tained" refers to the constitutive practices of phenomenology. Can Garfinkel really mean that rules and individual consciousness are the same thing? This would make it impossible to view them as involving different levels of analysis and would suggest a return to the individualism of Husserl.

This ambivalence about whether contingency is, in fact, an empirical or a presuppositional fact is even more strikingly revealed in the statement which immediately follows this introductory assertion. "Structural phenomena," Garfinkel suggests, "are emergent products of . . . accomodative work whereby persons encountering from within the environments that society confronts them with establish the social structures that are the assembled products of action directed to these environments." This is a profoundly ambiguous sentence, not simply a grammatically tortured one! If structural phenomena are, indeed, merely emergent products, then they are, it is true, simply the assembled products of action. In this case, it would be perfectly fair to conclude that it is individuals who establish social structures. But such purely contingent structures cannot, at the same time, confront individuals from without. They cannot, that is, be something with which society confronts individuals.

The complex, contradictory quality of these statements does not, then, reflect simply "bad writing." If a sensitive and expressive writer contorts his prose it is usually because there is something to be contorted about. The problem here is that Garfinkel has moved back onto the horns of the individualist dilemma. Though his discussion in the essay eventually will transcend the orthodox phenomenological position, he feels compelled to begin by paying it obeisance. To aver his commitment to individualism, he must make his descriptions of collective constraint extremely indeterminate. These opening sentences are foreshadowings. When Garfinkel defined ethnomethodology in the middle 1960s this ambivalence, this sense of regret about his ecumenical orientation, became much more intense. In the essays collected in *Studies in Ethnomethodology*, published in 1967, the strain is full-blown. Garfinkel in this middle period is still, tenuously, a student of Parsons, but he is also, very clearly, a student with a bad conscience toward Schutz. The automony of normative order is asserted in this work, but it is often explained in an extraordinarily indeterminate and confusing way. Contingency is also there, and it is much more fully embraced than in the essay on trust.

I want to begin by showing how *Studies* is continuous with the earlier work, for I do not believe that the new vocabularly Garfinkel introduced as "ethnomethodology" was written with individualism exclusively in mind.

There remains in *Studies* a strong thrust of valuable synthetic theory, concepts which are designed to articulate the extraordinary empirical investigations they inform. Garfinkel declares that the subject of ethnomethodology is "accounts." Actors believe that they must be able to account for new events. Whatever they may consciously assert, Garfinkel believes, they can do so only in terms of their prior expectations, which are normatively structured common sense. The irony, then, is that these accounts are actually constitutive of the settings they purport merely to describe. Motives are not responses to conditions: rather what appear as conditions are already subjective reconstructions of whatever is "out there." Precisely this circularity allows us to understand the reproduction of norms and rules in the face of continuously changing external events and situations.

By stressing accounts, of course, Garfinkel is just saying in another way that action is "indexical," a term, you may recall, that Husserl introduced. All new objects are treated as "signs," or indexes, of prior knowledge. Garfinkel sees "indexicality" as basic for the smooth, continuous functioning of normative order. It is not atomized individuals who must offer accounts and practice indexicality, but members of collectivities. It is through "members' practices" that social action is an "accomplished familiarity." With the term "practices," Garfinkel harkens back to Husserl. With the notion of "member," he opens himself to the collectivist tradition. Indeed, Garfinkel reminds his readers in a footnote that his use of the term membership is "intended in strict accord with Talcott Parsons' usage in *The Social System*."[2] All practices occur in relation to the structures of the collectivity of which they are a part, the

---

[2] Harold Garfinkel, *Studies in Ethnomethodology* (Englewood Cliffs, N.J.: Prentice-Hall, 1967), p. 57 n. 8. Hereafter page references to *Studies in Ethnomethodology* will be given parenthetically in the text.

"background assumptions" which are the society's normative order. It is for this reason that intentional actors, Garfinkel still often suggests, "consult institutionalized aspects of the collectivity." There is, he often still acknowledges, a "common culture" from which intentional action must draw.

In one of the empirical investigations Garfinkel reports in *Studies*, he investigates how the public health staff in a suicide prevention center categorized different types of death, a procedure which was part of their work on suicide prevention. What he found was a fundamental circularity. The staff categorized the deaths in terms of the classifications which were made available to them by the center's procedures. Yet these procedures were supposed to be rational, scientific responses to the nature of the suicides themselves. "The investigators's task," Garfinkel reports, "consisted of an account of how a particular person died in society that is adequately told, sufficiently detailed, clear, etc., for all practical purposes" (p. 15). By "practical purposes" he refers to the demands and practices of a particular organization. The accounts of the staff, in other words, were less objective descriptions of actual deaths than applications or specifications of the organization's rules. This self-referential, rationalizing character extended to every organization the staff had to answer to, not just their own: "Inquirers wanted very much to be able to assume that they could come out at the end with an account of how the person died that would permit the coroner and his staff to withstand claims arguing that the account was incomplete or that the death happened differently than—or in contrast to or in contradiction of—what the members to the arrangement 'claimed' " (p. 16).

To maintain their categories in the face of the subtle but often very definite differences between various kinds of deaths, the investigators used what Garfinkel calls the documentary method. They look at the actual scraps of evidence to "document" theories they already held. "Various ways of living in society that could have terminated with that death," Garfinkel asserts, "are searched out and read 'in the remains' " (p. 17). Rational procedures, then, bear resemblance to magical practices like reading fortunes in tea leaves. If we mean by rational thought objective, reality-determined generalizations, it never occurs. To the contrary, investigative evidence is "used to formulate a recognizable coherent story, standard, typical, cogent, uniform, planful, i.e., a professionally defensible, and thereby, for members, a *recognizably* rational account" (p. 17). Since this categorizing practice must be continuously creative, and since it cannot be predicted beforehand—in a formally rational way—what an account will be, Garfinkel calls it "ad hocing." Ad hocing, he suggests, is vital to the maintenance of every collective order.

But the most extraordinary studies which Garfinkel reports were experiments he carried out with students right here at UCLA. If the Nobel Prize were awarded for sociology, these experiments surely would have qualified. Garfinkel starts with a familiar problem: how "the common sense world is possible" (p. 36). Everyday life is familiar; it is viewed by "members" with a naivety which accepts the "natural facts of life" (p. 35). From a phenomenological point of view, however, such familiarity is not just there; it is "the product of activities." To find out what these activities are, and whether they are actually necessary, Husserl urged us to make the phenomenological reduction, to bracket the "realness of reality" and see how it is actually we who give this realness its due. But Husserl recommended this abstractly and philosophically. He had no suggestions about how such a method could become a method for making phenomenological investigations in a social scientific way. The result, in Garfinkel's view, is that there is available to the sociologist so inclined "little data and few methods" (p. 36). This lack is what Garfinkel seeks to redress. He does so through what he calls "breeching experiments." They employ the methodology of social disruption. "Procedurally," Garfinkel writes, "it is my preference to start with familiar scenes and ask what can be done to make trouble" (p. 37). Trouble-making produces sociological "reflections through which the strangeness of an obstinately familiar world can be detected" (p. 38).

In one experiment Garfinkel asked students to report common conversations by writing on the left side of a sheet what the parties actually said and on the right what they and their partners understood they were really talking about. I want to reproduce his write-up of a sample conversation (pp. 38–39) so you can see exactly what he has in mind.

	Actually Said	*Understood*
HUSBAND:	Dana succeeded in putting a penny in a parking meter today without being picked up.	This afternoon as I was bringing Dana, our four-year-old son, home from the nursery school, he succeeded in reaching high enough to put a penny in a parking meter when we parked in a meter parking zone, whereas before he has always had to be picked up to reach that high.
WIFE:	Did you take him to the record store?	Since he put a penny in a meter that means that you stopped while he was with you. I know that you stopped at the record store either on the way to get him or on the way back. Was it on the way back, so that he was with you or did you stop there on the way to get him and somewhere else on the way back?
HUSBAND:	No, to the shoe repair shop.	No, I stopped at the record store on the way to get him and stopped at the shoe repair shop on the way home when he was with me.
WIFE:	What for?	I know of one reason why you might have stopped at the shoe repair shop. Why did you in fact?
HUSBAND:	I got some new shoe laces for my shoes.	As you will remember I broke a shoe lace on one of my brown oxfords the other day so I stopped to get some new laces.

| WIFE: | Your loafers need new heels badly. | Something else you could have gotten that I was thinking of. You could have taken in your black loafers which need heels badly. You'd better get them taken care of pretty soon. |

What could provide a more compelling example of real events being taken as surface signs of culturally expected meanings and, therefore, of how understanding proceeds on the basis of active structuring mechanisms in the human mind? Listen closely to how Garfinkel himself analyzes (pp. 39–40) that exchange and you will see that he uses it to point simultaneously to order and individualistic contingency.

An examination of the colloquy reveals the following. (a) There were many matters that the partners understood they were talking about that they did not mention. (b) Many matters that the partners understood were understood on the basis not only of what was actually said but what was left unspoken. (c) Many matters were understood through a process of attending to the temporal series of utterances as documentary evidences of a developing conversation rather than as a string of terms. (d) Matters that the two understood in common were understood only in and through a course of understanding work that consisted of treating an actual linguistic event as "the document of," as "pointing to," as standing on behalf of an underlying pattern of matters that each already supposed to be the matters that the person, by his speaking, could be telling the other about. The underlying pattern was not only derived from a course of individual documentary evidences but the documentary evidences in their turn were interpreted on the basis of "what was known" and anticipatorily knowable about the underlying patterns. Each was used to elaborate the other. (e) In attending to the utterances as events-in-the conversation each party made references to the biography and prospects of the present interaction which each used and attributed to the other as a common scheme of interpretation and expression. (f) Each waited for something more to be said in order to hear what had previously been talked about, and each seemed willing to wait.

In his next experiment Garfinkel reversed this procedure, and he created trouble much more directly. Instead of asking conversationalists simply to write down the intended subtext of their discussions, he asked them to try and insert this subtext into the actual conversation. The experimenter (E) was to insist that the subject (S) clarify the literal sense of every commonplace remark (pp. 42–43).

(S):   Hi, Ray. How is your girl friend feeling?

(E):   What do you mean, "How is she feeling?" Do you mean physical or mental?

(S):   I mean how is she feeling? What's the matter with you? *(He looked peeved.)*

(E):   Nothing. Just explain a little clearer what do you mean?

(S):   Skip it. How are your Med School applications coming?

(E):   What do you mean, "How are they?"

(S):   You know what I mean.

(E):   I really don't.

(S):   What's the matter with you? Are you sick?

What seems to be happening here is that the subject's sense of reality is challenged because, suddenly, he cannot assume that his speech is treated as an "intended event" by the (experimenter) partner. What Garfinkel has done is to prevent the experimenter from employing normal constitutive practices. The result is that social order breaks down. Faced with disintegration, the personality experiences anxiety. Garfinkel reports (p. 43) how, in response to experimental questioning, one subject responded with "Why are you asking me those questions?" and repeated this two or three times after each question.

> She became nervous and jittery, her face and hand movements [became] uncontrolled. She appeared bewildered and complained that I was making her nervous and demanded that I "Stop it" . . . The subject picked up a magazine and covered her face. She put down the magazine and pretended to be engrossed. When asked why she was looking at the magazine

she closed her mouth and refused any further remarks. (p. 43)

Though Garfinkel conducted other experiments, the ones I have described to you certainly make his point. The orderly interaction of people, the stability of their personalities and emotions, the continuity of their symbol systems—all seem to depend on the actor's use of constituting procedures and on his assumption that they are equally employed by others. Whatever the eccentricity of Garfinkel's method and the iconoclasm of the ethnomethdological movement which took it up, this is the heart of its synthesizing achievement. And while I will suggest in a moment that this achievement is drastically undermined even in the book that most successfully displayed it, there are significant currents even in contemporary ethnomethodology which continue this attempt to link individual intentional techniques with a theory of normative culture.

In all of this work the attention on "members' practices" illuminates new levels of empirical analysis. It is not the basis for an alternative to collectivist sociology, not taken as the necessary presupposition for a completely individualistic understanding of social order. Perhaps the most systematicaly developed example of this nonindividualistic kind of ethnomenthodology is Cicourel's. In *Cognitive Sociology* he criticizes collectivist sociologies for "not address[ing] *how* the actor recognizes what is taken to be standard, 'familiar,' 'acceptable.'[3] He is suggesting the need for a new level of empirical analysis to be brought into play. I believe that Cicourel himself exaggerates the importance of such intentional rules. He argues that they supply the "deep structure" of norms and values and the "critical" feature of all role behavior. In doing so, however, he ignores the illuminations of intentionality which have been developed outside of the phenomenological tradition, for example, in Freud's theory of defense mechanisms or in Mead's theory of the act. Nonetheless, Cicourel has utilized Garfinkel's middle period ideas to explore significantly new aspects of normative order in the social world. In their study of mass media, sociologists like Molotch and Tuchman have similarly made good use of them. They have

---

[3] Aaron Cicourel, *Cognitive Sociology* (New York: Free Press 1974), p. 16; italics added.

suggested that newspaper reporters do not so much discover new empirical facts as normalize them, that they use the documentary method to demonstrate and specify preexisting expectations.[4] In a similar vein, Leiter has shown how teachers, without knowing their students, "read in" expectations in such a way that they interpret their students' actions in ways that sustain the often self-defeating normative order of the classroom.[5] Zimmerman has shown how welfare agencies transform client records that are fragmentary and contradictory into hard and fast records that simply reproduce conventional expectations about their behavior.[6] Kitsuse has shown how the social control of deviance involves finding ways of documenting prior expectations—a notion that converges with labeling theory, which I described earlier as a variant of symbolic interaction.[7] Pollner and Zimmerman have shown how supposedly objective social science relies on concepts which are indexical for both scientists and subjects and which, for this reason, often reproduce the commonsense knowledge of a given society rather than reveal how it works from a rational and independent position.[8]

My interpretation of such ethnomethodological studies seems obvious enough, but it actually bears little relation to how ethnomethodology has been viewed by most of its supporters and critics alike. As I have described these studies, they form a crucial supplement to the kind of voluntaristic and multidimensional theory that Parsons tried to lay out. Since it is my frank intention in these lectures to widen and elaborate such a theory—and in the process to go beyond Parsons' relatively narrow version of it—you might say my interpretation of ethnomethodology is itself merely an "account," as Garfinkel uses that term. Still, I think Garfinkel would himself once have agreed with my interpretation. In those

---

[4] Harvey Molotch, "News as Purposive Behavior," *American Sociological Review* (1974); 39: 101–112; Gaye Tuchman, *Making News* (New York: Free Press, 1978).

[5] Kenneth Leiter, "Adhocing in Schools," in Aaron Cicourel et al., *Language Use and School Performance* (New York: Academic Press 1976), pp. 17–73.

[6] Don H. Zimmerman. "Tasks and Troubles: The Practical Bases of Work Activities in a Public Assistance Agency," in D. A. Hansen, ed., *Explorations in Sociology and Counseling* (New York: Houghton Mifflin, 1969).

[7] John Kitsuse, "Social Reactions to Deviant Behavior," in Donald Cressey and David Ward, eds., *Crime and Social Process*, (New York: Harper and Row, 1969), pp. 590–602.

[8] Zimmerman and Melvin Pollner, "The Everyday World as a Phenomenon," in Jack Douglas, ed., *Understanding Everyday Life* (Chicago: Aldine, 1970), pp. 80–103.

earlier days he was hailing the convergence of sociology and phenomenology. This is not at all the case now. This shift has something to do with the way in which Garfinkel's work became involved in the rebellions of the 1960s. To understand how this might have occurred, however, we must try first to explain the shift intellectually, by scrutinizing the theoretical ambiguities, indeed the contradictions, in Garfinkel's most important work.

In the very midst of this rich and elaborate conceptualization of a new level of empirical analysis—the level of contingency which articulates culture and intentionality—Garfinkel suggests in *Studies* that ethnomethodology should, in fact, not be viewed as "empirical" illumination at all. He proposes it as a counter theory of order, as an individualistic theory that is an alternative rather than a complement to the collectivist Parsonian tradition. To understand the shift, we need only study closely Garfinkel's treatment—or rather his two treatments—of the intentional practice he calls ad hocing.

We have seen how Garfinkel utilizes this notion in a way that makes it parallel to what Mead, Peirce or Parsons would call signification. An actor, encountering an object, takes it as a sign, or symbol, which represents or signifies the relation of a more general system of meaning to his particular circumstance. To see the collective implications of this, just think, for a moment, how different it is from Goffman's dismissive reference to "signifying" in the early pages of *Presentation of Self* (see my discussion above, p. 231). By calling this use of symbols "ad hocing," however, Garfinkel is also calling attention to the fact that the meaning of contingent objects cannot be logically deduced beforehand, but must be constituted afresh in each situation. To engage in ad hocing, then, is to use some new object indexically. This approach to ad hocing clearly exemplifies Garfinkel's synthetic ambition. It neatly combines contingency with the importance of sustaining collective order. Garfinkel describes, for example, how a graduate student "coder" engages in ad hocing in the course of the research he is doing on a clinic's files. "He treats actual folder contents"— the material he is to code—"as standing in a relationship of trusted signification to the 'system' in the clinic activities—the organization to which the folder contents refer" (p. 22).

Because the coder assumes the "position" of a competent
member to the arrangements that he seeks to give an account
of, he can "see the system" in the actual content of the folder.
[The Coder] must treat actual folder contents as standing
proxy for the social-order-in-and-of-clinic-activities. Actual
folder contents stand to the socially ordered ways of clinic
activities as *representation* of them; they do not describe the
order, nor are they evidences of the order. It is the coder's
use of the folder documents as *sign-functions* to which I mean
to be pointing in saying that the coder must know the order
of the clinic's activities that he is looking at in order to
recognize the actual contents as an appearance-of-the-order.
(pp. 22-23)

Yet only a few pages later, Garfinkel tries to break this vital
connection between the practice of ad hocing and the broader,
cultural referent upon which it is based. "Suppose," he writes, that
"we drop the assumption that in order to describe a usage as a
feature of a community of understandings we must at the outset
know what the substantive common understandings consist of" (p.
28). To drop this assumption, however, is not a casual thing. It
has enormous implications. It would mean that the whole theory
of symbolism would be eliminated, for symbol theory assumes a
social-cultural referent for gestures and acts. Garfinkel realizes this.
Indeed, it is just what he intends: "With it, drop [also] the assumption's accompanying theory of signs, according to which a
'sign' and 'referent' are respectively properties of something said
and something talked about, and which in this fashion proposes
sign and referent to be related as corresponding contents" (p. 28).
To cut the relation between what is said and what is talked about
is to sever the relation between individual action and collective
order. Garfinkel knew this as well: "By dropping such a theory of
signs we drop as well, thereby, the possibility that an invoked
shared agreement on substantive matters explains a usage." We
are left with Goffman's pure manipulations of impressions, for all
that is left, of course, is the individual's intentional practices themselves: "If these notions are dropped, then *what* the parties talked
about could not be distinguished from *how* the parties were speaking" (p. 28; italics mine).

In this statement Garfinkel makes a sharp and, I believe, fateful move toward individualism. He is suggesting that the contents of what people talk about—the meaning of what they are saying— can be understood without reference to the broader normative or cultural framework within which they speak. If the sign can be separated from the cultural referent, then to understand the meaning of the sign we are left only with the techniques of individual consciousness. Garfinkel now maintains that the meaning of a sign is the simple and direct product of such interactional techniques. To understand meaning he refers to the constitutive gestures Husserl called analogy and pairing, to which Garfinkel adds some more of his own.

> An explanation of *what* the parties were talking about would then consist entirely of describing *how* the parties had been speaking; of furnishing a method for saying whatever is to be said, like talking synonymously, talking ironically, talking metaphorically, talking cryptically, talking narratively, talking in a questioning or answering way, lying, glossing, double-talking, and the rest. (p. 28–29; italics mine)

"The recognized sense of what a person said," Garfinkel now concludes, "consists only and entirely in recognizing the method of this speaking, of *seeing how he spoke*" (p. 29).

This movement embraces individualism as a presuppositional position rather than simply as a level of empirical analysis, and it transforms a path-breaking, synthetic insight into a dubious, one-sided presumption. The fact that a speaker uses synonym, irony, and metaphor, it seems to me, actually tells us nothing about what was said; it simply allows us to understand how this "what" was produced. It is precisely by this insistence on breaking apart signs and their referents—practices from rules—that Garfinkel can insist in *Studies* that social structures are completely emergent from individual gestures. What follows from this is decisive for the theoretical tradition he founded: ethnomethodology need not follow "sociology" in the attention to rules and institutionalized culture. "Organized social arrangements," Garfinkel now writes, "*consist of* various methods for accomplishing the accountability of a setting's organizational ways" (pp. 33–34, italics mine). This kind of one-sided phraseology came to typify ethnomethodology in its sectarian phase.

With this radical individualism, Garfinkel moves away from Parsons and Schutz, and back toward the "pure" phenomenology of Husserl. Whereas the synthetic strand of his work extends and makes much more substantial Mead's understanding of attitude, this individualistic strand takes a more Blumerian turn. For here Garfinkel wants to locate meanings in situationally specific individual response. When he argues, for example, that "recognizable sense . . . is not independent of the socially organized occasions for their use" (p. 3), he is denying the collective implications of indexicality which he had earlier labored to conceive. According to the notion of indexicality, a priori, situationally independent sources of sense are precisely the background for ascertaining the meaning of any particular occasion. Similarly, when Garfinkel argues that "rational features [of an organization] *consist of* what members do" (p. 3; italics mine), he is eliminating the very collective referents which had allowed him to avoid the randomizing, asocial qualities of earlier phenomenology. In his studies of coding and suicide, by contrast, he had assumed that cultural rationality set a standard of legitimate order to which ongoing "members' actions" constantly repaired. Now he has reduced his theory to a pragmatism of the purely experiential kind. He wants to eliminate from it culture, rules, symbols, and even "common sense." All that is left is action and experience. As he writes in the very first line of *Studies,* introducing a chapter that was clearly written just before publication: "The following studies seek to treat *practical* activities, *practical* circumstances, and *practical* sociological reasoning" (p. 1; italics mine). This reduction to the practical makes Garfinkel's later work fundamentally similar to the tradition of symbolic interactionism which it had sought to replace.

This turn in Garfinkel's work established the official self-understanding of the ethnomethodological movement. To see why and how this happened we need some historical background. Garfinkel named this movement during the early 1960s, and it was during this same period that the movement became enormously controversial. This controversy—and the anti-Parsonian alternative the movement apparently offered—attracted younger students, whose support pushed ethnomethodology further in an anti-collectivist direction. Much more than Garfinkel himself, these younger students viewed "ethno" as a reaction against the reigning functionalist sociology of the day. This aspect is what allowed it, after all, to assume a rebellious and even revolutionary thrust. There is an irony here. For as ethnomethodology became more individualistic and anti-normative—more anti-Parsonian—the potentially most significant parts of Garfinkel's theory melted away. To champion ethnomethodology now became equivalent to rejecting sociology, which was quite rightly identified as a discipline with a more collectivist thrust. Whether or not such pure individualism actually characterized ethnomethodological studies in fact, it certainly came to inform their understanding in theory. Indeed, while each of the studies I have referred to above—by Cicourel, Zimmerman, Kitsuse, Pollner, Leider, et al.—does contain a significant reference to collective norms, each presents the "revolutionary" nature of its findings not in terms of the relation between intentionality and belief but in terms of its illumination of individual practices alone.

When I discussed the other individualistic challenges to Parsons' theory I showed how each sought to justify itself by constructing of Parsons a "straw man." This was necessary, first, simply because every new movement in the postwar period had to deal with the hegemony of Parsons' work. You could not ignore Parsons; you had to criticize him and build your alternative directly upon this critique. For this reason, Rex had to construct a "Parsons" of his own. This "conflict Parsons" was not necessarily Parsons himself; in the real theory, after all, quite a bit about conflict can be found. Much the same strategy was invoked by his individualistic challengers. Parsons was anti-individualistic only in the presuppositional sense. In principle, his theory allowed contingency and individuality to be inserted at the level of the empirical unit act, as Garfinkel's earlier phenomenological sociology amply showed. To justify their radical version of individualism, however, Parsons' challengers felt compelled to present their work as the only possible path by which contingency could be conceptualized. This meant they had to present Parsons as if he allowed no individual freedom at all.

We meet this straw man in the heart of Garfinkel's *Studies*. While he never names Parsons directly, the reference was obvious not only to his students but to the sociological profession as a whole. What Garfinkel says is that "social science theorists" have created the image of the actor as a "dope." They have used the "fact of standardization"—the fact that action does follow norms and does reveal collective order—to judge the character of actions "that comply with standardized expectancies." Social science theorists have, in other words, used the fact of norm compliance to assume that action has a compliant character, that it is passive and conformistic rather than active and constructing. Theorists have "neglected the fact that by these same actions persons discover, create, and sustain this standardization."

> By "cultural dope" I refer to the man-in-the-sociologist's-society who produces the stable features of the society by acting in compliance with preestablished and legitimate alternatives of action that the common culture provides. The "psychological dope" is the man-in-the-psychologist's-society who produces the stable features of the society by choices among alternative courses of action that are compelled on the grounds of psychiatric biography, conditioning history, and the variables of mental functioning. The common feature in the use of these "models of man" is the fact that courses of common sense rationalities of judgment which involve the person's use of common sense knowledge of social structures over the temporal "succession" of here and now situations are treated as epiphenomenal (pp. 66–67).

Garfinkel wants us to believe that Parsons sees actors as dopes. He presents established theory as if it portrays people as utterly determined by society, as following a rule for its own sake without interpretive, personalizing work. In fact, Garfinkel implies, Parsons did not really care about actors or action at all; he viewed culture and society as being carried out automatically, with actors as a mere passive medium. This is much the same anti-collectivist straw man that we found in Blumer's and Homans' accounts. It is a far cry from what I described as the "level of analysis" critique which, rather than attacking Parsons as anti-individualist, applauds his inclusion of the actor while insisting that the level of contingency is not by any means adequately spelled out.

Garfinkel's straw man was eagerly seized upon by his followers and students. In a widely cited article from 1970, for example, Wilson claimed that there were two completely different paradigms in sociology, the normative and the interpretive. He associated the normative with Parsonian functionalism, and he described it as conceiving of the actor's relation to norms in a completely fixed, rigid, and formal way. Wilson claims, by contrast, that ethnomethodology sees meaning as resting entirely on actors' interpretations, not on the fixed meaning of norms themselves.

> In the interpretive view of social interaction, in constrast with the normative paradigm, definitions of situations and actions are not explicitly or implicitly assumed to be settled once and for all by literal application of a preexisting, culturally established system of symbols. Rather, the meanings of situations and actions are interpretations formulated on particular occasions by the participants in the interaction and are subject to reformulation on subsequent occasions.[9]

Even Wilson, however, cannot escape the individualist dilemma. He wants to include collective elements, but he can do so only in a residual way.

> Role-taking in interaction is a process in which the participants engage in documentary interpretation of each other's actions such that the underlying pattern consists of the context of their interaction, . . . of which the particular actions are seen as expressions. . . . Moreover, this context itself is seen for what it is through the same actions it is used to interpret. That is, on any particular occasion in the course of the interaction, the actions that the participants see each other performing are seen as such in terms of the meaning of the context, and the context in turn is understood to be what it is through these same actions.[10]

This is thoroughly indeterminate. You cannot, I believe, have it both ways.

[9] Thomas P. Wilson, "Normative and Interpretive Paradigms in Sociology," in Jack Douglas, ed., *Understanding Everyday Life*, p. 69.
[10] *Ibid.*, pp. 68–69.

The notion that functionalism viewed meaning as fixed and formal, as basically identical with rules in the written, bureaucratic, and legal sense, became firmly entrenched as ethnomethodology flourished in the 1970s. The straw man even creeps into Cicourel's work, which in other respects seems to offer such a sensible, level-of-analysis critique. Justifying his more interpretive, action-oriented position, he suggests that, contrary to Parsons' view, actors do not have "scripts" which outline their roles "in detail." He scores Parson for implying that action is guided by "explicit norms or rules."[11] The most elaborate application of the straw man justification appeared in the first real textbook of ethnomethodology, which was written by Leiter and appeared in 1980. "Conventional sociologists," Leiter writes, "view rules as objective statements with meanings that are clear and precise." From this bold proposition, he goes on to describe functionalist theory, in the person of Robert Merton, as proposing "that the objective consequences of action are independent of the subjective meanings that prompted them." Finally, he draws the logical conclusion that for mainstream sociology meaning does not actually matter at all. It is completely objectivist, caring not a wit for "what the members of an organization think."[12]

It seems absurd to me to understand the functionalist approach to meaning in this way. As I indicated in one of my early lectures, Parsons came to the notion of norm through his conception of the actor as continuously engaged in interpretation. He inferred, quite legitimately, that interpretation involves standards, and he called these standards norms. It is true, of course, that Parsons spent most of his career describing systems of norms and their interrelation with other systems and gave little attention to the process of interpretation itself. This does not mean, however, that he severed the relation between norm and interpretation. Nor does it mean that he conceived rules as somehow outside the actor; that would have given them exactly the kind of determinate, objective status that Parsons reserved for material things. In his ethnomethodology textbook, Leiter argues that "norms, rules, [and] motives"

---

[11] Cicourel, *Cognitive Sociology*, p. 17.
[12] Kenneth Leiter, *A Primer on Ethnomethodology* (New York: Oxford, 1980), pp. 18, 16 and 17.

are not "causal agents," suggesting instead that "they are tools societal members use to create a sense of social structure."[13] He cites Blumer and Turner as among the few established theorists who might agree. In fact, it would be hard to find a statement that better fitted Parsons' own theoretical program!

Armed with this straw man, and the sense of revolutionary mission it justified, ethnomethodology became known primarily for its radically contingent thrust. In the 1960s and early 1970s this image often camouflaged more truly synthetic work. In the subsequent period, image and conduct became more closely aligned. Two different strands of individualistic theorizing have emerged. One concerns itself with meaning orientation, the other more with situated, material practice.

Pollner's recent work follows closely Garfinkel's later individualist turn, and it also continues to preoccupy itself with meaning as such. In an article provocatively entitled "Explicative Transactions: Making and Managing Meaning in Traffic Court," Pollner gives us an elegant, rich ethnography of the enormous interpretive efforts that everyday life entails, even in the well-institutionalized location of a court of law. Because action is temporal, Pollner insists, it is also contingent, and actors must employ a repertoire of techniques to enable meaning to proceed. They make examples of legal points; they take exception in a vocal and often dramatic way; they make issues visible and concrete; they arrange and rearrange temporal sequences; they carefully try to maintain the consistent "horizons" of their actions. Yet Pollner wishes to do more than describe intentional techniques in an ethnographic setting. He believes he is analyzing how the meaning of the courtroom experience is created as such. He proposes that the meaning of what goes on in a traffic court is, quite simply, the product of the interactive techniques so described. "What one does next," he writes, "will be seen as defining the import or significance of what another did before."[14]

But can significance—"what one does"—really be so shorn of collective referent? A succeeding action can define my own only

---

[13] *Ibid.*, p. 192.
[14] Melvin Pollner, "Explicative Transactions: Making and Managing Meaning in Traffic Court," in G. Psathas, ed., *Studies in Everyday Language* (New York: Irvington, 1979), pp. 227–255.

insofar as both mine and the succeeding act refer to, and can be clearly interpreted by, an elaborate and complex cultural system of prior, supra-interactional meaning. Is the judge in a court "constituting" meanings, as Pollner suggests, or is he, with significant individual variation, "enacting" them? Let's take the judge who expresses incredulity in response to an advocate who has reacted to a guilty plea in an acrimonious, uncivil way. Is this judge "inventing" the meaning of "legitimate" legal behavior, or is he merely using normalizing techniques to ensure that ongoing events conform to well-established norms about what legal behavior "should be"? Pollner concludes his paper by lauding Mead's insistence that the meaning of an act is determined by the response. You may recall that I identified this radical pragmatism in Mead's work as a regretable departure from his more synthetic thought. This reference to Mead shows how later ethnomethodology has moved back toward the individualist tradition which it originally opposed.

In the later period of his career Garfinkel himself has published relatively little. He has confined his public efforts, in the main, to being a *maître* of students who themselves have articulated his later position in effective ways. What he has published, however, indicates not only a more contingent but a more "material" approach. Garfinkel and his students now study what they call "work," the details of practical action in highly circumscribed natural settings. An essay published on science in 1981 throws some light on what his new vocabulary actually implies. In studying how the initial scientific observations of the optical pulsar came to be made, Garfinkel, Lynch, and Livingston insist that they are concerned only with the "*in situ* . . efficacy" of the scientists' actions. Without reference to scientific norms, either formal or informal, or to the paradigmatic or thematically prior expectations of the scientists themselves, they suggest that "the properties that their [the scientists'] competent practices have in local production" are completely "interactionally produced." Their study focuses on the tools and instruments the scientists used, the words they spoke and the notes they took, on the "worldly objects" that allowed "embodied practice." It was this physically embodied practice, they claim, that allowed "the pulsar's existing *material* shape."[15] What could be further from the cultural reference of early ethnomethodology? In this later work, actors do not internalize culture or rules. They react to physical things which are outside of them, things to which their creative action gives some orderly shape.

Probably the most conspicuous corpus of later work which has given up the theory of cultural signification is the "conversation analysis" first initiated by Sacks and Schegloff. According to this perspective, it is entirely the nature of the conversational situation that determines the actions of each speaker. This situation consist of speakers, the visibility or lack of visibility of those conversing, and of such interactional exigencies as the necessity for alternating speakers without excessive gaps or overlaps or for changing a subject without losing continuity. Not only is the culturally prescribed, a priori meaning of language considered irrelevant, but meaning itself has dropped completely from concern. This branch of later ethnomethodology is more positivistic and latently materialistic than any other, though it can range from the focus on individual decisions to a more collectivist concern for the "speech exchange systems" which allocates turns in an "economy of interaction."[16]

There is a certain sense in which Garfinkel's entire career embodies the strains of the individualist dilemma. He began with a firm conviction about the constituting activity of the individual, but for a long time he showed a remarkable ability to constrain this thrust within a framework that acknowledged the independent power of collective norms. In this phase of his work the tension produced by the dilemma proved enormously productive. It motivated Garfinkel to articulate the individual-society relation in a profound and original way. Even in this early work, however, claims about the ultimate determinacy of individual behavior were not entirely repressed, and in the turmoil of the 1960s they came to

[15] Harold Garfinkel, Michael Lynch, and Eric Livingston, "The Work of a Discovering Science Construed with Materials from an Optically Discovered Pulsar," *Philosophy of Social Science* (1981, pp. 131–158, italics added).

[16] Anita Pomerantz, "The Social Organization of Enforcement Systems," Department of Sociology, UCLA, 1980; and Harvey Sacks, Emmanuel A. Schegloff, and Gail Jefferson, "A Simplest Systematics for the Organization of Turn-Taking for Conversations," *Language* (1974), 50:696–725.

the surface and began to dominate the work. As Garfinkel became more of an individualist, his references to collective order became more indeterminate and ad hoc. Later, when individualism became more unequivocally accepted, the theory was rethought so that it could display the contingent sources of order in a more consistent way.

There is no doubt that this later thrust represents a genuine humanism in an ideolgocial sense. It embodies the revolutionary vision of the 1960s: structure is completely open for human beings to shape and control. Whether this moral humanism is theoretically justified, I have suggested, is something else again.

LECTURE SIXTEEN
CULTURAL SOCIOLOGY (1): THE HERMENEUTIC CHALLENGE

WE HAVE SPENT some time on the postwar challenges to Parsons—more time, by now, than on Parsonian theory itself. You should have some sense of the "theoretical structure" of the postwar period. This may be a good time to take stock.

The story of sociological theory after World War II is, in one sense, the story of the rise and fall of the "Parsonian empire." But Parsons' "fall," of course, was also a rise, for it was brought about by new theories that gained intellectual popularity and authority in their own right. Despite their opposition to functionalism, however, all these theories have been tied to Parsons' in central ways.

The irony of this postwar period is that Parsons was hoisted by his own petard. He set theoretical standards for good theory which he himself could not meet. He demanded that theory be ecumenical and synthetic, that it incorporate, through its analytic virtuosity, rational and nonrational elements of action and voluntary and coercive aspects of order at the same time. But Parsons himself, we have seen, was not quite up to this task. While setting forth a multidimensional standard, he slid back toward a more exclusively normative kind of analysis, and he never filled out the nature of individual effort in anything like a substantive way.

The theories which challenged Parsons' hegemony did not develop purely for theoretical reasons. Institutional and ideological forces had changed. There were new sociology departments in the

United States, and European sociology had begun to revive. By the end of the 1950s, optimism about the welfare state had begun to fade.

But whatever the nonintellectual sources that fueled these challenges, they could only proceed upon the terrain of theory itself. Parsons' challengers confirmed his own theoretical ambitions in an ironic way: each of the movements we have considered focused on a segment of Parsonian theory which had not, in their view, received a "balanced" treatment from Parsons' himself. Rex and Homans challenged Parsons' conception of action, arguing that it did not pay sufficient attention to rational efficiency. Yet, while they agreed about action, they mounted their criticism from very different positions about order. For Rex, a good theory aggregates individually rational actions and focuses on the objective conditions which restrict them, conditions which Rex called systems of allocation. It is this collective force which allocates the means for individuals. Homans, by contrast, talks about rationality in terms of efficient individual action itself. His focus is rationalizing effort, and it is efforts, not systems, which are the crucial determinant of means.

If we put Homans and Rex together we have the theoretical elements of effort, means, and conditions. Because these represent only a subset of the components of the "unit act" Parsons identified in *The Structure of Social Action,* you might well ask, what exactly has been gained? My answer would be that, in principle, nothing at all. But *only* "in principle." The great multidimensional status of the "unit act" was a promise never fully carried out. Because it was not, post-Parsonian theorists interested in what was neglected had to start over again. They did so, however, without Parsons' ecumenical commitment to theoretical integration—"in principle." Their theories were reductionist. They concentrated on certain presuppositional commitments over others, and they vied for theoretical domination by claiming that their particular part was more important than any whole.

Where one challenge to "functionalism" emerges from instrumentalist theories which take different approaches to order, the other arises from individualistic theories which adopt different approaches to action. Interactionism, ethnomethodology, and exchange theory all challenge the reality of Parsons' commitment to the individual. All three emphasize effort in the sense of free will, a pure rather than qualified voluntarism. Interactionism and ethnomethodology are not concerned, as Homans is, with effort as efficiency, but with effort as interpretation. People act on the basis of their subjective expectations—the ends to which they are personally committed—rather than in terms of objective conditions. Actors are concerned with ends, not means. These challenges, then, add a crucial element to the theory deposited by the instrumentalist challenges—the notion of effort as the pursuit of ends. We now have effort, means, ends, and conditions.

By reconstructing these challenges to Parsons in this quasi-cumulative way we have, I think, discovered something quite striking. On the one hand, each challenge sought to best Parsons' system by emphasizing the overriding importance of a particular part. These universally one-sided emphases led to a terrific revival of the "warring schools" which Parsons sought to avoid. Ignoring, for the moment, the anti-Parsonian ambition of these theories, it is easy to understand how such one-sided theorizing comes about. Reality is multivalent. At first glance it seems to be composed of objects which differ widely from one another and are, therefore, in great disarray. It is for this reason that "partial theories" always arise. On the other hand, if we put these partial theories side by side we can see not only that each contributes to our understanding of reality in a different way, but that, taken together, they provide an outline of the larger whole itself. Reality, it seems, is multidimensional. If one theory becomes influential by taking up one part of reality, a succeeding theory will have to move toward an emphasis on another. Yet, judging from this postwar period, the possibilities for emphasis are far from infinite; indeed, they are relatively simple and few. When Parsons set out to investigate reality, he pointed to certain elements. His critics, when they set out to challenge his theory, ended up by pointing to the same things in different ways. This convergence helps convince us that effort, means, ends, and conditions really are "there." If they are not conceptualized from the outset by an act of ecumenical synthesis, they will all be brought back in the end through theoretical critique.[1]

---

[1] In *Theoretical Logic in Sociology* (Berkeley and Los Angeles: University of California Press, 1982–83), I showed that the students of Marx, Durkheim, Weber, and, indeed, Parsons, all tried to revise their masters' work by emphasizing the dimensions of reality which they themselves had underemphasized.

But if reality is really so multidimensional, and if it is really so structurally simple at the same time, you might well ask what has happened to the element that Parsons called norms? This, of course, was precisely the element that Parsons most emphasized, so it is no wonder that if norms are an issue in post-Parsonian disussion they would come in only at the very end. That norms "really" are there is demonstrated by the way in which their exclusion created problems for the post-Parsonian theories we have considered thus far. Rex tried to exclude the "superstructure" from conflict theory but in his attempt to explain the truce brought common culture back in by the side door. Homans attacked the very existence of norms but found that, in spite of himself, he had to relate discrimination and value to traditions and to peer group culture. Blumer tried to relate action only to self-interpretation but even he acknowledges, periodically, that culture and values actually exist outside the individual. Just so, Goffman could not discuss idealization without also referring to the value of which action was supposed to be the idealization. Garfinkel, at least through his middle period work, found it impossible to deal with practices without rules; his insistence on doing just that in the later writing made culture a residual category and ethnomethodology an internally contradictory, much more narrowly defined tradition.

Each of these post-Parsonian theories, then, has made culture into a residual category. That this has been necessary demonstrates that there is, indeed, an empty space to be filled. Each theory has been forced, in its own ad hoc way, to cover the missing "general," the supra-individual collective element which orders action in a nonmaterial way. Either because of an insistence on the purely efficient character of action, an emphasis on the individual character of order, or both, none has been able to acknowledge this element forthrightly.

Whether post-Parsonian theory really adds up to a reconstructed (and better) version of multidimensional theory—a new theoretical synthesis—depends on whether we can also find in this movement a new way of talking about normative culture. Has there been a post-Parsonian theory which has, in fact, made culture its object? I believe that there has. In the midst of the theoretical challenges I have described there developed a critique from a different direction altogether. Rather than accusing Parsons of being anti-individualistic, this critique accused him of not being anti-individualistic enough.[2] Rather than seeing him as anti-instrumental, this critique accused him actually of being too utilitarian.[3] This was the cultural critique of Parsons. It can be seen as a revival of the ancient "hermeneutical" tradition, and it provides just the kind of critical, normative revitalization we have sought. It is no more synthetic than the other theories we have examined, but the residue it leaves—a strong "theory of culture"—will allow us to complete the multidimensional theory which we have been rebuilding from the critiques each side of the anti-Parsonian movement has developed in turn.

In describing this hermeneutical tradition I will draw on various sources, on the German philosopher Wilhelm Dilthey, who wrote in the late nineteenth and early twentieth centuries, on the contemporary writings of the French phenomenologist, Paul Ricoeur, and on the American cultural anthropologist, Clifford Geertz. Dilthey's writings set the formal course for this tradition, and in modern thought the philosophical justification of hermeneutics remains rooted in German idealism. Germany is the country that reacted most strongly against the individualistic and rationalistic tendencies of the French and English Enlightenment. From Hegel onward, German philosophers argued, against the Enlightenment's democratic theory, that individuals should not be considered the basic units of the state. They argued, to the contrary, that individuals are bound by traditions and the "spirit," not merely by formal laws and explicit constraints. This romantic reaction against the Enlightenment was more broadly conceived as an attack on the materialism which German theorists found at the root of French and English arguments for the superiority of modern societies.

Toward the end of the nineteenth century, Dilthey systematized these ideas, developing an argument for a "cultural science" whose

---

[2] This is the charge against Parsons from the culturalist perspective of "structuralism." See Ino Rossi, in *From the Sociology of Symbols to the Sociology of Signs* (New York: Columbia University Press, 1983), e.g., pp. 91–95. I will refer to this particular version of the critique in lecture seventeen.

[3] This is the charge leveled by Clifford Geertz in "Ideology as Cultural System," in David E. Apter, ed., *Ideology and Discontent* (New York: Free Press, 1964), pp. 47–76. I will discuss this criticism as well in the lecture that follows.

mission directly opposed what he took to be the "materialism" of the natural scientific approach. Dilthey viewed natural science as embodying the abstract rationality of modern technology and materialism. The study of human societies, he believed, must be protected against this method; to do otherwise would be to fall victim to modern materialism itself. In the sciences which study man and society, the object is culture, something ideal rather physical. "The human studies," he declared, "must be related differently to the mental and the physical aspects of man."[4] Because natural science focuses on physical things, like spatial relationships, it can use exact methods of measurements—its objects are visible to the naked eye, and, therefore, move about in visible space. For the human studies, however, things are quite different.

> When we look at the procedure for singling out systems of interaction in the human studies we see the great difference from that which enabled the sciences to be enormously successful. The sciences are based on the spatial relationships of phenomena. The discovery of exact general laws becomes possible because what extends or moves in space can be counted or measured. But the inner system of interactions is superimposed by thought and its basic elements cannot be observed. (p. 201)

This distinction between the internal and external, between physical and emotional, pervades Dilthey's thought. He does not deny that physical things like technology exist, but he reduces them to mere conduits for the expression of subjective intentions and moods. For example, he acknowledges that "the chemical effects of gunpowder are as much part of the course of modern war as the moral qualities of the soldiers who stand in its smoke" (p. 172). He insists, however, that for human studies "there is a tendency, which grows stronger and stronger as they develop, to relegate the physical side of events to the role of conditions and means of comprehension." Make no mistake about it. Dilthey is not just engaging in description:

---

[4] Dilthey, "The Construction of the Historical World in the Human Studies," in H. P. Rickman, ed., *Dilthey: Selected Writings* (Cambridge: Cambridge University Press, 1976), p. 171. Hereafter page references to *Dilthey* will be given parenthetically in the text.

he is making a recommendation. He feels it is quite right not to analyze technology as a cause in itself, for it is, in his view, only the physical embodiment of an inward, mental state. The human studies must follow the "movement of understanding from the external to the internal." Technology—and other material expressions of life—should be studied not in terms of its physical impact but "in order to understand the mental content from which it arises" (p. 172). Compare Dilthey's "culturalist" perspective on political and economic phenomena that follows with the conflict and exchange perspective, which takes these same factors to be the central and constituting elements of social life.

> In history we read of economic activities, settlements, wars and the creating of states. They fill our souls with great images and tell us about the historical world which surrounds us: but what moves us, above all, in these accounts is what is inaccessible to the senses and can only be experienced inwardly; this is inherent in the outer events which originate from it and, in its turn, is affected by them. The tendency I am speaking of does not depend on looking at life from the outside but is based on life itself. For all that is valuable in life is contained in what can be experienced. (p. 172)

Dilthey, then, has a resolutely anti-instrumental perspective on action. He presupposes action as creative and emotive. This perspective leads him to an irredemiably subjective approach to the objects of knowledge. Because experience is the central fact of life, the first and in some ways the most important thing we ever try to understand is ourselves. "Though experience presents us with the reality of life in its many ramifications," he writes, "we only seem to know one particular thing, namely our own life" (p. 186).

This anti-instrumental subjectivism sounds much like the self-indicating action of Blumer and like various forms of phenomenological theory as well. Hermeneutics has, indeed, often been placed in the same "interpretive" camp. But Dilthey is really getting at something quite different. For him the actor's subjectivism is the beginning, not the end. If our primary experience is of ourselves, he asks, how do we—either as actors or analysts—ever find our way to understanding one another? How is it possible, moreover, for us to become part of organizations outside of ourselves which require cooperation? This is the problem of order, and what Dilthey is asking is whether the radically subjectivist approach to action necessitates an individualist approach to order. His answer is that it does not. The subjective nature of experience and the search for personal understanding are inherently related to the possibility for cooperation. Because we are primarily *experiencing* the world, Dilthey insists, we are always trying to understand others, not only ourselves. This leads us to strive for common knowledge and to construct general categories. "Understanding alone surmounts the limitation of the individual experience," Dilthey believes. "Extending over several people, mental creations and communities, it widens the horizon of the individual life and, in the human studies, opens up the path which leads from the common to the general" (p. 186).

Idealist theory, then, holds that experiencing and interpreting the world are the individual's primary interests. It is for this reason that the object of the human studies is meaning, not rational, objective motive and the interest it creates. But this is not meaning in an individual sense. The quest for experience generates a high degree of mutual understanding and common, generalized categories. If hermeneutical theory, then, like interactionism and Ethnomethodology, postulates nonrational action, it differs at least from the contemporary strands of these traditions by insisting on collective order. "Every individual," Dilthey writes, is a "point where webs of relationships intersect; these relationships go through individuals, exist within them, but also reach beyond their life and possess an independent existence and development of their own." Individual action is deeply affected by public, generalized "assertions about the passage of life, judgments of value, rules of conduct, definitions of goals and of what is good. . . . As custom, tradition and public opinion they influence individuals and their experience; because the community has the weight of numbers behind it and outlasts the individual, this power usually proves superior to his will" (p. 179).

This anti-individualistic approach to understanding has also been asserted in the formative writings of contemporary hermeneutical work. This is, for example, precisely what Geertz is driving at when, in his influential early essay, "Ideology as a Cultural System," he insists that we can understand the world only through "models" of experience not—as Blumer would have it—simply through making sense of experience in itself. Thinking, in Geertz's view, is hardly the self-referential process it is for Blumer, much less the rational, materially oriented process that Homans assumes. It is, rather, the "matching of the states and process of symbolic models against the states and processes of the wider world." What Geertz's conception does bear a relationship to is the phenomenological, especially the ethnomethodological variant in its early, collectivist form. Every conscious perception, Geertz suggests, represents a pairing, in which an object is identified by placing it against the background of an appropriate symbol. Like Garfinkel, Geertz uses the example of a road map. Culture is like a map, for "it transforms mere physical locations into 'places.'" In contrast to early ethnomethodology, however, Geertz—at least in this earlier work— moves from this collectivist focus to symbols themselves rather than to the process of symbolization. Hermeneutical analysis is the study of symbols, for these symbolic maps provide the "extrinsic sources of information in terms of which human life can be patterned— extrapersonal mechanisms for the perception, understanding, judgment, and manipulation of the world."[5] To Garfinkel, what is interesting about maps is how they are used, how rules are elaborated in the face of the real world's contingency. He is not interested in the rules themselves. That is why ethnomethodology, even in its profound early form, illuminates the actor's cultural capacity for relating general to specific while contributing virtually nothing at all to our understanding of the general in itself.

For hermeneutics the very opposite is the case. Once again, we must return to Dilthey for the most striking formulation. Whereas phenomenology finds the miracle of understanding in the mental capacity for generalization, Dilthey makes it clear that hermeneutics finds it in the phenomenon of cultural generality itself. A child "learns to understand . . . gestures and facial expressions, movements and exclamations, words and sentences," Dilthey insists, "only because it encounters them always in the same form and in the

[5] Geertz, "Ideology as a Cultural System," p. 61.

same relation to what they mean and express. Thus the individual orients himself to the world of objective mind" (p. 221–222). This presentiment of an objective mind bears a strong resemblance to the collectivist strains in Mead's thought. Indeed, Mead used the same Hegelian phrase. For Mead, as for the early Garfinkel, this collective presuppositional stance is combined with an empirical focus on individual expression. For Dilthey, by contrast, it leads to a focus on the most supra-individual empirical forms. Mead, moreover, sometimes, slips into a much more individualistic way of theorizing, suggesting that gestures can be understood only in terms of the contingent responses of other individuals, a theme which later interactionism raises to a central position. This individualistic pragmatism, we have seen, joins exchange theory in its denial of the actor's past. The hermeneutical insistence on collective meaning, in contrast, brings history into the center of interaction itself. Dilthey contends that "the past is a permanently enduring present for us" (p. 221). It is with the objective and binding form of society, not the subjective mind of the individual, that hermeneutics is concerned.

> The greater outer reality of mind always surrounds us . . . from a fleeting expression to the century-long rule of a constitution or code of law. *Every single expression represents a common feature* in the realm of this objective mind. . . . We live in this atmosphere, it surrounds us constantly. We are immersed in it. We are at home everywhere in this historical and understood world; we understand the sense and meaning of it all; we ourselves are woven into this common sphere."
> (p. 191)

Today we would not use the awkward phrase, "objective mind," but in important respects we might mean the same thing. What Dilthey calls objective mind is, it seems to me, very much what Geertz calls a "cultural system." Though Geertz emphasizes the cultural much more than the functional, his first teacher was Parsons, and in his early writing, at least, he maintains Parsons' systems vocabulary. What is systemic about culture, in Geertz's view, is that it consists of "patterns of interworking meanings." But while Geertz insists that culture has a structure, the fact that this structure consists of interrelated meaning suggests that it is "complicated."[6] Though culture is a whole, the whole consists only of parts. By referring to complication, Geertz suggests that the meaning of a cultural order is difficult to understand. The collective definition of culture, then, raises the problem of interpretation. This leads from cultural theory to cultural method.

The problem of "what is culture" is inseparable from the problem "how do we study it?" Hermeneutical theory is connected to hermeneutical method. We have made some first steps toward coming to grips with the theory. It is an idealist one. It holds that action is nonrational and experiential, that order is collective and binding vis-à-vis the contingencies of individual life. But if we want to go further, if we want to find out just what, exactly, this order is really made up of, we see that there is still much to learn. We must move from general, presuppositional statements to the level of a more empirical model. We have learned that culture is interrelated symbols. But it is not just symbols thrown together in this way or that. It is a system that has a certain form. Only when we try to examine this form empirically, in a more specific way, can we discover what it is. This leads us to reflect on the method of cultural analysis itself.

In much the same way as controversies over cultural theory, discussions over cultural method revolve around the implications of subjectivity. The case which must first be made, of course, is that cultural methods are, indeed, subjective ones. This argument can be made in the following way. To explain what a cultural system is, we must find out the *meaning* of action. Action is meaningful because it is experiential, and experience is disciplined by general categories. To discover what these categories are, we must enter into the experience of actors. Homans insisted this was not possible, that only "observables" can be admitted for scientific study. This objectivist methodology corresponds to his objectivist presuppositions, his belief that action is rational, determined by calculations about external, material conditions alone. Hermeneutics takes the opposite, subjectivist position. Because actors are motivated by meaning and not by efficiency, more intuitive and less

6 Geertz, "Ideology as a Cultural System," pp. 56 and 57.

observable things like experience must be the main focus of its science. Because "the inner system of interactions is superimposed by thought," Dilthey writes, "its basic elements cannot be observed." You simply cannot "observe" the mental connections a person is drawing between—the thought he is superimposing over—discrete impressions or events. The evidence for any hermeneutical statement, any cultural interpretation, is, therefore, irredemiably subjective. Dilthey insists that "only what has proved itself in [the actor's] thoughts is true" (p. 201).

But, if all evidence is subjective, does this mean that hermeneutical argument is simply a matter of personal opinion? Are the rational standards of science to be abandoned? Science, we must remember, searches for truth by establishing intersubjective standards which are binding on all who participate in scientific argument. Hermeneutics seems much more personal than that. This gulf between scientific and hermeneutic methods can be seen in the fact that the latter have been called "interpretive," the former "explanatory." In a famous justification for hermeneutics, Geertz emphasizes just this point. Because "man is an animal suspended in webs of significance he himself has spun," he writes, "I take . . . the analysis of [culture] to be therefore not an experimental science in search of law but an interpretive one in search of meaning."[7] The relativity implied by this position is, apparently, not something that Geertz wants particularly to escape. Natural science looks for "covering laws," general propositions which predict, or cover, an entire class of more specific events. Geertz acknowledges that such coverage is impossible within an interpretive genre. "Cultural analysis," he admits, "is intrinsically incomplete." "Worse than that," he continues, "the more deeply it goes the less complete it is. . . . It is a strange science whose most telling assertions are its most tremulously based, in which to get somewhere with the matter at hand is to intensify the suspicion, both your own and that of others, that you are not quite getting it right."[8]

Geertz notes "there are a number of ways to escape this—turning culture into folklore and collecting it, turning it into traits and

---

[7] Clifford Geertz, "Thick Description: Toward an Interpretive Theory of Culture," in Geertz, *The Interpretation of Cultures* (New York: Basic Books, 1973), p. 5.
[8] *Ibid.*, p. 29

counting it, turning it into institutions and classifying it, turning it into structures." But he insists that "these *are* escapes." To face the truth of the interpretive method is to accept that all scientific assertions are "essentially contestable."[9]

It seems clear, then, that hermeneutics must eschew what appears to be the incontestable objectivity of natural science, though this objectivity may not actually be as indisputable as positivistic (and even hermeneutic!) accounts of natural science make it seem. For all of this, however, the hermeneutic method may not be completely relativistic. If it were, cultural analysis would be much more like writing a novel than doing physics, and I think it is actually something somewhere in between. To see why radical relativism need not be embraced, we must recall that meaning formation is not itself radically individualistic. Only if it were would complete relativity be implied, for then the only method would be empathy. The task would be quite straightforward, if utterly impossible, namely, to "get inside the heads" of the actors under study. This is just the technique, of course, recommended by interactionists like Blumer and by phenomenologists of a similarly individualist bent.

If, however, meaning is not individually and contingently created but is, rather, the product of collective currents, then empathy cannot really get at its source. Dilthey saw this in a particularly clear way. He called the effort to reconstruct individual mental processes psychological rather than cultural. To illustrate this objection, he pointed to the problem of analyzing the meaning of an artistic work. Consider, for example, Goethe's *Faust*. Dilthey maintains that you would understand very little about the meaning of this work by making Goethe himself the object of the analysis, even if you had a full report of his creative activity while writing this text. It is the work, not the writer, we are interested in, and the latter, Dilthey believes, gives us very little information about the former: "If we only had the writers' reports on their creative activity, and all their works were lost, how little would these reports tell us."[10]

---

[9] *Ibid.*, italics added.
[10] Dilthey, *Gesammelte Schriften* (Leipzig and Berlin: Teubner, 1914), 7:321. Quoted in William Outhwaite, *Understanding Social Life* (London: Allen and Unwin, 1975), p. 30.

Dilthey's own attempt to use the hermeneutic method began with his biography of the early nineteenth-century philosopher and theologian, Schleiermacher, and he took one of Schleiermacher's statements as a motto of his own, anti-individualistic position. "The task," Schleiermacher said, is to understand the discourse "even better than its creator."[11] If empathy were the main hermeneutic method, the task would be different—to understand the discourse as well as its creator. Through empathy, one can only get at an actor's psychology, his understanding of himself. The goal of hermeneutics, however, is not individual psychology but the nature of the cultural order: not the author but the text. Let's return to Dilthey's discussion of the artistic text "Literary history and criticism," he writes, "are only concerned with what the pattern of words refers to, not—and this is decisive—with the processes in the poet's mind but with a structure created by these processes yet separable from them" (p. 174).

For literary studies this crucial distinction between author and text seems straightforward. It can relatively easily be transposed to some historical texts as well, for example, to historical documents like diaries, letters, or even constitutions. It seems much more difficult, however, to understand how this distinction can relate to the kinds of things sociologists usually study, namely the movements and gestures of real men and women. The challenge for a cultural or hermeneutic sociology is to find the social equivalent of the text. To find this social text, or, more accurately, a way to reconstruct something like it, is to describe the "objective mind," the intricate whole within which actors, events, and social structures are the meaningful parts. To do this we must find a way to describe the cultural system without referring to the intentions and interests of actors or institutions.

This is a difficult trick to turn. It is so difficult, in fact, that many cultural specialists recommend that it not be tried at all. Better, they say, to stick to written documents or things like conversations, which can be transcribed in a written form. There are other interpretors who do succeed in treating actions as texts

---

[11] Fr. D. E. Schleiermacher, *"The Hermeneutics:* Outline of the 1819 Lectures," *New Literary History* (1978) 10:1–16.

but who have not reflected on this method in a theoretical way. The one theorist who has fully come to terms with this problem is Paul Ricoeur, a French philosohcr who is one of Dilthey's most important successors as a philosopher of the human sciences. As Ricoeur sees it, whether or not actions can be viewed as texts is the litmus test for hermeneutical social science. "The human sciences may be said to be hermeneutical (1) inasmuch as their object displays some of the features constitutive of a text as text, and (2) inasmuch as their methodology develops the same kind of procedures as those of . . . text-interpretation."[12]

Ricoeur argues that both these conditions can be achieved. He does so by drawing an elaborate contrast between spoken discourse and written language. When you engage in spoken discourse you face an immediate situation, usually another person. Understanding the situation, then, becomes crucial for deciding exactly what is said, both for you and for anyone who wishes to interpret your speech. Because the significance of such situational contingency usually convinces the analyst that situation and contingency are all that really matter, scientific attention is paid primarily to the subjective intention of the speaker and the demanding nature of his or her environment: "The subjective intention of the speaking subject and the meaning of the discourse overlap each other in such a way that it is the same thing to understand what the *speaker* means and what his *discourse* means" (p. 534, italics mine). Thus, the French expression for asking "what do you mean?" is "qu'est-ce que vous voulez-dire," which translated literally means "what is it that you want to say?" When analytic attention is focused in this way on intention and/or situation, however, you have psychological or social but not cultural analysis.

Ricoeur then compares this popular and commonsensical approach to speech with what goes on in a written text. He points out that in the latter case the connection between meaning and the intention of some contingent actor is broken. With writing you have "intentional exteriorization." The event—the act of writing—"surpasses itself in meaning." A written text must be addressed to

[12] Paul Ricoeur, "The Model of a Text: Meaningful Action Considered as a Text," *Social Research* (1971) 38:529. Hereafter page references will be given parenthetically in text.

whomever knows how to read, and to whomever may read it in the future. It must have an objective quality: "The text's career escapes the finite horizon lived by its author." With this use of the term horizon Ricoeur turns the phenomenological approach to the concept on its head! How individual writers navigate contingency by extending the horizon of action from moment to moment must not be our concern. It is the horizon itself which must be studied. "What the *text* says," in Ricoeur's words, "now matters more than what the author meant to say" (pp. 533–534).

Having established the distinction between discourse and text, Ricoeur can make his principal point: meaningful action must be considered as a text. Action, even spoken action, must rise above the immediate situation. Because the parties in real life rarely know one other very well, they must rely on common parlance. They must speak, in other words, as if they were writing for an unknown audience. This necessity allows the "emancipation" of meaning "from the situational context" (p. 543). Cultural analysis must act as if "interaction is overcome," as if action is "no longer a trans-action [but] a delineated pattern" (p. 538). Husserl urged us to bracket the realness of social life and to pretend for the sake of argument that an actor has to construct this reality entirely on his own. Ricoeur wants us to do precisely the opposite. We must bracket contingency, and for the sake of cutural analysis treat contingent action as if were a written text.

These are not picayune points. They reflect fundamental differences in theory. Ricoeur sees action as guided resolutely by supra-individual, cultural order. It is this belief in the objectification of meaningful subjectivity that allows an "interpretive science" to proceed on something other than completely relativistic (because completely subjective) grounds. "Meaningful action is an object for science," Ricoeur says, "only under the condition of a kind of objectification which is equivalent to the fixation of a discourse by writing" (p. 537). Thus, hermeneutic interpretation can test itself by "what is really there"—and publicly be held accountable to it—in just the same way that literary analysis can be tested against a written text which is there for all to see. Because people must use common and depersonalized symbols if their subjectivity is to be understood, the symbols used to achieve understanding are, in principle, accessible to a wide variety of other people. There is, therefore, an objective, nonrelativistic element to hermeneuticial interpretation. How different this is than the situationally specific, thoroughly relativistic ethnograpy suggested by interactionism and the later ethnomethodology! Their individualism makes methodological objectivity impossible.

But the objective dimension that a collective reference provides does not mean that hermeneutics can escape subjectivity altogether. Far from it. The "parts" of a meaningful structure are, indeed, really there. Acts, words, gestures, and events provide visible, objective components of a cultural text whose real existence cannot be questioned. What whole these parts finally add up to, however, is another question. Wholes—the meaningful *themes*, the common symbol *systems*—take their shape, for the actor and the analyst alike, only as the result of generalizing thought. For the observer, these wholes must be constructed from an interpretive reservoir of previously sensible themes, from his or her own intuitive experience about how things "fit together" in cultural life.

But interpretive analysis gets even stickier than this. The meaning of the individual parts themselves can, in the last analysis, only be understood by seeing them already as parts of a larger whole. We must see parts as representing or exemplifying broader themes if we are to make any sense of them. The problem with this is that I have just finished telling you that wholes are themselves not "really there," that they, too, depend upon a leap of imagination from the parts. Wholes are constructed from thinking about the relation between meaningful parts, but the meaning of parts can only be approached if we assume some already existing whole!

If you think this reasoning is circular, that it makes interpretation inherently relativistic, you are right. Indeed, Dilthey said that all interpretation involves just this kind of "hermeneutical circle," a circle from which there is no escape.

Let's say that you see men in striped pants on a field wearing gloves and swinging bats. How are you to interpret this observation? Are they baseball players or lunatics? The objective facts of the situation are significant and they certainly limit your interpretation in decisive ways. You know, for example, that these men are not swimming in the ocean or conducting a meeting in an air-conditioned room! But you still do not know just what they *are* doing.

What they are doing depends on the whole you posit as the background against which to view their activity. If the field is well manicured and it is enclosed by a stadium with thousands of cheering people, the nature of this background presents itself to you (if you are an American) in a rather obvious way. If, by contrast, the men are by themselves in a park which has no specific markings, the part/whole problem becomes much more difficult. You must still interpret the background, but you can probably do so only by trying to "read" it as itself part of some larger whole. You have moved from part (player) to whole (park), and now you must make this whole a part again. You have looked at the players' surroundings, but if this whole is simply an unmarked lawn in a park what they are doing still doesn't "make sense." You cannot yet interpret the "meaning" of the men in striped pants. You must try, then, to construct a larger whole from the parts you have available— the unmarked lawn, the park, the men. You may also try to find out what time of day it is, study closely how these players stand and move, find out exactly where this field is located in relation to other things. You try to get the feel of the situation.

In making this construction you are relying on your repertoire of general cultural forms. It is a subjective, interpretive process, and your particular sensitivity to cultural nuance obviously plays a most important role. If you have never seen a baseball game, you are in trouble! You are also in trouble if you have never observed the mentally ill or had any experience with parks or lawns! Assuming you have had these experiences, however, there is a good chance that other, equally experienced observers would arrive at similar conclusions about what is before you. In the first place, these observers would be limited by the same "objective" parts. In the second place, they would share your, and the players', common experience, the repertoire of cultural forms from which wholes are constructed. If the men in striped pants are lunatics, of course, you will not be able to share some common experience, a fact which may lead you to decide that they are not baseball players after all!

This example of the men in striped pants points to the complexities of the interpretive task. On the one hand, you have a limited number of parts to which to refer and some shared experience upon which to draw. These provide elements of objectivity. On the other hand, in most situations there are many more parts to refer to than any single interpretation could possibly include. For this reason, the objective status of available parts does not provide an awfully strict limit on subjectivity. Moreover, the overlap is never complete between your experience of life, the experience of these whom you are observing, and the experience of other observers on or off the scene. No two experiences of life, after all, are ever exactly the same. This is even more true for modern, differentiated, and segmented societies. This meaning gap only increases when the subjects of observation are dead and when the material upon which you must draw to understand their intentions is fragmentary. You probably know from your own experience just how hard it is to know what somebody "really means," even when this somebody is a close friend or family member. Imagine, then, how much more difficult it is to understand people you do not know well or, indeed, have never even met. No matter how much we can modify the subjectivity of hermeneutics, then, we can never eliminate it. While there are significant methodological limits to relativism because of the existence of objective texts and shared experience, the necessity for interpretation to proceed inside a hermeneutical circle makes it impossible to remove speculation entirely.

Another limit to relativism comes from theory. We are not only methodologists, interpreters who approach the world with wide eyes, open questions, and the hermeneutical circle in hand. We are also social scientists who already have well-developed ideas about how this world works. We have presuppositions about how people act and about how actions are ordered into patterns. We have ideologies which incline us—before we ever encounter the person or event—to evaluate them in certain ways. We have models which outline the expected relations of empirical things in simple but often highly predictive forms, and we have a large body of what we take to be factual knowledge about the world. What these theories amount to is a particular, professional specification of the "common ideas and experience" carried around by every actor in the world. This specialized subset of ideas is carried by theoretical traditions which are the products of disciplined thought, intellectual argument, cumulative empirical observations, and conceptual refinement.

Because of these traditions social scientists approach cultural texts with definite expectations about how they work. These expectations provide us with widely shared and quite specific "wholes" against which to read the parts of social life. While Ricoeur doesn't speak about theories, he does refer to the "constitutive rules" of particular areas of social life, and Dilthey writes about the "laws" which govern the different areas of our interpretive interest. Indeed, in his discussion of literary analysis, Dilthey links his critique of psychologism and his claim for an autonomous text to the notion of such organizing laws.

> Literary history and criticism are only concerned with what the pattern of words refers to, not—and this is decisive— with the processes in the poet's mind but with a structure created by these processes yet separable from them. The structure of a drama lies in its particular combination of subject, poetic mood, plot and means of presentation. Each contributes to the structure of the work according to a law intrinsic to poetry. (*Dilthey*, p. 174)

This notion of laws ordering particular forms of symbolic organization is, in my view, not much different than the suggestion, which Geertz derived from Parsons, that there is a thing called a "cultural system."

Proponents of the hermeneutical position often neglect the tremendous significance of this theoretical reference for interpretive work. By doing so, it seems to me, they see themselves as stepping into the hermeneutical circle virtually unarmed. Still, while the omnipresence of sociological theories may change the way we think of subjective interpretation, they certainly cannot neutralize it altogether. Scientific theories are a subset of common ideas, and they play exactly the same role. They suggest wholes against which to see parts—parts being the "data" of scientific life—but exactly which parts they will be used to explain or understand is very much a matter of subjective choice. Because theories themselves, moreover, consist of manifold levels and nuances, the background wholes to which they supply interpretation are themselves open to selection.

Even when theorists accept the same components of a theory—the same paradigm—subtle shades of difference exist in how these components will be understood from one theorist to another. A scientist's understanding of the subset of shared ideas called theory is affected by his more general experience of life, and there is no more "common experience" between social theorists than between other kinds of people. If there is one thing you have learned from this course so far, it is that theoretical assumptions vary widely even when they are aimed at the same empirical phenomena and reflect the same historical climate. Given such widely divergent wholes, it is no wonder that social scientists so often find their interpretations of the same objective world to be so different, and why they often find it just as hard to understand one another as people do in less scientific walks of life.

Every person who is committed to rationality wishes that this kind of relativism could somehow be escaped. We want to agree with each other, and the possibility for progress and cooperation— between individuals as well as between groups—often depends upon being able to agree on the nature and meaning of social facts. If interpretations are relative, then facts become divergent, and trust eventually breaks down. The methods of science and the theories of science are efforts to combat this problem, but they can never entirely succeed. The interpretive method is necessary because people *experience* life; they do not just *react* to it in a mechanical way. As people experience life, they try to find its meaning. It is because meaning is subjective that the method of discovering meaning must be subjective in turn.

LECTURE SEVENTEEN
CULTURAL SOCIOLOGY (2): CLIFFORD GEERTZ'S REBELLION AGAINST DETERMINISM

IF PARSONS CLEARLY articulated the need for a multidimensional, synthetic sociological theory, he certainly did not provide a satisfactory conceptualization of how this might be done. Indeed, each of the elements upon which he sought to forge his master synthesis can be shown to have serious deficiencies. "Effort," for example, remains virtually unexplored, and means and conditions are seriously underplayed. Post-Parsonian theory, I have suggested, can be viewed as addressing each of these weaknesses, and in this sense each can be viewed as an advance. Yet precisely because each emerged within the context of a polemical dialogue with Parsons' original theory, each strand is one-sided and remains limited in turn.

Only when these various sides are brought together can a truly satisfactory post-Parsonian theory emerge. Where each single theory represents what Hegel called an abstract negation, this post-Parsons synthesis would represent a more dialectical, concrete negation of his work. It would attempt to build upon his accomplishments even while rejecting his theory taken as a whole.

Until we considered hermeneutic theory we had left the cultural element of Parsons' original synthesis untouched. While every other element had been thoroughly criticized, each had been premised on the assumption that Parsons had done at least one thing right: he had analyzed "values" in a systematic way. What conflict theory, exchange theory, interactionism and ethnomethodology were saying, in effect, was that Parsons had done too much of this good thing. He had given values too much prominence, spent too much time analyzing how they worked and not enough time on how they were limited or promoted by the other dimensions of social life.

I began my first lecture on hermeneutics by suggesting that this working assumption was incorrect. The explosion in the late 1960s and 1970s of "cultural studies" has called for a much more intensive analysis and conceptualization of meaning than Parsons allowed. If this hermeneutic revival is taken seriously, I suggested, we might find in it the resources to reconstruct the final element in Parsons' original theory, the element of values. In this way, a genuinely different, fully multidimensional theory might be achieved.

In this second lecture on cultural theory, I would like to do three things. First, I would like to show you that this hermeneutic revival was, indeed, a genuine confrontation with Parsons' work. It was not simply the revival of an earlier strand of classical theory independent of any reference to Parsons as such. Why is this important? Because this kind of direct relationship allows us to make the theoretical confrontation between a "culturally shallow" multidimensional theory and a "culturally deep" one more clear cut. It also makes the argument I am producing for postpositivist theoretical "cumulation" more concrete and accessible. Finally, not least, it sustains my historical account of the polemical path that postwar sociological theory has taken.

The second thing I will try to show you in this lecture is just what kind of contribution a reinvigorated cultural theory can make, how, that is, it "fits in" with the multidimensional theory I have been trying to reconstruct. The third point I will try to show you runs in quite the opposite direction. It is that hermeneutic theory, taken by itself, is a limited and ultimately unsatisfactory form of sociological analysis. I will try to demonstrate that, like each of the other post-Parsonian theories we have considered, its one-sided character leads to dismaying theoretical contradictions which are inherent in the very structure of hermeneutic theorizing itself.

Let's begin, then, with the relation between this hermeneutic revival and Parsons' work. After all, much of what I discussed in my last lecture had nothing to do with Parsons. Dilthey wrote long before him, and Ricoeur seems to have worked in an intellectual climate which is completely independent of Parsons' influence. Most of what passes for cultural studies today, indeed, has little relation to Parsons or to sociology. It finds its place in disciplines like symbolic anthropology—with theorists like Victor Turner and Mary Douglas—and in special fields like "structuralism" and "semiotics." Much of it never steps outside of philosophical argument at all.[1]

There have, however, been "culturalist" developments within sociology itself, and the most significant of these have, in fact, often been forged in polemical response to Parsons' work. These polemics provide the direct links we are looking for. It is by seeing what they contribute, and what they do not, that we will be able to establish the relation between cultural studies and multidimensional theory.

The cultural critique of Parsons is a bit different than the other polemics because it was carried out primarily from the inside. Perhaps this is not so surprising as it seems, since in the field of sociology it was primarily the "Parsonians" who took the idea of culture seriously in the first place. The most important figure here is Clifford Geertz. I discussed some of his ideas in my first lecture on hermeneutics, particularly his notion of culture as a system and his acceptance of the relativism of the interpretive method. What I want to do now is put such positions into a historical perspective.

Geertz initially developed his "interpretive" position in a pair of essays which simultaneously elaborated and critiqued Parsons' theory of culture. For reasons that will become clear later, I will not talk about the first of these essays, "Ideology as a Cultural System," at this point. Instead I will focus on the powerful argument in "Religion as a Cultural System," published in 1966.[2] Here Geertz set himself the task of developing an anthropological theory of

---

[1] See, for example, Victor Turner, *The Ritual Process* (Ithaca: Cornell University Press, 1969), and Mary Douglas, *Purity and Danger* (London: Penguin, 1966). For structuralism, see Claude Lévi-Strauss, *The Savage Mind* (Chicago: University of Chicago Press, 1966). For an influential semiotic study, see Roland Barthes, *The Fashion System* (New York: Hill and Wang, 1983). For one of the most widely read (along with Ricoeur) philosophical treatments of hermeneutics, see Hans-Georg Gadamer, *Truth and Method* (New York: Crossroad, 1975). I will talk more about structuralism and semiotics later in this lecture.

[2] Clifford Geertz, "Religion as a Cultural System," pp. 639–688, in Donald Cutler, ed., *The Religious Situation* (1966; Boston: Beacon Press, 1970), and Geertz, "Ideology as a Cultural System," pp. 47–76, in David E. Apter, ed., *Ideology and Discontent* (New York: Free Press, 1964).

religion which could forcefully describe the "autonomy" of cultural elements without adopting an idealist position. He complains that no progress has been made in theorizing about religion since the classical writings of Durkheim, Weber, and Freud, and he attributes this lack of progress to the reductionist bent of most social science analysis. It is necessary, he argues, to see that there are specifically cultural problems that religion addresses, problems that have to do directly with the "meaning of life." Though Geertz refers here to Weber, we hear echoes of Dilthey's hermeneutic emphasis on experience and meaning. Cultural autonomy is secured, then, because meaning is taken to be central. From there, Geertz suggests that the symbols which address meaning perform tasks which, taken together, create a cultural system. How these tasks are performed, he adds, is affected by more mundane psychological, political, and economic concerns. He is not arguing against the influence of other dimensions but simply that religion, and culture more generally, cannot be reduced to them.

Does this sound familiar? It should. It is precisely the position that Parsons himself worked out, the three-system theory about the autonomy and interpenetration of personality, society, and culture. In this essay, at least—and you will see later that his subsequent work changes in this respect—Geertz does not hesitate to admit he is following Parsons' lead. Faced with the different directions that an argument for cultural autonomy may take, he writes that "for my part, I shall confine my effort to developing what, following Parsons and Shils, I refer to as the cultural dimension of religious analysis." The point of Parsons' three-system theory, you recall, was that every concrete, or empirical, action involved different analytic dimensions. This is what allowed him to suggest that a multidimensional argument was possible, for he could describe the autonomy of cultural organization without reducing action to a mere cultural embodiment. Geertz wants to follow Parsons in this insistence, and it is precisely here that the uniqueness of his hermeneutic position rests. He insists that "cultural acts . . . are social events," while adding that "they are not, however, exactly the same thing." His point is that "the symbolic dimension of social events is, like the psychological, itself theoretically abstractable from those events as empirical totalities." Doing cultural analysis, then, is not necessarily to oppose culture and society, but to abstract one dimension for the purposes of analysis: "No matter how deeply interfused the cultural, the social, and the psychological may be in the everday life of houses, farms, poems, and marriages, it is useful to distinguish them in analysis, and, so doing, to isolate the generic traits of each against the normalized background of the other two."[3]

Is Geertz, then, simply reiterating Parsons? Not at all. Parsons, while insisting on analytic autonomy, concentrated on the "interfusion" of culture, personality, and society. This is why the brunt of his cultural analysis is concerned to demonstrate that values play an indispensable role in regulating social life and forming personalities. Yes, it is the existence of "relatively autonomous" values that makes the relation of personalities and social systems to values of central importance. But it is the relation itself—for the social system, "institutionalization," for the personality, "socialization"— not the nature of value systems per se which is Parsons' primary interest. Not only is Parsons not particularly interested in the origins and development of values themselves, but by concentrating on values he is discussing only one small part of cultural systems. Parsons himself is aware of this: he is emphatic that sociologists should not focus on "symbol systems" in general, but rather on values. He identifies values as the subset of symbols which are institutionalized—in other words, symbols which have become part of the social system.[4] Values are symbols which directly relate to the problems of social system and psychological action, hence their definition in terms like equality and inequality, achievement and ascription, spontaneity and control.

Geertz's own analysis of cultural systems, by contrast, refers to values not at all. It is not to specifically social problems that he sees symbols as directed, but specifically cultural ones. In the case of religion, it is, as I have said, the problem of meaning. Even in this multidimensional phase of his analysis, then, Geertz differs from Parsons by giving cultural systems something distinctively

---

[3] Geertz, "Religion as a Cultural System," p. 641, 644–645.

[4] Talcott Parsons and Edward Shils, "Values, Motives, and Systems of Action," in Parsons and Shils, eds., *Towards a General Theory of Action* (Cambridge: Harvard University Press, 1951), pp. 162–163.

"cultural" to do. This allows him to justify the analysis of symbol systems per se. Symbol systems have distinctive tasks. These tasks are related to their distinctively cultural aim. In the case of religion, the goal is to address the meaning of human existence in its broadest terms. What follows is Geertz's distinctive definition of religion, which because of its clarity and elegance has since become famous. "Religion," he writes, "is (1) a system of symbols which acts to (2) establish powerful, pervasive, and long lasting moods and motivations in men by (3) formulating conceptions of a general order of existence and (4) clothing these conceptions with such an aura of factuality that (5) the moods and motivations seem uniquely realistic."[5] Cultural analysis of religion should be directed toward explaining how each of these tasks is carried out. In this way it will describe, more strongly than Parsons himself, the internal structure and independent effects of symbol systems on social life.

Since Geertz may well be the most significant American who figures in the revival of hermeneutical work, it seems clear enough that this revival has been, at least in part, significantly concerned with positioning itself vis-à-vis Parsons' theory. That Geertz is an anthropologist rather than a sociologist is beside the point. Sociological theory—our topic in these lectures—knows no disciplinary bounds. It is a theory of society as such. This is demonstrated by the fact that the book of Geertz's collected essays of which the essay on religion was such an exemplary part, *The Interpretation of Cultures,* was given the most prestigious award—the Sorokin Prize—of the American Sociological Association. But this initial, brief discussion of Geertz shows, I hope, something more as well. It begins to suggest just how a strong theory of culture might be integrated with a multidimensional analysis.

Geertz was not the only student of Parsons who played a crucial role in developing the case for cultural studies. Geertz's friend and fellow student, Robert Bellah, was also important, and Bellah has been much more central to the specific discipline of sociology. In broad outline, Bellah's thinking follows rather closely the path laid out by Geertz. In part this has to do with the strong collegial relation which existed between the two men. More importantly, it

[5] Geertz, "Religion as a Cultural System," p. 643.

resulted from the interaction between the internal "logic" of sociological theorizing and a particular kind of extra-theoretical intellectual climate. Even when they were more or less satisfied followers of Parsons, Geertz and Bellah had a strongly cultural bent. In the face of the social turmoil of the 1960s and the emergence of strongly anti-Parsonian movements, they sought to differentiate themselves from Parsons in much the same way. They called for a strong form of cultural analysis without abandoning multidimensional work.

For Bellah this conspicuous break comes three years after Geertz's essay on religion appeared, in an article, written in 1969, which he entitled "Between Religion and Science."[6] For many years, Bellah had theorized about the sociology of religion under the rubric of Parsonian theory. In keeping with Parsons' own views about the progress of sociology under his leadership, he had viewed the discipline as gradually incorporating the multidimensional synthesis which Parsons had laid out. By 1969, however, this was no longer possible.

In "Between Religion and Science," Bellah condemns sociology for its failure to appreciate the relative autonomy of the symbolic, cultural realm. Most contemporary and even classical sociology, Bellah now suggests, engages in "symbolic reductionism." This argument echoes Geertz's. Symbolic reductionism occurs when symbols are explained by reference only to their social and psychological roots. Reductionists can accept cognitive culture because it refers to the kinds of purely rational beliefs, like science, which are treated as objective reflections—reductions—of external reality. In opposition to this position, Bellah proposes "symbolic realism." Symbols must be seen as expressing a reality of their own, as addressing a realm that is not, in the first instance, the social or the psychological. This makes culture partly "constitutive" of society and personality, not simply their reflection. What it constitutes is their meaning, or more accurately, the symbolic context within which their meaning can emerge. The emphases in Bellah's definition of religion—autonomy and multidimensionality—are very much like Geertz's:

---

[6] Robert N. Bellah, "Between Religion and Science," pp. 237–257, in Bellah, *Beyond Belief* (New York: Harper and Row, 1970).

"Religion [is] that symbol system that serves to evoke . . . the context in which life and action finally have meaning."[7]

How does all this relate to Parsons? Bellah's position has a certain ambiguity. He developed the notion of symbolic realism to oppose what he described as the dominant orientation in Western sociology, and it was certainly Parsons, more than any other figure, with whom Western sociology in the postwar period was identified. The implied critique is underlined by the circumstances of this phase of Bellah's work. In 1967 he had moved from the sociology department at Harvard, long dominated by Parsons, to the one at the University of California at Berkeley. In his preface to *Beyond Belief*, the collection of essays he published in 1970, Bellah describes this move as a transition from a strait-laced intellectual atmosphere to a "wide-open" one. Berkeley, you might remember, was at the center of the 1960s social and cultural upheaval, the same social changes that formed the backdrop to the anti-Parsonian challenges in sociological theory. Bellah makes the link explicit. In the same preface, he writes that in the few years since his move, "my thinking has . . . been influenced by the emergence of a counter-culture."[8] And he makes no bones about the change in his relation to Parsons, recalling, in an introduction to one of the earliest essays in that volume, that at the time he had written it he "was still caught in the unfolding of the Parsonian theoretical scheme."[9] Bellah's new emphasis on symbolic realism, then, must at least in part be viewed as a rejection of Parsons, an attempt to create a really strong theory of culture that Parsons did not have.

Yet Bellah does not want to reject Parsons entirely. In the preface to which I have just referred, he adds, after his declaration of independence from Parsons, that while he has "shifted some of the emphases," he considers his later essays "more a development than a repudiation of Parsonian theory." In the pivotal essay on symbolic realism, moreover, Bellah places Parsons in the avant-garde of anti-reductionist theorizing rather than in the mainstream of contemporary sociology. He writes that "to some extent what I have said parallels the famous argument of Talcott Parsons in

[7] *Ibid.*, pp. 252–253.
[8] Bellah, *Beyond Belief*, p. xvii.
[9] Bellah, "Appendix: The Systematic Study of Religion," in *Beyond Belief*, p. 260.

The Structure of Social Action," and he insists that Parsons, too, speaks of "symbol systems as partly autonomous."[10]

There are, it seems to me, clear theoretical reasons for this ambivalence. It is a strongly cultural theory, not an idealist one, that Bellah is after. Just as social systems find meaning from within cultural systems, symbols must always be seen as lodged within social structures. In an earlier essay he revised for the 1970 collection, Bellah makes this multidimensional, typically Parsonian position perfectly clear. Sociological theory must distinguish, he insists, "between cultural system in a pure sense and [how culture works] in a social system." Cultural systems refer to "symbol systems . . . more or less in themselves." These pure symbols are the subject of "cultural history" or the "history of thought." Sociological theory is concerned with something different, with symbol systems only insofar as they are part of the social system. Bellah writes that "within the social system there are cultural elements that are partly constitutive of that social system," and he calls these, following Parsons, the "social value system."[11] He wants to use the notion of constitutive symbols—the notion which is crucial for his later conception of symbolic realism—in a socially related, not an idealist way. Though Bellah, like Geertz, eventually devotes himself to symbol systems and not just to values, he clearly sees no incompatability between strong cultural theory and a multidimensional frame.[12]

In its initial sociological version, then, cultural studies took over key elements of hermeneutics while rejecting it as a general theory. It created a new theme in the anti-Parsonian movement, but it did so without entirely rejecting Parsons' work. Drawing on hermeneutics, Geertz and Bellah deepened their understanding of the nature and force of symbol systems. As they developed a new, more hermeneutic emphasis, they pushed meaning much more clearly to the fore. By making meaning more central, they made culture more important, and this new importance made it essential

---

[10] Bellah, "Between Religion and Science," pp. 240–241.

[11] Bellah, "Values and Social Change in Modern Japan," in *Beyond Belief,* pp. 114–115.

[12] The best example in Bellah's later work of a multidimensional approach to symbolic as opposed to value analysis is his "Civil Religion in America," in *Beyond Belief,* pp. 168–189.

to find a stronger cultural theory. Sociology, to use the concept of Ricoeur's I introduced in my last lecture, would have to be more concerned with action as a text, but it should not forget context in the process.

It would be nice if we could just stop right here. This middle position, in my view, is just where sociological theory ought to go. This is not, however, where the hermeneutic revival in sociological theory eventually stayed. The multidimensional position is notoriously difficult to maintain, even in the best of times. This was not the "best" of times in sociology, not best, at least, for theoretical positions in any way associated with Parsons' work. The hermeneutic revival was, indeed, caught up in the polemic against Parsonian theory. Like each of the other challenges to some one-sided Parsons' emphasis, this strand of post-Parsonian theory itself began to show a one-sided slant.

One way of explaining this is to say that rather than being satisfied with critique and revision, the proponents of cultural theory sought to present a fundamental theoretical alternative. For cultural analysis to offer such a completely different perspective, it would have to build a theory of the whole society upon its insight into the importance of a single part. But if the part becomes the basis of the whole, the complexity of the whole becomes sacrificed to the simplicity of the part. Social theory would have to be related to cultural elements alone.

Insofar as cultural analysis becomes one-sided, or "culturalist," it gets itself into the same kinds of problems as theories that are materialistic or individualistic. By emphasizing one part over others, significant aspects of reality are ignored. When this happens, however, the other aspects of action and order will find their way back in a residual form. This is the fate of every culturalist theory. It becomes inextricably caught up in what I will call the "interpretive dilemma."

Insofar as sociological theory becomes one-sided in a cultural way—insofar as it seeks to form a purely hermeneutic analysis—it argues not only that there is always a cultural reference for every action but that there is only a cultural reference. Every change in action, every source of stability, everything that works for the good, everything that works for the bad—all must be explained in terms of the search for meaning itself. Every culturalist theory is, as I argued in my last lecture, a form of sociological idealism.

Now the idealist notion that action takes only a nonrational form is not unique to hermeneutics. We have found it also in phenomenology and interactionism. What makes hermeneutics different, as I also pointed out in that earlier lecture, is that it insists that meaning takes a collective form. Interactionism and ethnomethodology face what I called the individualist dilemma. They cannot explain nonrandom, social order and remain within the framework they seek to maintain. This is not at all the case for hermeneutics. It assumes that order is collective. It "reads" action as if it were a text, as if it followed a script composed of supra-individual themes. This makes it a much more culturally satisfying theory. What interactionism and ethnomethodology can introduce only in a residual way, hermeneutics can take up in an explicit and systematical way. The problem of order is solved by asserting the existence of cultural structure. Dilthey explained how the search for experience leads to common understanding and the objective mind. Geertz described this collective order as a cultural system. Ricoeur likened meaningful action not to a spoken discourse but to a literary text. The explanation of order, then, is collective ideals.

Yet this very advantage can also be a deficit in disguise. The problem is that within the context of an idealist theory this collective emphasis presents the spectre of determinism. If action is converted into a text, what remains of the actor himself, or of the exigencies of interaction? Parsons acknowledged the element of cultural control, and he called it the cultural system. But he insisted also on the significance of interaction in concrete situations—on social systems—and on the purely particular, individual level of the personality. The cultural referent in theory makes it voluntaristic only if the status of concrete, individual actors is clearly acknowledged. Only if culture is conceived of as being internalized by personalities can it be seen as an expression of will, as a manifestation of individual purpose and identity. Only if it is connected with purpose and identity, moreover, can it be linked to the search for meaning which, hermeneutic theory tells us, is at the basis of culture to begin with. Collective idealism, then, threatens to undermine the very basis upon which the hermeneutic position rests.

It also makes it very difficult, we will see in a moment, to explain changes in social order and action which are not already part of the cultural system itself.

The history of cultural analysis has manifested a strong tendency for such ideal reduction. We have already observed the normative slant of Dilthey's hermeneutics in Germany. In France, at about the same time, Ferdinand Saussure created a "science of symbols" on a different empirical basis but along much the same theoretical lines. He named this science semiology, and he based it on an analogy between individual symbols and the words of a language. He argued that actions must be converted into "systems of signification," or signs. The distinctive accomplishment of semiotics since then has come from its ability to do just that, to show that an order which appears to be governed by contingency and material constraints may actually be viewed as an emanation of cultural structures unrecognized by the actors involved.[13]

The other significant contemporary form of collective idealism has been anthropological structuralism. Claude Lévi-Strauss, the founder of this movement, transferred the language analogy to the study of myth, viewing the actions of primitive man as elaborating the structures of myth. To find the symbolic arrangements which composed them, Lévi-Strauss insisted that myths must be studied completely independently of their social and psychological moorings. Changes in culture, moreover, can be traced to internal structures and internal strains alone; they unfold independently, without input from other levels of social life. Myths "think themselves," Lévi-Strauss claimed in a slogan that has become emblematic. They do so, moreover, in a manner unaffected by the passage of time. Indeed, Lévi-Strauss attacked the very idea of history, arguing that social science had to be "synchronic," static and systematic, rather than "diachronically" oriented to change and contingency. That such a deterministic approach undermines the relation of cultural analysis to meaning is an implication from which

[13] Ferdinand Saussure, *Course in General Linguistics* (New York: New York Library, 1960), especially the introduction. This book was based on lectures Saussure gave in the first decade of this century. See also, in this regard, Roland Barthes, *Elements of Semiology* (London: Jonathan Cape, 1967), especially pp. 23–34, and Marshall Sahlins, *Culture and Practical Reason* (Chicago: University of Chicago Press, 1976), especially pp. 166–204.

structuralism does not shy away. The object of structural analysis, Lévi-Strauss suggests, is a "totalizing entity"—that is, a collective form—which is "outside (or beneath) consciousness and will." It is "human reason which has its reasons and of which man knows not a thing."[14]

Ideal determinism, then, constitutes an ever present possibility for a purely hermeneutic position. Indeed, I will go out on a limb and suggest that determinism is inevitable if collective order is embraced in a purely cultural way. A cultural theorist cannot avoid determinism if he does not wish to step outside of hermeneutics itself.

Does this mean, then, that all who take the hermeneutical path are cultural determinists? "Logically" it does. But you have probably noticed in these lectures that theorists rarely remain satisfied with the logical implications of a one-sided position. Because reality has a multidimensional quality, rival theories can take up arms against this position in the name of those aspects of reality it has neglected. When this happens, a theorist finds his own polemic quite a bit less satisfying! At this point he starts working to find some way around the "iron logic" of his work. For culturalist theories there is a more specific element at work as well. This has to do with the tension between cultural idealism and the commitment to theorizing in a sociological way. Those who study society—who are not simply students of literary texts—are rarely entirely comfortable with a completely symbolic explanation. Even if their explicit commitments have become idealistic, they do not want to leave institutions, interaction, and personalities completely behind. Just as phenomenological sociologists are "theorists with second thoughts" because as social scientists they cannot really accept order in a random form, so do hermeneutic sociologists have regrets because they cannot entirely ignore more typically social references.

In principle, hermeneutics denies individual contingency and material environment. Individualists have criticized it in the name of contingency, and materialists condemned it in the name of social change and a more "realistic" conception of constraint. In response to these pressures, and because of their own internal doubts as

---

[14] Lévi-Strauss, *The Savage Mind*, p. 252.

well, hermeneutic theorists have usually tried to alter their theories without acknowledging they are doing so—probably even to themselves. They do so by tacitly referring to the very dimensions their presuppositions force them explicitly to ignore. We have seen the result of such efforts before. It is the introduction of residual categories, with all the theoretical indeterminacy this implies.

Hermeneutical theory produces two kinds of residual categories. The first seeks to incorporate contingency. When a hermeneutician wants to escape the influence of cultural "codes" without acknowledging that he is doing so, he will suggest that the "meaning-creating" quality of action makes it impossible to predict. Yet because he has not given up on his explicit commitment to collective order, the relation between contingency and cultural control cannot be specified in a theoretical way. Contingency is residual to the analysis, not a systematic part of it. The relation between this open, indeterminate element and the culture which is supposed to determine it becomes anybody's guess.

The other residual category introduced by the cultural analyst with second thoughts concerns the material realm. When they want to posit a source of disorder or constraint outside of self-referential cultural patterns, the hermeneutic theorists sometimes point vaguely to material conditions. Such conditions, of course, are not "in principle" part of hermeneutic theory, and it possesses no theoretical resources for conceptualizing their role in a systematic way. But how and why such conditions arose, not to mention what their precise relation to culture might be, is not the hermeneutic theorist's concern. It is precisely because they are outside of cultural theory that they are pointed to in the first place. They can do something that cultural theory cannot. But just because then can do so they must remain untheorized, that is to say they must remain residual to the analysis.

The interpretive dilemma is the choice between cultural determinism and residual category, of either a contingent or a materialist sort. A dilemma is a choice between two equally unsatisfactory alternatives. What is special about a "logical dilemma" is that the escape from either pole implies the other. The only way to avoid the horns of a dilemma in theoretical logic is to step outside the overarching theory itself.

Ironically, if the interpretive dilemma is to be avoided without giving up on cultural analysis altogether, the radically culturalist position must be dissolved. The relation between culture, contingency, and material constraint can be theorized in an explicit way only from a multidimensional and synthetic position. Dilthey was forced to relegate the analysis of economic and political phenomena to natural science because his idealism led him to understand such processes in an anti-cultural, mechanistic way. They could never be anything but residual for his hermeneutic analysis. Parsons argued that this was not necessary. Noncultural processes can be conceptualized analytically—conceived as a level of analysis—and in this way studied independently of other variables. In empirical terms, however, they must be viewed as occurring within the framework of some cultural order. There is never, in empirical terms, purely economic or political process as such. For this very reason there is no necessity to isolate the analysis of culture from the systematic study of other, more material concerns.

But if Parsons outlined the way to avoid the interpretive dilemma, he did not develop a strong enough cultural theory to make this alternative particularly convincing. Indeed, for theorists who were becoming increasingly sensitive to the cultural dimension, Parsons' argument for interrelation often seemed like an attempt to undermine the analysis of culture itself. For this and other theoretical and social reasons, some of Parsons' cultural critics came to believe that hermeneutic analysis would have to be pursued for its own sake. The most notable of these was Clifford Geertz.

In my earlier discussion of the emergence of anti-Parsonian cultural sociology—the developments which occurred among Parsons' students in the course of the 1960s—I suggested that in this initial phase Geertz had developed a strong cultural position without abandoning a multidimensional frame. He demonstrated that religion was an internally complex cultural system which formulated general conceptions of the meaning of life and established powerful moods and motivations in individuals. Yet he was careful to insist that cultural symbols were not by themselves constitutive of persons, structures, or events. On the one hand, the latter are "external" to cultural patterns; on the other hand, it is only by passing through cultural patterns that such processes "can be given a definite form."

Nor, because of this multidimensionality, did Geertz feel the need to dissociate contingency from cultural order. To the contrary, following the logic of his approach to more material processes he insisted that contingency could emerge only within the context of cultural life. "Man depends upon symbols and symbol systems," he wrote, "with a dependence so great as to be decisive for his creatural viability." It is precisely because of this that "even the remotest indication that they [the symbol systems] may prove unable to cope with one or another aspect of experience raises within him the gravest sort of anxiety" and, in turn, becomes the basis for creative change. The challenge for "the comparative sociology and psychology of religion," therefore, is not at all to find "correlations between specific ritual acts and specific secular social ties." It is something quite different, namely, to understand "how men's sense of the reasonable, the practical, the humane, and the moral is colored by men's notions, however implicit, of the 'really real' and the dispositions these [religious] notions induce in men."[15]

There is one other thing I hope you will recall about this early essay. While Geertz was clearly embarked on a strong version of cultural sociology, far from repudiating Parsons' framework he actively embraced it. It is precisely a shift in his public attitude to Parsons that alerts us to a new phase in Geertz's work. "Ideology as a Cultural System" was presented as a companion piece to the essay on religion. It was published two years earlier but I would guess it was actually written some time after.[16] It became by far the better known of the two essays, and the reason is not hard to find. In the midst of the social and intellectual upheaval in Western sociology, it takes a much more explicitly anti-Parsonian stance.

It may come as something of a surprise to you to find in this essay that Geertz lumps Parsons in the same theoretical boat as Marx. He calls both symbolic reductionists and he claims that both are equally barriers to the development of cultural analysis in sociology. True, Marx produced what Geertz calls an "interest"

---

[15] Geertz, "Religion as a Cultural System," p. 645, 652–653, and 683.

[16] Whether or not this is actually true, of course, is something we would have to ask Geertz himself. The timing is not crucial for what follows. For one thing, I am primarily interested in theoretical logic, not historical sequence. For another, the pattern I am describing in Geertz's work becomes increasingly apparent from the late 1960s on, as we will see.

theory approach, while Parsons developed a more complicated theory of ideology as "strain." But all Geertz means by this is that, while Marx envisioned the economy as the only source of reduction, Parsons viewed ideology as reflecting the psychological strain produced by the interaction of social structure and personality. "Both interest theory and strain theory," he insists, "go directly from source analysis to consequence analysis without ever seriously examining ideologies as systems of interacting symbols, as patterns of interworking meanings."[17]

This is a theoretical strategy with which, by now, you should be thoroughly familiar. Geertz has set Parsons up as a straw man. We know from our experience with other anti-Parsonian efforts that such distortion precedes, and legitimates, the effort to establish a theory which is presented as a necessary alternative. This, indeed, is also the case with Geertz. His aim, he tells us after that initial critical discussion, is "to construct an independent science of . . . symbolic action." Social science until now, Geertz suggests, has been "virtually untouched" by the important work which has already proceeded along these lines. He cites, by way of example, the writings of estheticians and philosophers on metaphor, and he tells us that "few [social scientists] seem to have read much of it" (pp. 57–58).

In contrast to his essay on religion, in other words, Geertz now wants to establish an entirely new social scientific theory, one that will focus exclusively on symbols. What will this new symbolic science look like? Geertz argues that it must be centrally concerned with tropes, with rhetorical devices such as metaphor, analogy, irony, ambiguity, pun, and paradox—in a word, with style. At first it looks as if this emphasis, though idealist, will constitute an elaboration of Geertz's theory of cultural systems. Rather than simply elucidating interworking themes, Geertz suggests, we should understand that these themes must always have an esthetic form. Tropes provide this form. They give a shape to cultural discourse; a new wrinkle to the interpretive approach. We must learn to examine the relative power of the tropes which a particular ide-

---

[17] Geertz, "Ideology as a Cultural System," p. 56. Hereafter page references to this article will be given parenthetically in the text that follows.

ological statement contains. If a metaphor is lame—trite and un-inspiring—it may undermine the shaping power of an ideological system even if the other elements of this system have powerful thematic relevance (p. 59).

As we continue to follow Geertz's argument, however, we find that the further elaboration of cultural systems is hardly his point. Indeed, what he pursues with great energy in the remainder of the essay is not how tropes structure symbolic patterns but how they emerge from symbolic action. We must take more seriously, perhaps, the initial definition of the science that Geertz has said he wants to found. His interest is not in a science of symbols or symbolic patterns but in a science of symbolic action. While it is true that every social theory must take a position on action—and even a collective theory can examine individual action from the empirical point of view—Geertz has something quite different in mind. What it involves, in my view, is a shift—within the context of nonrational action—from a collective to an individual under-standing of order. From this point on, his essay is much more about the contingency of meaningful action than about the structure of meaning itself.

If the theoretical logic I laid out earlier holds, Geertz turns to contingency and action because he does not wish to accept the deterministic, objectivist consequences of the pure hermeneutic position he has undertaken. In a crucial passage in the ideology essay, we can find, I think, just this reluctance, and the resulting shift to more action-oriented theory. In what seems, at least retro-spectively, to conclude the more collectivist phase of his analysis, Geertz articulates the notion of tropes in action. He suggests that "the semantic structure" of tropes creates "a configuration of dissimilar meanings out of whose interworking both the expressive power and the rhetorical force" of ideology derive. To understand tropes, in other words, one must look at them as types of symbols and see how they work within the internal structure of symbolic systems themselves. Yet in the very next sentence Geertz seems to say that this is precisely the position he does not want to accept. He insists that the interworking he has just referred does not have to do with symbolic processes internal to cultural systems but with "a social process." It is not something "in the head" but in the "public world where people talk together, name things, [and] make assertions." In the sentence that follows, Geertz reiterates his commitment to "the study of symbolic action" (p. 60).

To maintain the internal intracultural reference, it would seem, provides too mentalistic a picture for Geertz to swallow. With the phrase "in the head," Geertz is telling his readers, and no doubt himself, that he recognizes the idealism of a purely culturalist position. By asserting the need for social and individual process, he is making it clear that he does not want to deny the meaningful intention upon which hermeneutic analysis rests. Since he has abandoned multidimensional theory, however, he can avoid this situation only by embracing contingency. He moves, therefore, from an internal, purely cultural analysis of systems to an internal, purely cultural analysis of action.

We should not, of course, expect Geertz to recognize his inconsistency or to tell us he is changing his mind. Does Rex tell us that "truce" violates the materialism of his conflict theory? Does Homans announce that his theory of distributive justice undermines his insistance on exchange? Geertz, too, remains ostensibly loyal to his general theory, never renouncing his hermeneutic position despite his underlying awareness of its now unattractively collectivist cast. What he does, instead, is to shift the nature of his analysis in a camouflaged way. It is this camouflage, of course, that creates the problems and confusions in a theorist's position. Since theorists cannot fundamentally change their theory without explicitly renouncing it, they change it through the introduction of ad hoc, residual categories.

The closest Geertz comes to actually acknowledging his difficulty occurs in the paragraph immediately following the one I have just discussed. Geertz suggests here that the effort to develop an independent science of culture—"asking the question that most students of ideology fail to ask"—"gets one . . . very quickly into quite deep water indeed." How will he extricate himself from this dangerous situation? By developing, he writes, "a somewhat untraditional and apparently paradoxical theory." The point of this theory is, once again, to insist on human thought as a "public" activity. Only if we do so might we "find our way back from the elusive world of symbols and semantic process." To escape from the dangers of cultural theory, Geertz will turn from the analysis of symbols in themselves to the analysis of symbols as public action.

What follows is a discussion that borders on the phenomenological. "The defining propositions of this sort of approach," Geertz writes, "is that thought consists of the construction and manipulation of symbol systems." This insistence allows him strenuously to differentiate his approach from any hint of idealism. Public thought, he explains, "consists not of ghostly happenings in the head." It directs theory to individual action and away from collective order, to how an individual "match[es] the states and processes of symbolic models against the states and processes of the wider world" (pp. 60–61). Geertz is interested no longer in the structure of symbolic models themselves but rather in how, given their existence, an actor makes use of them to understand the wider world. His subject, he declares a bit later, is "the *construction* of ideologies" (p. 63; italics mine).

I suggested earlier that this resort to contingency leads to indeterminacy. This is true in both a substantive and a more formal sense. Contingent action is by its very nature indeterminable, as ethnomethodologists like Garfinkel have spent their careers pointing out. Equally significant for our interests here, however, is that Geertz cannot even make this contingent action the point of more systematic analysis. Ostensibly, his theory still remains a hermeneutic one. That he does not wish to interpret cultural systems cannot be explicit. Contingent symbolic action must, for this reason, remain a residual category. These difficulties lead, in turn, to another. If a theorist is forced to explain the success or failure of an ideology only by reference to contingent action, and if even this reference cannot be systematically developed, his theory will be able to say very little about ideology indeed. Faced with this prospect, the theorist might well try to step entirely outside of cultural studies itself, shifting his analysis not just from collective to individual order but into the world of purely material processes and things. This, as I mentioned much earlier in this lecture, is the second type of residual category to which hermeneutics falls prey. It introduces another layer of indeterminacy and makes the interpretive dilemma that much harder to bear.

Geertz gets caught in this theoretical whipsaw when he tries, in the later part of his essay, to analyze a particular piece of ideology.

Looking at the problem of Indonesian political ideology in the postwar period, he acknowledges that there was a cultural system already in place. His analysis of this Hindu-Islamic belief as an "exemplary center" is, however, brief. What he is interested in is action, not order, the "search for a new framework" (p. 65). His subject is the Indonesian President Sukarno's attempt to develop a political ideology called Pantjasila. He sees Sukarno as having employed tropes—particularly analogy and metaphor—as "means" to "construct . . . a new symbolic framework." The new ideology failed to hold; it did not achieve the popular consensus Sukarno sought. The question is why, and in the realm of contingent action this is a difficult question to answer. Contingent action is indeterminate. Geertz praises Sukarno's effort as "ingenious," but says little more about the action itself. Why such a clever effort failed, and whether something even more ingenious might have succeeded, Geertz cannot say. Contingent action is a residual category: it cannot be analyzed in a systematic way.

Geertz is caught within the interpretive dilemma. Since he cannot return to the strains and thematic conflicts within the cultural system itself, he has very few options left. One is simply to embrace indeterminacy. The search for a new framework, he suggests at one point, was "intense—but indeterminate" (p. 65). At another point he explains that the reasons for failure were "many and complex." The other option is to step outside of cultural analysis itself. Indeed, in the end Geertz suggests that, after all, "only a few" of the reasons for failure "are themselves cultural" (p. 68). He wants us to believe that it was mainly political and economic developments which eventually caused the whole cultural pattern to dissolve. "The failure to create a conceptual framework in terms of which to shape a modern polity," he argues in his conclusion, "is in great part itself a reflection of the tremendous social and psychological strains that the country and its population are undergoing" (p. 70). This argument is perplexing, if not downright depressing. It would seem to reinstate the very notion of ideology as strain that Geertz designed his essay to refute. It is—there is no getting around it—a reflection theory of culture, not a theory of relative cultural autonomy. Geertz seems, essentially, to have thrown up his hands. No doubt he would tell us that it is a matter of his empirical material. In my view, however, it is the difficulty of his theoretical situation, not the nature of the empirical case, which makes a more satisfactory analysis impossible to attain.

This essay on ideology marked a turning point in Geertz's career. Throughout the social sciences it was seized upon as a definitive statement of the new cultural approach. That it clearly defined the cultural thread of the anti-Parsonian movement I would certainly agree. Geertz emerged as the "cultural spokesman" for social theory in the contemporary period. You will not be surprised, therefore, when I tell you that the strains in his work were never confronted. Rather than being resolved, they were actually deepened. The theoretical position which caused them—the forced choice between idealism and indeterminacy—was increasingly presented by Geertz as the best of all possible theoretical worlds.

In my analysis of the ideology essay, I tried to show how theoretical logic worked, ineluctably, to create a distinctive movement in Geertz's work. Because he intends to produce an independent cultural theory, he begins with a caricature of Parsonian thought, refuting it as a reductionist theory of strain. Still, while he can no longer pursue the multidimensional framework, he does not want to give in to cultural determinacy. The result is that he turns to contingency and indeterminacy, which eventually leads him back to strain theory in an ad hoc, residual way.

I will try to show that exactly the same logic unfolds in an essay which appeared eight years later, the famous ethnography of a cockfight in Bali. This ethnography, "Deep Play: Notes on the Balinese Cockfight," formed the conclusion to *The Interpretation of Cultures*, the collection of essays which has gained for "cultural theory" a growing audience in American social science. For this and other reasons, it is a fitting conclusion to our discussion of his work.

In the background of this essay, if less explicitly, perhaps, than in the earlier work, there lies the same polemic against "functionalist sociology," which is held to treat symbols in a highly reductionist way.[18] Though he acknowledges the role of psychological strain and

---

[18] Geertz, "Deep Play: Notes on the Balinese Cockfight," in Geertz, *The Interpretation of Cultures* (New York: Basic Books, 1973), pp. 412–453. This essay was first published in 1972. Page references to "Deep Play" in the quotations that follow will be given parenthetically in the text.

social structure, Geertz insists he will not himself be guilty of construing culture as their reflection. Again, it is an independent cultural theory that he wants to construct. Yet, as before, Geertz insists that his own version of cultural theory will not be deterministic. His new approach is different. It "shifts the analysis of cultural forms [away] from an endeavor in general parallel to dissecting an organism, diagnosing a symptom, deciphering a code, or ordering a system" (p. 448). He will not, in other words, spend much time trying to understand the internal structure of a cultural system. It is action, nor order, that will draw his attention.

We have been here before. Geertz acknowledges that Bali has an overarching cultural and religious order and that the cockfight is related to it. The men who bring their fighting roosters into the ring sense they are dealing with "The Powers of Darkness." Geertz goes so far, indeed, as to suggest that "in the first instance" a cockfight is a kind of blood sacrifice, complete with ritual chants and oblations to religious demons, and he notes that numerous sacred occasions include such fights as a matter of course (p. 420). Beyond these tantalizingly undeveloped references, however, we find in this later essay virtually nothing at all about the cultural order within which the cockfight rests. Indeed, Geertz makes even shorter shrift of the cultural system here than in the essay on ideology. In forty some pages of text, his thematic discussion of Balinese culture is limited to a single footnote (p. 446, n.34).

It is betting, Geertz believes, that is the key to interpreting the Balinese cockfight. He sees the money which changes hands during the fight as symbolizing its "moral import," but it is the act of betting itself to which he means to attribute morality. Not the structure of meaning but its creation is what he is after. "The imposition of meaning on life," he insists, "is the major end and primary condition of human existence" (p. 432). We are back to contingency, and the indeterminacy that implies.

But Geertz is not simply a phenomenologist. He brings to contingent action his theory of tropes and the imposition of esthetic form. He likens the cockfight to an "art form." It is a "means of expression"—a fiction, a metaphor, an allegory—that gives to Balinese life "a dramatic shape." As a trope in action, the cockfight "catches up [the] themes" in Balinese culture. It "puts a construction on them, makes them . . . visible, tangible, graspable." In fact, the power of this esthetic action is such that, at one point, Geertz describes it as "ordering [the themes] into an encompassing structure" (pp. 443–444).

What is this structure? Even if it is viewed as the result rather than the cause of action it would be very interesting to find out. Unfortunately, Geertz cannot tell us. To do so would evidently bring him too close to ordering a system or deciphering a code, the determinateness he has promised to avoid. Instead of an exposition of interworking themes we are given a litany of indeterminate lists. I can find at least three:

(1) "In the cockfight, man and beast, good and evil, ego and id, the creative power of aroused masculinity and the destructive power of loosened animality fuse in a bloody drama of hatred, cruelty, violence, and death" (p. 420).

(2) "[The cockfight] catches up these themes—death, masculinity, rage, pride, loss, beneficence, chance" (p. 443).

(3) "Drawing on almost every level of Balinese experience, [the cockfight] brings together themes—animal savagery, male narcissism, opponent gambling, status rivalry, mass excitement, blood sacrifice" (p. 449).

Each of these lists contains elements the others do not. If one accurately names the themes caught up by the Balinese cockfight, then the others cannot. This is the first vagueness—an indeterminacy within an indeterminacy! But there is another, much more important one. This is, quite simply, that each list is only a list. A list is not an interpretation of the interworking themes of cultural life.

I suggested earlier that at the end of his essay on ideology Geertz may have sensed the frustration of such a contingent analysis and that he sought to justify it in empirical terms. "Things do not merely *seem* jumbled—they *are* jumbled," he wrote at that time.[19] Here he does exactly the same thing. Though he insists that "any expressive form lives only in its own present—the one it itself creates," he adds that in Bali "that present" is even more contingent and ephemeral than anywhere else. It is "severed into a string of

---

[19] Geertz, "Ideology as a Cultural System," p. 70.

flashes . . . all of them disconnected, aesthetic quanta" (p. 445). In response I would like to bring in something esthetic of my own. To quote Shakespeare, "the fault lies not in the stars but in ourselves." It is Geertz's own theoretical framework, not the facts of Balinese society, that makes a strong cultural analysis so difficult to sustain.

Indeed, right in the midst of his argument for esthetic action and contingent indeterminacy, Geertz suggests that the powerful attraction of the cockfight for the Balinese can only be understood by linking culture to noncultural things. "The question of why such matches are interesting—indeed, for the Balinese, exquisitely absorbing—takes us out of the realm of formal concerns into more broadly sociological and social-psychological ones" (p. 432). He argues that for the Balinese cocks are symbols of sexual organs— "psychologically an Aesopian representation of the ideal/demonic, rather narcissistic, male self." But the social source of attraction is, in his view, even more powerful than this—"sociologically it is an equally Aesopian representation of the complex fields of tension set up by the controlled, muted, ceremonial, but for all that deeply felt, interaction of those selves in the context of everyday life" (p. 436).

What we have here is strain theory in its most explicit form. To understand the Balinese cockfight one must read in it not the interworking of cultural themes but the tensions of the social system. The secret to the symbol is social status. It is "a simulation of the matrix, the involved system of cross-cutting, overlapping, highly corporate groups . . . in which its devotees live" (p. 436). What follows this statement is a succinct description of the status structure of Balinese society, followed by several pages of one-to-one correlations between this status structure and the pattern of betting in the cockfight itself.

Do you remember how Geertz attacked the idea of correlating symbols with social and psychological things in "Religion as a Cultural System"? He insisted, at that time, that what cultural analysts should do instead is to trace how cultural notions color people's sense of what the "really real" psychological and social things are (see above, p. 317). What he has done here is quite the opposite. He has described the status structure as if it were, in fact, really real—as if it were formed, that is, without any cultural mediation—and he has suggested that this entirely social thing determines the basic pattern of culture in turn. But he cannot really do anything else. At this later point in his career, he has no description of "cultural notions" to draw upon. Because he abandoned the multidimensional frame of that earlier essay, he cannot allow himself to reconstruct a cultural system. For this reason he has turned to contingency, and it is because of his unease with indeterminate contingency that he has embraced the "really real" level of social and psychological strain. The interpretive dilemma is, for hermeneutic theory, impossible to escape.

The same reduction of symbols to noncultural status structures occurs in Geertz's more recent book-length treatment of nineteenth-century Bali, *Negara,* and the same resort to contingency and indeterminacy marks his most recent collection of essays, *Local Knowledge.*[20] The title of this last collection, it seems to me, tells us quite a bit about where Geertz's response to the interpretive dilemma has taken his work. In concluding this lecture, I would like to develop this point.

In the introduction he supplied to the first collection of his essays, the collection which stretched from cultural system to cockfight, Geertz tried to describe the position at which he had finally arrived. He criticized the argument that culture should be treated "purely as a symbolic system" and scrutinized for its "underlying structures." What's wrong with such an approach is that it turns cultural analysis away from "its proper object," which Geertz describes as nothing other than "the informal logic of actual life." It is "behavior" that must be attended to, because it is "through the flow of behavior" that "cultural forms find articulation." It is not from their intrinsic relationship to one another but from their "use" in social life that cultural forms "draw their meaning." The social scientist, therefore, gains access to meaning "by inspecting events, not by arranging abstracted entities into unified patterns."[21] A more anti-analytical, anti-collectivist, indeed anti-textual perspective

---

[20] Geertz, *Negaria: The Theatre State in Nineteenth-Century Bali* (Princeton: Princeton University Press, 1980); Geertz, *Local Knowledge* (New York: Basic Books, 1983).

[21] Geertz, "Thick Description: Toward an Interpretive Theory of Culture," pp. 3–30, in Geertz, *The Interpretation of Cultures.*

on culture would be hard to find. In his early essay on religion as a cultural system, of course, Geertz took a completely different position. Abstraction was precisely what the interpretor must do. From this perspective, events are the bane of cultural analysis, which seeks, to the contrary, to convert social action and events into a cultural text.

In my view, it is no accident that in that earlier effort Geertz also took a very positive attitude toward the possibilities of cultural theory. The notion that culture is abstractable from events assumes that meaning has an objective dimension, an element which actors have in common, that because it is social serves to regulate contingent interaction. Because theory is simply one form of such objective culture, to believe in the possibility for cultural abstraction is to believe in the possibility for cultural theory. No wonder, then, that in the introduction he writes to the collection of essays which includes "Ideology" and "Cockfight" Geertz announces that theory is impossible. "The terms in which such formulations can be cast," he writes, "are, if not wholly nonexistent, very nearly so."[22] Theoretical terms are nearly nonexistent because they are general terms, and in his turn to contingency Geertz assumes that generality beyond concrete events is hardly possible. The goal of cultural analysis must now be interpretation, not theory.

The title of that first introductory essay was "Thick Description." It was description, not generalization, that Geertz had come to think that cultural analysis must do. By the time he writes the introduction to his second collection of essays, this attack on theory has become more confident and explicit. "Calls for 'a general theory' of just about anything social," Geertz argues, "sound increasingly hollow, and claims to have one megalomanic."[23] Once again, the turn from theory to description is tied to the critique of cultural generality itself. "The shapes of knowledge," Geertz insists a paragraph later, "are always ineluctably local, indivisible from their instruments and their encasements." He concludes that "one may veil this fact with ecumenical rhetoric or blur it with strenuous theory, but one cannot really make it go away."

[22] *The Interpretation of Cultures*, p. 24.
[23] Geertz, "Introduction," *Local Knowledge*, p. 4.

With this turn from theory, we must ourselves turn reluctantly away from Geertz. I say "reluctantly" because nobody in the postwar period has taught us more about the case for a strong cultural theory than he. More than any other body of work, his writing has inspired the revival of cultural studies. If a strong cultural theory is actually to be made, however, and if cultural studies are not only to be revived but really carried out, the analysis of culture must proceed within a much more consistently multidimensional frame.

LECTURE EIGHTEEN
MARXISM (1):
THE LEGACY AND THE REVIVAL

MOST OF MY discussion in these lectures has been about what might be called the technical aspects of social theory. I have been primarily concerned with social theory as explanation. Of course, the elements I have focused on have been extremely general ones. My focus has been on "presuppositions," and as I have defined them they are far removed from empirical facts. Still, they are assumptions which are made with an explanatory purpose. To try to explain why something happens in society we must ask what kind of action makes it go and what kind of order makes it hold together. What is presupposed by these assumptions are certain things about the constitution of the world. Presuppositions are oriented to what is.

There is a very different kind of assumption which has received much less attention here. These are notions about what society should be rather than notions about what it is. In these lectures I have referred to such elements as ideological assumptions rather than as presuppositions, though—like other theoretical elements, for example, models and methods—they are just as "presupposed." Now, I certainly have not neglected ideology altogether. I have stressed that Parsons' commitment to liberal political ideals was critical to the formation of his theory, and that his movement in the postwar period toward a more quiescent, self-satisfied liberalism significantly effected his later work. One of the significant themes in my subsequent discussion, moreover, has been how ideological disillusionment in the post-1960 period significantly undermined the legitimacy of Parsonian theory. Parsons not only explained the world in a certain way, but he wanted a certain kind of liberal world to exist. As this kind of world seemed less possible, to many the liberal position began to seem less desirable as well. This ideological confrontation between two different visions of what ought to be, I have argued, fueled the controversies over different presuppositions about what is.

For all of this, however, ideology has not assumed center stage in my discussion. The reason is straight-forward enough: ideology has not, I think, been the central point of the theories we have discussed. All theories have ideologies and presuppositions, but they do not play the same role in every theoretical work. Indeed, what distinguishes sociological theory from, say, moral and political philosophy, is the different roles ideological assumptions play in these different kinds of work. The ambition of most sociological theory is "scientific" in the sense of being committed to explaining, as objectively and neutrally as possible, the structure and workings of the world. That sociological theory itself can, in fact, never be scientific in the positivist sense of producing explanations which simply mirror the world does not delegitimate this scientific ambition. The "theoretical work" of Parsons and his anti-Parsonian successors has been scientifically ambitious in this sense. Though implicit ideological commitments have had their effect, the argument on both sides has been about the right way to explain, not to evaluate, the world.

This relative emphasis, however, should not blind us to the fact that even scientific, sociological theory is a form of self-reflection and not simply explanation. Even if theorists do not make evaluation their primary task, the existential relevance remains. Explanatory theory cannot be reduced to values, but it is inextricably related to them. A theorist's presuppositions structure his explanatory theory, and as do other cognitive commitments, but this theory will not be of much interest unless it can be used to understand the world in a value-related sense. Parsons did not adopt a collectivist perspective on order simply because he disliked laissez-faire capitalism and the values associated with it. At the same time, one of the major reasons he so valued his collectivist frame of reference was because he could use it to work out a morally acceptable alternative to the free market system. While in the beginning of his career Parsons was quite sensitive to this ideological ambition of his sociology, in his later work he seems to have quite forgotten it.

Marxism, by contrast, is the theoretical tradition which never forgets. What differentiates it from other forms of contemporary theory is not its presuppositions but its ideology, and, of course, the different empirical models and insights which this combination of presupposition and ideology implies. It is not simply the nature of Marxist ideology, however, that distinguishes it from other theory. It is also the role that this ideology plays. Marxism is the only form of sociological theory which wears its moral commitments on its sleeve. Its ambition is as much evaluative as explanatory, its goal and self-conception as much political as scientific. I do not think this makes Marxist sociological theory less scientific than others. "More than scientific" might be a better phrase. If we want to understnd why such self-consciously critical theory revived in the contemporary period, then, we will have to deepen our understanding of the ideological background of sociological work.

Since the beginning of the nineteenth century, three fundamentally different ideologies have been in conflict in the Western world. Left-wing, radical ideology and right-wing, conservative ideology both have had an explicitly critical, transcendental purpose.[1] Liberal ideology, the position in the middle, has had a more incremental approach. Liberal ideology has accepted "bourgeois individualism" and sought to increase it. Left- and right-wing ideologies have usually rejected it and sought to restore some version of community. Liberal ideology has accepted the irreversability of many facets of historical "progress" in the modern world, not only individualism but also industrialism, rationalization, differentiation, and secularization. It has tried to change things but rarely in anything more than a piecemeal way. Conservative and radical ideologies, by contrast, have seen such "modern" developments as neither inevitable nor as entirely progressive. They have asked whether modern

---

[1] I should say right away that these labels of liberal and conservative are historical. They do not necessarily apply to the divisions in contemporary American and European politics. In America, for example, conservatives and liberals are both "liberals" in the historical sense which I develop below.

rationality is really rational, whether individuation actually frees the individual or merely binds him or her by a more alienating if less visible chain. Their ambition, then, is to overcome the contemporary phase of modernity rather than to change it in an incremental way.

But the similarities between left and right ideologies should not be overdrawn. There are parallels in their objections to liberalism but there are crucial differences as well. Radical theories seek to transcend the historical process in a forward direction. They accept key segments of modernization, like rationalization, industrialization, and secularization, but believe these can be combined with less individualism and more community. Their version of community, moreover, is egalitarian rather than hierarchical. Conservatives, by contrast, seek to transcend contemporary history in a backward direction. They want to restore essential characteristics of pre-modern times, often opposing, for example, secularization in the name of religious authority and rationality in the name of tradition. For this reason, while radicals have sought to transcend the status quo by increasing equality, conservatives have tried to negate it by restoring hierarchy.

In the course of the nineteenth century intense competition developed between these ideological movements. Liberalism made its seemingly (to its protagonists) "inexorable" progress with the rise of laissez-faire and utilitarian ideologies in England and the United States. Conservative themes, as reactionary and romantic ideologies, became increasingly powerful in Germany and Central and Eastern Europe. Radical ideologies, like Marxism, anarchism, and utopian socialism grew in various countries not only among the working but the middle and upper classes. Until the first World War, liberalism looked as if it were the ideology on the ascendance, the American and French revolutions having led the way. From 1917 until the end of World War II, however, radical and conservative ideologies had their day. The period was bounded by the Russian and Chinese revolutions, which ushered in communism, and its middle years were filled with a series of revolutions from the conservative right, which ushered in the Fascist regimes of Germany, Italy, and Spain.

These victories were, of course, short lived. Fascism and Stalinism appeared to discredit left- and right-wing ideologies for good. In the postwar period, the lesson seemed to have been learned that transcendence was impossible. Incremental liberalism, which to be sure had its own political variations, seemed the only viable option left. The vast majority of conservatives, socialists, and centrists alike now accepted its tenets. "Modernization" would be accepted, while being ameliorated and reformed from within. Those who wished to change society would stick with the day-to-day struggle over the distribution of wealth. They would recognize the necessity for social conflict without transcendence. They would accept the inevitable individuation of society without necessarily abandoning community. They would resign themselves to the inevitability of hierarchy without totally negating equality.

This liberal consensus, we have seen, was a personal stimulus to Parsons' later social theory. Because it reflected Western society in a particular historical juncture, it also defined the empirical reference points for his systematic analysis. Liberalism, finally, provided the ideological sources for the strong resonance of Parsons' theory in this postwar period. Parsons wanted to go beyond individualism toward community and social integration, but he held that individualism could still be maintained. He wanted to go beyond instrumental, anti-human rationality, but he believed that more value-infused rationality could still be at the center of modern society. Individuality, even if social, still exists; rationality, even if relative, is still possible. The antitheses of modern society cannot be abolished but, if both sides are embraced, they can be brought into contact and made to qualify each other. For example, the differentiated autonomy of various spheres, like economy, culture, and polity, cannot be rejected if freedom and flexibility are to obtain, but there must be quite a bit of integration, or interpenetration, between these spheres if the freedom is to be liberating and the flexibility is not to lead to stalemate.

Parsons was not, of course, the only important liberal sociological theorist in the postwar period. Raymond Aron, the French liberal who was a leading anticommunist intellectual, held much the same views. Parsons' theoretical influence, however, meant that it was his work which, in sociology, came to be identified with liberalism as such. As we have seen, however, liberalism was not just an ideological value for Parsons; in his later writings he came increasingly to view liberalism as an accomplished fact, as having an empirical rather than a normative status. In France, Aron employed liberalism in a critical way to warn his fellow citizens against the stalemate that pluralism could induce and to urge, in turn, the appropriate incremental reforms.[2] Parsons would have none of this. For him liberalism was institutionalized in American society in the postwar period. It identified U.S. society as then constituted. In this way, liberalism became for Parsons not just an ideology but an ideological bias, indeed an evaluative straightjacket. How would any future problems of American society, therefore, be evaluated and explained? By identifying his explanation of society so closely with his evaluation of it, Parsons became unable to provide a standard for self-reflection on his own time. When the strains and conflicts of the postwar period began, his theory became existentially irrelevant. The stage was set for the Marxist challenge to Parsonian theory, but it did not come right away.

But while Parsons was by far the most influential postwar liberal theorist, many of his early critics were part of the liberal consensus as well. Most postParsonian theory challenged significant aspects of Parsons' ideological vision without ever stepping outside the boundaries of an incrementalist, liberal version of progress. They departed from Parsons in their confidence in the ability of liberalism to be institutionalized or in their acceptance of the precise balance he gave to liberalism's different elements. They did not, however, give up liberalism completely.

At first glance you might think that this was certainly not true of conflict theory. Rex, whose work we discussed at length, certainly gave up on Parsons' presuppositional idealism and narrowed rationality in an instrumental way. If rationality is not a value but an instrumental motive, it would seem, in addition, that Rex would have to give up on the liberal idea of community as well. Indeed, Rex's actor is very much the selfish atom pursuing his own interests,

---

[2] Raymond Aron, "Social Class, Political Class, Ruling Class," *European Journal of Sociology* 1 (1960):260–281. Aron's *Progress and Disillusion* (New York: Praeger, 1968), written in the midst of the social conflicts of the 1960s, exemplifies how liberal sociology can be remarkably critical of the liberal society of its own time. The difference between this kind of liberal sociology and Parsons' by then quiescent liberalism is marked. In the 1960s, Parsons could never have written such a critical book.

not the individual who is socialized to act and feel in an altruistic, morally obligatory way. This turns out, however, to be the basis for a different version of liberalism, not the foundation of an alternative ideology.

Rex sets up his conflict model of society so that there is a strong and independent working class to challenge the selfish and dominating elite. The achievements of this working class, in his view, have much to their historical credit. They have laid the basis for a liberal, pluralistic society within the context of capitalism by sustaining the egalitarian "truce" between classes. With luck, Rex believes, this balance of power may eventually neutralize the class war. This hope leads him to the liberal belief in the necessity of preserving the institutions of Western capitalism rather than transcending them.

The other contemporary theorists we have considered—Homans, Blumer, Goffman, Garfinkel, and Geertz—each depart more fundamentally from Parsons' liberal theory. Insofar as each embraces individualism, each gives up on the community which, according to Parsons' liberalism, is necessary for a modern democratic society. This individualism reflects, in part, a retreat—in the face of growing conflict and change—from Parsons' confident assertions about inclusion and reconciliation between citizens and social groups. The focus on individual action at the expense of collective order also reflects the greater pessimism in this late postwar period about the ability of sociological theory to handle the "big issues" like the relationship between power and equality and the nature of a liberal culture.

Yet even these theorists are still liberals. They believe that individuality can and must be realized in modern society. They describe individual integrity as the basis for social process and order. They believe that the individual's interpretive ability is more or less rational and his common sense in good working order. True, their easy acceptance of rationality, as either inborn efficiency or natural common sense, points to weaknesses in their liberal ideals. When Blumer and Garfinkel urge that we need simply to get inside the heads of actors or accept "members' rationality," they have abandoned the capacity of liberalism to constitute an independent standard of ideological judgment. Geertz's situational relativism does much the same thing. The cynicism and privatism which pervade Homans' and (some of) Goffmans' views of interaction make it difficult to believe that rationality and community could ever be social ideals. These theoretical perceptions point to the danger of apolitical withdrawal from the project of incremental reform. Still, these theorists all believe that, for better or worse, in the society in which they live individuals can control their fate and that cooperation is possible.

By the late 1960s, however, this kind of ideological equivocation wasn't enough. For many, especially younger theorists, a deep sense of social crisis had taken hold. If liberalism was not wrong in itself, these disaffected theorists were convinced it was grossly in error as a description of American and Western European society. Many, moreover, had become quite persuaded that liberalism was wrong in a more fundamental sense. It was in these circumstances that Marxism attained an important position in contemporary sociological theory. Drawing upon European sources such as the Frankfurt school and the work of once marginal American radical social scientists like C. Wright Mills, Paul Sweezy and Paul Baran, Marxism moved from the periphery to the center of theoretical debate.

It was not, I believe, its specific presuppositional or empirical elements but more its ideological resonance that explains Marxism's initial theoretical attraction. For Marxism, fundamental alienation was a given in capitalist society. The calm of the postwar period, far from indicating the inherent progress of liberal society, was an anomaly, the calm before the storm. Parsons took the postwar welfare state as the symbol of contemporary society, and predicted there would be more of the same. Marxism took the Great Depression and the world war which succeeded it as typical, and also predicted more of the same. The growing individuality which Parsons lauded seemed to Marxist theorists only the artifice of market economics. The rationality he saw increasing they claimed to be the false consciousness produced by advanced technology.

It is important to understand, of course, that Marxism is much more than an ideology. If we are to perceive its achievements and limitations, the internal strains that create its theoretical dynamic, we must be clear about its presuppositions, models, and empirical predictions as well. Stripped of its unique ideological position,

Marxism is actually conflict theory of a particular type. Action, at least in capitalist society, is viewed as instrumental in the extreme. Order is viewed as collective, so the individual stands to society in a dominated way. In terms of model, society is seen as composed of two parts, superstructure and base. The base is composed of the forces and relations of production—technology and division of labor on the one hand, legal relations of property on the other. The superstructure consists of political, cultural, and intellectual ideas and institutions, and it is considered by Marx to be a mere reflection of the structure of the base. The way property articulates economic forces defines the class structure of any economy. Classes respond to the way property distributes economic forces, their ideas being the product of their rational interests so formed. Economic forces have an internal dynamic of their own, and as they evolve they will eventually come into conflict with the given property relations of that historical period. The contradiction between the forces and relations of productions is the motor of history. Class struggle and revolution is the result. The history of all societies, Marx believed, is the history of class struggles.

What I have sketched here is the "orthodox" sociological theory articulated by Marx and his immediate followers. As you can see, it has a spectacularly deterministic logic. Part of this is presuppositional. As we learned from our discussion of conflict theory, instrumental action plus collective order equals anti-voluntary control. Part of it, however, is the special kind of model Marx employed, which both draws from and informs empirical findings that are particularly disastrous for the future of Western society. In this sense, the explanatory elements in Marx's theory go well with its strongly critical ideology.

There is another sense, however, in which the determinism of the theory contradicts the ideology. For Marxist ideology is not only a value system of critique. It is also an ideology of transcendance. It eschews liberal incrementalism because it sees the possibility of a dramatically different world. The extraordinary suffering which Marx felt to be humankind's fate is matched only by his extravagant hopes for its salvation. If you are thinking that I have made Marxism sound a bit like religion, then I am making my point. As I see it, Marxism presents a secularization of the most radical strands of the Judeo-Christian tradition. Transcendance has, of course, been a major thrust of Western religion from the beginning, and in the form of God's will it has often provided the standard for vigorous critique of human morality. This devaluation of the contemporary world has been combined with strong millennial currents, the belief that at some future time God's kingdom will be realized on earth. Sometimes the means to achieve this salvation is earthly activity; more usually it is the appearance of a savior.

Marxism continued the transcendance of the Western tradition, applying its millennial hopes to purely earthly activities. In each age, Marx believed, the vehicle for salvation is the oppressed class. For capitalism this means the proletariat, the "working" class dependent for its survival on factory labor. For Marx and his socialist and communist followers, the working class was truly an object of ideological veneration. In it they invested their hopes for world transformation and the advent of the postcapitalist utopia, the kingdom of God on earth. They believed that despite, or indeed because of, its initial degeneration, the proletariat would soon become a source of vitality and criticism. It would come to possess a consciousness of its own, and through its strength of will transform the relations of production—the laws of private property—and create a new world.

Marxist ideology, then, has an extremely voluntaristic aspect to it. The explanatory theory, however, is completely different. It is as deterministic as can be. This contradiction sets the stage for fundamental conflicts within Marxist work. By now it will come as no surprise that I will define these conflicts as theoretical and ideological dilemmas.

The ideological dilemma is internal to the evaluative dimension of Marxism itself. While salvation through world transformation is predicted, it has never come. Western countries have proved much more resistant to revolution than Marx ever imagined. Indeed, there has never been a socialist or communist revolution in the more developed nations, where Marx thought they would occur. Instead, the first and by far the most intellectually consequential revolution in the twentieth century occurred in Russia, and every one since has taken place in equally undeveloped countries. The communism which has resulted from these revolutions has, from the beginning, been deeply intertwined with national interests, particularly with the interests of Russia. Because of the ways these communist nations have developed, moreover, Marxism has been seen, at least in the eyes of many Western intellectuals, as associated with dictatorship rather than liberation and with a commitment to industrialization rather than to going beyond it.

These facts—that Western revolutions never came and that the Eastern ones differed markedly from what was expected—have presented tremendous difficulties for Marxist ideology. One typical response has been simply to give up the belief in transcendance all together. In the early 1950s, an international group of former communist intellectuals published a book called *The God That Failed.* They confessed their disillusionment with radical utopianism and explained why this had led them to liberal, and even in some cases relatively conservative ideologies. But what if a theorist does not want to abandon the hope for radical transcendance? What will he do if, in other words, he wants to remain within Marxism? In this situation, the Marxist theorist, I believe, is bound to accept one of two ideological choices, neither of which will ultimately prove satisfactory.

One choice is to put revolution off into some indefinite future. It will come eventually, but we don't know when. In the meantime, of course, there is no point in engaging in revolutionary activity. This has been the tack taken by Marxist theorists of what has come to be called the "social democratic" type. An evolutionary rather than revolutionary view of the present period, it was first articulated by the leaders of the great German Social Democratic Party, the largest socialist party in Europe before the first world war. Since then it has been taken up by the socialist and working class parties which today hold substantial power in capitalist countries around the world. The problem with this resolution of the ideological dilemma, however, is that it leads to apoliticism and resignation. Putting the revolution off into the indefinite future may at first allow the transcendental idea to be maintained, but eventually it undermines the vitality of the idea itself. When this occurs, Marxist ideology comes dangerously close to the liberal incrementalism it was designed to displace.

In reaction against this choice and to the problems it implies there arises—both logically and historically—the movement back toward an activist alternative. This movement, of course, must still face the fact that revolution has not occurred. But its response is completely different. Instead of arguing that revolution simply cannot be made, it is argued that revolutionaries have just not tried hard enough. This hyper-voluntaristic choice has taken different forms. When Lenin designed the Bolshevik party, the conspiratorial, vanguard structure that eventually made the Russian revolution, he rejected the passivity of the Russian workers and the German socialist party alike. "The strength of the modern movement lies in the awakening of the mass," he wrote; "its weakness lies in the lack of consciousness and initiative among the revolutionary leaders." The Bolsheviks, he argued, against the evolutionary passivity of social democracy, "are dissatisfied with this submission to elemental forces, i.e., bowing to what is 'at the present time.' "[3]

"Leninism" became associated with the belief that revolution could be induced through the exercise of political will and disciplined struggle. Trotsky, the great Marxist leader and intellectual theorist who aided Lenin before becoming the enemy of his successor, Stalin, argued that the Russian revolution would never achieve real communism unless there was "permanent revolution" on a world-wide scale. He was perhaps the first to respond to the disappointment of the Russian revolution, and turning away from the incrementalist pole he was doing so in a typically Leninist way. In doing so, he had a similar response to the frustration of revolutionary failure.

"Maoism," the revolutionary theory created by the leader of Chinese communism, Mao Tse-Tung, can also be understood in this manner. Frustrated with the slow pace of socialist change after the Chinese revolution and determined to avoid the "conservatism" of the Russian example, Mao initiated movements like the Great Leap Forward and the Cultural Revolution. Mao's intention was to transcend the supposedly deterministic "laws of history" which Marx himself had conceived and, thereby, to bring an immediate transformation of Chinese society. Similar efforts—often called

---

[3] V. I. Lenin, *What Is to Be Done?* (1902; New York: International Publishers, 1929), pp. 31, 26 respectively.

"leftwing communism"—developed in Western countries in response to growing frustration with the absence of revolutionary change. Rosa Luxemburg, for example, developed the notion of "spontaneity" and in the aftermath of the first world war tried to organize a putsch-like revolution in Germany. Most of the Western movements for immediate action, however, came from radical movements like anarchism which were outside of Marxism itself, for reasons I will discuss later.

This cult of action is ultimately no more satisfying than the evolutionary choice. Will and determination are not enough to transcend earthly conditions, even if they are enough, sometimes, to make revolutions. If "objective conditions" in the West have not allowed a revolution to be made, it seems that conditions in the East have condemned them to disappointment, no matter what the hopes of their leaders. It is possible that Lenin himself learned this lesson when, in the final years of his life, he saw the radical, critical spirit of the Russian revolution perverted by the brutality of Stalin. After Lenin's death, Stalin harnessed Russian communism to the murderous effort to make Russia an advanced industrial and military country. Trotsky and Mao, no matter what their earthly disappointments, never changed their secular millennial views. They continued to believe in the transcendent power of will to the day they died.

But the personal reactions of these leaders cannot negate the internal logic of the ideological dilemma. Their followers in the communist movement have often learned opposite lessons from the past. Since the mid-1930s, communist parties in the West have largely ceased to foment revolution. Today, communist Marxism— and we will see in the lecture which follows that in the contemporary period communism is hardly identical with Marxism as such—has developed a "Eurocommunist" branch which seeks active cooperation with liberal movements. The post-Mao leaders of China, for their part, are much more chary of willed transcendence than their founder, and they seem now to be setting a conservative, incrementalist course. While the frustration with reformism leads to activism, the disappointment with activism leads back to reformism. This dilemma cannot be escaped without stepping outside of Marxist ideology itself.

As compared to this ideological dilemma, the theoretical dilemma of Marxism initially develops from problems generated by its explanatory presuppositions. I explained much earlier in these lectures that conflict theory tries to escape objective determinacy in various ways. It is difficult, indeed, for any theorist of human behavior to accept complete external determination in a consistent and unequivocal form. This latent dissatisfaction is exacerbated for Marxism because deterministic presuppositions are here in dramatic tension with ideological hopes.

The determinacy of Marxist theory is difficult for even evolutionary ideologies to maintain. Even as incrementalists, they must maneuver through the day-to-day world of political struggle, and this war of maneuver convinces them that every action involves some choice. Determinacy is virtually impossible to accept for theorists in the more radical camp. On both sides, then, Marxist theorists have continually sought to introduce voluntarism into the original theory. They can do so, of course, only by altering their presuppositions about action and order. They give action a less instrumental, more interpretive and emotional hue, and they suggest that collective order be conceived in a cultural and not just a structural form.

The problem is that, if these theorists are to remain loyal to "Marxism," to the systematic determinism which set Marx's original work so distinctively apart, they cannot make such fundamental alterations in an explicit way. They must camouflage their revisions, and because they must do so their new concepts are rarely more than residual to the orthodox parts of their work. The presence of residual categories, of course, makes theory vague and uncertain. A residual category is rarely systematically developed, and its relation to the body of the theory is, by definition, impossible to make explicit. If these categories were precise and specific, the challenge to orthodoxy would be too explicit to be ignored.

This sets up one side of the theoretical dilemma. Theorists dissatisfied with systematic determination may choose to refer to "voluntarist" and "idealist" elements in a residual and indeterminate way. The other side of the dilemma appears because indeterminacy and residual category are, for any theorist worth his salt, not a very happy place to be. They are not satisfactory in themselves, and they uncomfortably imply a certain disloyalty to orthodox theory. For both of these reasons, every "Marxist with second thoughts" ends up by trying to reintroduce orthodox determinism at the same time. In one form or another, every Marxist theorist I know of—even the most original and ambitious—ends up by suggesting that economic forces are, in fact, determinate "in the last instance."

Marx's own coworker, Frederick Engels, first set out the poles of this dilemma. Responding to academic criticisms of the systematic determinism of their original work as well as to the practical demands of the day, he suggested that "various elements of the superstructure" like political constitutions, religious views, and traditions "play a part" in history independently of economic demands. Yet in the same breath he sought to make the contrary point that "the economic movement finally reasserts as necessary." Otto Bauer, an important Austrian Social Democrat, claimed the mantle of Marxism even while maintaining that nations are held together as much by "common morals and customs [and] common cultural tradition" as by common economic life. Lenin claimed that economic forces and class movements were the principal motors of history but argued at the same time that communist theory, a superstructural element if ever there was one, somehow also played an independent, central role: "The role of the vanguard," he wrote, "can only be fulfilled by a party that is guided by an advanced theory." Georg Lukács places alienated subjectivity and consciousness at the center of his theory of capitalist oppression, but he maintained that it was the objective class position of the proletariat which ensured that their consciousness would eventually be put right.

We have seen how Trotsky blamed objective conditions outside Russia for the Stalinist perversion—the "permanent revolution" he insisted was necessary never occured. But Trotsky also tried to explain Stalinism by the superstructural fact that the Soviet proletariat had "no tradition of dominion or command." In much the same way, Mao Tse-Tung asserted the general principles of economic determinism while embracing the idea that "the relations of production, theory and the superstructure" can sometimes play a "principal and decisive role." Antonio Gramsci, the founder of

Italian Communism, invented the notion of "ideological hegemony" to explain how the pervasiveness of capitalist ideology can make workers voluntarily committed to capitalism even without oppressive economic constraint, which represented a significant departure from one-dimensional theorizing. At the same time, however, Gramsci argued that the intellectuals who develop such ruling ideas always do so in the interests of a dominant economic class.[4]

I could go on to discuss the other major figures in twentieth-century Marxist thought, but, for all the value of their work, you would not learn anything new. The reason is that the underlying theoretical problem each faces is always the same. In trying to change their theory, Marxists face a problem of the most mundane sort, one which all of you can easily understand: they want to have their cake and eat it too. To avoid determinacy, they have tried to include in their theories an autonomous superstructure. None, however, have developed a systematic theory of how superstructures actually work. Why? Because to avoid turning their backs on Marxism they have had to make this reference residual and the forces of production most powerful in the end. Their work veers back and forth between the Scylla of indeterminacy and the Charybdis of the last instance. To avoid this deadly choice, to escape the theoretical dilemma of Marxism, they would have to dissolve the Marxist frame itself, and this is something they obviously cannot do.

I have spent some time describing the multilayered structure of Marxist theory. It was toward this theory, I have argued, that the delegitimation of liberal ideas in the postwar period eventually led. Parsons' critics never completely abandoned liberal ideology, even when they challenged functionalism in every other way. When the

---

[4] For Engels, see "Letter to J. Block, September 21–22, 1890," in *Marx and Engels: Selected Works* (1962), 1:448–490; for Bauer, see "The Concept of the 'Nation,'" in Tom Bottomore and Patrick Goode, eds., *Austro-Marxism* (London, 1978), p. 102; for Lenin, see *What Is to Be Done?* p. 28; for Lukács, see "Reification and the Consciousness of the Proletariat," in Lukács, *History and Class Consciousness* (1923; Cambridge, Mass.: MIT Press, 1971), e.g., p. 162; for Trotsky, see the selection from his *The Revolution Betrayed*, in Irving Howe, ed., *The Basic Writings of Trotsky* (New York: Vintage, 1976), p. 217; for Mao, see "On Contradiction," in Anne Fremantle, ed., *Mao Tse-Tung: An Anthology of His Writings* (New York: New American Library, 1962), p. 232; for Gramsci, see "The Intellectuals," in Gramsci, *Selections from the Prison Notebooks* (London: New Left Books, 1971), pp. 3–23.

ideological environment of sociology began to crumble in the 1960s, for the younger generation of theorists Marxism seemed like the only viable option to take its place. If I am to ask you to jump from the abstract delineation of Marxist theory which I have just given you to the revival of Marxist theorizing in the contemporary period, however, I must give this "general logic" a much more historical form.

To move from the theoretical logic of Marxism to the Marxist turn in contemporary theory you must see the difference between "Soviet Marxism" and Marxism as such. If the non-Marxist challenge to Parsons cannot be understood without seeing the peculiar character of the postwar period, neither can Marxism itself. To understand postwar Marxism, moreover, we must go back much further, to explore the ramifications of the Russian Revolution of 1917. This was the first revolution made in the name of Marx's communism. Henceforth, the Russian approach to communist action and the Russian approach to communist theory had tremendous prestige in the international Marxist movement.

Lenin himself, of course, had taken up the activist pole of the ideological dilemma. After 1917, however, international communism was designed to serve Russia's needs, not the needs of revolutionary movements in particular capitalist nations. By the late 1930s, moreover, Russia was not actively interested in promoting Western revolutions at all. Its goal was to stabilize its own international position. In order to do so, it sought to mollify, not antagonize, the ruling circles of capitalist nations. Communist theory accepted the structure of the world as it was. Fundamental transformations would inevitably occur, but they would be the result of very long-term shifts in the objective conditions of society. In the meantime the slogan would be live-and-let-live. Trotsky was expelled from the Communist International, exiled from Russia, and eventually assassinated by Stalin's agents. Mao was castigated as a "left-wing communist," a revealing epithet which, ironically, can be traced back to Lenin himself.

If the ideological shell of Marxism hardened, so did its presuppositions. First, the commitment to the status quo made the search for a voluntaristic Marxism seem less urgent. Most of the great revisions of Marxian orthodoxy, moreover, had come from Western

Marxists outside of Russia. Russian Communists sought to delegitimate these theoretical revisions in order to maintain their intellectual hegemony over Marxists in other countries. Finally, there were theoretical issues specific to Russia itself. Understandings of Marx usually grew out of perceptions of Hegel, Marx's great philosophical forebear. Western Marxists typically read Hegel in a subjective way, and upon this understanding they built a subjective reading of Marx. The perception of Hegel in Russia, however, had taken on extraordinarily objectivist tones. The political tasks of Russian Communism, moreover, focused much more on economic success than on changing political or cultural conditions. It was perfectly natural for its Marxism to be of an economically reductionist sort.

Under these intellectual influences, Russian Marxism became exceedingly mechanistic. This mechanism, moreover, presented itself in a much more simplistic way than in Marx himself. Stalin wrote tracts which took economic determinism and a faith in the objective laws of nature to ludicrous extremes, and major Marxist intellectuals in Western countries either bowed to his word or exited the Communist Party. Bauer was written off as a social democrat. Lukács was induced to make a humiliating confession about the "idealist" errors of his early work. Gramsci's theory was interpreted in a way that undermined its challenging intent. Karl Korsch, a philosopher who in the 1920s had also helped to fuel the voluntaristic revision, retired to a timid political economy in his later work. The Marxist social scientists who made significant contributions in the 1930s and 1940s, and there were many, did so under the banner of an orthodox economic determinism.

By the beginning of the postwar period few self-respecting intellectuals were attracted to Marxism. Not only had it lost its revolutionary ambitions, but with the revelations about Stalin's brutal dictatorship an intellectual sacrifice for mother Russia seemed pointless. The apparent degeneracy of Russian Communism made the possibility of transcendence seem well-nigh impossible. Theoretically much the same kind of repulsion occurred. There were not only ideological reasons for intellectuals in the postwar world to hope that human intention counted and that subjective hopes could be fulfilled. Freudian ideas about the power of the unconscious were at that time increasingly popular, and anthropological ideas about the pervasive influence of culture were taking the day. These, of course, were factors in Parsons' growing influence as well. When a new generation of Marxists finally arose, they often blamed Parsons for the denouement of Marxism in the postwar period. But this put the cart before the horse. The same intellectual climate which nourished Parsons' influence made the popularity of an orthodox, mechanistic Marxism impossible.

The nadir of Marxist theory—which occurred not coincidentally at the same time as Parsons' ascendence—was short lived. Twenty years after the end of World War II Marxism would ride again. It would do so because the ideological climate was transformed and the theoretical geography had undergone an extraordinary shift. Marxism was thus enabled to contribute, in a particularly vivid way, to overcoming the theory which had tried to take its place.

MARXISM (2):
THE CRITICAL THEORY OF
HERBERT MARCUSE

I HAVE CALLED the sociologists who challenged Parsons in the 1960s the younger generation of postwar theorists. They were young, however, only by comparison to the reigning functionalists of the day. They did not actually grow up in the decade in which they launched their critiques. This, I believe, is precisely the reason that their challenges remained presuppositional in form, why they did not challenge Parsons' theory in an ideological way. They were surprised, stimulated, sometimes disturbed, often pleased by the emerging social conflicts of the day. They did not, however, completely identify with them. Their world view had been formed in an earlier time, and they continued to hold to some fragment of the liberal tradition and to some hope for its consensual reconstruction.

The situation was entirely different for the generation of the 1960s themselves. I am speaking here of the young intellectuals who were just then attending college and entering graduate training. They experienced social turmoil at a much more formative period in their development, and their disillusionment with liberalism was much more profound. Indeed, throughout the leading centers of sociological activity, in France, Germany, England, and the United States, it was often young sociologists who led the social movements of the day. Humiliated by their nations' participation in colonial wars, terrorized by the spiralling arms race, inspired by the struggles of minority groups for civil rights, and caught up in the romantic idiom of youth culture itself, the initial alienation of young intellectuals often ripened into a feeling of genuine moral and political antagonism to the established order.

Many of these young radicals were theorists. Indeed, their estrangement from the present order made them much more interested in theory than many of their sociological teachers. In theory they could be more speculative and imaginative; it would be more possible in theory to find a way to transcend the contemporary world. It was in this younger generation, then, that the Marxist challenge to Parsons first took hold. It was from within this generation as it matured that the program for contemporary Marxist theory took off.

Insofar as the generation of the 1960s engaged Marxism, they engaged its theoretical and ideological dilemmas. The positions they adopted, of course, reflected their intellectual and moral experience. The postwar consensus was built upon the widely shared rejection of revolution from the left or right, and this was a premise the generation of the 1960s did not accept. They wanted to change society now, and they wanted to do so in a fundamental way. At the same time, however, while disengaging from capitalist liberal society, they could not accept Marxism of the Soviet sort. The Soviet Union had betrayed revolution ever since the late 1930s. Their own revolution was a totalitarian disaster. Their Marxism, if it could be called Marxism at all, denied transcendence as thoroughly as the capitalist West.

The 1960s generation developed a new kind of Marxism, which they called "New Left" to differentiate it from the older "left" theory of the Communist International. Since that time it has also come to be called "Western Marxism" to distinguish it from the Marxism that developed in the communist East. In the first years of their generational rebellion, in fact, young radicals were hardly Marxist at all. They talked about participation, community, and humanism, and the liberation which they envisioned had more to do with utopian democracy than economic communism. C. Wright Mills, one of the sociological godfathers of the movement, attacked orthodox theory in *The Marxists*. He and many of the other older supporters of the early movement warned that the path of Soviet development would make a viable Marxism virtually impossible.[1]

---

[1] C. Wright Mills, *The Marxists*. New York: Dell, 1962.

When Marxism did finally become the theory of the student movement, its leading spokesmen were intellectuals who had once been old leftists and who were determined not to make the same mistakes. The first important American New Left journal was *Studies on the Left*. One of its editors, James Weinstein, actually championed the American Socialist Party over the Leninist, American Communist Party which after 1917 had taken its place. Another editor, Eugene Genovese, made an outspoken effort to revive the "idealist" writings of Gramsci over the theorizing of leading members of the American Communist Party.[2] In England, at about the same time, *The New Left Review* sought to rebuild Marxism on the foundation of Lukács, Gramsci, and Sartre, the French intellectual who tried to reconstruct Marxism in an existentialist way. As New Left theorists became more sophisticated, they dedicated themselves to what they called "the unknown dimension" of twentieth-century Marxism. This was, of course, the transcendental, voluntaristic, multidimensional Marxism that the International Communist movement had fought so hard to ignore.[3]

I have described in my last lecture the many important efforts at revision which challenged Marxist orthodoxy in the twentieth-century. Most of these, however, were isolated efforts. Up until the postwar period, at least, there had been only one line of Marxist thought outside of Communist orthodoxy which had been able to sustain a real intellectual tradition. This was the Marxism of the "Frankfurt School," often called simply "critical theory." Begun by Horkheimer and Adorno in the 1920s, it kept abreast of the most significant "subjectivist" currents of the day, from psychoanalysis to phenomenology and anthropology. It had been founded on skepticism about the Russian revolution and proletarian orthodoxy, and its aim was to establish a different kind of Marxist theory of its own. When Nazism emerged in Germany, the Frankfurt theorists moved to New York, where they joined the New School for Social Research. But they disliked capitalism as much in America as in Germany, and after the war they returned to Europe as transcendental in their hopes for world transformation as before.

---

[2] Eugene Genovese, "On Antonio Gramsci," *Studies on the Left* 7, no. 2 (1967).
[3] Dick Howard and Karl Klare, eds., *The Unknown Dimension: European Marxism Since Lenin.* New York: Basic Books, 1972.

It was a member of the Frankfurt School who remained in America, Herbert Marcuse, who provided the first and most important model of Marxist theory for the New Left.

Like the other members of the Frankfurt school, Marcuse drew a sharp line between what he called "positive theory" and "critical theory." Positive theory accepts the world as it is, without any belief in the possibility of transcendence. Critical theory, by contrast, makes such transcendance its point of departure. This was the central message of Marcuse's first major work, *Reason and Revolution.* Published in 1941, at a time when most intellectuals had either taken up the Soviet Union's call for defending the socialist motherland or had given up on socialism altogether, this work called for a transcendental social theory and condemned mere "explanatory" theory as inherently conservative. Marcuse related this ideological critique to fundamental conceptions of rationality, arguing that transcendental theories work with a notion of "critical reason," positive theories with an impoverished concept of merely "technical reason."

In a later book, *Soviet Marxism,* Marcuse attacked the Marxist theory promulgated in Russia on much the same grounds: it was a conservative, economically deterministic theory which had lost touch with the possibilities for real social transcendance. In *Eros and Civilization,* published in 1955, this critique was applied to the foundations of liberal rather than communist society. On the one hand, Marcuse used Freudian ideas to attack the justifications for liberal ideology in the postwar period. The rationality and individuality which were so prized—by Parsons and other liberal thinkers—as postwar achievements were described by Marcuse as the stunted consequences of the "surplus repression" of sexuality demanded by capitalist society. Radically different possibilities of motivation and selfhood were actually available, he claimed. Possibilities like polymorphous sensuality and organic community would be achieved after capitalism was abandoned. On the other hand, Marcuse attacked the use which liberal theory had made of Freud. Liberals, like Parsons, had claimed that Freud's theory of introjection allowed one to understand the basis for value commitment in the modern world, how culture molds psyche in a positive way. Marcuse, by contrast, argued that Freud considered introjection a negative phenomenon, that he saw it as the internalization of parental threats which were surrogates for oppression in an unpleasant and ultimately unsatisfying world. Rather than promoting autonomy, such introjection undermined the possibility for individual separation from the world upon which transcendance depends.[4]

Is it any wonder, then, that Marcuse provided the perfect intellectual foil for the alienated students in the 1960s? He provided a radical critique of liberal society and he firmly believed in the possibility of transcendance. Not only was the suffering of younger people confirmed and legitimated, but salvation was considered possible. Salvation would be achieved through socialist revolution.

When masses of striking students and young people marched through the streets of Paris in the near revolution of 1968, they carried banners heralding the "3 Ms"—Marx, Mao, and Marcuse. Marx had provided the original theory of transcendance. Mao had just initiated the Cultural Revolution in China, which was designed to avoid the mistakes which had prevented the Russian revolutionaries from carrying this transcendance out. Marcuse was the theorist who had made the most trenchant critique of contemporary Western society, a critique which would allow salvation to be achieved at home. Though they had been influenced by all of Marcuse's work, the critique to which these striking students most especially referred was included in the one major work of his which I have not yet mentioned. It was *One-Dimensional Man*, the book which embodied Marcuse's sociological critique of capitalism in the contemporary period. It was published in 1963 and immediately became the most important theoretical work of the New Left. This is the work to which I will devote most of the rest of my lecture.

It is clear from the very beginning of Marcuse's discussion that he is not at all satisfied with the orthodox determinism of Marxian theory—he, like other Western Marxists, was strongly influenced by a subjective reading of Marx's Hegelian frame. When Marcuse describes capitalist society in the nineteenth century, for example, he presents a much more voluntaristic and multidimensional picture

---

[4] Herbert Marcuse, *Reason and Revolution* (1941; Boston: Beacon Press, 1960); Marcuse, *Soviet Marxism* (Boston: Beacon Press, 1958); Marcuse, *Eros and Civilization* (Boston: Beacon Press, 1955).

than Marx himself. "The way in which a society organizes the life
of its members," he writes, "involves an initial choice"—a declaration of intentional control which steps completely outside the
external control that Marx sought. To include choice in historical
development depends, for collective theorists at least, on positing
a relationship between individual action and culture. This is precisely what Marcuse does. The choice about social organization
which every society makes, he argues, is "between historical alternatives which are determined by the inherited level of material
and intellectual culture."[5]

When Marcuse actually discusses the nature of this inheritance,
moreover, we find a far from hierarchical image. Rather than
imposed, social order in this early capitalist period is conceived as
the result of more or less equal forces. In fact, Marcuse drastically
alters Marx's original theory of the connection between forces and
relations of production. Marx, you recall from my last lecture, was
insistent that the forces of production—the economic and technological elements—were all powerful vis-à-vis the relations, the
latter being the legal rules, particularly property laws, which provide
the content for the economic forces to operate. At first, then, the
forces and relations of production would be mutually reinforcing.
The capitalist forces of production, however, are inherently dynamic. Always changing, they will eventually come into conflict
with the more restricted relations of production. In what does this
conflict consist? With the increasing division of labor, capitalist
forces of production become ever more "socialized" and interdependent. Capitalist relations of production, by contrast, remain
rigidly privatistic. The expansive, social character of the forces of
production contradict the privatistic relations. The result is economic depression and class conflict, and the eventual overthrow of
the system.

Marcuse turns this original theory quite upside down. First, he
defines the relations of capitalist society much more broadly to
include not only legal life but the spheres of family life, politics
and private life generally. These are the elements which Marx

---

[5] Marcuse, *One-Dimensional Man* (Boston: Beacon Press, 1963), p. xvi. Hereafter
page references to *One-Dimensional Man* will be given parenthetically in the text.

placed not in the mode of production—for him composed of both the forces and relations of production—but in the superstructure. These superstructural relations of production, Marcuse then suggests, existed prior to the forces of capitalist production itself. Capitalist forces of production were introduced into relations which already existed. Far from being determined by the capitalist forces of production, these relations at least initially hemmed them in. "Individual," "private," "family," even "class" itself, Marcuse maintains, at first "denoted spheres and forces not yet integrated with the established conditions" (p. xiv).

Far from top-down domination, then, the early stage of capitalism was characterized by "spheres of tension and contradiction." Such a situation allowed, even encouraged, a sense of inner autonomy and the expression of independent thought. Individuals and groups possessed an "inner dimension" which was clearly distinguished from, and even antagonistic to, the external exigencies of economic life. "The private space in which man may become and remain 'himself,' " Marcuse maintains, really existed in that earlier period (pp. xiv and 10). This extended to political activity. "Independence of thought, autonomy, and the right to political opposition" were powerfully exercised (p. 1), and they possessed a highly critical edge. It was no wonder that it was in this period that, Marcuse argues, critical social theory was first developed (p. xiv). The result was a triply disjunctive society. There was the critical consciousness of alienated and forceful intellectuals; there was the political opposition, based on liberty and the autonomy of private life, of powerful social groups; there was, finally, the objective inequalities and instabilities which provided a real motor for continuing discontent and agitation.

As long as Marcuse confines his analysis to the nineteenth century, there seems nothing particularly dangerous—in theoretical terms, I mean—about this analysis. To analyze the contradictions of capitalist society, he has tried to develop, like other important Marxists before him, a distinctively more voluntaristic theory than the original. In his case, as for many others before him, this revision is motivated by an attempt to bring critique and transcendence much more directly into the capitalist period itself. Theoretical danger does arrive, however, when Marcuse changes his focus to the present day. Here he is analyzing not social contradictions but a society which is much more stable.

Marcuse realizes that this contemporary society—Western capitalism in the 1950s—is in relative equilibrium. Certainly it is without any significant revolutionary challenge. There is subjective acceptance of basic institutions. If this is so, however, might not his voluntaristic theory of capitalism lead to the conclusion that contemporary capitalism is not that alienating after all? If society is based on choices, and if there is an inner autonomy that makes these choices really free, then it is only logical to argue that the behavioral acceptance of contemporary institutions tells us that actors have found something in them they want to preserve.

Marcuse is quite aware of the dramatic changes which have occurred in the last one hundred years. Rather than poverty, there is a high standard of living, an "ever-more-comfortable life for an ever growing number of people." Rather than class strife, conflicts are "modified and arbitrated." Indeed, Marcuse acknowledges, "capitalist society shows an internal union and cohesion unknown at previous stages of industrial civilization." It is quite true that the state often serves today as a neutral and respected mediator for economic disputes, that individual rights and liberties have become widespread, and that change and reform are the rule rather than the exception (pp. 8, 21, and 23).

Perhaps, then, the critics of nineteenth-century society succeeded in attaining their goal. Maybe the fighting working class, the reforming middle class, and the critical intelligentsia had some effect? Perhaps capitalism has evolved into a more differentiated society, characterized by the inclusion of outgroups and pluralization rather than by ruling class superordination? This was just what Rex implied when he discussed the possibility of permanent truce, with mutual satisfaction, though far from mutual ecstacy, being found on both sides of the class divide. If individuals really retained their autonomy, as Marcuse's theory of early capitalism said, then their contentment with the contemporary scene may indicate some active and voluntary change in the capitalist system. Individual achievement in an open society is, of course, just what Parsons himself had in mind in his contrast between the postwar welfare state and the laissez-faire "business system" he had criticized in his prewar work.

I am sure it will come as no surprise when I tell you that, in fact, Marcuse does not draw such conclusions from his observations of stability and acceptance in contemporary society. The reason is not, I believe, simply because such conclusions would be empirically inaccurate. We must, for the moment, leave the issue of empirical accuracy somewhat aside. The reason Marcuse does not draw these conclusions is because they would be theoretically dangerous. To do so would be to undermine the integrity of Marxism as a theoretical system, and to compromise it ideologically as well. To reason in a consistent way from his earlier discussion would be to place motives, culture, and subjectivity in the forefront of his analysis of contemporary capitalism as opposed to the analysis of capitalism's material base.

Marcuse's multidimensional theory of early capitalism took up only a few pages. Though I have shown how radically different it was from Marx's own work, Marcuse himself never made this explicit. To draw such conclusions would be to make his differences with Marx dramatically apparent. It would show that Marx's theory of capitalism was inaccurate because, by denying the significance of consciousness, it proved unable to envision the possible subjective acceptance of contemporary life. More than this, it would threaten the millennial hope for world transformation that is at the back of critical theory. If social structures have intentional roots, and if contemporary structures seem to be willfully accepted, what hope, indeed what rationale would there be, for revolutionary transformation?

Simply to ask this question shows how contrary such conclusions would be to the entire thrust of Marcuse's intellectual career. He wrote his early sketch to fix a point of departure, perhaps even to gain a measure of intellectual independence, but certainly not to step outside of the Marxist tradition itself. It is quite possible, indeed, that he himself conceived this sketch as a simple elaboration of Marxian theory. It is not, of course, but the implications of this "not" must be sharply curtailed. The voluntaristic and multidimensional elements of Marcuse's early theory will never appear again. The elements themselves, moreover, are left in a vague and indeterminate state. We will see that Marcuse declares contemporary society to be hierarchical and coercive in the extreme. How it got from there to here is never explained. Perhaps we are being asked to assume that the awfulness of contemporary society can explain itself. For his part, Marcuse leaves his earlier analysis dangling. It becomes a residual category.

Marcuse is caught on the horns of the Marxist dilemma. Unwilling for ideological and theoretical reasons to step outside the Marxist circle, he has been forced to make his reference to voluntaristic effort vague and indeterminate.

But one horn of the dilemma always implies the other. Marcuse makes the voluntaristic theory residual because he must present himself as accepting Marxism in an orthodox form. For this same reason he must reject even the indeterminate reference which remains, and he must embrace material determinism. He theorized that contemporary society is actually one dimensional. In doing so, he finds a way to assert the power of economic hierarchy and anti-intentional motivation in the last instance.

Marcuse first puts collective, external order back in place. He does this in a way that is just as determinate as Marx but still different in a revealing way. What has changed as compared with earlier society, Marcuse insists, is the power of technology. Technical innovations like automation have made the machinery of production so powerful that the other social spheres no longer have any chance. Technological needs determine economic organization; they provide the goals of political life and the nature of political discourse; they determine the form and content of cultural life as well. Because of the power of technology, all the differentiations of earlier society have been broken down. Technological determinism fuses the subsystems under its command. There is only the "omnipresent system," a one-dimensional society (pp. xvi, 11, 23–35).

Marcuse has moved back to determinism with a vengeance! It might even be said that he outdetermines Marx. Marx said that it was the mode of production that determines the superstructure, and he insisted that this productive mode was a product both of technological forces and particular property relations. Marx was not, in other words, a technological determinist. To the contrary, he wanted to suggest that technology—the force of production— could be used in a benign way if only it were filtered through productive relations which were socialist in form. Earlier, of course, Marcuse went much further even than this in isolating and neutralizing the effects of technology per se. He argued that relations of production could exist completely independently of technology and economics.

The description of one-dimensional society, then, not only reverses Marcuse's earlier model of subsystem relations but actually becomes more unidimensional than Marx. Technology is now equated with the mode of production itself, and productive relations are considered completely subservient to it. But if relations are no longer independent, then the differences between capitalism and socialism become moot, for it was the change of property from private to public that was intended by Marx to usher in the Golden Age. Indeed, one of the striking departures in Marcuse's Marxism is that it speaks less about capitalism or socialism than about "advanced industrial society." Marcuse insists that in a society with a technologically sophisticated industrial system, "the technical apparatus of production and distribution (with an increasing sector of automation) functions, not as the sum-total of mere instruments which can be isolated from their social and political effects, but rather as a system which determines *a priori*" the other elements in the system. Because they cannot be isolated, Marcuse can emphasize the "similarities in the development of capitalism and communism (pp. xv–xvi).

Where once there had been a choice between systems, technological power has made choice irrelevant. Marcuse speaks about "the slaves of developed industrial civilization" who "exist as an instrument, as a thing." This, he writes, is servitude in a "pure form." Far from being the driving force for social liberation, as Marx once thought, technology "serves to institute new, more effective, and more pleasant forms of social control and social cohesion." Marcuse calls this "the totalitarian tendency (pp. 32–33, xv).

The earlier theory is now defunct. Rather than autonomous spheres and individual privacy, there is economic domination. "The productive apparatus," Marcuse insists, "obliterates the opposition between the private and public existence, between individual and social needs." Rather than conflict and disjuncture, there is conformity and harmony. "Under the conditions of a rising standard of living," he writes, "non-conformity with the system itself appears to be socially useless, and the more so when it entails tangible economic and political disadvantages and threatens the smooth operation of the whole." The autonomy of culture from material base no longer exists, or, to be more precise, the split itself is superseded by technological control: "The apparatus imposes its economic and political requirements for defense and expansion on labor time and free time, on the material and intellectual culture." The result is not surprising: the possibility for transcendence has disappeared. "Today's novel feature," Marcuse writes, "is the flattening out of the antagonism between culture and social reality through the obliteration of the oppositional, alien, and transcendent elements" (pp. xv, 2–3, 57).

How did this happen? How has Marcuse moved from a theory more voluntaristic than Marx's to one that is decidedly more deterministic? If you were to ask Marcuse himself this question, there is no doubt what his answer would be. He would insist that it is empirical reality that has changed, not his theory. Technology has changed and the structure of society along with it. But according to his earlier theory, economic forces—much less technologies—can hardly be determinate forces. If we presuppose that earlier theory, the growth and power of technology cannot by themselves be grounds for the totalitarian transformation of society. Technology would have to be interpreted according to nontechnological standards, and this interpretation might well produce protective action from the relatively autonomous political, intellectual, and familial spheres.

Empirical transformation cannot, then, so radically shift the grounds for the analysis of action and order even in capitalist society. The alternative, of course, is to suggest that this account of pure technological determination results rather from a change in theoretical perspective itself. It is not so much one-dimensional society as one-dimensional theory which explains the later account.

We must look to presuppositional and ideological reasons if we are to understand the way in which Marcuse has chosen to portray modern society. He is caught on the horns of the Marxist dilemma. I suggested earlier that to explain the vague and residual status of his earlier multidimensional account, we must appreciate how Marcuse was caught in the same dilemma as Marx's other revisors. I want to suggest to you now that this same situation explains his movement toward theory in a one-dimensional form. If Marcuse does not want to transform Marxism, he must not only make his voluntaristic innovations vague and residual but he must invoke economic determinism in the last instance. There is an iron logic at work from which he cannot escape.

One indication of the stature of a theorist, we have seen throughout these lectures, is that he senses the dangers to his position and tries to respond to them. If Marcuse is to successfully invoke the last instance, he must convince us that it is an empirical change which has really occurred. Now Marcuse has argued for a determinate, indeed a totalitarian technological order. What might cast doubt on this statement? Certainly, the attitudes and feelings of the actual human beings in this technological society would be significant. Marcuse must insist that people today are not the same as those who peopled earlier capitalism. Those earlier people cared deeply about their autonomy, were committed to transcendent cultural ideals, and resisted all material control. If "action" were still presupposed in this way, it would challenge the vision of technological order. Marcuse seems to sense this problem. Action and order must be made compatible. He moves, therefore, to revise his earlier theory of action as well.

Marcuse's challenge is to create a subservient and passive actor. He does so in two ways. The first is simply by going right back to the instrumental-material actor of Marx. What is different now is simply that the actor lives in a super-affluent society. The greater ability for this technological society to deliver the goods makes people more satisfied, indeed leads them to be enslaved to the apparatus that delivers them. C. Wright Mills called postwar Americans "happy robots." This nicely characterizes the implications of Marcuse's materialist solution as well.

But there is a much more subtle way in which Marcuse pacifies the actor. At first blush, indeed, it seems that with this second strategy he does not actually step outside his earlier theory at all. He adopts the same central notion from Freud that helped Parsons to formulate his voluntaristic theory—the notion that the personality is formed through introjections, or internalizations, of social objects which were originally outside the self. In a multidimensional theory, this recognition of internalization leads to the autonomy of the actor. Since what the actor introjects is culture, and since culture is relatively independent of material structures, internalization leads to the ability to act against structural imperatives. The way Marcuse now conceives the social situation, however, means that introjection has the opposite result. Rather than being separated from material structure, culture is determined by, indeed identical with it. What is introjected is not transcendent culture but the technological apparatus itself.

Marcuse cannot go back to the voluntarist pole. He has invented one-dimensionalized society to get away from it. In fact, if he allowed internalization to sustain autonomy he would not even be back where he started from: this autonomy would then be seen as occurring in the present stage of capitalism and not just in the past. This would make the last instance impossible to evoke and Marcuse would have definitively stepped outside of Marx's original theory. Marcuse wishes to remain inside Marxism, so some last instance must be found.

An empirical, historical transformation must be posited so that theoretical logic can be served. The transformation is technological domination. Because of this omnipresent control, internalization leads toward passivity, not away from it. It is "social controls" which have been introjected. It is the political needs of the state which have become individual needs. What internalization accomplishes is to convert the individual into a piece of technology; it amounts to the "implanting of material-intellectual needs" in the human being (pp. 9, ix, 4).

One of Marcuse's early descriptions of this phenomenon deserves quoting in full.

> [Individual] needs have a societal content and function which are determined by external powers over which the individual has no control; the development and satisfaction of these needs is heteronomous. No matter how much such needs may have become the individual's own, reproduced and fortified by the conditions of his existence; no matter how much he identifies himself with them and finds himself in their satisfaction, they

continue to be what they were from the beginning—products of a society whose dominant interest demands repression. (p. 5)

With this diabolical sense of internalization, Marcuse has found a foolproof way to avoid the theoretical embarassment of present-day individuals expressing satisfaction with the present order. Even if they do so, it doesn't matter. It would be the technological order speaking, not themselves.

It is revealing, it seems to me, that Marcuse picks up the Marxist idiom of "last instance" to make this point: with this transformation of action, he feels, material determinism is finally securely in place. "In the last analysis," he allows, the question of whether individual feelings are their own or simply introjections of the dominating system "must be answered by the individuals themselves." He warns, however, that this is true *"only* in the last analysis; that is, if and when [individuals] are free to give their own answer"! At the present time, nothing which individuals say about their lives can be used as evidence that they have helped to constitute them in an autonomous way: "As long as they are kept incapable of being autonomous, as long as they are indoctrinated and manipuated (down to their very instincts), their answer to this question cannot be taken as their own" (p. 6). Marcuse is arguing that multidimensional theory—a theory that separates subjective motivation from institutional determination—is impossible in a one-dimensional society. I would argue, to the contrary, that he makes this very suggestion because he himself is unable to sustain a multidimensional theory.

It is a fairly straightforward matter to see how this vision of one-dimensional society would appeal to the young radicals of the 1960s. Because they felt excluded from society, they felt that their freedom was greatly constrained. What is not so immediately clear, however, is why such a theory of domination would inspire these alienated students to rebel against it. To see why, you must only remember that a theory is more than presuppositions, models, and empirical descriptions. It is also ideology. Marcuse not only tried to explain one-dimensional society, he also evaluated it. When he did so, he started from the Marxian premise that transcending the present order really was possible.

But as I suggested in my preceding lecture, this confidence in transcendence has not been easy for twentieth-century Marxists to sustain. The communist revolutions in the East have been great disappointments, and the promised revolutions in the capitalist West have simply failed to occur. Marcuse is sensitive to these problems. It would be fair to say that the difficulty of revolution stands at the very center of his work.

Indeed, Marcuse's theory of one-dimensional society seems designed to serve a double purpose. A response to presuppositional exigencies, it has an ideological function as well. It explains why the Marxist messiah, the revolutionary proletariat which was supposed to be empowered by the development of advanced capitalism, has instead virtually disappeared. It is not that things are now so much better than expected. It is rather that things are so much worse. They are so bad that "the subject which is alienated is swallowed up by its alienated existence" (p. 11). Under the impact of technological domination, Marcuse believes, "the laboring classes in the advanced areas of industrial civilization are undergoing a decisive transformation." The mechanization of the labor process, he writes, "modifies the attitude and the status of the exploited." Because work is less difficult and physically demeaning, workers do not feel as resentful and the prestige of their work rises. The power of technology, moreover, ties the worker more closely in an objective sense to the process of production. For all these reasons, Marcuse concludes that "the new technological work-world thus enforces a weakening of the negative position of the working class: the latter no longer appears to be the living contradiction to the established society" (pp. 24–31).

While Marcuse has used a different theory to reach these conclusions, in themselves they are not different from those which most other twentieth-century Marxists have reached. Indeed, it is only after seeing that there are good reasons for the failure of revolution that Marxist theory engages what I earlier called the ideological dilemma. There are two possibilities. On the one hand, Marxist theorists can put off transcendence to some distant future, becoming "meliorists" who implicitly make their peace with the present day. On the other, they can take up a much more activist stance and seek, through the assertion of voluntary will, to overturn the meliorating tendencies which they themselves have described.

One-Dimensional Man explores both these possibilities. Remember, though published in the beginning of the 1960s rebellions it was composed during the period of extraordinary postwar calm. Marcuse has described a technological system of almost omniscient power. It is not surprising that his thinking about future possibilities is influenced by this fact. There is one strand of this work which takes up the resigned, apolitical pole of the ideological dilemma. "On theoretical as well as empirical grounds," Marcuse laments, "the dialectical concept [of critical theory] pronounces its own hopelessness." With the growth in the technological conquest of nature, after all, there "grows the conquest of man by man," and this latter conquest "reduces the freedom which is a necessary *a priori* of liberation." It is not possible for those subjected to technological control to gain any independent material force, and "without this material force, even the most acute consciousness remains powerless." More significantly, however, radical consciousness has, at least for the masses of people, itself become virtually impossible: "The power and efficiency of this system, the thorough assimilation of mind with fact, of thought with required behavior, of aspirations with reality militate against the emergence of a new Subject."

Marcuse even goes so far as to suggest that a thorough-going democratization of the economy—the actual goal of Marxian communism—would not be liberating. This notion is valid only where laborers are "the living denial and indictment of the established society." In the present situation, however, "their ascent to control would [only] prolong this [technological] way of life in a different setting." This is a gloomy assessment. While Marcuse insists that "dialectical theory is not refuted," he acknowledges that "it cannot offer the remedy" (pp. 252–253).

But if Marcuse had chosen only this side of the ideological dilemma, his theory would not have appealed to the New Left. Though he acknowledges a certain despondency, he is fiercely critical of the left-wing movements who have adopted the meliorist stance. He scorns the "collusion and alliance between business and organized labor" in the United States, and he claims that "the British Labor Party, whose leaders compete with their Conservative counterparts in advancing national interests, is hard put to save even a modest program of partial nationalization" of the means of production. In West Germany, meanwhile, the Social Democratic Party "is convincingly proving its respectability." Even among the left parties which are explicitly communist, which have remained part of the Communist International founded by Lenin, reform and world acceptance are the primary goals. "As for the strong Communist parties in France and Italy," Marcuse writes, "they bear witness to the general trend of circumstances by adhering to a minimum program which shelves the revolutionary seizure of power and complies with the rules of the parliamentary game" (pp. 20–21).

The organized movements for left-wing reform must be rejected because they are not left-wing enough. They lead toward greater integration with this world, not the transcendence of it. But Marcuse recognizes that the relative conservatism of critical movements is not an accident. It reflects the feelings and hopes of the masses of oppressed people. He does not shrink from the logical conclusion: if transcendence is to be obtained, the majority's feelings and hopes must be disregarded. "The fact that the vast majority of the population accepts . . . this society does not render it less irrational and less reprehensible," he insists (p. xiii).

Though Marx was as committed to transcendence as Marcuse, his theory of capitalism allowed him to tie its transformation to the expressed dissatisfactions of the majority of its people. The working class would experience capitalism's contradictions themselves, and they would rise up against them to build a new system. Marcuse is aware that quite the opposite has occurred, and he has built his theory of the one-dimensional society to account for it. The key to seeing through the contentment of the majority is to distinguish between true and false needs. Technological domination has brainwashed the population so that it needs only what can be provided and feels no need for what human beings should actually desire. The majority, even the left-wing majority, is contented only because it has been provided with a sense of false needs.

We may distinguish both true and false needs. "False" are those which are superimposed upon the individual by particular social interests in his repression: the needs which perpetuate toil, aggressiveness, misery, and injustice. Their satisfaction might be most gratifying to the individual, but this happiness is not a condition which has to be maintained and protected if it serves to arrest the development of the ability (his own and others) to recognize the disease of the whole and grasp the chances of curing the disease. (pp. 4–5)

This solution to the reformism of the time seems at first glance legitimate. If the majority's experience of contentment is corrupt and manipulated, there remain justifiable grounds for rebellion and, one hopes, social transformation. If you think about it a little more, however, I think you will agree with me that Marcuse's distinction between true and false needs raises more questions than it resolves. The problem, in a nutshell, comes down to this: where will the standard of true needs come from? Marx employed a standard of judgment which was there for all to see. He thought you would simply have to look at the feelings and actions of the people involved. But where will Marcuse get his standard of critical judgment? The source of this standard is absolutely critical, of course, for it establishes not only the grounds for critique but the conditions which define transcendence for the particular social system.

The danger is that Marcuse can establish the critical standard in only a highly subjective way, that it will be the revolutionary theorist himself who decides what people truly need. Marcuse explicitly rejects this possibility. "What tribunal," he asks rhetorically, "can possibly claim the authority of decision?" He answers that "no tribunal can justly arrogate to itself the right to decide which needs should be developed and satisfied." He concludes that "any such tribunal is reprehensible." But in the very same sentence he adds that, nonetheless, "our revulsion does not do away with the question: how can the people who have been the object of effective and productive domination by themselves create the conditions of freedom" (p. 6)?

In truth, Marcuse cannot escape embracing the tribunal he knows is wrong. Rejecting the judgments of the masses of people, his only alternative is the judgments of particular individuals. These individuals, not surprisingly, are intellectuals like himself, and the standard they employ is critical theory. Marcuse insists that the judgments of critical theory have "objective validity." The historical possibilities which are available to any given society are real, and the social structure which exists must simply be measured against them. He makes such comparisons on the very first page of his book, though he never returns to them again. Present-day society is irrational, he writes, because in it "production destroys the free development of human needs and faculties," because peace is "maintained by the constant threat of war," because happiness and sexuality represent only "repressive desublimation" (pp. ix–xi). But these judgments are, in fact, highly personal and subjective ones. Could there ever be a society without demands for work? If there could not be, can "free development" be defined in such radical opposition to social control? On what grounds can sexual desublimation be called repressive? If it does not challenge social structures, then might it not be equally valid to suggest that it is the structures themselves which are not repressive rather than the sexuality which is? Finally, on what grounds does the maintenance of peace through the threat of war constitute an indictment of technological civilization per se? Has this situation not been frequent throughout the history of human societies, and if it has been how can it provide the historically specific grounds for criticizing this one?

Marcuse would undoubtedly reply that my own reasoning here is biased in a liberal, this-worldly way. I would not deny this charge, though I would deny that this bias undermines the possibility for social criticism and significant reform. But this underlines my more general point: critical judgments are rather personal things. This is unavoidable. What is dangerous is when this subjectivity is camouflaged, and when the judgments so arrived at are recommended as bases for mass, revolutionary activity. This leads to authoritarianism and elitism, to the denial of the very ideals which the left has always stood for against the right.

We have seen earlier that Marcuse rejects democratic, participatory reform. The problem is that, because they have introjected civilization, these reformers might not know good needs from bad.

His conclusion follows logically: only by standing ouside society can a valid standard of judgment be attained. This leads back to intellectuals themselves. It is why Marcuse has written his book. The alienated intellectual stands outside society, and he is in touch with the tradition of critical theory which makes social understanding possible. Alone, however, intellectuals are not enough. They must find some social force to ally with, a group that has not yet been civilized. Marcuse searches, therefore, for groups which "exist outside the democratic process." He finds them in "the substratum of the outcasts and outsiders" which forms the fringe of every society. They are radical because they are completely unsocialized. Because they do not know democratic procedures, they constitute "an elementary force which violates the rules of the game and, in doing so, reveals it as a rigged game" (pp. 256–257).

Marcuse is caught inside the ideological dilemma. No matter what the social circumstances, Marxist theory is bound to alternate between uncomfortable reformism and radical transcendence. On the one hand, because it is a reforming social movement, Marxism will be inclined to conditionally accept the world as it is. Because it is also a secular religion, however, it will feel compelled to reject world acceptance and to insist on salvation no matter what the consequences.

In the 1960s Marcuse's radical solution to the dilemma seemed appropriate, and it inspired not only the social movements but the theorizing of the New Left. As the 1960s turned into the 1970s, however, the familiar frustrations of the transcendent position once again reappeared. First and most important, of course, was that there had been no revolution. Instead, backlash movements developed against the young revolutionaries, movements whose goal was to transform society in a right-wing, rigid and authoritarian way. The frustrations of revolution, moreover, had consequences for left-wing groups themselves. They became more inturned and less interested in making alliances. As their hopes were dashed, they, too, became rigid in their denunciations and more extreme and violent in their methods. If outcasts are revolutionaries, revolution can become a frightening mockery of itself.

In response to the failures of New Left Marxism, two new and powerful theoretical traditions evolved in the 1970s.[6] One was inspired by the already established work of the French "structural" Marxist, Louis Althusser. The other was a new form of critical theory, led by a younger member of the Frankfurt School, Jürgen Habermas. Both theories, each in their own way, returned to fundamental elements of Parsonian work. This is not so surprising as it may seem. It was the radical reaction against liberal theorizing which led New Left Marxism not only into the search for transcendence but to the eventual denial of voluntaristic social order itself. Only if elements of liberal theory were re-incorporated, its successors might reason, could the dangerous dichotomies of that earlier Marxism be avoided. Parsonian theory, of course, remained the premier liberal theory of the day.

Although Althusser actually began composing his theory much earlier, his "structural Marxism" only achieved widespread popularity as the 1960s waned and the 1970s began. Structural Marxism developed a more supple and nuanced model of the capitalist system than the Marcusean version. It made a point of the relative autonomy of political and culture subsystems, arguing that there had, indeed, been the kind of internal differentiation which Parsons had described. This complex understanding of causality led to the notion that the major contradictions in capitalism must be "overdetermined," that is, they must be the result of overlapping strains in different subsystems of the capitalist whole. This theoretical subtlety, moreover, was combined with a much more evolutionary view of how social systems change. There would be changes and disbalances, but rarely upheavals shaking the foundations from the bottom up.[7]

---

[6] I should emphasize "new" and "theoretical," for there was certainly another form of Marxism which developed in the aftermath of New Left theory and practice. This is what might be called empiricist Marxism. These Marxian sociologists focus on what they take to be clearly delineated research problems. In general, however, this empirical work occurs within an orthodox framework which tends to ignore the most important revisions of Marxist theory. It becomes, in this way, merely another form of conflict theory, one with an evolutionary and economic thrust. Yet, while these empirical Marxists eschew the problematics of "grand theory," they can hardly escape from theoretical logic itself. I believe that their work, too, is beset by the strains of the dilemmas I have described.

[7] See, for example, Louis Althusser, *For Marx* (London: New Left Books, 1969) and Louis Althusser and Etienne Balibar, *Reading Capital* (London: New Left Books, 1970).

By the end of 1970s, however, the structuralist alternative had worn thin. Althusser's rendering of Parsonian multidimensionality was not entirely satisfactory. The reason was that, because Marxism was never given up, the myth of the last instance was invariably invoked. This led to a curious kind of theoretical indeterminacy, a sense that Althusserian Marxism could never be precisely pinned down. Still, it was not so much the explanatory but the ideological aspects of structural theory which was to blame for its declining popularity. Structuralism had sent radicals back to study Parsonian theory, and various kinds of Marx-Parsons syntheses have in the meantime been produced. The problem was more that structuralist ideology was simply too conservative. The familiar dialectic of Marxist ideology was still in play. Reacting against transcendence, a reformism was instituted which was often so anti-transcendent that it protested against efforts at radical change. Althusser was himself a member of the French Communist Party, and his theory was often associated with the anti-revolutionary ambitions of the Communist International. New Left Marxism had been rejected, but at least for Western intellectuals Communist Marxism was not about to take its place.

The new version of critical theory which Habermas proposed has avoided these difficulties with more success. Habermas, too, reacted against the ideological excesses of the 1960s. He condemned New Left students for authoritarianism and argued that the search for alternatives must never endanger democracy. Habermas rejected Marcuse's rejection of liberalism. He argued that radical alternatives would have to build on the accomplishments of liberal society. The liberal recognition of individual rights, and its encouragement of rationality, Habermas viewed not as false slogans but as real embodiments of a progressive society. For Habermas, therefore, the search for a critical standard of judgment did not provoke nihilistic despair. These standards, he reasoned, could be found within the ideals which liberal society, and liberal social movements, set for themselves.[8]

Habermas has also been much more successful than Marcuse in maintaining a voluntaristic and multidimensional explanatory ap-

---

[8] Jürgen Habermas, *Towards a Rational Society* (Boston: Beacon Press, 1970).

proach. Indeed, his model of contemporary society resembles in many respects the conflictual, pluralistic model which Marcuse reserved for capitalism in its earlier state. Habermas tries to build interpretive action into his theorizing about rationality, and he tries to link actors' efforts to realize their ideals to the operation of society's subsystems themselves. The fact that such emphases push questions about subjective motivation, culture, and learning to the forefront of critical theory do not bother Habermas nearly as much. As his work has progressed, he has cared much less about maintaining the orthodox Marxist legacy, and for this reason he has felt much less compelled to evoke determinism in the last instance. In his later work, in fact, he has suggested that the basic strains of capitalism are rooted in experiences of psychological and moral development and that fundamental social change will be gained through a kind of social learning.[9]

I do not think that Habermas entirely succeeds in this reworking of the critical map. One can still find in his work strong residual loyalty to the Marxist tradition, and this commitment sometimes leads him to invoke "capitalism" in instrumental and coercive ways. This latent ambivalence makes it hard for him to make his multidimensional theory specific, for fear of embracing too openly not only liberal ideology but also liberal (and Parsonian) theory. These commmitments, and his effort to supplant Parsons as the most significant social theorist of the day, have led him to engage in serious distortions of Parsons' work. This straw man, in turn, has made it more difficult to build sociological theory in a truly multidimensional way.

Still, if Habermas has not fully succeeded, his work points in the direction which every effort at critical theory must go. It also points to what every more explanatory theory must never forget, namely that any effort to explain society must also be an effort at moral self-reflection and, at least for those who are not completely satisfied with society as it is, a contribution to critical renewal as well.

The histories of postwar Marxism and postwar sociological theory are curiously reversed. Sociology began from a multidimensional

[9] Habermas, *Legitimation Crisis* (Boston: Beacon Press, 1975); Habermas, *Communication and the Evolution of Society* (Boston: Beacon Press, 1979); Habermas, *The Theory of Communicative Action* (Boston: Beacon Press, 1984), vol. 1.

theory and in the course of its antagonism to Parsons created tendencies which went off in various one-dimensional directions. Marxism, by contrast, started from one-dimensional theories and sought to reinvigorate multidimensional frameworks. Both efforts came to grief because of exaggerated responses to their points of origins. Contemporary sociological theory has failed because of an exaggerated antagonism, postwar Marxism because of too much loyalty. Postwar sociological theory often subordinated its better judgment in the effort to hermetically seal itself off from Parsonian ideas. Postwar Marxism withdrew from the logic of its own conclusions in the effort to maintain the distinctive ideas of Marx himself. The very real innovations of both traditions, in other words, have failed for the same reason: they have not been able to build upon a multidimensional base. The path for both efforts, then, would seem to lead back to Parsons, or, to be more historically accurate, to the theoretical framework Parsons ambivalently sought to build.

LECTURE TWENTY
SOCIOLOGICAL THEORY TODAY

IN MY OPENING LECTURE I suggested to you that sociological theory, like the medieval kings of old, has "two bodies." It is, on the one hand, abstract and transcendental, a timeless search for the fundaments of action and order in human societies. Yet this "pure" dimension always takes on a second, historical form. We do not simply study "theory," but "theories" in a particular time and space.

This stereophonic sense has guided me throughout these lectures. I have discussed intellectual movements in a particular time and place. At the same time, I have tried to make the universal relevance of these movements clear as well. You should continue to keep these two bodies of social theory in mind today. In this last lecture, I will try to sew the different parts together as neatly as I can.

When I look at my discussions in this course, I see that sometimes I have talked of "anti-Parsonian" movements and at other times about "post-Parsonian" theory. With both terms, of course, I have been referring to the same movements—the developments in conflict theory, exchange theory, interactionism, ethnomethodology, hermeneutics, and Marxist theory which emerged in the period after Parsons' postwar hegemony. The first term, however, has been a way of characterizing these theoretical movements from the point of view of their emergence in the 1960s and 1970s. The second term characterizes them from the perspective of the theoretical situation today. "Anti-Parsonian" sees Parsons still as very much an actor; he is what the "anti" side is rebelling against. "Post-Parsonian" implies that Parsons has been superseded, at least in historical terms if not in theoretical scope.

I am not parsing words. What I am getting at is that the theoretical struggles I have described in these lectures occurred within a bounded period of time. The story of Parsonian theory and the challenges which were mounted against it is a historical one. Historical stories have dates, and the dates of this one are, very roughly, 1940 to 1980. Sociological theory today is no longer engaged in the effort to dethrone Parsons. It is post-Parsonian, not anti.

Why is the anti-Parsonian movement over? The answer is very simple: because it won. Parsons' theory was ambitious and in many ways profound. It had, as well, fundamental shortcomings which can be traced to deep ambivalences on Parsons' part. Given the different social, cultural, and intellectual climate which emerged in the 1960s, these shortcomings were bound to come out, and the ambivalences made it impossible for Parsons—and, thus, very difficult for his students—to alter his theory in any significant way. The challengers had picked on significant issues and the best among them made a formidable case. By 1980 the battle was won. The challengers were no longer challengers: they had established themselves as major traditions in their own right.

Indeed, by 1980 these theoretical movements constituted the principal forces in sociological theory. Estranged from two generations of theorists—the liberal revisers and the Marxists—functionalist theory had undergone by the late 1970s an almost total eclipse. An Englishman reporting on several books about Parsons began his review with the question, "Who now reads Parsons?" This was a mocking echo of the question Parsons himself asked about Spencer fifty years ago when he began his famous attack on utilitarian theory in *The Structure of Social Action*. "Who now reads Spencer?" Parsons asked on the first page of that book, and what he meant by that was that nobody did. Of course, people do still read Parsons. But that such a question could, even rhetorically, be asked indicates that an era has certainly come to an end.

In the last few years, it seems to me, a new phase of sociological theorizing has begun. Now that the dust has settled, it has become increasingly clear to many that Parsons' successors failed to develop a satisfactory alternative theory themselves, and for precisely the same reasons that they succeeded in displacing Parsons' own influence: their theorizing had a highly polemical bent. The result was that, challenging Parsons' one-sidedness, their work evidences a clear one-sidedness of its own.

The generation of theorists which has succeeded the liberal revisors and Marxists—the new "younger generation" in sociological theory—has been able to avoid this trap. Because they have grown up in an environment in which Parsons simply does not matter as much, they are less invested in either side of the battle. For this reason, they have been able to get a little more perspective on the war itself. This new generation of theorists have made efforts to close the dialectic, to provide a "third way" that takes the best of each side. Some pay a great deal of attention to Parsons, others do not. Still, theirs is exactly the same course that long ago Parsons set for himself: to end the "warring schools" by developing a synthetic theory which incorporates the partial theories of the day.

This new theorizing has unfolded in two forms: as systematic theorizing and as reinterpretation of the classics. Both forms have, however, had the same ambition, and they have often been parts of the same theorist's work. The overriding systematic, or analytic, issue has been to reintegrate subjective voluntarism and objective constraint. Since for much of post-Parsonian theory subjectivity has been conceived in an individualistic way, it is not surprising that this newly synthetic effort has often been directed to constructing, or restoring, the link between "micro" and "macro." Exchange, interactionism, and ethnomethodology have usually been characterized as "micro" traditions because they are concerned with the microscopic focus on small, or individual units. Conflict theories, Marxism, and functionalism, by contrast, are conceived of as "macro" because they are concerned with units of larger size, like institutions or whole societies.

The effort to close the micro/macro gap is, then, an effort to relate individual action and interaction to theorizing about social structure. When you recall that the individualistic challenges to Parsons, and the hermeneutic challenge as well, labeled him as a structuralist insensitive to action and subjectivity, and that conflict and Marxist critiques saw him as too subjectivist in turn, you can see how this recent insistence on linking action and structure, subjectivity and objectivity, marks an effort to supersede the terms of the earlier debate. It is also, of course, an effort that directly echoes the earlier ambition of Parsons himself.

In 1981, a significant volume appeared which made this ambition explicit. It was organized by ethnomethodologists and included essays by Marxists and functionalists, and its aim was to find a way of bridging the micro-macro divide.[1] The most important and widely discussed reinterpretation of the pragmatist tradition in recent years has exactly the same intention.[2] Its authors argue that pragmatic theory was not so purely individualist in intent as Parsons' challengers assumed but was, in fact, internally divided and actually contained a strong collectivist dimension. Because the modern interactionist tradition which emerged from Blumer has ignored the collectivist strand, they suggest that it must be rejected. They see a closer connection, in fact, between collectivist pragmatism and the purportedly antagonistic traditions of Durkheim and Parsons. An important German reconsideration of Mead makes a similar point, arguing that Mead is hardly the individualist that contemporary interactionism portrays and suggesting that a synthesis between Mead and neo-Marxist theory can be established.[3]

The same kind of synthesizing movement can be discerned in recent developments from the other, structuralist side of the great divide. The most significant younger proponent of conflict theory, Randall Collins, began in the late 1960s as a sharp critic of culturalist, voluntaristic, and Parsonian theories. In recent years, however, this clean-cut antogonsim has begun to blur. Collins has made a concerted effort to link structural theory to ethnomethodological, Freudian, and Durkheimian ideas, and he has even begun to acknowledge the pivotal effort that Parsons made in the same direction. In his most recent book, *Three Sociological Traditions*, Collins suggests that there should be a new synthesis between the conflict, Durkheimian, and microinteractionist traditons, so that "the weak-

[1] Karen Knorr-Cetina and Aaron Cicourel, eds., *Advances in Social Theory and Methodology: Towards an Integration of Micro- and Macro-Sociology* (London: Routledge and Kegan Paul, 1981).

[2] J. David Lewis and Richard L. Smith *American Sociology and Pragmatism* (Chicago: University of Chicago Press, 1980).

[3] Hans Joas, *G. H. Mead: A Contemporary Re-examination of His Thought* (London: Polity Press, 1985).

nesses of one set of ideas can be discarded, and its strong points built up and integrated with the strong points from elsewhere." In fact, he believes that this is already underway, and that "the future will show us even more of the same." In a recent review of my own work, indeed, he has taken over the term "multidimensional"—the term I use to define the standard set by Parsonian theory—as his own, arguing that a revised conflict theory can be more multidimensional than theory of any other type.[4]

The career of Anthony Giddens, perhaps the leading younger English theorist, presents a similar contour. Giddens' first book, *Capitalism and Modern Social Theory*, took an explicitly anti-Parsonian position on the classics, arguing, for example, that Durkheim was not interested in "order" but "change." As soon as this work was completed, however, he began to extricate himself from the Parsons/anti-Parsons debate. He argued that the distinction between conflict and order was fundamentally misconceived, and in a series of works that appeared in the 1970s and early 1980s he insisted that sociology reorient itself to the task of interlinking "agency" with "structure." To accomplish this, Giddens, like Collins, has drawn increasingly on ethnomethodological and phenomenological work, and he has tried not only to link these to Marxist structural concerns but also to certain kinds of cultuiral work.[5]

I have already referred, in the lecture preceding, to similar developments in the neo-Marxist theorizing of Jürgen Habermas. In his earlier writings Habermas expounded Marxist critical theory. He tried to elaborate on the voluntaristic dimension of Marxism

---

[4] For the new synthetic link, see Randall Collins "On the Microfoundations of Macrosociology." *American Journal of Sociology* (1981), 86:984–1014; for the reference to Parsons' pioneering work on the micro-macro link, see "The Durkheim Tradition in Conflict Sociology," in Jeffrey C. Alexander, ed., *Durkheimian Sociology* (New York: Cambridge University Press, 1987). The quotations are from Collins, *Three Sociological Traditions* (New York: Oxford University Press, 1985), p. 233; the reference to multidimensional conflict theory can be found in Collins, "Jeffrey Alexander and the Search for Multidimensional Theory," *Theory and Society* (Fall 1985) 14:877–892.

[5] Giddens, *Capitalism and Modern Social Theory* (London: Cambridge University Press, 1972); for the dismissal of the conflict/order distinction, see "Four Myths in the History of Social Thought," *Economy and Society* (1972), 1:357–385; for the agency/structure link, see Giddens, *New Rules of Sociological Method* (New York: Basic Books, 1976), and Giddens, *Central Problems in Social Theory* (Berkeley and Los Angeles: University of California Press, 1979).

and seemed content to defend Marxism against itself. Though recently he has acknowledged having been influenced by Parsons even at that point in his career, scarcely a mention of Parsons appeared. As the 1970s progressed, however, Habermas' interest in subjectivity and motivation became more serious and explicit. Eventually he came to reject completely the Marxism versus sociology divide and has tried to reinterpret the classics, and critical theory, to make them more accessible to one another. From Weber he draws a theory of rational morality, from interactionism, phenomenology, and Durkheim a theory of the intuitive, emotional, naturally democratic "lifeworld." In this whole later development, moreover, Parsons has played an explicit and central role. He has provided a model—as well as a foil—for Habermas in his effort to conceptualize the relationship between structural systems and lifeworlds.[6]

Need I add that I see my own work as part of this intellectual movement? In a series of earlier efforts I went back to the classics and tried to develop the basis for a new, more synthetic kind of collectivist theory. In later essays I took up more directly the micro-macro link, arguing, for example, that the "individualist" traditions of both phenomenology and interactionism contain significant collectivist strains and that these can be integrated with the subjective dimensions of the collectivist tradition. Most recently I have tried to work out a more systematic account of the relation between contingency and ideal and material structures. Though I have worked much more closely with the Parsonian tradition than the other theorists I have mentioned, my interest in overcoming the antagonism of the previous period, while not in any way negating its accomplishments, is, I believe quite similar to theirs.[7]

[6] See, particularly, Jürgen Habermas, *Reason and the Rationalization of Society* (Boston: Beacon Press, 1984), vol. 1 of *Theory of Communicative Action*. Steven Seidman's *Liberalism and the Origins of European Social Theory* (Berkeley and Los Angeles: University of California Press, 1984) represents another powerful argument against the Marxism versus sociology divide which so inspired the anti-Parsonian Marxism of the 1960s and 1970s.

[7] For the rereading of the classics, see Jeffrey C. Alexander, *Theoretical Logic in Sociology*, 4 vols. (Berkeley and Los Angeles: University of California Press, 1982–83); for the micro-macro concerns, see Alexander, "The Individualist Dilemma in Phenomenology and Interactionism: Towards a Convergence with the Classic Tradition," in S. N. Eisenstadt and H. J. Halle, eds., *Macrosociological Theory* (Los Angeles and

My goal in these lectures has been to develop an argument for what Hegel would have called this "concrete negation" of postwar theorizing in both a systematic and historical way. I have done so, of course, through a process of interpretation. As you learned from the lectures on hermeneutics, however, to conduct an interpretation you must step into the hermeneutical circle first, that is, you must first have some interpretive standard in mind. The standard I developed in my first lectures was a frankly ecumenical one, derived from the spirit, and in part from the letter, of Parsons' earlier work. Multidimensionality, I believe, is the only position which can explain the social world in a thorough, consistent, and satisfying way. It is also, I have tried to demonstrate, the only perspective from which the full variety of competing sociological theories can be fairly interpreted without shunting one or another of their partial interests aside. In theoretical interpretation, the prior commitment which draws the hermeneutical circle is a theory itself. If my interpretations have been good ones, however, I have justified my initial theory in (relatively) more empirical and inductive ways.

Though I started with a general and abstract multidimensional position, I have tried to specify the particular elements of a multidimensional theory through my interpretations of postwar work. My strategy has been to convert the concrete emphasis of each one-sided theory into analytic elements of a larger whole. Other paths are certainly possible. I hope, however, that I have convinced you that the interpretation and reinterpretation of past theories is one way that the new movement in sociological theorizing might proceed.

London: Sage Publications, 1985), pp. 25–57; Alexander and Bernhard Giesen, "The Long View of the Micro-Macro Link," in Alexander, Bernhard Giesen, Richard Münch, and Neil J. Smelser, eds., *The Micro-Macro Link* (Berkeley and Los Angeles: University of California Press, 1987); and Alexander, "Action and its Environments," in *ibid;* for my argument for continuing a critically revised Parsonian tradition, see Alexander, ed., *Neofunctionalism* (Beverly Hills and London: Sage, 1985); see also in this regard, the recent work of Richard Münch.

INDEX